War and Peace in Vietnam

By the same author

An English Journey
Sketches from Vietnam
Victory in Vietnam
Tito

WAR AND PEACE IN VIETNAM

RICHARD WEST

SINCLAIR-STEVENSON

First published in Great Britain in 1995
by Sinclair-Stevenson
an imprint of Reed Consumer Books Ltd
Michelin House, 81 Fulham Road, London SW3 6RB
and Auckland, Melbourne, Singapore and Toronto

Copyright © 1995 by Richard West

The right of Richard West to be identified as author
of this work has been asserted by him in accordance
with the Copyright, Designs and Patents Act 1988.

A CIP catalogue record for this book
is available at the British Library
ISBN 1 85619 523 6

Phototypeset by Intype, London
Printed and bound in Great Britain
by Mackays of Chatham plc, Chatham, Kent

Contents

	Prologue	1
1	South Vietnam: 1966–7	7
2	The Collapse of the Americans: 1968–72	54
3	Cambodia, Laos and Thailand: 1972–3	94
4	Vietnam Without the Americans: 1973–4	124
5	The Fall of South Vietnam: 1975	157
6	Thailand, the Refugees and a Guided Tour of Vietnam: 1975–80	181
7	Vietnam in Books and Film	213
8	Thailand, Vietnam and the Missing in Action: 1988	248
9	From Hanoi to Saigon: 1990	278
10	Vietnam: 1994	326
	Epilogue	355
	Index	361

Prologue
First Visit to Indo-China: 1963

Over forty years ago, I made a long train journey with nothing to read but a copy of *Newsweek* containing a special report on French Indo-China. I read it several times so that by the end of the journey I knew at least which of the countries were Vietnam, Laos and Cambodia. I did not try to remember the names of the various kings and politicians but something about the different countries stuck in the memory. I knew from then on that Laos and Cambodia, like neighbouring Thailand, were romantic countries of bells, gongs, gilt barges, bonzes, elephants and royal intrigue. From then on I knew that the Vietnamese were a stern people, ready to fight for their independence, and drawn towards Communism. This impression was reinforced in 1955 when I read Graham Greene's new novel about Vietnam, *The Quiet American*, and then Norman Lewis's great travel book *A Dragon Apparent*.

During the 1950s and early 1960s, I slowly made a name as a writer who liked to wander round Britain and Europe, but it was not till 1963 that I got a chance to see Indo-China. A Sunday magazine had commissioned a series of articles from Japan, Hong Kong and India, while the *New Statesman* suggested I go to Saigon. In Hong Kong, I applied for a visa for South Vietnam, but this was only a fortnight after the *coup d'état* and the murder of President Ngo Dinh Diem, so the consular staff were refusing entry to journalists. A few days later I heard the news of the killing of President John F. Kennedy, but did not see the connection between the two events. I decided to spend two weeks in Thailand and Cambodia.

On this journey I carried a book of the Joseph Conrad stories *Youth, Heart of Darkness* and *The End of the Tether*, all three of which became part of my Indo-China experience. In *Youth*, Conrad describes a first trip to the East, to 'Bankok, blessed name', on a freighter that sinks and leaves the sailors to row to shore on the Malay peninsula:

> We drag at the oars with aching arms, and suddenly a puff of wind, a puff faint and tepid and laden with strange odours of aromatic wood, comes out of the still night – the first sigh of the East on my face. That I can never forget. It was impalpable and enslaving, like a charm, like a whispered promise of mysterious delight.

Arriving by plane at Bangkok airport was hardly like rowing ashore to a silent harbour; moreover at thirty-three I was hardly a youth, yet Conrad's story continues to work its fascination. Bangkok in those days was only a third of its present size and population, and still had as many canals as roads. You could walk down a lane behind the high-rise office blocks on Silom Road and discover a farm with pigs and a duck-pond. The little hotel where I stayed was in Patpong Road, before it became an international red-light district of brothels, live-shows and massage parlours, supplemented by two adjoining roads for Japanese and homosexuals. During the few delightful and languorous days I spent in Bangkok, I dined with friends in their wooden house on the Chao Phraya River; I watched the sun go down in front of the Oriental Hotel, where Conrad may have stayed; but even the charms of Bangkok faded after my ten-day sojourn in Cambodia. Later I wrote of that visit:

> I remember Phnom Penh as a city of broad streets, trees, flowers

and flamboyants; serene and smiling people; dusk at a café beside the river and after dark the floating dance halls where Vietnamese girls, insubstantial as shadows, swayed in the moonlight to music I had never before heard or imagined. In the mornings I sat under the green awning at La Paillotte in the market-place, drinking orange juice and bitter tea, watching the slow crowd by the food-stalls crammed with the abundance of a fertile land. There were Vietnamese lunches and French dinners and late at night a soft tap on the door from a barefoot girl who smiled as you unwound her from her sarong.

After a few days in Phnom Penh I took a Chinese bus to Siem Reap, near the temples of Angkor, the most famous monument of the East. I remember the first sight of paddy fields in which water buffalo grazed, almost every one with a white egret perched on its back picking at insects; of vegetation so bright and green that it hurt the eyes; of waits at ferries beside broad rivers the colour of *café crème*; of gaudy pagodas and wooden homes on stilts, surrounded by dogs and ducks; of the steaming atmosphere, the ripe smells and water everywhere, giving a sense of fecundity, of nature spawning, flowering, ripening and on heat. The peasants laughed and yelled when they saw me sitting up near the driver, and sometimes demanded he stop the bus to give them a better look at the white man. Once we were stopped at a check-point and given injections against a disease, the whole bus sharing the same unsterilised needle. At first I meant to object but could not deny the pleasure and laughter with which my fellow passengers watched the orderly plunge the needle into my arm. This was twenty years before AIDS.

Cambodia at the time had broken off diplomatic relations with most of the nearby countries, including Thailand, so there were few other tourists in Angkor, the city of temples spread over an area about the size of Manchester. The largest and most important temples, such as Angkor Wat and the Bayon, with its forty leering Buddhas, were tidy and clean and ready to be inspected; however, I found it amusing to wander in search of smaller ruins.

It was my first time in a jungle (even then they were growing rare in South-east Asia) and I was awed by the rank stench and the hubbub of screeches, purrs, twanglings and yelps – like a dog run over by a motor car. Once, turning a corner, I came on a troop of monkeys and once on a TV actress from New York, but nobody could complain that Angkor was spoilt by tourists. The jungle was too powerful to be tamed, the temples too fearsome to be vulgarised.

The British anthropologist Geoffrey Gorer bracketed Angkor Wat itself with Greenwich Hospital as one of the world's two most beautiful buildings. However, it has to be said that Angkor is rather a frightening place. It was started during the twelfth century AD by one of the last Khmer rulers before the empire was crushed by Siam, and I wrote after that first visit that 'only a mad Cambodian Stalin' could have begun a project on so vast a scale with so little variety of invention. This was before I had seen the temples at Sukhothai, in Thailand, expressing a grace, humanity and even humour utterly lacking in Angkor. This was before I had seen that the Khmers could produce a real-life twentieth-century Stalin of their own. Beautiful as they are, the temples at Angkor and even the statues and friezes are endlessly repetitious in concept and detail. The mind becomes dulled by the hundredth identical Buddha, with lips set in unchanging smile, by the dancing girls with their arms ever akimbo so that you come to believe that they never danced.

Cambodia then, as once again at the time of writing, was under the wise but eccentric rule of the man who later became my one political hero, Prince Norodom Sihanouk. Having come to the throne in 1944, the young Sihanouk characteristically took both sides in turn in the war of the French against the Vietnamese Communists. With independence in 1954, he abdicated his crown and governed the country instead as its Prince and Prime Minister, making alliances both with the French and the North Vietnamese against the South Vietnamese and Thais. At the time of my visit in late 1963, the Prince was having one of his fits of xenophobia. The crisis erupted when one of his foes made a broadcast from Saigon, including some sexual innuendo, and the enraged Prince himself went on the air for hours on end, screaming abuse in his piercing falsetto. I wrote in my diary at the time that he sounded less like a head of state making a diplomatic *détente* than a schoolgirl hockey player accusing another of 'sticks' in a vital match.

In his fury against the Saigon government for the shelter it gave to his slanderers, Sihanouk came out in support of the Communist South Vietnamese, or Vietcong. He went on to attack the Americans, who were supporting Saigon, and therefore enemies by association. In a series of noisy pronouncements, he nationalised trade and banking, asked for support from Communist China, turned down American aid and finally shut the US Embassy. Although I had not intended to write any newspaper articles, I thought I should ask Prince Sihanouk for an interview, and by way of reply found a front-page lead story in next day's *Dépêches de Cambodge* denouncing those journalists who thought they could see Prince Sihanouk without having applied months in advance. The same issue carried a long attack not merely on the Americans, but, ominously, on 'the Anglo-Saxons . . . who have put about the rumour of a mad Sihanouk'.

Indeed such rumours were going about. At the US Embassy I was told that nothing could keep Cambodia from instant and total bankruptcy; that all foreign investment would be withdrawn; that the Red Chinese would soon be in charge of the army and the police; and that Sihanouk was off his rocker. In part I believed this and wrote an article to the same effect in the *New Statesman*, which luckily did not use my name, or I might never have got another visa to go to Cambodia. In those days, I supported America's policy in South-east Asia, and I had not come to understand Sihanouk's wisdom.

From 1963 onwards, I longed to return to Indo-China, and during the 1960s I found myself in the happy state of having the means to travel and write about anywhere in the world. Sensing, correctly, that I would not for long remain in the favour of newspapers and magazines, I took the chance to explore as much as I could of Britain, Europe, Latin America and Africa before I felt free to indulge my craving for South-east Asia.

It was in May or June 1966 that I made up my mind to pay a long visit to South Vietnam, where already the number of US troops had risen to 200,000, and soon would be more than half a million. For fifteen years, since doing my national service in Trieste, I had observed the confrontation with Communism, first in Eastern Europe and later in Latin America, Africa and the Middle East. Already I had reported on what Marxists called their 'liberation struggle' in Angola, Aden, the Congo and the Dominican Republic. Inevitably I was drawn to the part of the world where liberation struggle had turned into full-scale war.

One Wednesday in June 1966 I found myself at a *Private Eye* lunch at the Coach & Horses in Greek Street, sitting next to Gerald Scarfe the cartoonist, then employed by the *Daily Mail*. Since I admired his drawings and guessed that he might excel at descriptive illustration, I suggested our going to Vietnam. Gerald liked the idea and persuaded the *Daily Mail* to send him there to do some drawings for which I would write the appropriate text. We also obtained a commission from the publisher Jonathan Cape to produce the subsequent *Sketches from Vietnam*. To cover my fare and living expenses, I also obtained commissions from the *Sydney Morning Herald* and the *New Statesman*, but as it turned out, Vietnam was cheap. When I was not staying free in a tent or hut, by courtesy of the US forces, I paid only a few dollars a night at M. Ottavj's Royale Hotel, Saigon, my home from home over the next eight years.

1

South Vietnam: 1966–7

When I got off the plane at Tan Son Nhut airport one afternoon in July 1966, and found a taxi to lead me into the tumult of Saigon's traffic, I had no idea that this was a city where I would live for much of the next ten years, and pine for ever after. What at first seemed only a jumble of crowded and noisy streets, eventually took shape in my mind as a distinctive community, clustered around the nineteenth-century French colonial city, and its most famous thoroughfare, once Rue Catinat, now renamed Tu Do.

This long, narrow street, stretching north-west from the river to the red-brick Roman Catholic cathedral, with its colonnade of tamarind trees and its fashionable cafés, reminded the French of the Canebière at Marseilles, or the Corso Napoleone at Ajaccio in Corsica. Most of the action of Graham Greene's *The Quiet American* takes place in Tu Do, beginning with a first, fateful encounter at the open-air terrace café of the Continental Hotel, one evening 'in the momentary cool when the sun has just gone down, and the candles were lit on the stalls in the side streets'. The Continental and the Majestic Hotel, at the bottom of Tu Do facing onto the river, both played a part in my long experience of the city, but first I should like to describe the modest Royale Hotel, which was my base in South Vietnam until the death in 1974 of Jean Ottavj, its much loved proprietor.

The Royale Hotel stood in a side-street, Nguyen Thiep, connecting Nguyen Hue, with its flower market, photography shops and Corsican restaurants, with Tu Do, known to the French as Rue Catinat, which still had the main hotels, boutiques, nightclubs, airline offices and Indian bookshops, also dealing in dollars and gold. In Nguyen Thiep Street there was Brodard's Café – a haunt of disgruntled Vietnamese politicians and journalists, a pastry shop and a number of girlie bars, run by Corsicans for the US troops and construction workers.

The Royale itself was a corner of quiet and demureness among the surrounding bawdy houses. The barmaids were chaste, or did not go out with foreign men, so there were no GIs in the Royale clientele. No juke box rent the air, and even the gramophone was broken. The loudest noise was the clank of a ceiling fan, the shrill cry of a gecko or, late in the evening, the rusty squeak of the shutting metal doors. The restaurant food was the French equivalent of the chicken curries and rice puddings served to the British in India, a bastardised cuisine of *soupe chinoise, bifteck au riz,* and tomato salad, taken with red North African wine that was shipped to Saigon in bulk, bottled in Cholon, the Chinese quarter, and drunk with plenty of ice.

Like most of the buildings near to the Saigon River, the Royale Hotel was infested with rats, which rushed to and fro through a hole in the bar, without attacking the legs of the drinkers. There were bats in the trees outside that sometimes entered the bedrooms and flew around with the overhead fans; there used to be swallows as well until the street urchins obtained a ladder to steal their nests and eggs. You could bring in a girl if she was not a prostitute or a troublemaker; since the Royale Hotel respected the privacy of its guests. If there were telephones, I cannot remember ever making or taking a call.

The proprietor of the Royale Hotel, Jean Ottavj (pronounced *Ottavy*), was born on a mountain above Ajaccio in 1897, and he and an old Corsican lawyer would argue for hours as to which of their villages boasted the deeper and richer wells. Conscripted into the First World War, M. Ottavj was twice wounded and learned from the British Tommies the tune and words of 'Tipperary', which he would sing at parties – but otherwise spoke not a word of English. After that war he stayed in the army and served in Senegal (*quand j'ai fait l'Afrique*), in Syria, where he remembered the full moon rising above Aleppo, and then Vietnam, where he spent two years before taking a local demobilisation. 'Ah, Monsieur West,' he would say, pronouncing my name *Oo-oo-est*, 'I came for two years and stayed forty. I never went back. The Orient draws one, Monsieur West.' The former Sergeant Ottavj went to Phnom Penh as a white hunter attached to one of the tourist hotels, then joined the Majestic beside the Saigon River, whether as *maître*, or reception clerk or waiter, I never discovered.

When France fell in 1940, the Japanese moved into Indo-China, billeting some of their officers in the Majestic Hotel so M. Ottavj, who was a Gaullist (or so he said), decided to move to the Hotel des Nations, including the present Royale. He was jailed for a time by the Japanese, and found that his hotel lay on the flight-path of Allied planes attacking the docks. 'One bomb hit the Opera House and the whole building shook' – here M. Ottavj shook – 'while another hit the former British Consulate killing six senior Japanese at dinner. Unfortunately one of the same stick of bombs fell on the Graal Hospital.' In March 1945, the Japanese rounded up and interned the French, some in the Hotel des Nations, where they were crammed in six to a room.

In August that same year, 1945, the British arrived and the Communists started to agitate for an end to French colonial rule. The British tried to suppress the Communists, then armed the Japanese prisoners and released the Vichy French. After the French had massacred some of the Communists in the Town Hall, at the top of Nguyen Hue Street, a mob plundered the French suburb of Roux, killing and wounding dozens of people. 'The Vietnamese women drank the blood of the French,' M. Ottavj used to assure me, whispering so he was not overheard by his Vietnamese second wife.

Anarchy stalked the city and M. Ottavj's hotel: 'One night I was in my room when my dog growled' – here M. Ottavj growled – 'and I fired my revolver. The man in the window fell five metres but when I looked down he had gone. Another time a burglar who had stolen a pile of linen was escaping along the wainscot. I fired twice but he kept running toward me and fell into the road. The police came and took him to hospital where they found that he had been shot through the chest but was still holding the linen.'

By the late 1940s, Vietminh bomb attacks and assassinations had made life difficult for the Saigon hotelier. One of M. Ottavj's regular guests and partner at cards was a French major who was apparently very hirsute and hired a Vietnamese barber to shave his torso. One day M. Ottavj heard dreadful screams, saw the barber running out of the building, then went upstairs to find his friend 'clutching his tripes' and dying. The barber, a Vietminh agent, had drawn his razor across the major's belly. M. Ottavj's only son was killed at about this time when a mortar attack was launched on an estate at Tay Ninh. According to M. Ottavj: 'When the first mortar fell my son ran out of the building to take shelter, then realised that his girlfriend was still inside. He went back to fetch her just as the house received a direct hit.'

M. Ottavj was short in stature and walked with a stick but held himself straight and gave an impression of dignity and authority. Each morning at ten and each evening at half past five he would limp downstairs to shake hands with the guests and enquire after their health, the news and gossip. He always wore a long-sleeved white shirt, a faded tie, black baggy trousers and sometimes a jacket for special occasions such as a dinner party, a Mass or memorial to the dead. 'As a rule,' M. Ottavj used to say, 'I hate going to ceremonies. *Mais pour les morts...*' M. Ottavj greatly honoured the dead. Once a year, on the Buddhist Day of the Departed Spirits, M. Ottavj invited his Vietnamese staff to a feast, leaving one chair free for the souls of the dead. Once an English journalist, who had been celebrating his safe escape from a battle, came wobbling up to the table and plumped himself down in the chair of the Spirits. It was typical of M. Ottavj's tact that he managed to get the journalist out of the chair and into another without offending either him or the superstitious staff.

M. Ottavj's face was creased with a hundred lines, like the map of some mountainous region, and when he winked to bring home the point of some joke or a story, both eyes closed tight, like asterisks. His lower lip had a permanent swelling, as happens to trumpet players, however in M. Ottavj's case this was due to the opium pipe. When I first knew him, M. Ottavj used to frequent a den in Cholon, to which he on several occasions took me. Although I enjoyed a few pipes and the dreams that followed, I also noticed the deleterious side-effects.

As long as I knew M. Ottavj he used to complain of inferior opium, adulterated with rubbish. 'Ah, M. West, you should have savoured the true opium, the opium of Laos and India. If I could go to Laos now, and smoke some of the real stuff, my illness would disappear.' Through an American photographer, Sean Flynn, I got some high-grade opium which M. Ottavj enjoyed, but then Flynn was killed and M. Ottavj was once more disappointed. He tried morphine and poisoned himself. He tried but did not enjoy marijuana, which made him tipsy. Opium eased the pain in his limbs and freed his imagination to wander among the memories of his eventful life, his favourite books and superstitions.

M. Ottavj also talked of his fellow opium-smoker Graham Greene, who was here in Saigon in the 1950s, but somehow the memory of the author became confused with Greene's Indo-China novel *The Quiet American*. 'Of course M. Greene was right to have the American killed. The man was ill-mannered enough to steal Greene's girl from under his eyes,' M. Ottavj would comment. 'By the way, did Greene ever take that girl back to England with him?' Although not a reading man, M. Ottavj had formed his philosophy out of the Bible, certain histories of old Egypt, Thucydides and above all Nostradamus, the French astrologer who had predicted that Paris would burn to the ground in 1999. M. Ottavj used to explain all world events, from the First World War to '*Hitler et compagnie*', through a study of these pages. '*Nostradamus a tout prévu*,' he would say at the news of every disaster in Indo-China. 'He said that in the twentieth century a mighty country would be overthrown by a small country. *C'est le Vietnam, Monsieur Oo-oo-est!*'

Although he thought the United States had betrayed the French in Indo-China, he never complained of the well-meaning Americans who squeezed his rheumatic hand and addressed him as Jean (pronounced Gene), having seen his Christian name on the hotel menu. 'America has not sent here its cream,' he would say. Violent and burly American drunks would leave the hotel quietly after a few words, in a language they did not understand, from an old man they could have knocked down with a finger. Once a Korean major dragged into the restaurant a confidence trickster, at whom he pointed a pistol, meanwhile ordering food and drink for himself. The military police were afraid to interfere in this argument but M. Ottavj approached the Korean, bade him good day and persuaded him to release the little swindler.

When I went to Vietnam in July 1966, for a two-month visit, I did not imagine that I would come back for Christmas, then for extended stays in 1967, 1968, 1969 and all but one of the subsequent years before the débâcle of 1975. Like M. Ottavj, I came to feel the addictive power of Vietnam: *'L'Orient attire, Monsieur Oo-oo-est.'* Yet Saigon, in the rainy season of 1966, during the build-up of US military men and *matériel*, was a feverish, raw and alarming city.

Already hundreds of thousands of country people had come to Saigon to escape the war, especially the ever-increasing American air and artillery strikes. They went to the noisome shanty towns beside the Saigon River and the adjoining canals, or looked for work in the new military suburbs around the Long Binh base and Tan Son Nhut airport, which had overtaken Chicago as the busiest in the world. Wherever you went there were torn-up streets, piles of rubbish and building cement, with all the concomitant dust, noise and ugliness. The characteristic sight of new Saigon was a half-finished girlie bar surrounded by barbed wire. Convoys of old American trucks added their black diesel effluence to the stench of the bastard petrol used in Vietnamese motor cars and scooters. The chemical pall that hung all day over the city was briefly dispersed by the afternoon storms of the rainy season; then built up again in the steam.

The building, the traffic, the fumes and the din were especially troublesome in a city that works and lives in the open air. In row after row of outdoor workshops, mechanics hammered and welded automobile parts, bicycles, kitchen equipment, electric fans and air-conditioning units, clocks, transistor radio sets and record players. As well as the Central Market, there were many streets specialising in sales of clothes, books, musical goods or photographic equipment. Among them, multitudinous food stalls offered the basic rice with fish sauce, soups, vegetables, nuts, oranges, tea and soft drinks, as well as more piquant dishes like quail, frog and eel in garlic, pungent enough to arouse the Saigon appetite jaded by heat and 'spring fever', a term that encompassed most diseases from colds to malaria.

Besides the traditional Saigon business there was a growing black market in US military *matériel*, from combat boots to tinned Christmas pudding, from talcum powder to air-conditioning units and even trucks. Much of the stuff on sale was stolen; more was fake. The bath-tub distillers who once sold home-made hooch to the French as Pernod were now selling the same rice spirit as Scotch or Bourbon.

American journalists and visiting congressmen used to denounce the ingratitude of the Vietnamese in exploiting US military aid, especially when it was rumoured that black marketeers were selling arms to the Vietcong enemy. To answer the critics, the Saigon government sometimes made an example of black marketeers, and even put on a public execution by firing squad at dawn – or rather a half hour later, when it was bright enough for the TV cameras. The Americans were not impressed; indeed they claimed to know that the black market was run by senior Saigon politicians and generals, who cornered the sale of goods like cement, barbed wire, canned beer and antibiotics. Although at the time I believed in the venal character of the South

Vietnamese leadership, I now think that the allegations were largely unfair.

Even in the 1960s I understood that the biggest war profiteers were the Texan and Californian firms that held the concessions for building military installations such as roads, bridges, airstrips, docks and communication systems. Beside the 5,000 engineers on government contract were many more sales representatives, automobile dealers, sellers of unit trusts and others who normally worked at US oil installations abroad. A high proportion of those I met were refugees from the Internal Revenue or the Californian divorce laws.

These civilian Americans were for the most part older, sadder and much more belligerent than the fighting men. One of them told me how he had watched a napalm strike and found it 'really a lot of fun'. Another regular at the Royale Hotel wanted a nuclear strike against Communist China to bring its 800 million people to death by starvation. A third man told me: 'I'm going to Hong Kong and I'm going to fix me a divorce. Then I'm going to Los Angeles and I'm going to commit mass murder – my wife, my two exes and two son-of-a-bitch attorneys. Have you ever seen a Chinese fall down two floors of an open elevator shaft? It happened in my hotel last night. Real funny. Mind you, it was his fault. This American couldn't get the elevator door open, so he just picked this man up and threw him down.'

The American government tried to prevent civilians as well as servicemen from bringing over their families, because of the shortage of lodgings and schools as well as the possible danger. A few civilians smuggled over their wives, a few found mistresses, but most, like the GIs, had to make do with prostitutes. Almost all agreed in disliking Vietnamese women. 'If you go into a bar in Korea,' I used to be told by an engineer, 'a man like me of forty or forty-five, and you want to meet a girl there, she's probably aged about twenty, and she wants to learn everything you know. She wants to learn from all those years of experience of yours. She becomes like a servant to you. There's love and devotion such as you've never experienced.'

Puccini's opera *Madame Butterfly* tells how Lieutenant Pinkerton loved and then abandoned his faithful Cio Cio-San; yet many real-life American occupation troops in Japan after the Second World War fell in love with and wanted to marry their Japanese girlfriends, against army regulations. This was the subject of several tear-jerking novels and films. American popular fiction also extolled the beautiful and submissive Filipino and Thai girls, contrasting them with their aggressive, neurotic and frigid American counterparts. Yet for a long time the only Vietnamese woman in popular fiction was Bloody Mary, the market mammy of James Michener's *South Pacific*. Thousands of Americans who had been to bed with a Vietnamese were later killed in action, yet no liaison inspired a tragic romance such as *Love Is a Many Splendoured Thing*. Much of the Western world lusted or wept for the unbelievable Suzie Wong, a Hong Kong prostitute, but no heroine ever appeared among those Vietnamese girls who sold themselves to Americans.

Many years after the war, the British musical *Miss Saigon* adapted the story of Madame Butterfly to the events of 1975, yet as I had found out during the 1960s, the Vietnamese women seldom identified with Cio Cio-San, but rather with Kim Van Kieu, the heroine of an eighteenth-century poem, who sacrificed her chastity and her life for the sake of her family. In modern adaptations of Kim Van Kieu, a girl who wished to marry a poor but romantic Vietnamese was obliged by her parents to live with a rich American. The theme appeared in the popular novel *War*, written by Chu Tu, a Saigon psychologist, of which I was given a summary by a woman friend.

The heroine Dao is a southern girl who has gone to a French school and whose modern ideas disagree with those of her very conservative parents. She falls in love with Hiep, an idealistic refugee from the north, who in turn is in love with another girl, Huyen. In the confused politics of the time, the late 1950s and early 1960s, Huyen is tortured and raped by pirates, while Dao has to marry a Communist to protect her family. Both girls now feel disgraced. After the death of the Communist villain, Dao 'in her complete despair' meets a former girlfriend married to an American. The friend advises her to do the same: 'A foreign husband will not investigate your past like a Vietnamese would. He has lots of money, he knows how to please his wife, how to love. And when you are tired of each other, you can always live peacefully. When one's past is not so pure, it is disastrous to marry a man of the same country.'

Dao, in the novel, asks her friend to find an American – and Casey appears. Big, handsome and moustached, Casey is fascinated by the delicate, beautiful girl with her fatalistic and *risquée* air. He blushes 'like a little child' (a feature of Westerners that astonished the Vietnamese) and, being intelligent, knows that Dao is not really in love with him. 'I am sad,' he tells her, 'because your voice reveals that you are not in love, yet I don't want an affair without love. And I don't believe that Vietnamese are only in love with money. You are an irresistible woman and I will make you love me.' Dao reminds herself that 'I only wanted to marry a foreigner for money but he is not stupid and I'm afraid that I might fall in love with him. However, I will despise myself if I love a foreigner.' But when Casey kisses her, she realises that she is not in love with him or Hiep or any man – but only with herself. Another girlfriend tells Dao:

> I have had many foreign lovers and I have found out that I have never loved any of them sincerely: whether the foreigner loves me truthfully or not, I never know. We are Vietnamese to our very bones and our very soul. Maybe we can love a foreigner but that is not the same kind of feeling we have for a Vietnamese.

At the end of the novel, Dao gets a letter from Hiep who is in exile in Cambodia. Telling Casey that she must make a business trip, Dao goes to join Hiep for a last meeting, after which she will take her own life. So the book ends in a classical Vietnamese tragedy. But the author Chu Tu has added a second alternative ending in the form of an epilogue years later. Dao has married Casey and lives with him in a big villa on Nguyen Du Street.

Hiep, who has lost his ideals, now teaches at a private school in another part of Saigon. He sees Dao only to borrow her card to shop at the US army store, the PX, to buy a bottle of whisky and 'get drunk and forget about life'.

From various Vietnamese women, including the one who gave me the résumé of the novel *War*, I tried to understand how they felt about marriage, love and American men. It soon became clear that although Vietnamese women enjoyed sexual love, and talked about it with candour and even earthiness, they did not see it as any more than a pleasant bonus to a romantic affair or marriage. They were not obsessed by sex, as many Americans were even then, in the mid-1960s, before the full impact of the Permissive Society. However, Vietnamese women were capable of tremendous rage and even physical violence against unfaithful husbands and lovers.

The Americans in Vietnam were obsessed with castration dread; not the psychological phobia but the actual fear that their girlfriend might castrate them. I heard it said by one American, married to a Vietnamese, that he went to bed each night in terror of losing his genitals. 'He nearly loses "It" ' was the famous *Vietnam Guardian* headline over the story about a woman who just failed to sever her husband's penis.

One respectable Saigon housewife told me (rather too often) the tale of a woman

> who took a knife and went to her husband when he slept and cut off his sexual organs. As he woke up roaring with pain and staggered toward the door, she continued pricking him with the knife so that he died a lingering death. In court she defended herself by saying that his behaviour over the last few years had been a slow death to her.

Even as early as 1966, the war had devastated the family system of South Vietnam, creating a class of 200,000 child delinquents. There were seventy-seven orphanages, though a survey revealed that three-quarters of those inside had one or both parents living.

The American troops, being lonely and starved of family life, smothered these orphans and pseudo-orphans with money and gifts. 'Their over-generosity doesn't always help,' said an American adviser who showed me around some orphanages. He had had the same problem during the war in Korea, when the GIs made a pet of some particular child: 'One little kid of five had his own little uniform with sergeant's stripes, hand-made combat boots, two lockers (one of them filled with candy), a private room with a folding bed and his tailored uniforms on a clothes-rack. Nice deal!' The South Vietnamese were less indulgent, yet nevertheless, 'At every damned orphanage in this country you can see American servicemen giving money or surplus food to the kids.'

Thousands of Americans, both in Vietnam and in the United States, were keen to adopt Vietnamese children. The wish was no doubt prompted by pity for children they saw on television; also perhaps by guilt, as American bombing had helped to create these orphans. However, the Saigon government was most reluctant to let any children leave the country, and it had banned adoption of all but a very few. Many Americans helped a needy Vietnamese child by making monthly payments to its family, and the child in return wrote a monthly letter of thanks, often in stilted, old-fashioned language: 'There have been two serious fires in my area recently . . . The noise of children singing loudly is coming through my window . . . My siblings are all fine.'

Some of the orphans and pseudo-orphans ended up in the children's wing of the state penitentiary at Thu Duc, north of Saigon. One of the boys I met there was only eight years old and serving a sentence for pickpocketing. He stood rigidly to attention and regarded me with the shifty eyes and tight smile of an old lag. His gums and mouth were a mass of rotting, white infection and his voice had a hoarse, wheedling tone. Two of the boys had been sentenced for murder. One had killed his best friend with a kick in the genitals. The other, aged thirteen, had a tattoo on his arm saying: 'I hate the girl who betrayed me.' Yet even the lower depths of South Vietnam, in 1966, were not as appalling as what was to come with the drug epidemic.

Already, in 1966, Saigon was overwhelmed by the presence of so many foreigners. There were few cafés or dance halls just for the Vietnamese themselves, nor regular ballet and theatre in the Vietnamese style. One of the few places of entertainment just for the Saigonese was Phu Tho race-course, where meetings were held on Sundays. During the 1930s, M. Ottavj told me, Phu Tho was almost as elegant as Longchamps in Paris. There were European and Arab horses, and he himself had owned a fine chestnut, which had been poisoned by enemies on the eve of a race. By 1966, the yellow and red cement grandstands had started to crumble. The scrubland inside the circumference of the track was so overgrown that a Vietcong regiment could have sheltered there without the spectators noticing. Swarms of dragon-flies blundered around the paddock, in parody of the helicopters that chattered overhead. When I saw the jockeys weighing in, I thought that there must be a change of programme and this was a children's gymkhana. The average jockey, in boots and holding his saddle, weighed in at about thirty kilos, the largest tipping the scales at thirty-five kilos, and weighing himself no more than four stone. These tiny boys were said to be fifteen years old but they did not look more than six. The horses themselves were several hands smaller than their European equivalents, as well as being rangy, bad-tempered creatures that kicked the spectators whenever they got the chance. One of the horseshoes would fit quite easily into a man's palm.

The starting point for the races was on the other side of the mile-long track, and as these ponies were led across I wondered how many would have the energy left to gallop back to the finishing post. This proved an accurate speculation because, by the end of the first race, the field had slowed down to a kind of half-canter. The baby jockeys whipped their horses across the head and even, in fury, whipped each other. Three were disqualified in the first race, including the ones I had betted on in the incomprehensible French *pari-mutuel* system. There was much shouting and tumult among the standing crowds but calmness reigned in the reserved stand and bar, where big Chinese, in sharkskin suits, ties and hats, sipped real Scotch whisky and puffed cigars.

Whenever Saigon became depressing, I went to the zoo at the other end of the avenue from the President's palace. The lawns were well watered and tended; the trees and shrubs were worthy of what began as botanical gardens; the pagoda and the museum on either side of the entrance gates were well painted and cheerful. The Saigonese appreciated all these things, so that the zoo was well patronised. Even on weekdays one generally had to queue for an entrance ticket, while after the weekends the animals did not need to be fed because of all the peanuts and bamboo-shoots they were given by visitors. Since few Americans went there, foreigners were welcome. A group of young women would ask you to take their photograph, and the children who spoke to you were not, for once, trying to pick your pocket.

Even the zoo had had its darker episodes. The Japanese put an ammunition dump there, and Diem used part of it as a prison. Although some of his victims claimed to have been held under the tigers' cage, they were in fact in the director's office. The tigers were still an object of terror to many Vietnamese who thought that they had the evil eye. Visitors preferred the lions, which had come from Africa via Japan. I heard it said in Saigon that 'the lioness makes love like a woman, lying on her back'. This odd belief may have explained the constant crowd in front of the lions' den. The Vietnamese enjoyed watching the apes, and comparing them with Americans because of their long arms and hairy bodies. The snake house was popular during feeding-time when the keepers put live ducks in the cage, and impatient boys threw stones to wake up the pythons.

The zoo director, Vu Ngoc Tan, told me that most of his animals came from South Vietnam, the most valuable imports being the zebra, the chimpanzee and the monkey-eating eagle from the Philippines. He was especially proud of the chimpanzee: 'It is not so tame as yours in London. It likes to chew children's fingers. I prefer them like that. We are not in the circus business here.' According to Mr Tan, the human beings as well were sometimes vicious. One of his apes had died after eating a bun containing ground glass, and some children had stoned a crocodile to death.

There used to be herds of elephants in the Saigon region but their number had been reduced to one shackled animal that hobbled restlessly about its cage. War had made animals costly, Mr Tan said; the tigers from Tay Ninh were now frequently shot and sold to the Americans. However, he did his best to make the zoo a commercial venture. There was quite a demand from foreign zoos for the ridgeback dogs native to Phu Quoc island. Moreover he bred the hog deer and the spotted deer: 'They are very resistant to disease and we give them to underdeveloped people instead of cattle. Also the horns are very popular in oriental medicine and if we cut them off they may sell for three times the price of the deer.'

Like other correspondents in South Vietnam, I tried to work up an interest in its political life, although this was dull compared with the early 1960s when Buddhist monks were burning themselves to death, and general succeeded general in a series of military *coups d'état*. President Nguyen Van Thieu was effective but bland, while his rival, the flamboyant air force marshal Nguyen Cao Ky, had ceased to make outrageous remarks such as how he admired Hitler. Every now and then there were press conferences given by trades union leaders, or politicians claiming to represent a 'Third Force' between Communism and capitalism, but it was hard to take these things seriously. Or perhaps we all suffered from 'spring fever'.

Some of the foreign correspondents continued to hope for a story from the fanatical monks of the An Quang Pagoda. This group of buildings looked more like a run-down school than a principal holy place of the Saigon Buddhists. The walls were peeling and decked with rusty barbed wire. The courtyard was dusty on dry days and flooded on wet days, so that you had to cross on stepping stones. Even inside the pagoda itself, the children begged for cigarettes, made faces and tugged at the hair on your arms. However, there were always a few surly and slovenly men in Boy Scout uniform, to drive the children away with blows of a rolled-up newspaper.

Some of the monks, with shaven heads and orange robes, were working at typewriters or telephones, but most of them loafed about, grinning and simpering. To persistent journalists, hoping to get an interview with an abbot, they repeated their few phrases of French or English, 'No understand', 'I forget' or 'Come back at eight'. Their obtuseness maddened the foreigners, who hoped to see them burning to death. 'All I want to know, Venerable,' said one angry and sweating American, 'is whether we can expect a self-immolation. You see we have a deadline to catch.' Then in an aside to a colleague: 'Goddam it! How am I going to explain to this mother-f—er what deadline means?'

Soon after Gerald Scarfe arrived in Saigon, he got a series of telegrams from the *Daily Mail*, commanding him to proceed to 'the front', followed by further queries on why he was not yet 'frontward'. We duly went to stay with a US unit in a rubber plantation near An Loc, about fifty miles north of Saigon, and came back to find another pile of telegrams for Gerald telling him not, on any account, to go near the 'front'. It seemed that the *Daily Mail* had discovered he was not insured against death or injury in a war zone. I, as a freelance, did not matter.

Saigon itself was never remote from the war, or 'behind the lines'. In fact there were no real lines, and Saigon became a battlefield twice in 1968. Even in the centre of town you could hear the noise of bombing and artillery fire from the surrounding plain, and occasionally rockets or mortars would fall on the city at night. There were many places in South Vietnam that seemed remote from the war, but Saigon was not one of them.

And yet in Saigon I cannot remember feeling afraid or uneasy, as sometimes later in Belfast during the 1970s, let alone Beirut. Saigon was not undergoing the terror attacks that M. Ottavj recalled from the 1950s. During the 1960s the Vietcong succeeded in blowing up a US officers' hostel, a floating restaurant and part of the old American Embassy, but these incidents were as isolated and rare as the *plastique* bombings in Paris at the end of the war in Algeria, or IRA bombings in London.

Saigon was the base of the South Vietnamese army (ARVIN), the Air Force (VEENAF) and Navy, whose ships were moored in the river in front of the Majestic Hotel. Saigon also contained the headquarters of the US Military Assistance Command (MACVEE) and its propaganda division, the Joint United States Public Affairs Office (JUSPAO). At five o'clock each evening, JUSPAO conducted a briefing for the foreign correspondents, generally known as the 'five o'clock follies'.

At these performances, a series of officers representing different arms of the services came out one by one onto the dais like carved evangelists on a medieval clock tower. Each read out his news and answered questions. 'Could you clarify on the intensity of the strike on Thursday. Was it the hardest sortie-wise?' 'Yes, sortie-wise, I should say it was one of the hardest, Ted.' Markers on the wall-maps showed the progress of Operation Paul Revere II or Operation Game Warden or Operation Masher. Sometimes the reports had a surreal quality, like the announcement of an air strike on 'a Vietcong terrorist squad graduation ceremony'. 'Could you clarify as to the result of the body count the next day?' 'Negative to that one, Joe. A body count was impossible owing to the fact that the vicinity was under water.' 'Could you clarify if the Vietcong terrorist squad graduation ceremony was being held under water?' 'Negative to that one, Mike.'

It was at JUSPAO that journalists got their accreditation and booked themselves onto flights of the US Air Force to travel about the country. You could also travel by Air Vietnam and on the CIA's Air America, but it was safest to get on one of the low-bellied C123 or C130 troop transport planes, which seemed to be able to land in a short forest clearing. The army clerks at JUSPAO loved to frighten the new correspondents with stories of who had been 'zapped' in the last few weeks. 'How did the *Look* man get zapped?' 'He just happened to be in the wrong place at the wrong time.' 'There was a little Malaysian newsman got zapped on his third day. That was last week.' In spite of such stories, most correspondents liked getting out of Saigon.

At this stage of the war, between 1966 and the Tet Offensive in early 1968, the American troops were generally well officered, disciplined and prepared to fight. For example the unit that Gerald Scarfe and I visited near An Loc had just suffered casualties but the morale was excellent. The commanding officer spoke of his men with emotion: 'You hear people say how proud they are of their troops and you think it's all bullshit, but I felt like crying fifty times yesterday. You can't ask for better citizens. They're going against everything that's natural, doing their job. I can't get over some of these people, I mean a wounded guy apologising for leaving the battle, someone coming up and thanking me.'

In the tent where I stayed, the young soldiers looked solemnly at the empty beds of their comrades who had been killed. A lieutenant came in from the shower, naked except for his round, owlish spectacles, and delivered a patriotic speech that might have been part of a Hollywood war movie. He said he was going to suggest that at the funeral service, a rifle and bayonet should be stuck in the earth in honour of each of the dead.

A sergeant interrupted to say that the unit was short of equipment for this project; but he too was proud and patriotic. Reading this in my diary long after the war, it occurred to me that these officers and the sergeant, only a few years later, would have risked getting fragged (that is, killed by a fragmentation grenade) by their own troops, if they had been so eager for combat.

The American troops round An Loc and all along the Cambodian border were mainly trying to stop the influx of soldiers, arms and supplies from North Vietnam, along the 'Ho Chi Minh Trail'. Most of the US forces were in the north-east coastal plain, around the naval and air force base of Danang, the second city of South Vietnam, where the first US troops, 3,500 Marines, had waded ashore on 8 March 1965 to meet a battery of photographers. The Marines were assigned the defensive task of guarding depots and other military installations, but soon they began offensive 'search and destroy' operations, first in the populous coastal plain, and then in the mountainous rain forest near to the border with Laos. By July 1966, the US Marines ran most of the operations in I Corps, and also the Danang Press Centre, providing the correspondents with guides, air and road transport, sleeping accommodation, hamburgers, chilli con carne and Scotch on the chlorinated rocks.

Danang had become an American naval base and port, although Vietnamese fishermen still cast their nets among the rusting hulls of the freighters, tankers and frigates. Danang was also a major air base, claiming to have the only parallel runway for jets in Asia. The Vietcong, from their hide-out up in the nearby Marble Mountain, frequently pounded the airfield with rockets and mortars and sometimes machine-gunned planes on take-off and landing. Three US planes crashed at Danang during the first three days I spent there, and several more helicopters were wrecked by enemy fire, just some of the more than 4,000 American aircraft lost in the Vietnam War.

On the main street running beside the waterfront stood evidence of the profusion and waste of industrial military matter. Alps of ammunition were joined to an Andes chain of crates and containers of tinned food, soft drinks, plastic boots, transistor radios, electricity generators, air-conditioners, heavy artillery pieces, tanks, trucks, baseball bats, candy and pulp magazines. Every company in the United States appeared to have dumped here its surplus goods, soon to become garbage. The prodigious build-up of military matter had spread over the waterfront and cast its dust over the villas, parks and avenues of the residential district. Barbed wire and cement blocks served as fences to guard the dumps and the building projects, but since the American soldiers were friendly, sociable people, they allowed the Vietnamese to wander among the military installations. Old women squatted next to the crates of ammunition; children, many of Vietcong age, clustered around the sentry posts to cadge cigarettes, to peer at the sentries' comic books and practise their scraps of English. At forward units in battle zones, I noticed peasants grazing their cattle among the artillery and mortars, and even beside a general's tent.

Danang was overwhelmingly ugly, but it had moments of charm. I saw a Vietnamese girl of about sixteen – in trailing *ao dai* dress, in pantaloons and a conical hat – who rashly started to walk across a freshly tarred road. After a couple of footsteps, one of her sandals stuck. She stopped to extract it, and as she did so the other sandal stuck. At every slow step across the road she looked more vexed and more desperate, like a white butterfly caught in a pool of jam. Then, just as she was nearly across, she chanced to look up and see me watching her progress. Her rosebud mouth, which had been pursed up with worry, suddenly split in a smile; she leaned back, took off her conical hat, brushed the back of her hand against her forehead and said in a nasal, plaintive and altogether enchanting voice: 'Number ten' – the American-Vietnamese for 'bad'.

It was in Danang that I met for the first time a Vietnamese who really loved and admired the United States. She was a woman of thirty or forty, a Roman Catholic from an aristocratic family in Hue, and she liked to wear a dark blue *ao dai* in the quiet, almost sombre style of Annam, or central Vietnam. Although she pretended she was poor, she also remarked that when her cousin was going to Switzerland, she asked her to bring back diamonds because they were cheap there. She let one of her villas to the Americans, and owned a number of restaurants and a cinema. 'If I was not so poor,' she said, 'I would build a big cinema.' Her house in Danang was planned in the usual Vietnamese fashion, having a humble, shabby exterior and entrance, leading on to a lavish front room and elegant bedrooms, then to a kitchen and bathroom and finally to the servants' quarters out in the yard. It was like a Victorian London house, but built on a horizontal instead of a vertical plane.

Madame Danang, as I thought of her because she reminded me of the late President Diem's sister-in-law, the elegant Madame Nhu, served delicious meals of crab or meat-noodle soup, fried fish, slices of pounded and spiced steak, stewed duck and rice, followed by lotus fruit stuffed with nuts. In Vietnam, as in China, the meal was intended to follow rather than fuel the conversation, which took place earlier. Madame Danang talked mostly about the United States. She did not like France, where her husband was living, or by association, Europe. She liked Japan and had learned Japanese during their wartime occupation, but Japan did not gratify her romantic imagination.

America, and above all Hawaii or California, was where she wanted to live 'because American women do not have to work and are very pretty'. When she said this I understood the significance of the strange picture that hung in the corner behind her chair. It was an oil painting, eight feet high, of the film actress Sandra Dee. When one of Miss Dee's films had been showing at Madame Danang's cinema, she 'saw how beautiful she was and asked a Chinese artist to make a portrait'. The final result was astonishing. The huge pouting lips, the blank, bulging eyes and eyelashes as big as quill pens, lowered with colossal cuteness over the room. On the other side of the door there was another work by the Chinese painter which I thought I recognised as a portrait of Brigitte Bardot. I praised the likeness but happily Madame Danang did not understand, for this was a portrait of her sister as seen through the artist's imagination. All Madame Danang's decorations showed the same taste. There were cheap nude statuettes of nymphs and playgirls, ornamental bottles of whisky, souvenir ashtrays from Texas and Honolulu, phials of scent and glossy American magazines. Madame Danang had fallen in love with America, just as many Westerners fall in love with the East. Her decorations and taste were chinoiserie in reverse. Just as an English girl at the turn of the century might have been painted with pigtail and slanted eyes and a dashing kimono, so Madame Danang's sister appeared with a pert pout and round, saucy eyes.

For most of the Vietnamese in Danang, Americans meant the US Marine Corps, the legendary 'leathernecks' who, in the words of their stirring song, had fought their way 'from the halls of Montezuma to the shores of Trip-o-lee'. For those of us who wanted to see the war, the Marines were our guides, protectors and friends in I Corps. From the Danang black market, we kitted up with a uniform, boots, poncho and if we were extra cautious a steel helmet and flak-jacket, though these were insufferable in the heat. When fully equipped we would go for day sorties out to the battles going on in the rain forests, or longer stays in the coastal belt where Marines were engaged in 'pacification' or 'winning the hearts and minds' of the village population.

On the first of these trips I followed the coastal route to the border with North Vietnam, along what used to be known to the French as the 'Street Without Joy'. This was also the title of one of the books by Bernard Fall, the French historian who had witnessed the war in the 1940s and 1950s, and came back repeatedly when the Americans were there. I met him in Saigon early in 1967 with Mary McCarthy the novelist, who was one of our grander colleagues. A few days later, Fall went back to the 'Street Without Joy' and was killed by a land-mine.

From Dong Ha, the northernmost port in South Vietnam, I went by truck to Con Thien, where the Marines were fighting the North Vietnamese in the mountainous rain forest. We could not see the enemy undergoing artillery shelling and napalm strikes from the air, but we heard their voices chattering over the field radio. What were they saying? I asked an American colonel, but he did not know as they had no interpreter present. However, he thought that the enemy understood American orders in English. He showed me some of the recently captured North Vietnamese weapons, apparently home-made mortars and ancient machine-guns mounted on bipods. In those days, the Americans and the South Vietnamese had an immense advantage in fire power, the Northerners having virtually no heavy artillery, let alone tanks and aircraft. Nevertheless the Marines took casualties, as I saw from the body bags on the plane going back to Danang.

When they were not involved in these pitched battles against the North Vietnamese Army out in the forests, the Marines were combating the local insurgents, or Vietcong, in the villages of the coastal plain. I once spent a week with one of these units in Quang Nam Province, south-west of Danang, and found the

Marines to be far removed from their grisly, robotic reputation. The officers had studied the problems of Vietnam and read even the arguments against American intervention. Many Marine other-ranks had college degrees or were planning to go to college later. A number had learned the Vietnamese language, putting to shame us journalists, who never imagined we would be staying long enough in the country to make the effort worthwhile. Clearly the arduous training and discipline had not produced a corps of automatons, but on the contrary, self-reliant men with confidence in each other as well. The old-style braggarts and chest-bangers were mostly the older men who had re-entered the Corps from retirement, typically because they were 'mad at the draft-card burners and bastard Vietniks'.

The new Marines engaged in pacification had to study to be gentle with civilians, and this produced a certain neurosis, particularly as their duties were often dangerous. Mines and boobytraps were the principal killers, still more since the Vietcong had acquired a supply of 'Bouncing Betties', small grenades that jump to explode at groin level. The sergeants and warrant officers in my hut were confirmed sleep-talkers. The man who sat up most of the night obsessively cleaning his pistol would say in his dreams that 'it's all very complicated'. Even the crackshot sniper in the corner would say, 'I can't do it'; he had a horror of having to shoot a woman. By day he was full of reasoned advice on his trade: 'At one hundred yards you aim at the crotch and hit the chest cavity. At three hundred yards you aim at the head and hit the chest cavity.' But he was living on his nerves. Stress and danger may have accounted for some of the troubles of the Marines, but so too did the strain on a lion obliged to lie down with the lamb.

One instrument of pacification was the County Fair, which was both a civic and military operation. I attended two of these near Hill 55 in a strongly contested area. A lieutenant explained to me the principle of the County Fair: at midnight a company of Marines would surround a village, preventing all movement of people in and out. At first light a company of the South Vietnamese Army (ARVIN) would sweep through the village arresting known or suspected Vietcong, searching for tunnels and other hide-outs and forcing any armed enemy to make a dash through the cordon of waiting Marines. Meanwhile the villagers would be led to a neighbouring camp where they would see some of the benefits of loyalty to the Saigon government.

I got on the first of four lorries bringing the ARVIN soldiers early next morning. A tank and a mine-clearer went on ahead – more than twenty Marines had been killed or wounded by mines in the previous week – and our progress was so slow that dawn had broken before we reached the village half a mile away. The ARVIN soldiers smoked and giggled, and I was startled to notice one of them masturbating. When we got to the village, the US Marine corporal in front of me took great care not to step on the young lettuce plants in the furrows, and walked with a curious splay-legged gait. 'This is a real poor village,' said a sergeant. 'The shelters are no good. No head covering.' Even the smallest hut in this part of Vietnam had its family shelter against the bomb and howitzer shrapnel.

As an ARVIN officer tried to get the villagers to leave, a burst of automatic fire came from the tree-line over the paddy fields, and I joined two Marines taking cover behind a bank. One, a black man, was reading a paperback, while his white comrade was keeping his head down and laughing. They had two more days in Vietnam and were 'demob happy', as British soldiers say. The ARVIN soldiers searched the village and then in turn were searched by their officers to make sure they had not stolen chickens. The villagers trooped off with their wailing children and squawking ducks, and the ARVIN soldiers discovered a Vietcong hide-out which they destroyed with dynamite. The snipers across the wide paddy field kept up a sporadic fire.

After the village was cleared, the two or three hundred old men, women and children who had been found there went to another camp for the County Fair, a mixture of medication and propaganda. Health orderlies treated skin ailments, cuts and minor shrapnel wounds, distributed chewable vitamins and pulled a few teeth. An army lieutenant and graduate of the John F.

Kennedy School of Psychological Warfare at Fort Bragg put on a Walt Disney film about hygiene. He had forgotten to bring any Vietnamese music, therefore he played Bob Dylan protest songs instead. The Americans and Vietnamese listened in equal boredom to wailing denunciations of the Vietnam War and mournful thoughts on 'the eve of destruction'. By the afternoon, the heat was fierce but the Marines persuaded a few children to join in a sack race, with candy bars for the finishers. They even persuaded the old men to join in a three-legged race, for cigarettes as prizes.

By the end of the County Fair, tempers were running short. The women fought for the hand-outs of rice. Cripples brandished their crutches. The children stole. But at least one of these fairs I attended was deemed a success. A Marine officer said they had caught two VCesses, or women Vietcong: 'They were sort of prostitute age and we think they were banging for the VC... We know one of them is a cadre but we don't know which one.' The psy-war lieutenant, his big blue eyes gleaming with satisfaction, said that the war 'was like trying to grab smoke, when you open your fist there's nothing there'.

Critics of the American role in South Vietnam said that the military fought the war at long range – and above all by airplane – rather than staying with the peasants. However in 1966–7, the Marines had a policy of installing Combined Action Companies (CACs) in villages taken from the Communists. I visited two of these CAC teams in districts captured during the previous year. Both teams were commanded by sergeants and worked with local auxiliaries of the Popular Force. A sergeant at Dai Loc said there had been heavy fighting at first: 'A lot of the people were killed by the VC, and a lot by us. We've made a lot of friends out here. At first they were frightened because the VC said we were going to kill their buffaloes and rape their wives... But we're the good guys now and so they're with us.' This sergeant was rather amused by his new job as administrator and do-gooder: 'I was in Korea when I was eighteen years old and then you didn't see any civilians. Anything that moved you shot.'

On one visit to Quang Nam Province, in 1967, I met an eccentric Marine lieutenant-colonel, W. R. Corson, who advocated pacification through free trade economics. He was a devotee of Adam Smith, and was writing a history of the Imperial Chinese monetary system. He spoke or understood several Asian languages and had recently challenged the local Vietcong at Elephant Chess. In the course of a conversation that took in the Enclosure Acts, William the Conqueror and eighteenth-century Vietnamese history, Colonel Corson told me his plans for introducing the profit motive: 'Do you know that bit in *The Brothers Karamazov* when Dostoevsky says "Scratch a peasant and you'll find a petty bourgeois"? Well I'm scratching like mad! I'd sure as hell prefer a petty bourgeois to a peasant... Maybe the Lord loves a giver but the recipient doesn't. I despise charity in any form, and that goes for the USAID mission... We're going to build a pig pen here and when it's finished I want to see a twenty-two-inch dollar sign bolted over the door.'

Colonel Corson had taught the villagers to fish in the river with stun grenades, and to get a good price for the catch. He had started a lumber business at Phong Bac, where he commanded a tank battalion. He had also founded an apiary: 'Bees will literally work themselves to death for you. Yet nobody in USAID knew about bees. But I read an article in the *Wall Street Journal* (I have an airmail subscription) about how to keep bees, and we're going to make mead. A friend of mine who's a director of Sears Roebuck said, "We could almost replace sacramental wine if we could get Phong Bac mead." '

Partly because of the articles later written about him by others, including Mary McCarthy, Colonel Corson became the head of the CAC team operation in I Corps. Making allowances for his pawky humour and fondness for shocking liberal opinion, I thought Corson and others like him were doing a good job. In common with other journalists I poked fun at some of the dottier aspects of County Fairs, CAC teams and Corson himself; however, in retrospect, I think that I underestimated their achievements. The Vietcong (as opposed to the North Vietnamese) were by no means finished, as they showed in the two uprisings of

1968, but now I can see that the mass of peasants in South Vietnam were already turning against the Communists, and hoping to better their lives under the market system. This was in large part due to America's pacification programme, particularly by the Marines in I Corps.

There were no US Marines and virtually no Americans in Hue, the former imperial capital, north of Danang. Because it was risky to drive there on the winding road through the mountains, then controlled by the Vietcong, I normally flew there by Air Vietnam from Saigon. And I went there often, for Hue was at that time the only city that still retained an exclusively Vietnamese character.

The name of the Perfume River, dividing Hue, was often the subject of crude and obvious jokes about sewage; however, in fact the musty smell of the river was more of mud and weeds, and it was not polluted by chemical or industrial waste, like most of our rivers in Europe. Standing on the bridge one day, I watched two herdsmen taking a dozen water buffaloes across the river. The men wore solar topees but their bodies were almost invisible under the surface; the buffaloes swam with only their muzzles above the water. The crossing took almost half an hour since the front buffalo wanted to head downstream while the beast at the back, with a small calf paddling at its side, was equally keen to go in the other direction. The herdsmen clutched at the animals' horns and necks and shouted abuse from under their hats, but all the commotion did not disturb the nearby fishermen.

Like most university cities, Hue had a rowing set, but most of the members seemed to be young women. The girls were not very proficient in using either the oars or the sliding seats, sending the boats spinning round in circles, their long hair falling over their knees, and the splashing water darkening their white *ao dais*. When things went badly wrong and the skiffs were about to sink, the girls abandoned ship and slid, with their tresses hanging behind them, into the Perfume River, doing the breast-stroke to the bank.

In the hot summer months the people of Hue sometimes spent the night in a sampan in order to get the benefit of the river breeze. The Hue sampans, like the Venetian gondolas, had a romantic and even erotic reputation. Scandalous stories from Hue were popular in the Saigon newspapers. 'A southern country boy whose local girl fiancée talked him into spending a pre-betrothal night aboard a sampan on this romantic city's lovely River of Perfumes barely escaped from his breeches,' according to the reporter of the *Saigon Daily News*. 'The soldier had such an exhaustingly good time with his girlfriend that he fell into a deep slumber' – or as the rival *Vietnam Guardian* described the occasion – 'that night for the first time she did not refuse anything to him who immediately fell sound asleep after proving his virility repeatedly.' The soldier awoke to find that the girl, his jewellery and 70,000 piastres had all vanished.

Southerners often referred to Hue as the 'City of the Dead', and when it appeared in the news in those days, the agencies called it the 'ancient imperial capital', a mistranslation of *ancienne* (former) *capitale impériale*. Early in 1966 the Buddhists of Hue had risen against the Catholic military and in the course of the subsequent riots had burned down the American Information Centre; but calm had returned to the walled imperial gardens where the young people took their leisure. The students of Hue University read on the parapets of the Ngo Mon Gate, and beside the lotus ponds. A spooning couple, both in military uniform, peeped out from the shadow of a stone ornamental dragon. I noticed graffiti along the outer wall of the citadel, including algebraical signs and fragments of French, such as '*Liberté, qu'est-ce que c'est?*' and the poignant '*Amour?*'

Through English friends, I got to know a widow of Hue who ruled over a household of handsome and beautifully mannered sons, daughters, nephews and nieces. Their living quarters backed onto the family tailoring business, and centred around a low, black-varnished table-cum-bed, on which I was sometimes invited to sleep the night, but made excuses, preferring a hotel sprung mattress. This family of tailors was to display great courage and dignity during the agony of Hue from Tet 1968 till the Communist takeover, followed by worse persecution. Even in 1966, the matriarch told me: 'I try to learn English' – she was speaking French – 'but I just don't like the Americans. I saw a film the other day which showed some dead American soldiers, killed here in Vietnam. I felt touched – but all the same I don't like them.'

Guests at the little hotel where I stayed on my first visit were recommended to take their meals at the Hue Club – formerly Cercle Sportif – over the road. Although *Le Monde* and *France Soir* were still available in the library, the club had lost most of its old French glory. There was dust on the piano, the fans in the ceiling were still, and the food was reduced to horrible fish soup, bits of tinned luncheon meat, and omelettes smothered with American bottled sauces. The bar smelt of old, unwashed dishes and pots and pans. The club servants dozed in the armchairs, ate snacks or joined in the ceaseless games of billiards. The swimming pool was only half full and its rich, green water looked more suitable to lotus-growing than taking a dip. At least half the two hundred members, so I was told, no longer bothered to pay their subscription, not because they were poor but because of Hue's notorious stinginess. The torpor was very agreeable after the frenzy of Saigon, and I loved to sit there in the evening, drinking a bottle of Tiger beer and looking out on the Perfume River.

One of the people I met at the Cercle Sportif was Jacques Sanlaville, a big, red-faced and hearty Burgundian who had lived twenty years in the country, first as a soldier and now as one of the management of the local power station. Through Sanlaville, I got to know some of his Vietnamese friends, who were mostly junior army officers and civil servants, as well as a few businessmen. The senior officers and the rich Chinese no doubt frequented a more exclusive club.

Occasionally, on the way to or from central Vietnam, I stopped at the coastal city of Qui Nhon in the II Corps military region which also included most of the Highlands. Since the adjoining province had always been heavily Communist, even in French times, the Americans had plastered it with defoliant poison, driving much of the population as refugees to Qui Nhon. The squalor of two camps run by the Roman Catholic Church was as grim as anything I had seen outside Calcutta. The alleys between the shacks were covered in dirt and excrement and guarded by ulcerous mongrels baring yellow fangs. Naked, scabrous and pot-bellied children approached with one hand over the groin (for modesty was remembered, even here) and one stretched out in supplication. After seeing the Catholic camps, I went to the Buddhist camp on the sea-shore, and perhaps because of my Western prejudice, I expected even worse. It was, on the contrary, one of the smartest refugee camps I have ever seen. The huts were clean and sweet-smelling, each having its hammock and wooden bed, its carved shrine, joss-sticks and offertory fruit. (Bananas were favourite, since Buddha was fond of them.) Many foreigners, and I was guilty of this, were inclined to underestimate the Buddhists because of their querulous politics and their odd, giggling manner.

In the summer of 1966, I stayed several days with the South Korean Tiger Division, controlling much of the province behind Qui Nhon. The colonel who gave me a briefing wanted to rebut the allegations recently published by *Time* magazine that troops of the Republic of Korea (ROK) had flayed a Vietcong prisoner as a reprisal. 'There is no truth whatsoever in the stories that we have taken people's skin off,' he said, then went on to claim that the Vietnamese in the northern part of the Tiger's district had begged to be ruled by Koreans instead of their own troops. Another information officer said that the Vietcong themselves regarded the ROK troops as on the side of the Vietnamese people against the Americans: 'This is because the Korean soldiers are doing very kindly things to the Vietnamese. We have never shown any cruel deed to them. This is the Vietcong way of explaining the kindness of the Korean soldiers.'

The Tigers took me to see one of their 'psy-op' markets, at which women from Vietcong areas were encouraged to trade their fish and crabs for rice, salt, joss-sticks and factory-made goods. Tiger medical orderlies handed out pills and smeared salve on barbed-wire cuts. The Korean troops were amazed by the Vietnamese conical hats and how they were used to measure amounts of rice. They guffawed with joy when a pretty young woman filled her hat at a tap and drank from the brim. The Korean 'psy-op' included 'Elder Respect Parties', 'Sister Village' projects, and the teaching of Tae Kwon Do to the Qui Nhon High School girls. The Vietnamese appeared hopelessly frail for this bone-crushing business, and giggled and chattered during the lesson. The Korean battle grunt emerged from their mouths as a plaintive wail. Their behaviour infuriated the black-belt ROK officer next to me: 'They do it like a dance.'

During my stay with the Tiger Division I watched many displays of Tae Kwon Do. One sergeant broke through five thick tiles with a thrust of his outstretched fingers; another chopped four heaped bricks with the side of his hand; a third broke five bricks with a butt of his forehead. One afternoon I was watching a group of artillerymen practising Tae Kwon Do, when a special order was given and they rushed, still wearing pyjamas, to load the guns. I imagined this was a standard drill to keep them alert and ready for action. However, they fired off many rounds of 105 howitzer shells, to my great astonishment, for there was no sound of action nearby, and they were aiming in the direction from which I had just come. Later I wrote: 'When you listen to the psy-op briefings given by the Americans or the Koreans or the Australians, and then listen to the Vietnamese, you are struck by one supreme difference. The outsiders are eager and energetic. The Vietnamese do not care very much any more. The French, Japanese, Chinese, British, Americans, Australians and now Koreans have all lorded it here during the last twenty-odd years. Perhaps the Japanese were the most liked. The Koreans now are not unpopular. But the Vietnamese are tired of them all.'

From Qui Nhon it was easy to get a lift by plane or helicopter to one of the towns in the central Highlands, the region of rolling hills and savannah, occupied by the Montagnards, as they were called by the French and then the Americans. They were different from the Vietnamese in language, race and even appearance, generally broader in frame and plumper of face. Some anthropologists think that some of the Montagnards descend from the

Chams, who were driven from the coast by the Vietnamese about six hundred years ago; others believe they descend from Polynesians who sailed to the continent more than three thousand years ago. Until colonial times the Montagnards had lived undisturbed and ignored in the hinterland of North and South Vietnam, and in similar highland parts of Cambodia and Laos. Most of the Montagnard tribes had a way of life based on hunting, 'slash and burn' agriculture and matriarchy. They usually dwelt in thatched, wooden long-houses raised on stilts; they wore sarongs, enjoyed the music of gongs, drank rice wine through straws and went in fear of evil spirits, which they placated by animal sacrifice.

The most popular town in the Highlands was Dalat, a hill station cold enough for tourists to wear a three-piece suit. The dripping pine trees, the stone walls, the chalets with overhanging eaves, had been to the French what Simla had been to the British. The Palace Hotel had a hallway panelled in dark wood; antlers and horns on the wall; a glass-cased library of old French novels, along with *Kim* and *King Solomon's Mines*; and even a duck press in the dining room. The lady mayor of Dalat asked me to tea and sang a mournful Vietnamese lament: 'The rain-drops falling on the banana leaves, drop by drop, mean the beginning of autumn.'

As soon as the novelty of the coolness died away, I grew tired of Dalat, and wanted to get to Ban Me Thuot in Darlac Province by the Cambodian border. The Americans there, as in the rest of the Highlands, greatly preferred the Montagnards to the Vietnamese, who ran the administration, the army and much of the commerce and agriculture. Americans who would not have drunk from the tap in Saigon were ready to swill crude rice wine, topped up with river water. Those who rejected Vietnamese pork, duck and rice with fish sauce, were ready to try Montagnard grasshoppers and leopard meat. Most Americans in the Highlands wore one or several copper bracelets given by Montagnards to their blood brothers. They affected not to be shocked by animal sacrifice. 'They tie the cow up and beat it to death,' an American told me. 'It's brutal but it's kind of exciting.' A CIA agent at Ban Me Thuot confided in me: 'When we pay for a sacrifice, as Civic

Action, we say to the Montagnards, "We respect your customs but it's our custom not to torture animals." So we tell them that when they have a sacrifice, it's not to last more than five minutes.'

The sacrifices constituted a problem to the Evangelical missionaries around Ban Me Thuot, who otherwise found the Montagnards receptive to Protestant teaching. An American, Robert Ziemer, who had translated all the New Testament into the Rhade language, said there was difficulty in distinguishing between the sacrifice of a buffalo and that of Christ. 'They paint a house with blood after building it,' he went on. 'We have the blood of the Lamb. But we teach them it's no longer necessary to have sacrifices because this Sacrifice has already been offered.' Also, he said, the Montagnards were once rather deficient in a sense of sin but this too had changed for the better. 'My predecessor said to me: "You will find the people here will not weep over their sins." But I've lived to see it. Now they weep.' Thanks to Mr Ziemer and his colleagues, many Montagnard women now wore black brassières, though many wore them around the neck, leaving the breasts exposed.

Some Montagnards believed that their ancestors lived on the coast, near modern Nha Trang, from where they were driven westward into the mountains. The legend may well be true of the Polynesian tribes, in which case it was appropriate that Nha Trang was the base during the 1960s for the American Special Forces, or Green Berets, who befriended and took up the cause of the Montagnards. The rise and fall of this famous corps was important not just to the Montagnards but to the course of the Vietnam War and even to the history of the Americans, who lost with their faith in the Green Berets some of their faith in themselves. Until about 1968, the Green Berets were identified in the public mind with the classic American heroes and frontiersmen, with Daniel Boone, with Davy Crockett, with Gary Cooper in *The Westerner*, with John Wayne in *Stagecoach*. They were the only troops in Vietnam to inspire a patriotic and best-selling novel, a famous song and a Hollywood epic, all entitled *The Green Beret*.

The Special Forces were formed in 1952 as the secret military arm of the CIA in combating Communism, and many recruits were East European refugees, to be trained as guerrillas behind the Iron Curtain. They first went to Vietnam during the rule of Diem, who was murdered after a *coup d'état* ordered by John F. Kennedy, three weeks before Kennedy's own assassination on 22 November 1963. Since American troops at that time served in an advisory capacity, each twelve-man 'A' Team under a captain was technically answerable to a Vietnamese military counterpart, but it had the authority to recruit and command a 'civilian irregular force defence group', almost invariably from the Montagnards or the Cambodian minority. This hiring of non-Vietnamese to defend Vietnam was not as absurd as it sounds, since the Green Berets were mostly deployed in the Highlands and near the Cambodian border. This arrangement caused bitterness between the Green Berets and their counterparts in the Vietnamese Army, but it seemed to the US government of the time that friction with Saigon was a reasonable price to pay to obtain a string of Green Beret 'A' Teams, each with its band of mercenaries, to guard the cities and rice paddies of coastal Vietnam and the Mekong Delta. When a jealous American general in 1961 attempted to ban the symbolic green beret, President Kennedy cancelled the order and urged the Special Forces to wear the headgear with pride as 'a trade mark of distinction and a badge of courage in the difficult days ahead'.

That it became so was largely due to the author Robin Moore who wrote the best-selling novel *The Green Beret*. The idea for this came to him while he was writing a book about counterinsurgency in the Caribbean. He approached the then Vice-President Lyndon Johnson, who was visiting Jamaica, and through him was offered assistance in his research, provided he took the whole Special Forces training course of parachute-jumping, jungle manoeuvres, unarmed combat and armed combat with gun, crossbow, longbow and garrotte. Having passed the course and received his wings – quite an achievement for a man in his late thirties – Moore went to Vietnam to spend six months with various 'A' Teams, taking part in their many engagements. The fact that Moore was befriended and given a green beret by the men he had come to observe lends authority to his fictionalised account. The novel, which must have been read by tens of thousands of servicemen in Vietnam, offers a neat kit of received ideas about the war, the Vietcong, ARVIN, the French, the Montagnards and such delicate moral issues as torture. Many times in Vietnam, I heard incidents from the novel repeated as recent fact, and I even read them reported as news in the local press.

The hero of one of the episodes of the book is a gigantic Finn, Captain Kornie, who has to defend his camp not only against the Communists but the perfidy of his allies. 'By God damn! Those Vietnamese generals – stupid. Two hundred fifty my best men that sneak-eyed yellow-skin bastard corps commander take out of here yesterday – and our big American generals! Politics they play while this camp is zapped!' Captain Kornie is furious that he is not allowed to chase the Communists into neutral Cambodia, a prohibition he circumvents by hiring bandits to cross the border. The Green Berets interrogate a Vietcong infiltrator by driving a long, heavy pin into his thumb, forcing him to reveal that the camp will be attacked the next day. When the narrator is asked by Captain Kornie, over a schnapps, what he thinks of this style of interrogation, he answers: 'It's always grim but I've been around some damned crude sessions.'

In one adventure, the 'A' Team uses a beautiful Vietnamese woman to lure a Communist general into a kidnapping. In another, an 'A' Team crosses illegally into Laos. (A Special Forces officer once, drunkenly, offered to take me on such a mission, but I was sober enough to refuse.) In the novel *The Green Beret*, the South Vietnamese troops are shown as venal cowards, who take delight in torturing prisoners – in contrast to the Americans who do not enjoy it – but they are not as villainous as the French. Moore tells the reader as 'basic fact' that most French rubber planters were Communist sympathisers, that French hotels such as the Continental paid VC tax, and that one of the top Communist officers was a huge Frenchman who went into battle, stripped to the waist and wearing levis and a cowboy hat. The Montagnards are shown as humorous, brave and loyal.

During a stay in Ban Me Thuot in 1967, the photographer Philip Jones Griffiths and I got to know several Americans working with the Montagnards, including a man called Mike Benge, who virtually lived out in the long-houses. From him we heard of a Special Forces 'A' Team near the Cambodian border at Ban Don, who were said to be using elephants to get about the country. Since Philip, like myself, was preparing a book and did not have to meet any newspaper deadlines, we were able to wait a week for permission to go to Ban Don and then to wait a further week for an elephant ride.

The Special Forces 'A' Team did indeed use elephants to transport supplies through the forests, the turbulent streams and head-high brush of the Darlac countryside. The team commander said that the beasts could make a journey in six to eight hours that would need a day and a half for a man on foot. An elephant and her handler hired out at three or four dollars a day compared to as many hundred dollars to carry the cargo and personnel by helicopter. Furthermore the use of the elephants helped the local economy.

The Special Forces had closed their first camp at Ban Don in 1964, after a Montagnard rebellion against the Saigon government. Returning in August 1966, they found there were no elephants left after the US Air Cavalry had killed three or four, and the villagers had let the rest go free. Since the North Vietnamese and the Vietcong both used elephants on the Ho Chi Minh Trail, the animals were routinely strafed by American helicopters and dive-bombed by planes. The Special Forces Civic Action officer Captain Jerry Walters said they had tried to get the word back to the pilots not to regard all elephants as 'unfriendly', but as a precaution he took the American flag and spread it out on an animal's back as soon as he heard an approaching aircraft.

Captain Walters carried the Stars and Stripes on the elephant convoy with which we travelled from Ban Don to the village of Buon Brang Pak about eight miles to the north. We had four cow elephants and their three young calves which the village chieftain said would have to go along with their mothers. Vietnamese elephants, unlike their Indian cousins, do not kneel to enable the rider to mount, so that you have to step on the animal's head from a suitable platform such as the top of a truck or a raised long-house. You then balance yourself by placing a hand on the driver's shoulder, stepping on to the elephant's back and making yourself as comfortable as possible in one of the wooden baskets on either side. Since our convoy had only a small escort of Montagnard troops to defend it, Philip and I were obliged to arm ourselves with captured Chinese sub-machine-guns.

Connoisseurs say that travelling on elephant-back is rougher but less nauseous than on camel-back. The elephant keeps up a moderate speed but stops every few minutes to chew off a tasty shrub. There are incidental hazards such as the red ants that fall off the branches onto your hair and shirt; sometimes the elephant turns to spray you with phlegm or dust; but after a time the ride acquires its own rhythm and beauty. We forded a shallow stream in which the animals drank, showered and enjoyed themselves. We passed through a plain of tall elephant grass, which the Vietcong in these parts used as a shelter for ambushes. The driver pointed out gaudy lizards and stick insects on tree trunks and branches. The Americans and the Montagnards had lit many brush fires in the forest to rob the Vietcong of their shelter and once, when a gust of wind brought a ripple of flame to the convoy, the elephants reared on their hind legs, uttered a trumpeting squeal and bolted into the bamboo bushes, but luckily none of the riders lost their balance.

After three hours' riding and one hour on foot, we reached the pretty village of Buon Brang Pak, where the local chief received us in his long-house of cool, woven bamboo and reed. The American doctor who had come with us inspected some sick children and dished out pills, while Captain Walters distributed blankets, food, sweets, towels, balloons (in the yellow and orange colours of South Vietnam) – and plastic toy elephants. 'One time I gave them all bars of soap,' said Captain Walters, 'and when I went down to the river to bathe I could hardly get near the water. There were three or four hundred people wanting to try out their bars of soap. I wanted to get them towels too, so I wrote to my church back home, in Coal Grove, Ohio, asking the minister if he could get the people to give us 354 flowered towels for the women and 180 striped towels for the men. I also asked him to get people to send pipes because these Montagnards just love American pipes, even the corncobs. He wrote back to say he'd be sending the towels but he added a page and a half explaining why it was against his principles to send pipes because he was against smoking.'

As in every Montagnard village that I had visited, the people of Buon Brang Pak pressed us to drink their rice wine, squatting around the jar. The Americans, who were used to getting through four or five pints during a tour of the villages, would not risk more than one pint before mounting an elephant. The loads were lighter on the way back, but the beasts were tired and so it was dark before we made camp. The forest was suddenly loud with bird cries on a cracked, falling scale, and the smouldering pine trees glowed like beacons in the night. We were dusty, bruised and cramped when we at last jumped off the elephants onto an army truck, and made for the shower and the mess tent.

There was no sign of the Vietcong or the North Vietnamese during the week Philip and I spent at Ban Don, which was just as well, for some of the 'A' Team did not inspire any confidence as fighting men. Several had been seconded from other regiments of the army and had not done the parachute jumps or combat training entitling them to a green beret. Three at least of these men were overweight, dull and lazy, as well as complaining of sickness, apparently from the mass of chlorine they put in the drinking water.

Captain Walters, the tough and likeable man who had taken us on the elephant journey, was one of the old-style Green Berets, like one of the characters in the Robin Moore novel, and actually thrived on life in the forest. Besides his military duties, he used to go hunting at night with a rifle or crossbow. When I had got to know him better, Walters confided to me his fears that the army commanders wanted to close down unconventional regiments such as the Special Forces in Vietnam. 'The brass are trying to get rid of us. LBJ [President Lyndon Johnson] doesn't like us. Nor does the other Johnson, the army chief of staff [General Harold K. Johnson]. What they're doing is filling up the "A" Teams with men from other regiments. Most of them have never jumped. Some of them are no good at all.' As he said this, he nodded towards the mess tent that we had just left. Since Walters had spoken in confidence, I did not refer to his fears in subsequent magazine articles on the Green Berets and the elephants. However in the following year, 1968, it was evident that his worst misgivings were justified.

Even in 1967, there were certain Green Berets who were bringing their regiment into disrepute, as Philip Jones Griffiths and I discovered in IV Corps, the military region comprising southwestern Vietnam, including most of the Mekong Delta. This was the part of the country you first saw, flying in from Bangkok, and from a high altitude it looked both flat and colourless. The mighty Mekong and Bassac rivers, as well as the hundreds of streams and canals to which they are joined, appeared like the grey or dull brown tracks of worms and crustaceans upon an oily seashore. This was my first thought on seeing the Delta, and I recall the shock when the American sitting next to me on the plane pointed downwards and said: 'That place could be a tourist paradise except for the war.'

A few weeks later, I found out that the Mekong Delta was in fact a place of great charm, particularly if you travelled through it by water. Staying in An Giang Province, one of the safest areas because it was populated by anti-Communist followers of the Hoa Hao religious sect, I made a number of boat trips that were better than any holiday. The rivers were then at their highest level and almost rose to the top of the wooden stilts, supporting the houses on the banks. The great pigs, whose sties were also on stilts, were reposing almost at water level. Enormous water jars, which are said to have a religious significance as guardians of the family spirit, stood like sentries in front of each house. The villagers smiled at us from the banks, and travellers on other water taxis shouted greetings as they passed. Every now and then we met a boat full of twittering, laughing girls, with their white *ao dais* trailing on either side in the breeze, their conical hats tipped back on their heads, and their purple parasols twirling above them.

Not all the Mekong Delta was as delightful as An Giang Province, and even there, staying with a team of Australian doctors and nurses attached to Long Xuyen hospital, I witnessed plenty of casualties of the war. However, the Delta did not live up to its reputation as a hot-bed of Communist discontent. That reputation was earned in 1930, and again in 1940, when Ho Chi Minh's Communist Party led peasant revolts in the Mekong Delta. During the Second World War, the Japanese and then the Vietminh Communists encouraged the peasants to seize the land from its owners. Peasant grievances against the rack-renting landlords, usurious rice millers and government taxmen revived again after the Second World War when France attempted to re-impose colonial rule. The British authors Norman Lewis and Graham Greene, who went to the Mekong Delta in the early 1950s, have told of the terror stalking the countryside during the hours of the night.

In the late 1950s, when the United States began to send army advisers to bolster the crumbling forces of President Diem, most of the battles they fought were in the Mekong Delta. American journalists like David Halberstam and Neil Sheehan got most of their first experience of the war in the Mekong Delta, and also a poor opinion of South Vietnam's ability to resist the Communists. The idea was instilled in the minds of subsequent correspondents that IV Corps, the Mekong Delta region, was heavily Vietcong.

Perhaps because of these preconceptions, many reporters refused to acknowledge the real success of pacification in the Delta. We refused to believe the evidence of what we saw and heard. In particular we did not credit the economic revolution bringing prosperity to the peasants. Since the government had secured the main road through the Delta, leading to My Tho and Can Tho, the peasants were able to send their produce by truck as well as by boat to the rich and growing market of Saigon. American aid officials at My Tho, who wanted to break the dependency of the peasants on rice, had seen the road as a way of encouraging market gardens. In the My Tho area I met an onion farmer who had grown rich from a plot of a hundred by ten metres in size, and a water melon farmer who netted 300,000 piastres a year from an investment of only 30,000 piastres.

In An Giang Province, I met a farmer now preparing to join with some friends in buying a tractor. He had just built and furnished a fine house for himself and his charming family. His five dogs were well fed and friendly, and the Chinese rats (like our guinea-pigs) were kept as pets rather than food. He also had a large and well-stocked carp pond. He told me that when he had gone to Saigon to look at tractors: 'I was very careful about money. I went everywhere on foot so as to save the money for a cyclo, and I always kept a hold on my pocket.' The American aid advisers crowed over such instances of the capitalist mentality, and one of them told me he wanted to see the Mekong Delta become 'a get-up-and-go, greedy society, where every peasant has a second motor-scooter in his garage'. I rather priggishly disapproved of remarks like that.

In the same way, I could not believe that America was 'winning the hearts and minds' of the Mekong Delta peasants. A US information officer in Can Tho – this was in 1967 – told me the Vietcong in the Delta were so desperate that they had started to mortar provincial capitals:

> We're going to get it in Can Tho soon. There's nothing to stop them. This is a sign of defeat for the VC. All their idealists have now gone. All that are left are a few people who've spent their lives in the movement and have to go on living for it because they can't face up to the murders they've committed. The mass of the peasants are still not excited about the government. They still won't denounce the VC. But anyone who thinks the people still like

the VC is deluding himself. We emphasise in our propaganda that the VC are fighting against *people*.

Reading that, nearly thirty years later, I think that the information officer was right, and that I was wrong to disbelieve him. Later I went north from Can Tho to stay in a district said to be one-third controlled by the government, one-third by the Vietcong, and one-third contested. As elsewhere, most of the population lived in the first third, while ARVIN and their American advisers tried to extend their influence in a circle outwards, to where the Vietcong lived in huts or sampans. The size of the circles corresponded to the range of the howitzers firing from the district headquarters, in this case Co Do village. The political geography of the Delta could be compared to beermats on a bar, the mats corresponding to regions of government power, while the Communists lived in the gaps in between. These gaps were 'free strike' or 'select strike' zones, liable to artillery or aircraft attack.

The four US advisers at Co Do were quite exceptionally pleasant and intelligent, and I am sure that they did not abuse the 'free strike' zones to fire at civilians, as happened later in many parts of the Delta. They were much more popular than ARVIN, and seemed to get on especially well with the dark-skinned Cambodians. Although many peasants complained of rents and taxes, and did not want to contribute to the cost of a new bridge, I noted that most of them lived well: 'They have their rice and ducks; their fish in the wet season, their rats, snakes and snails in the dry. The tradesmen at Co Do have never enjoyed such affluence.'

With a small escort of the Americans, ARVIN and local Popular Force auxiliaries, I travelled at length along the canals to visit villages near to the Bassac River, even in districts said to be Vietcong controlled. At a Popular Force blockhouse which had been recently overrun, with many casualties, the survivors were much more cheerful than those in the watch-tower described in Greene's novel *The Quiet American*. They joked about one of their sampans getting upset by a buffalo. They peered at a new grenade-launcher and watched with amazement when US and ARVIN officers took pot-shots at the larks on the barbed wire, grazing a couple, but not enough to stop them singing. It occurred to me that I never saw in the Vietnam Delta the herons and egrets so common upstream in Cambodia. Birds hate noise, and I have read that migrants stayed away from London during the Blitz and for many years after the war.

Although I spent several nights at Co Do, I did not sense the fear and menace reported by Lewis and Greene in the 1950s. One evening, the Americans showed a movie in their sitting room, projecting it on a muslin screen in the window. They and their ARVIN guests sat in easy-chairs to enjoy the show. After a few minutes I noticed signs of another audience. There were muffled laughs, cries of delight or fear and a mutter of comment and conversation. Then I realised that scores or even hundreds of village people had gathered outside in the courtyard to watch the obverse side of the film through the muslin. The American next to me smiled: 'They like cowboy movies best. They laugh and giggle at love scenes.'

They laughed and giggled a lot at the film we saw that night called *Women of the Prehistoric Planet*. It was a bad but strangely disturbing film with all sorts of implications for Vietnam. The space fleet of a very advanced galaxy has come to the aid of the dark-skinned, fragile Santorians (I cannot vouch for the spelling), whom they consider backward and ungrateful. 'You take everything from us and give nothing in return.' The whites are appalled by the jungle terrain of Santoria, the pterodactyls and rivers of boiling mud that have to be crossed on a log – like the bamboo-pole bridges over the Delta canals. 'The air is so humid it's liquid,' says one of the whites.

There was one part of the IV Corps region where, even in 1967, the US forces were seen as brutal aggressors rather than friends of the Vietnamese. This was the island of Phu Quoc, thirty miles west of the Vietnamese mainland, and holding a population of barely eleven thousand. Few foreign journalists went to Phu Quoc, which did not even appear on the map of the country handed to visiting dignitaries. However, Philip Jones Griffiths and I had heard reports that the Special Forces 'A' Team sent to the island the previous summer had gone berserk and were murdering civilians. Our experiences on the island and above all Philip's extraordinary photographs would many years later provide some of the inspiration for Francis Coppola's film *Apocalypse Now*.

Phu Quoc was renowned for its fish sauce, ridgeback dogs and pepper plantations. The *nuoc mam* that accompanies every meal in Vietnam is made by putting anchovies into a huge vat until they rot and foment. Philip and I inspected this evil-smelling factory and heard the owner's complaints about the lack of salt and the shortage of 'coolies'. The famous dogs, which were sold to foreign zoos, appeared to be treated as pets and I even noticed a child leading a puppy on a string. The Green Berets did not approve of the animals. 'Sometimes we try to creep up on the VC at night,' one of them told us, 'but we hear them banging their cow horns as a signal, and if they don't bang the gongs then the dogs start barking.'

The Americans and the Vietnamese authorities complained that the VC tax on the pepper crop was a prime source of their revenue for the Mekong Delta region, and they had tried to stop its collection by making the farmers spend each night in the main village of Duong Dong or one of three smaller hamlets. Anyone staying outside needed a permit valid for only four nights, and nobody was allowed to take more than half a kilo of rice into the countryside, in case it went to the VC. The American Special Forces team had dedicated itself to killing those who remained illegally in the countryside.

Even before we went to the 'A' Team headquarters, Philip and I were aware of the impact made by the Green Berets on Phu Quoc island. On the way from the airport to Duong Dong, our ARVIN interpreter, a Saigon man with a New York accent, had pointed out to us the fishing junks in the bay and the hideous marble statue of the Madonna above the village: 'Very beautiful, sir, here you can see red sails in the sunset. That's the whorehouse, sir, just four girls for seven or eight companies [he meant the Chinese and Hoa Hao auxiliaries with the Special Forces]. But this town is no good, sir. They're eighty per cent VC.'

It was rough out in the bay that evening, and so the Special Forces were not able to practise their favourite sports of water-skiing and surfing out on the ocean. So instead they were water-skiing along the narrow river that runs through Duong Dong village, swerving among the sampans, creating a violent wake and terrifying the villagers. I wrote at the time: 'The children thought it was fun to splash in the water and watch the huge blond men sweep by at the end of the rope, but the old people glared and muttered. Even in South Vietnam I have never felt so detested because of my size and colour.'

When they were not surfing and water-skiing, the Green Berets made sorties into the island to root out the pepper growers living illegally in the countryside. They told us they had killed 192 Vietcong since the previous September, 'more kills than any "A" Team in IV Corps area'. A Green Beret officer gave us this justification:

> If people are around in the countryside, the VC have someone to tax, someone to give them food and someone to teach their bullshit to. We don't take prisoners here. If we did, we'd interrogate them for two days, then the Vietnamese [army] would give them a going over for one day, and then they'd go to a rehabilitation centre for three months, and after that they'd go back to where they came from and next thing, they'd kill us.

After meeting the Green Berets, Philip and I got a lift on a US Coast Guard vessel to visit the US Navy base at An Thoi, a village on the other side of the island. All but a few of the two thousand three hundred villagers were Roman Catholics who came in a group from North Vietnam after the country was divided in 1954. They were anti-Communist, friendly to the American Navy, and as cheerful in character as the Duong Dong villagers had been morose. The neat houses and clean streets were proof of their own contentment. It was Sunday morning when we arrived and a naval officer took us to one of the three celebrations of Mass at the local church, where burly American sailors, with sweat-stains spreading across the backs of their shirts, knelt clumsily beside the Vietnamese. An officer read one of the lessons in English: 'Two hundred pennyworth of bread is not sufficient to them that everyone can take a loaf.' It was the moral of USAID, Philip whispered.

The kind old village chief Ngo Dinh Ho plied us with beer after the service and said what an honour it was to talk French with a man from London. Before the war he had worked as an international radio operator in Hanoi. That was before 1946 when he started ten years of 'earthly hell' under Communist government. Most of the villagers had been fishermen back in North Vietnam, and had chosen to come to Phu Quoc because there was empty land and fish in the sea and a beautiful climate that never got cold. 'When we came here, there was nothing but snakes and grass,' he said, 'but the villagers are very hard-working and tough. Now we have rice fields and orchards – this red earth is very good. If only we could get rid of the Vietcong it would be just like heaven – just like a dream of women . . . I'm very grateful for the help given us by the United States.'

The navy men said that the army had given too high an estimate of the VC support on the island. If there were 2,000 anti-Communists in An Thoi alone, the rest of the island must be totally VC to provide an eighty per cent figure. And this was clearly not true. Why, then, should the Special Forces at Duong Dong wish to exaggerate the hostility? Was it in order to justify their brutal style of pacification? The naval officers at An Thoi made this very complaint against the Green Berets, and told us that they had threatened to shell the 'A' Team headquarters. These were the words of one naval officer, denouncing his army colleagues on Phu Quoc island:

> They are licensed killers. It's gun law. They shoot at everything that moves outside the four hamlets. But there are only a few VC

on the island. I've been shot at more in — [he named his home town]. None of them speaks Vietnamese. They call the Vietnamese 'slopes' and 'slant eyes' but I really like the Vietnamese and I know that one Vietnamese is worth ten of those assholes. More than half the VC they claim to have killed were farmers. One of them [he named one of the Special Forces officers] tells how an old man in a blue shirt knelt down in front of him holding his hands together in Vietnamese fashion – and he put five bullets through his head. The old man had no weapon. There was nothing wrong with his papers. He just didn't like the look of him . . . They have a joke that their idea of Chieu Hoi [the programme of encouraging defectors from the VC] is a mortar. They know that if they take a prisoner and the Vietnamese clear him he'll return, so they kill him first. They want to show they're real hard . . . Look at the way they go water-skiing through the village, setting up a wake and frightening old women in their sampans . . . When those monkeys clear a hamlet they burn down the houses and then make the villagers walk home. They don't do anything for them. They want to do it the hard way. If that's the war I don't want any part of it.

The Green Berets must have heard that Philip and I had talked with the navy, for when we got back to Duong Dong, one of their officers warned us in no uncertain terms to get a plane out of the island, at once. Later, the Special Forces on Phu Quoc would come to be seen as typical of the Americans in Vietnam, as caricatured by Colonel Kurtz and Colonel Kilgore in *Apocalypse Now*. However in that year, 1967, the navy men we met at An Thoi were more representative of their countrymen.

2

The Collapse of the Americans: 1968–72

During the Tet, or New Year, celebrations on 31 January 1968, the North Vietnamese Army and the indigenous Vietcong launched an offensive throughout the south of the country, capturing Hue and Ban Me Thuot, threatening to overrun the US Marine outpost at Khe Sanh, and venturing into the heart of Saigon to storm the American Embassy. An astonished world read and saw images of the South Vietnamese General Loan firing his pistol into the head of a Vietcong prisoner, the US Marines attacking the fortress at Hue, and the flattening of a Mekong Delta town because, in the words of a US Air Force spokesman, 'it was necessary to destroy Ben Tre in order to save it'.

At the time of the Tet Offensive, I was in Communist Eastern Europe, engaged on a cold and unprofitable journalistic assignment. From the East German, Yugoslav and Bulgarian newspapers, it seemed as though Communist tanks were rolling all over South Vietnam, that MIGs had the mastery of the air, and that Saigon was soon to be renamed Ho Chi Minh City, as it was seven years later. Determined to get back there, I got a journalistic assignment in Kenya, which seemed to be on the way, and then the promise of going to Cambodia in the summer, so that by early April I reached Hong Kong and a few days later was back at M. Ottavj's Royale Hotel.

The Collapse of the Americans: 1968–72 55

Among those present were Philip Jones Griffiths and another old friend, the Australian Murray Sayle, a tall, hawk-beaked scholar-adventurer, who had recently made a name for himself as a journalist by feats such as sailing single-handed across the Atlantic, and climbing most of the way up Everest. Like Philip, he is a splendid travelling companion, forever inquisitive, patient, amused and unafraid. During a flight to Danang on a C130 troop plane the pressurisation failed and most of the young GIs collapsed or fainted from lack of oxygen, and I too felt weak, when Murray came up, smoking a big cigar, and asked what was wrong with all these fellows.

Just over two months after the start of the Tet Offensive, the I Corps of South Vietnam was still in a state of shock. Although the US Marines had held Khe Sanh and helped to retake Hue, they had suffered a blow to their pride, or their arrogance as it was seen by other regiments. 'The Marines don't dig!' was the angry answer given to any suggestion that they protect themselves in trenches or shelters. As a result they suffered severe and pointless casualties from the NVA's artillery, rocket and mortar power, now much more formidable than when I had been there first in 1966.

Some Marine units were so depleted that they had been replaced by their hated rivals the First Air Cavalry. There were alarming rumours in I Corps that the Marines and the 'Air Cav' were shooting at each other's helicopters, as if there was not danger enough from the NVA's increasingly accurate ground fire. A new 'Americal' Division, cobbled together from infantry units and mostly made up of unhappy conscripts, had taken over part of the I Corps, and later disgraced itself by the My Lai massacre. Soon after the Tet Offensive, the MACVEE high command seized its chance to close down all the pacification projects such as the CAC teams in I Corps, preferring to fight in conventional set-piece battles out in the rain forest.

Many years later, American military writers came to see that this was a strategy wished on them by the North Vietnamese General Vo Nguyen Giap. Having defeated the French in 1954 by trapping an army at Dien Bien Phu in north-west Vietnam, Giap drew the Americans into another, apparently similar battle at Khe Sanh, once again close to the border with Laos. The Americans gladly took up the challenge, confident in the air power that the French had lacked. It later became clear that Giap had never hoped or even intended to take Khe Sanh, but was using it as a feint to draw attention away from the main Tet Offensive against the populous coastal plains, and even against such towns as Ban Me Thuot, Hue and Saigon itself.

Since the US commanders had studied conventional warfare at West Point, during the Second World War and then in Korea, they gladly accepted the NVA's challenge, even although this meant fighting battles on the terrain of the enemy's choosing. The futility of these operations was soon apparent in 1968. Each spring and sometimes at other times of the year as well, the Americans launched their offensives into the misty jungle of hills and ravines, stretching west from the coast towards Laos. It was assumed by the Marines at the Danang Press Centre that every journalist wanted to join these military operations, so that, willy nilly, I sometimes had to go.

On one such occasion, in April 1968, I asked at the Danang Press Centre if I could get a ride to Phu Bai, the nearest military airport to Hue. 'Sure, sure,' said the sergeant and drove me out to the airport, where I met a sad-looking group of newspaper men and was put with them on a helicopter that went to a desolate place called Camp Eagle. Becoming suspicious, I asked once more if there would be a helicopter taking me to Hue and the same sergeant replied: 'Sure, sure.' Ten minutes later I was aboard a much bigger helicopter which set off in a westward direction as a half-witted officer announced that he could promise us a 'real good fire-fight' and added that eight American helicopters had been shot down that day round the place to which we were going. We arrived in the rain at a red earth clearing, raw as a wound in the jungle, which here consisted of dead and broken trees. Heavy guns were firing in all directions into the forest and it occurred to me that although these Americans probably did not know where the Communists were, the Communists probably knew where we were. And so they did, for within a few minutes mortars or rockets were crashing into our camp.

An American TV journalist (who was later killed in Cambodia) was not satisfied with the quantity of the attack and demanded to go to the next camp, which may have been called Bastogne, after a battle in the Ardennes, or even Khe Sanh itself, where the combat would be more spectacular. 'But this kind of war is meaningless,' I said to him, and he agreed but went on: 'My company just wants film with the most bangs and the most dead bodies, and I like to show the people at home how bloody and pointless this war is.' While this TV man was asking to travel westwards, I was asking to go back east to Hue, Camp Eagle or even back to Danang, which was where I was taken in the end. That evening the colonel in charge of the Press Centre found to his disgust that five of the reporters present were Europeans, a people he now distrusted. 'If I were President of the United States,' he informed the *Le Monde* correspondent, 'the first thing I'd do would be to drop a hydrogen bomb on Paris.'

Having failed to get to Hue by air and not wanting to risk the journey by road from Danang, I succeeded in getting a ride on a little ship of the US Navy. It was a squat, flat-bottomed, ugly vessel that did not inspire confidence. Nor did its crew. Except for the worried Negro captain, myself and Murray Sayle, who had turned up again at the Press Centre, there was not a sober man on board when we left Danang beach in the evening. Indeed some of the crew had arrived so drunk that they could scarcely board at all. They had brought liquor with them and probably drugs and they went below as soon as we set sail, leaving the deck, the bridge and the view of the lights of Danang to Murray, myself and the anxious skipper, who was grasping the wheel with both hands during the voyage.

Soon after dawn we reached the mouth of the Perfume River, about ten miles downstream from Hue. It must have been some Buddhist festival, for fishing boats carried streamers of green or red instead of the yellow-and-orange marzipan flag of the Republic of Vietnam. 'The fishermen are not hostile,' I was told by one of the crew who had come on deck for air to relieve his hangover, but shortly afterwards he and another sailor went to the lengths of manning one of the heavy machine-guns with which the vessel was armed. The first sailor took aim at a group of old women plodding along the northern bank and muttered a 'rat-a-tat-tat' from beneath his teeth. 'What are you playing at?' asked his friend, to which the first sailor replied: 'Playing war games, I suppose.' Further upstream, we started to pass wrecked and burned-out houses and pagodas, and over the paddy fields we could see the Phantom jets strafing the equally phantom Communists. 'Up here the people are VC,' the first sailor said, and went down to join the rest of the crew in the kitchen, or galley, the safest part of the ship, leaving the deck, the wheel and the guns once more to Murray, myself and the captain. Many years later, just such a trip up a Vietnamese river, with an intoxicated crew and a dour black skipper, featured in Francis Coppola's film *Apocalypse Now*.

From press reports of the Tet Offensive, I half expected to find Hue flattened like Hamburg or Dresden after the Second World War, but there was not much sign of damage. The one-storey wooden houses north of the river are almost as easy to rebuild as to knock down; the home of the matriarch whom I described in the previous chapter had suffered a hole in the roof, which was now repaired. She pressed me to stay to lunch. The former French and Mandarin part of the city south of the Perfume River had not suffered so much from artillery fire.

The home of Jacques Sanlaville next to the power station was overrun by the Communists on the first day of Tet but no harm came to him, his Cambodian wife or their many engaging children. The Communists stayed in his house, which later was bombed or shelled by the Americans with anti-personnel *fléchettes* – barbed, inch-long arrows of steel that explode in all directions from a canister with deadly force. Two months later Sanlaville showed me the trees in his garden, so profusely embedded with *fléchettes* that I gave up trying to count them. I am told the

Americans used these atrocious weapons wholesale in their bombing attacks on North Vietnam.

On this visit to Hue in April 1968, I found Jacques Sanlaville at his usual chair in the Cercle Sportif, which had several holes in the wall and had lost all its billiard balls to a looter. When Sanlaville raised his glass of beer in a greeting, I noticed that some of his fingers were missing but this was not a result of Tet, but an earlier ambush along the road from Danang. 'I managed to drive back to Hue,' he told me. 'My Vietnamese assistant, sitting next to me, wasn't touched but he spent two months in hospital suffering from shock.'

Most of the US bombardment after the Tet Offensive, including naval artillery used against individual snipers, had been directed onto the Citadel itself. This showed so little sign of damage afterwards that some Americans claimed that they had wanted to spare an historic monument, just as the Royal Air Force claimed to have spared Cologne Cathedral during the Second World War. The truth is that the walls of Hue Citadel had been built so strong that the shells scarcely dented them, just as the British bombs bounced off Cologne Cathedral.

During the Tet Offensive the Communists killed at least 2,000 political enemies, many of whom were later unearthed from mass graves. The massacres were discussed with remarkable lack of excitement. 'It was rather like France after the liberation,' said one Frenchman, not Jacques Sanlaville. 'The Communists had a list of people they thought were traitors, but others got killed for purely personal reasons. They were denounced by servants or by people with grudges.' A planter from near Khe Sanh, who had come to Hue that fatal Tet 'to get a holiday from the war', was staying with priests when the Communists came. 'They shot two priests dead, I was shot in the leg but they left it at that. They didn't kill me. Another priest was not harmed. He had a box with about 16,000 piastres which were the church funds. He tried to hide the box under his robes but the Communists told him to produce it. They took it and gave him a receipt. A few days later he was noticed by two of his former students who were serving with the Vietcong. They told their commander: "This is a friend of the Vietnamese. He was always good to his students." So then the priest produced his receipt and the Vietcong gave him his money back.' Most of the people killed by the Communists were policemen, politicians and civil servants but some priests, teachers and doctors were shot as well.

After the recapture of Hue at the end of February 1968, the South Vietnamese revenged the Communist murders. General Loan, who had been photographed in Saigon shooting a Vietcong prisoner, flew north to Hue to supervise the punishment of the Communists. One day, during our visit in April, Murray and I were walking across the Clemenceau Bridge, now partially wrecked and closed to motorised transport, when we passed an American and a Vietnamese soldier leading four Communist suspects, three boys and a girl, all of them blindfolded and handcuffed. The American told us that these suspects, who were aged about eighteen, had spent a few days in a police station and now were going to ARVIN for further interrogation. When I asked if these suspects would afterwards go to prison, the soldier looked at me with surprise before answering 'Maybe'. Murray and I followed the party into an ARVIN compound near the southern bank of the river where we met a second American, a corporal in intelligence. The first American said: 'I've brought you some more meat,' and the second one answered: 'Yeah, and I see some of it's female.' We saw the prisoners taken into a shed where a tough ARVIN man singled out one of the boys, gave him a violent boot in the testicles, punched his head, then kicked him again in the base of the stomach. This interrogation process, watched by those awaiting their turn, appeared to be quite routine, and at first Murray and I were too surprised to protest. When we did so, the intelligence corporal, who was a southerner, said with the natural courtesy of his people: 'I'd appreciate it if you gentlemen were to leave the compound.'

Later that day I fell into chat with a young US infantryman, who held strong views about Hue: 'You know that bridge that was blown up? They should clear it away and build a four-lane flyover. This could be a real nice city. It's a pity the people aren't civilised.' The South Vietnamese government did not take this young soldier's advice. The Clemenceau Bridge was later repaired by the same French Eiffel company that had designed it.

From Hue I went to Ban Me Thuot in the western Highlands, a town that had also been overrun in the Tet Offensive. Among the casualties was the American missionary Robert Ziemer, who had described to me the year before his efforts to make the Rhade people weep over their sins. When the Communists surrounded their mission compound, Ziemer came out of cover shouting, 'We are civilians, with women and children', and took a burst of shots in the chest, becoming the first of the six American missionaries killed that day in Ban Me Thuot. Another civilian American, Mike Benge, who had taken Philip Jones Griffiths and me round several Montagnard villages where he was treated as an honoured friend, had fallen into the hands of the Communists, and remained their prisoner until 1972. Perhaps because he had learnt to rough it among the Montagnards, Benge survived the diseases and poor diet that cost the lives of many American prisoners in the Vietnam forest.

The Special Forces, with whom I had gone on an elephant journey the previous year, were also among the casualties of the Tet Offensive. Just as MACVEE, the American high command, had used the military setback as an excuse to stop pacification in I Corps, it now saw a chance of closing down all irregular, non-conventional units. A good pretext came when the Green Berets were accused of throwing a suspected double agent out of a helicopter into the South China Sea, describing the murder as 'termination with extreme prejudice'. The euphemism appeared again in the film *Apocalypse Now*.

Early in May 1968 I went to Dalat, the hill station that had not suffered during the Tet Offensive. Whereas the Communists used the western part of the Highlands for distributing material brought down the Ho Chi Minh Trail, they did not bother to take control of the eastern towns such as Dalat. The Vietcong occasionally made a gesture in Dalat, as when they raised their red star flag over a cinema showing a Rock Hudson film, but they normally kept an informal truce with the Saigon forces.

However, when I was there in May 1968, a great many Communist troops in civilian clothes were thought to have entered Dalat, which sprawls over so large an area that one suburb does not know what is happening in any other. I was already the only guest in the large, silent Palace Hotel, whose receptionists in their brown sweaters were knitting intently and suffering *'beaucoup de peur'*. On 7 May the receptionists, the chef and still worse the barman failed to turn up for work because of their *'beaucoup de peur'*, and I was left alone with the porter in what had become an alarming hotel. Next morning, 8 May, I went for a walk to try to find out what was happening, until I was stopped by a kindly man who said: 'Get away from here, they're all VC.' This was how I discovered that the Communists had begun their second or May Offensive.

Because this May Offensive came at the time of riots and student excitement in the United States, Germany and above all Paris, it did not receive the same publicity as Tet. Perhaps, in retrospect, it should be seen as the second half of a desperate contest that ended with the defeat of both sides, the United States forces and the indigenous South Vietnamese Communists. Although the Americans lingered on in ever-decreasing numbers till 1972, the May Offensive coming on top of Tet had finally broken their will to fight. Yet at the same time, their futile sacrifice had broken the hearts of the Southern Communists, as they admitted twenty years later. This was really the end of the Vietnam insurgency. From now until the fall of Saigon in May 1975, the Vietnam War was once again part of the struggle for power between North and South that began as long ago as the sixteenth century.

That is how I see it with hindsight. No such thoughts were in my head on the afternoon of 8 May 1968, when I got a lift to Dalat airport, and found a seat on a gleaming silver plane belonging to President Thieu, which was just about to take off for Saigon. On the descent to Saigon's Tan Son Nhut airport, the pilot as usual executed a steep and alarming dive to avoid ground fire, and this time the precaution was justified, for the Vietcong had seized much of the south-west part of the city and were indeed firing at all arriving and departing planes, including ours as I was afterwards told.

At the Royale Hotel, I found my colleagues in shock. Four British and Australian journalists had been shot dead that morning while travelling in their jeep to a contested part of the city. According to a survivor, who had played possum, the journalists had yelled '*Bao Chi*' ('press') to the Communist officer, who merely laughed and then gunned them down. The US Ambassador condemned the killings as an atrocity but most of us regarded them more as a mishap. It was unreasonable to expect that the Communists in a battle should be able to tell the difference between the military and civilian white men, especially when so many journalists wore uniform and carried guns. A representative of one of the grandest American newspapers had helped to storm the Citadel at Hue, and in Saigon, during the May Offensive, a US photographer borrowed an M16 to 'avenge a dead buddy' and was himself shot dead at the old French cemetery. In all, seven journalists were killed in Saigon that week.

There was a curfew for all but a couple of hours a day, during which M. Ottavj would hobble off with his stick to buy food and wine for his customers. As usual in time of confusion and fear, M. Ottavj and the Royale Hotel represented order and confidence. Dinner was served in the small *salle à manger*, separated by iron lace from the large room in which the entire staff and all their families were lodged throughout the emergency. As we ate in the evenings, dozens of children in white pyjamas would stare at us through the partition.

On the evening of 8 May the mood was sombre until the arrival of one of the more flamboyant reporters, a huge and fiery-faced Irish Australian, Pat Burgess, who had just come back from the countryside and seemed not to have heard of the dead Australian and British reporters, nor of the curfew imposed on most public places. When he had taken a glass of wine, Pat announced his intention of going round to the nearby Princess Bar. We tried to explain that the bars were all shut but Pat affected not to believe us. His voice had a defensive tone as he went on to say: 'The cashier in the Empress Bar is the only Asian Sheila I've met who can exercise muscle control' – the last two words being heavily stressed. We gaped at him, for in those days the British were only starting to learn the Australian argot. We gaped still more when Pat went on in the same aggrieved manner: 'Well I don't know about you fellows, but it's six weeks now since I exercised the armadillo.' It took me years to understand that this had been part of the favourite Australian sport of baiting the British. The last time I met Pat Burgess, in Sydney in 1972, the bicentenary of the landing of Captain Cook, I heard him remark to a friend that Sir Joseph Banks, the scientist who went on the expedition, was without doubt a 'pooftah'. What proof did he have? 'Banks was a botanist and a Pommy – what more proof do you need?'

Two evenings after his failure to get to the Empress Bar, Pat Burgess himself was in sombre mood. He had gone out the previous day on a sortie with General Loan and was photographed standing beside the notorious Vietnamese as he, Loan, was shot in the leg. Pat was taken aback by his narrow escape and also by the publicity of the photograph, which soon became almost as famous as that of Loan shooting the prisoner. 'I know what people say about General Loan,' Pat confided to me, 'but as far as I'm concerned he's a plucky little bastard.'

The war was unpleasantly close in Saigon during the May Offensive. At seven o'clock in the morning on my first day back, Philip Jones Griffiths knocked on my door and asked if I wanted to visit the area of the fighting. He looked like a dog with a walking stick in its mouth that is eager to go for a run. Normally I try to avoid such things, for I never worked for a newspaper that offered the two things – money and fame – that compensate a reporter for the risks he takes. My only outlet for articles at the time was the BBC weekly *Listener*; and who would lay down his life for the *Listener*? But although most war is boring as well as frightening, a battle fought actually in a city would at least be interesting.

The Communists at this time held much of the south-west part of Saigon and its sister-city, the Chinatown of Cholon. The two sides were installed on either bank of the Saigon Canal, which is crossed at one point by the Y-Bridge, known formerly as the Bridge of Love. An island in the canal, also reachable from the bridge, was supposedly neutral territory. From the Royale Hotel to the Y-Bridge took only ten minutes by taxi, in spite of the thousands of refugees crowding the streets.

Near the Y-Bridge Philip and I joined a platoon of the Vietnamese Rangers who were going to make a sweep through a suburb that had first been occupied by the Communists then shelled and rocketed by the Americans. All civilians were ordered to leave the district, which had therefore become a 'free-fire' zone, meaning that anyone who moved there was presumed to be a Communist. The patrol set off in leisurely fashion, taking advantage of cover along each side of the street. An army cameraman joined at one point and two days later I saw on Saigon TV the very patrol of which I had been a part; on TV it looked very exciting – like one of those Westerns where Gary Cooper stalks the villains through a deserted town.

Behind the patrol came a van to collect the enemy casualties, most of them dead but a few only dying, who were picked up by the arms and legs and thrown in the back. One of the dead wore a handsome if rather blood-stained ammunition pouch in the VC colours, which I removed (and later gave to a Trotskyist young woman), but unfortunately one of the Rangers spotted me and immediately started to re-examine the bodies to find out what he had missed. Another Ranger present, a boy of ten or eleven enrolled as a mascot, uttered blood-curdling phrases of GI English: 'Yesterday I kill mother-f—ing VCess. No shit!' Philip proclaimed that the VCess, or female VC, was the boy's own mother, but nevertheless he was publicised in the government press as a symbol of youthful patriotism.

At one point during our slow progression I became detached

from the platoon and was startled to hear a voice behind me saying '*Bonjour, monsieur*'. A neatly dressed, elderly Vietnamese had come up a side-street to warn me, '*Attention*! There are two VC in the house opposite', then asked if I would do him the honour of visiting him at his home. 'But you're not supposed to be here,' I said, 'you could be bombed.' '*Monsieur*,' he retorted with pride, 'it would take more than these events to move me out of my house.' He invited me in, poured me a large whisky (very welcome that morning) and showed me photographs of his career as an NCO in the French Army. 'Fifteen years' service, *monsieur*, and if it was left to me I could clear these Communists out in a day.' However, it was noticeable that his family and the neighbour, whom he had bullied into staying, were far less confident than this fierce old soldier and kept on asking me what the situation was. Rather bewildered by this encounter, as by the whisky and the heat of May, I thought I had better rejoin the patrol before I got lost in a deserted city. The old soldier took me back to the corner where the VC were, and I saw the patrol in the distance.

Not all the casualties in the May Offensive were VC, and Philip Jones Griffiths took some distressing photographs of children killed by shelling or rockets from helicopters. The carnage had been especially bad on the island on the canal, which houses one of Saigon's largest municipal slaughterhouses. On the first day of the offensive, many people had fled the Communist zone to get away from the answering bombardment and had settled as refugees in the cattle pens and pig sties, from which they could see their houses burn a few hundred yards away. However, the VC had briefly come to the island, which therefore became a free-fire zone, although the bombardment came after the VC had left. The whole place stank of dead humans and animals and was loud with the noise of air strikes on the other side. Philip warned me that we might be attacked by the refugees if they thought we were American, so we said we were French, a more familiar people than the English. We were greeted with smiles and even invited to eat meals cooked in the stalls and sties.

At the time I thought that there must be some novelty of the macabre about a battle fought in a slaughterhouse but, as so often in Vietnam, it had all happened before. A year or two after the May Offensive I read George Rosie's book *The British in Vietnam* describing the months in 1945 when, by arming the Japanese and letting the French attack the anti-colonial Vietnamese, Britain sparked off the war that by now had lasted twenty years. The Vietnamese Communists seized and defended the Saigon Town Hall and called for an insurrection against the British occupation. They were poorly armed but managed to put up a fight in some districts. According to Rosie, one of the bloodiest battles between the Vietnamese and Indian Army troops took place at the very same slaughterhouse on the island in the canal.

The carnage in 1945 was slight by comparison to the May Offensive, for only fighting men were affected. From the Y-Bridge in 1968 I saw the folly and cruelty of unleashing technological war on a city. About 200 yards away a helicopter was firing rockets down into a large building, a factory that was said to contain VC. Flames leapt up, to cheers from the Y-Bridge, when a Vietnamese policeman approached and said there were no VC and that some of his colleagues were in the factory. Nobody paid him any attention, indeed there was no sign of an officer with the American troops and tanks on the Y-Bridge. The only man to exercise any authority was the English journalist Donald Wise who had served as an officer in the Second World War and then the Malaya Emergency before reporting the 'Wind of Change' in countries like Kenya, the Congo and later Uganda, Nigeria, Mozambique, Angola, Rhodesia and his native South Africa. Tall, thin, distinguished and almost a double of David Niven, the actor, Wise quickly imposed his will on the leaderless troops on the Y-Bridge, who even stood to attention and called him 'Sir'. This was comic, since Wise was then the *Daily Mirror* correspondent.

An American TV crew was filming the refugees who kept retreating over the bridge. The producer wanted more excitement and therefore grabbed an American soldier, pointed towards a building a hundred yards away and yelled: 'VC! Look, there!' 'Where, where?' asked the soldier, so the producer took his assault rifle and pointed it for him. 'Oh, yeah,' said the soldier, and though he was not really convinced, he squeezed off some rounds and soon other soldiers were firing at roughly the same target, which turned out to be a stable in which some civilians were sheltering. Perhaps a few horses and people may have been killed, but the TV producer obtained some memorable footage.

The only admirable people on this occasion were the Buddhist monks, who ventured deep into Communist-held districts to bring out wounded civilians. Foreigners used to sneer at these Buddhist 'boy scouts' (I did in *Sketches from Vietnam*) but there was no doubt of their courage on the Y-Bridge. One could not say the same thing of the US troops who came from the 9th Division, stationed at My Tho in the Delta. They skulked most of the time behind their tanks, whose turrets were crowned with Confederate flags and whose insides were crammed with looted drink and miniature TV sets. It was there, on the Y-Bridge in May 1968, that I first saw the collapse of morale in the US Army.

The loss of America's will to fight was one of the most important phenomena of the Vietnam War. As late as the end of 1967, most of the troops I met were patriotic, disciplined and willing to serve – in short 'motivated', to use the current jargon. Four years later, what remained of the army was drugged, depressed and even mutinous, its loyalty undermined by black and radical agitation. Some of the change could be attributed to the failure to win a clear-cut victory, although since most of the men were conscripts serving only one year, they could not plead battle weariness. Some of the symptoms of demoralisation, especially the epidemics of radical politics, drug abuse, sexual assaults on women and murder, were also found in 'the world', as soldiers called the United States. The social revolution that swept the West in the 1960s is now part of the history books. Among its expressions in the United States were the breakdown of taboos against extra-marital sex, abortion, pornography, homosexual behaviour and drug abuse. Having abandoned its Hays Code on sexual morals, Hollywood in 1969 allowed the glamorisation of drugs in the film *Easy Rider*. It was a decade too of increasingly violent political groups, many inspired by Castro's Cuba or by 'liberation movements' in Africa and the Middle East.

Later it came to be the accepted liberal wisdom that the tragedy of the Vietnam War was the cause of the social revolution in the United States; however, I think the reverse was true. The Americans brought their social revolution to Vietnam, not only wrecking their army but causing added misery to the country they once had wanted to help. The Vietnamese never accepted America's social revolution. Like most Asians, they hated the long-haired hippies, especially their blasphemous claim to follow Hindu or Buddhist religious beliefs. The Vietnamese never took to American pop music, greatly preferring the sad, traditional songs of the Hue poet-composer Trinh Cong Son. When a Saigon cinema put on a film of the Woodstock festival, the audience jeered and whistled. Although later, tens of thousands of Vietnamese were hooked on the heroin and other drugs introduced by Americans, there never existed a cult of the joys of marijuana, as in the film *Easy Rider*.

Apart from the bar girls, few Vietnamese women, even those who learnt English, adopted American attitudes to morality. They did not drink alcohol or smoke tobacco, let alone marijuana; they tried to be sexually chaste until marriage; at dances they stuck to the graceful tango, foxtrot or quick step. Above all they kept to their modest national dress. When *Playboy* magazine wanted a special issue on Asian girls showing representatives of each country naked or near-naked, the Vietnamese appeared in an *ao dai*, clothed to the tips of the neck, wrists and ankles. And even this lady, the actress Kieu Chinh, told me afterwards that she was furious at having been shown, even clothed, on the same page as girls in the nude. So conservative were the Vietnamese in their dress, that a proposal to lower the *ao dai* neckline by even an inch caused an argument comparable to that in the West over the topless swim-suit.

From 1968 until the withdrawal from Vietnam four years later, the American Army was clearly in disarray. A whole quarter of Saigon was taken over by US deserters, who posted permanent sentries against the Military Police. As fragging, or killing by fragmentation grenades, became widespread, one of the many underground newspapers that opened in military units called on its readers to murder their colonel. This increasingly drugged and demoralised rabble was no longer willing or able to fight the enemy, so turned its aggression instead against its own officers and the civilian Vietnamese. All these things reflected the social revolution in the United States itself.

The progress of demoralisation in the American forces has been recorded for future historians in the files of an unusual newspaper, the *Overseas Weekly*, Pacific Edition, edited for its first five years in Saigon by an enterprising young woman, Ann Bryan. The *Overseas Weekly* started in Germany after the Second World War as a newspaper for troops who wanted something besides the semi-official *Stars and Stripes*. It annoyed the Pentagon when it printed the story that a general had handed out leaflets on behalf of the right-wing John Birch Society. From 1966, when it began its Pacific Edition, the *Overseas Weekly* was banned from most of the PX or army stores and had to be sold by subscription or in the streets.

The files of the *Overseas Weekly*, which I examined in Saigon during the early 1970s, told the astonishing story of an army in decay. Much of this was based on the reports of court martials and factual inquiries among the men. 'Troops throw Frag Grenade at Lt Colonel,' said one typical headline (5 May 1969), or 'Angry GI guns down Captain with M16' (24 July 1971). An *Overseas Weekly* investigation (3 January 1972) showed that during the three years ending in 1971 there had been 500 cases of 'fragging' assaults with grenades or other explosive devices, most of them against officers or senior NCOs. 'From the Delta to northern I Corps,' the *Overseas Weekly* reported, 'fragging in Vietnam has become a way of life.' The court martial reports also describe attacks on civilians, for instance a bar girl, Miss Anh. 'We sat there for about fifteen minutes, then there was a shooting. Miss Anh was shot with a small gun. After he brought her tea, he says: "Are you shitting me?" Then he shot her.' The countless rapes of Vietnamese women, often forcing them to perform fellatio with a pistol held at the head, very seldom led to a prosecution and therefore a court martial.

The *Overseas Weekly* reported but did not comment upon the growing abuse of drugs towards the end of the 1960s. In one survey (23 August 1969) a soldier is quoted as saying: 'If it weren't for Mary Jane here I would have gone completely out of my mind.' And next week the same reporter observed: 'Many GIs feel that compared to the world, Vietnam is a head's paradise because of the relatively low price of grass and lax attitude towards pot users by the military.' The *Overseas Weekly* also recorded the increased use of stronger drugs, ranging from speed, through opium to heroin.

The *Overseas Weekly* appeared to accept the army view that drugs had a harmful effect on their users. In an article under the stark headline 'Why do our troops shoot each other?' (20 June 1970), it quoted an army doctor as saying that opium and racial tension were partly responsible for the fact that forty or fifty per cent of gun-shot wounds were inflicted on GIs by other GIs. The view of an army doctor might be discounted but any sample of *Overseas Weekly* articles bears him out. One man interviewed said he had grown paranoiac from marijuana, thinking that everyone was a Communist and trying to kill him. 'I even thought the dogs in the compound were Communists. They kept looking at me with their eyes. I thought about killing myself because I didn't want to be captured alive by the Chinese.' Here is the court martial report on two men who murdered a local civilian: 'Slicksleaves Kenneth E. Ritter and George English puffed on pot but they were far from relaxed. In fact they wanted a little action. The two troopers from the 335th Trans. Co. decided their idea of sport would be to go out and harass some Vietnamese people' (8 February 1969). At the trials of Lieutenant Calley and others for the My Lai massacre, it was stated in evidence that many if not most of the men responsible had been smoking marijuana not long before the shooting took place.

Liberal opinion blamed these atrocities not on drugs, pornography or other features of the American Permissive Society, but on the Vietnam War itself. In January 1971 a group called Vietnam Veterans Against the War held a hearing in Detroit at which more than a hundred members testified publicly to crimes either witnessed or committed by them in Vietnam – twenty-eight of which were documented in a subsequent film, *Winter Soldier*. These crimes included the splitting open of infants' heads with cans of food for which they were begging, the dropping of live prisoners from helicopters and the rape of a dying woman with an entrenchment tool. Gilbert Adair, the author of *Hollywood's Vietnam* from which I take this account of *Winter Soldier*, seems to accept that in some mysterious way the war itself obliged these men to commit such crimes: 'That for obvious reasons the movie can offer little in the way of visual evidence to support this testimony (though one of the witnesses had consented to be photographed in the act of torturing a woman) in no way diminishes its power: men who were self-confessed killers *then* we see, in agonising close-ups, to be ordinary God-fearing if profoundly troubled citizens *now*, painfully straining (many are poorly educated) to articulate the warped rationale behind their crime.'

It was an article of faith to the 1960s liberals, especially to those of the long-haired 'love generation', that marijuana and other drugs induced a spirit of gentleness. For this reason they welcomed the news that eighty per cent of the troops in Vietnam had at least tried 'Mary Jane'. Most foreign journalists in Saigon, even if they were years ahead of the 'love generation', refused even to argue the possibility that drugs could induce aggression, in spite of historical evidence that, from Indonesia to Morocco, hashish or bhang or marijuana was commonly taken by soldiers before battle, making them fearless and pitiless. There is evidence to suggest that drugs had the same effect in Vietnam. It was when I tried to report the harmful effects of drugs, pornography and radical politics in Vietnam, that I first encountered the liberal censorship that now would be called Political Correctness. Neither the *Listener* nor the *New Statesman*, for which I had written from Vietnam, would publish articles on this subject.

The Collapse of the Americans: 1968–72

Drugs and demoralisation made the Americans dangerous to the civilian population, but useless at fighting the North Vietnamese, or what remained of the local Vietcong. Those officers who were brave enough to risk getting 'fragged' could sometimes persuade their men to make a patrol or even search through a village, like My Lai, but most units stayed in their fortified camps or better still in an underground bunker. When an American unit came into contact with enemy troops, it seldom tried to engage them on the ground but instead took cover and called in an air or artillery strike. Relying on the accuracy of the targeting technology, the Americans frequently called in strikes on an enemy less than a hundred yards distant, often resulting in errors and deaths from 'friendly fire'. A television film on the subject that came out in 1979 claimed that, between 1968 and 1973, no fewer than 10,303 American soldiers were known to have died in Vietnam through 'friendly fire'. Moreover America's ever-increasing reliance on long-distance air and artillery fire, rather than fighting the war at close range, resulted in tens of thousands of largely civilian Vietnamese casualties.

Even before the Marines had landed in South Vietnam in March 1965, the United States had begun its carpet-bombing attack on the North, which eventually killed more than 100,000 civilians and left more than twenty-two million craters. Although some of the strikes were aimed at military targets along the Ho Chi Minh Trail, much of this long bombardment struck the populous region of North Vietnam. Since there were few factories or legitimate 'economic' targets, the US Air Force concentrated its venom on towns and villages in the coastal strip and the Red River Delta. Because there were few foreign reporters in North Vietnam, and even they remained largely in Hanoi, the capital, which did not receive an attack till Christmas 1972, the outside world knew little about this aerial atrocity. Here is one account of a series of raids on the village of Vinh Quang, just to the north of the 17th parallel, in July 1967, recorded by Stanley Karnow and reproduced in his *Vietnam: A History*:

The bombing started at about eight o'clock in the morning and lasted for hours. At the first sound of explosions, we rushed in to the tunnels, but not everyone made it. During a pause in the attack, some of us climbed out to see what we could do, and the scene was terrifying. Bodies had been torn to pieces – limbs hanging from trees or scattered around the ground. Then the bombing began again, this time with napalm and the village went up in flames. The napalm hit me and I must have gone crazy. I felt as if I were burning all over, like charcoal, and I lost consciousness. Comrades took me to the hospital, and my wounds didn't begin to heal until six months later. More than two hundred people died in the raid, including my mother, my sister-in-law, and three nephews. They were buried alive when their tunnel collapsed.

After the Tet Offensive, the Americans came to rely on air and artillery power, including the use of anti-personnel weapons, such as *fléchette* darts, to cow or punish the people of South Vietnam. During a stay in Danang in the summer of 1968, I called at the West German hospital ship then moored at the waterfront, probably in the hope of meeting one of the beautiful nurses said to be working there. Instead I was introduced to a large, disapproving matron, resembling an ageing Brünnhilde who had been cheeked by one of the junior Valkyrie. She gave me a tour which was thankfully quick, until we arrived at the napalm ward. As I forced myself to glance at, if not examine, those roasted, pain-racked bodies, mostly women and children, the matron explained to me: 'Almost none of the victims live more than three weeks even if they survive the burns. They die of poisoning of the kidneys.'

I was so shocked by the napalm ward that I did not think to protest when the matron said afterwards: 'I will now arrange for you to see the Vietnamese state hospital in Danang,' but it turned out to be less alarming. Like other state hospitals I had seen in the country, its lack of equipment and sanitation were in part balanced out by the friendly atmosphere, in which relatives of the patients could wander and even camp in the wards. Furthermore there were only a few napalm cases, since most of these went to the hospital ship, or as I suspected, were gently eased out of their agony. On this same visit to Danang I met two American military doctors who told me categorically that there were no civilian victims of napalm. They just would not believe what I had seen and been told at the hospital ship. They were humane, honourable people and I suspect that, knowing the horror of napalm, they could not live with the thought that their own country was using this weapon, even in error, to kill women and children. At about this time a group of American doctors toured Vietnam and later reported that all burns attributed to napalm were due to the use of 'unfamiliar cooking fluid'. Apparently they had not been told by their interpreters that the Vietnamese word for napalm was the same as for cooking fluid and gasoline.

The American Army's loss of morale and growing reliance on fire power was seen at its worst around My Tho, the Mekong Delta town where I stayed for a fortnight in February 1969, while making a television film for the BBC. The surrounding province of Dinh Thuong was one of the three in the Delta where the US Army and Navy sent in combat troops to support the ARVIN. American tanks – I noticed three in a row called Alcatraz, Assassin and Amputator – ground through the suburbs of My Tho between the hedgerows of barbed wire. Naval vessels patrolled the rivers and the canals to 'police up' (meaning to blow to pieces) sampans breaking the curfew. The artillery of the 9th Division pounded away at everything in the 'free-fire' zone, and many places outside it, so that at first I could not sleep at night because of the thunder of guns. Long after the war I learnt that this artillery barrage was part of Operation Speedy Express, whose mastermind, General Julian Ewell, believed in the merits of 'body count', even if some of the bodies were clearly civilian. In his debriefing report of September 1969, General Ewell wrote: 'I guess I basically feel that the "hearts and minds" approach can be overdone. In the Delta the only way to overcome VC control and terror is by brute force applied against the VC.'

All Ewell's battalion commanders had to carry a three-inch by five-inch card with an up-to-date, day-to-day, week-to-week, and month-to-month body count tally just in case the General happened to show up wanting to know. 'With the main motivator being body count,' wrote Colonel David H. Hackworth, who served for a time under Ewell, 'in my view the powers that be didn't give a damn whose body was counted, and a great many – too many – civilians in the Delta were part of the scores.' Most of the body count came from artillery strikes since few of the troops in the 9th Division were capable of combat. Colonel Hackworth himself has described the state of his own battalion when he assumed command in 1969:

> It was total disintegration. Throughout the fire base, amid the shit and the toilet paper and the machine-gun ammo lying in the mud, were troops who wore love beads and peace symbols and looked more like something out of Haight-Ashbury than soldiers in the US Army. All were low on spirit and a few were high, openly, on marijuana.

Another American officer who served in the Mekong Delta during the same year, 1969, has described in his memoirs how the collapse among the GIs made them brutal and arrogant towards the Vietnamese. David Donovan, the pseudonymous author of *Once a Warrior King* (incidentally one of the very best books on Vietnam), had been an adviser in Kien Phuong Province where there were no American units, for which he was grateful because it meant there were no needless casualties from 'H & I', or 'harassment and interdiction' shelling. He got on well with the 30,000 Vietnamese in his district and did his best to protect them from the savage attacks of the Communists. On his visits to Can Tho, My Tho and Saigon, Donovan was horrified by what had become of the US Army. He was shocked to hear servicemen talk of the Vietnamese as 'gooks' and 'slopes' particularly when the speakers were blacks who would be enraged at hearing the word 'nigger'. He thought that the Black Power agitation had caused 'an almost monolithic prejudice' against whites, provoking hatred in return: 'I remember thinking that it seemed as if we had two different armies based in Saigon, one white and one black.'

At My Tho, the home of the 9th Division, Donovan saw an American soldier pull an old woman off her bicycle and then ride away to the cheers of his friends. Donovan knocked the soldier off the bike, using his rifle-butt, to be met by the furious comeback: 'What's it to you? Who the hell are you? I was just playing a little. It didn't hurt anybody.' An artillery officer intervened, not to arrest but to take the side of this private soldier and his friends: 'They're just bored . . . I know this kind of crap causes a lot of trouble. But it's unmanageable, we can't do anything about it . . . If I started handing out Article 15s just because a guy is a shithead and doesn't like the natives, I'd probably be fragged within a week.'

These were my own impressions of My Tho in 1969 and how it had changed since I went there first:

> The coming of American troops had brought the usual abundance of barbed wire, black-market stalls, whores, bars and hatred to what had once been a quiet provincial town. Our small hotel was full of Koreans – the scowling variety, not the smiling – who spent most of their time walking naked along the corridor, screaming abuse at the staff or, to judge by the noise, smashing the furniture with their fists. On the waterfront street, an old hunchback had learned to cadge cigarettes with the new phrases 'Okay! Number One!' Café loudspeakers howled out the latest popular songs, which included one set to the accompaniment of revolver shots. Sometimes one heard real revolver shots. One night I saw a small child run over and killed by a US truck. When the mother complained, she was arrested by Vietnamese police for making a nuisance. All night My Tho shook to the roar of American guns.

The village of Xuan Dong, where I was making a TV film for the BBC director Richard Taylor, is about five miles from My Tho and lies on both sides of a deep canal joining the River

Mekong to Saigon. The 5,000 inhabitants, in seven hamlets, grew rice, coconuts, oranges and bananas. About three-fifths belonged to the Catholic Church, which also owned half the land, to the chagrin of the Buddhists, but this meant that the village was on the government side, and did not object to our filming there. Because of their loyalty, most of the young men stayed at home for their military service, to join in the local Popular Force. These 120 soldiers were not impressive – one of them got drunk at a wedding and marched with a sprig of bougainvillaea stuck in his carbine – but at least they were willing to fight for their homes and families, their church or their ancestral shrines.

When the Japanese surrendered in 1945, the Vietminh started a youth group in Xuan Dong, but with the return of the French next year, these Communists gave up their weapons or went off to join the guerrillas. 'From about 1960,' the headman told us, 'the Vietminh began again and since then about forty villagers have joined them, although six of these left last Tet. In a big granary, a few grains will fall through the floorboards, to feed the rats.' However, we soon learned that the largest hamlet, with more than a thousand inhabitants, was actually under VC control at night. I dreaded having to visit this hamlet, not because of the Communists but because it lay on the other side of a stream that had to be crossed by walking along a greasy tree trunk, a torment to those who suffer from vertigo. We called at one cottage inhabited by an old lady of eighty and her son-in-law, who told us: 'The VC don't come often, perhaps every two months, but the adult men are frightened of being caught and they cross the river every night. If the VC caught me they would burn me alive or cut my throat.' His mother-in-law, the old lady, had less to fear: 'When the VC knock on the door, I have to open up very quickly and then they look inside to see if there are any men in the house. They say "How do you do, madam" and leave.'

The VC were not always so courteous. In the 'secure' part of the village I met two sisters whose lives had been scarred by the politics of assassination. One of them, Vo Thi Kho, had been in the house two years before when the VC killed her father and two of his friends with a fusillade of machine-gun fire. 'It was an experience I shall never forget,' she said with typically Vietnamese understatement. She now kept a small shop selling sweets, biscuits, tinned meat and sardines, providing her with sufficient income. Her younger sister, Vo Thi That, had been widowed at twenty, two years before, when the VC ambushed her husband. 'Remarriage for me is a bleak prospect,' she said, 'for only a poor man would marry a widow.' There were seventy war widows in Xuan Dong, not counting the widows of men killed by assassination or stray bullets and shells, which cost the lives of about twelve people a year. In the less secure hamlets of Xuan Dong, each hut had some primitive dug-out shelter lined with wood, a car door or flattened beer cans soldered together. One old lady showed me her two means of protection – a shelter the size of a bath-tub and a packet of blood pressure pills.

During a week of research with Richard Taylor and then a week of filming with Chris Menges, I talked to many villagers and also to US officials engaged in aid, redevelopment, pacification and reconstruction. Even then I never quite grasped the difference between the Self-Government Pilot Scheme and the Revolutionary Development Self-Help Project, and now, a quarter century later, I understand even less. I also investigated two other programmes, more clandestine and political, that were active in the Delta at the time. The Revolutionary Development Scheme and Operation Phoenix had both been devised by the Americans on the principle that in order to fight the Communists one should borrow their tactics, their ruthlessness and even their style of dress. The 'RD Cadre Teams' were groups of young men and women in black pyjamas who lived in politically contested areas, serving as guards, police and advisers. Even the word 'cadre' came from the Communists, who had taken it from the French word for 'frame', and changed its meaning first to 'small group' or 'cell' and then to an individual 'agent' or 'activist'.

The RD Cadre Teams were used by the CIA to conduct Operation Phoenix, started in 1966 as a propaganda exercise but slowly becoming a murder campaign. Since Xuan Dong was classified as a 'secure' village, it did not have an RD team or agents of Phoenix. However, I met these people at neighbouring villages and at the small district town. An American there in civilian clothes explained the role of the RD cadres in Operation Phoenix: 'There are several agencies in this province engaged in going into VC areas and murdering people. It's called "eliminating the VC infrastructure". Hell, the other side do it to.' At the time I thought that Operation Phoenix was ineffective as well as immoral, but I was wrong, as about so many things.

Our TV crew was well received in the village, where everyone got their news from the BBC overseas radio service. We were asked to so many lunches, feasts and rice-wine parties that I, for one, gained about half a stone in a fortnight. However, the province chief and his US advisers were most unwilling to let us stay in the village at night. Surely, we argued, Xuan Dong was secure? Surely the VC knew we were British and would not harm us? At last we were given permission to stay one night in the village provided that ARVIN performed a sweep of the district beforehand and we were accompanied by a US official. This second condition annoyed us because we believed this man was a CIA agent; also he carried a gun. We were all invited to stay in the house of the priest, and the village chief gave us a dinner beforehand of dried deer and shrimp crackers, chicken and lettuce, sweet potato and port and rice gin. After dinner we went to the square in front of the church where some of the villagers had assembled to watch TV on a set donated by the American government. Perhaps for our benefit, the set had been switched to the US services station and it was showing a documentary on a Los Angeles public relations man: 'Let's talk to a man who's engaged in selling things and selling people.' This was followed by the comedian Dean Martin, who leered into the camera and said: 'I didn't sleep a wink last night, my jockey shorts were on too tight.' The audience understandably started to drift away and the US official (or CIA man) said to me that many people were frightened to watch TV for fear of attracting a VC rocket attack. The village had gone to sleep by the time we retired to our rush mats in the house of the priest, who appeared in his night-shirt to give us a drink of whisky. 'This village is safe,' he assured us, 'but if anything happens you climb up that ladder into the loft.'

Night in the Delta was louder than night in Saigon. There were natural sounds such as the trilling and twanging of crickets, and a noise like radio static as though the jungle mimicked man's technological world. Birds called continually *took-took-took* often ending on cracked or false notes. There were *plop* sounds of frogs diving or carp rolling for oxygen on the surface of a pond. There were warning sounds, given mostly by pigs, turkeys and dogs, of which the pigs were the noisiest – they must fight in their dreams – while the turkeys and dogs cried out only to other animals. There were also plenty of military sounds: the US artillery firing 'H & I'; distant bombs, less noise than physical tremor; the cough of mortars (everyone calls it a cough) and the clatter of sub-machine-guns. When the Vietcong were around, or were thought to be around, the noise of the war increased to Somme volume. Then there were signal sounds. The government troops signalled by firing their carbines in single shots or in bursts of up to seven. Sometimes they banged gongs as a warning, and from half past four in the morning I heard a great honking of car horns, which was eerie because there was no road from where the noise came.

Rivers and canals are the thoroughfares of the Mekong Delta, so by half past five I heard the first putter of outboard motors that by mid-morning became the background noise of the region. At six the church bell clanged and the choristers, carrying flaming brands, made their way to the church through the coconut groves and over the monkey bridge. They doused the brands in a heap in front of the church and started to chant in nasal plainsong. Meanwhile the priest had furnished us with a breakfast of bacon, a whole roast chicken, lettuce, radishes and tomatoes, salami, bananas and oranges, toast and butter, coffee, rum, whisky and banana liqueur. The US official (or CIA man) told us that he had 'thoroughly savoured' the experience of spending a night in the village but that he had not slept a wink – though not perhaps for the same reason as Dean Martin.

Richard Taylor's film included, besides my views on the Mekong Delta, a report on military operations by Peter Arnett, a New Zealander, and one on Saigon by Mark Frankland of the *Observer*. The three of us were filmed holding a stilted conversation on the terrace of the Continental Hotel. Taylor's film was refreshingly free of the pro-Communist bias normally shown by the BBC, and it therefore delighted JUSPAO, the Joint United States Public Affairs Office, or propaganda machine. Having previously been on the list of those with a 'negative publication pattern', I found myself now well regarded. However, I no longer had any outlets for journalistic work, at any rate not from South Vietnam, where most of the newspapers kept their own staff correspondents. Nevertheless, I kept returning to Saigon for long stays in 1969, 1970 and 1971.

The Royale Hotel became my base for visits to other countries in South-east Asia, and also to Papua New Guinea and Australasia, where I was doing research for a book on Rio Tinto-Zinc and the politics of mining. Looking through my old papers recently, I found a novel about Yugoslavia I wrote while staying in M. Ottavj's Royale Hotel in 1970, apparently never sent to a publisher, and then entirely forgotten.

Saigon was extremely cheap, and at that time it was still possible for a freelance writer to set his expenses abroad against tax. But most of all I had come to feel at home in this exhilarating city. '*L'Orient attire . . .*' as M. Ottavj said, or as Kipling put it:

When you've heard the East a-calling
You won't ever heed aught else.

As the war dragged on into the 1970s, American public opinion grew ever more angry and impatient. American politicians who prided themselves on obtaining quick results were enraged by the persistence of the Vietnamese Communists. President Kennedy had put his faith in gung-ho counter-insurgency groups like the Green Berets and when these made little impression, he ordered the *coup d'état* in Saigon that led to the murder of President

Diem. Perhaps as a punishment for his attempt to play God in the affairs of another country, Kennedy was himself assassinated three weeks later.

Frustration was followed by fury and a desire to punish the North Vietnamese. President Johnson was driven almost insane by what he called that 'damned little pissant country'. He told his press secretary: 'I feel like a hitchhiker caught in a hailstorm on a Texas highway. I can't hide. I can't run. And I can't make it stop.' President Richard Nixon forced his aides to join him in watching the film about General Patton, the blood-and-guts hero of World War Two. He indulged in what he called 'madman' fantasies of obliterating North Vietnam with nuclear weapons. His foreign affairs adviser, the sinister Dr Kissinger, grew apoplectic when talking about the North Vietnamese: 'They're just a bunch of shits. Tawdry, filthy shits.'

When Napoleon advanced through Russia in 1812, he ordered the burning of captured towns because of his failure to draw Kuznetsov into a pitched battle. Leo Tolstoy in *War and Peace* compared Napoleon's temper tantrum to that of a small boy who whips the floor on which he has fallen and hurt his knee. So, in their temper tantrums, Johnson, Nixon and Kissinger rained down bombs on the North Vietnamese. The bombing was almost certainly ineffective and probably counter-productive. It did not stop traffic along the Ho Chi Minh Trail. It did not destroy the morale of the North Vietnamese Army and civil population, and may have stiffened their will to resist. During the 1960s, both China and the Soviet Union for different and purely selfish reasons were putting pressure on Hanoi to come to terms. On at least two occasions, in 1965 and 1967, a Moscow peace proposal was scuppered by a renewal of bombing raids. At that time South Vietnam could have obtained a firm guarantee of its frontiers and sovereignty. But American politicians had now forgotten why they had entered the war. The aim of defending the South had given way to the aim of punishing the North.

The behaviour of the United States was all the more foolish because, by 1968, it had already achieved its ends in South Vietnam. The revolt of the Southern Vietcong guerrillas had virtually ended after the Tet and May offensives. In President Thieu, the South Vietnamese had found a solid if uninspiring leader. From I Corps down to the Mekong Delta, the peasants had come to accept if not like the Saigon government. The Americans had achieved their aims and might have obtained an honourable peace treaty. However, the pressure of public opinion at home and the US Army's inability to fight were forcing Nixon and Kissinger into a speedy withdrawal, on terms that could be dictated by Hanoi. By late 1971, the American troops in Vietnam were only a rearguard, thinking of nothing but their departure. This shabby betrayal was justified by the slogan of 'Vietnamisation'; however, the Vietnamese themselves were not deceived.

When I visited Hue, late in 1971, the wrecked bridge had been repaired by the same Eiffel company that had built the original and had also repaired it in 1945 when it was first blown up. The same French company had meanwhile constructed a second bridge, in a shallow and graceful arch a few hundred yards upstream. The contracts given to Eiffel were seen by some Americans as a deliberate snub but they pleased my old friend Jacques Sanlaville. Walking around the Citadel I noticed two slogans written in English, apparently by the same hand: 'Americans go home!' and 'Smash down the American attempt at Vietnamisation of the war!' Did the slogan writer demand that Americans go home yet continue fighting? Most Hue people I met feared that a new offensive was coming (it came four months later, in April 1972) and were not too confident of resisting it. In fact the Vietnamese Marines fought bravely, driving the Communists back up the 'Street Without Joy'.

Winter, which is both damp and cool in Hue, added an extra degree of melancholy to the Cercle Sportif. Drizzle and mist hung over the Perfume River, while indoors there sounded plaintive Vietnamese music from cracked and furry gramophone records. It was a Chekhov scene with Chekhov characters supplied by the Cercle Sportif. 'You're frightened of lung cancer?' a doctor asked, when I turned down his offer of a cigarette. 'Well, I can tell you in all my years of practice here, I've never seen one case of lung cancer. Cancer of the uterus and of the breast, yes, but here in Vietnam there are too many other things from which to die. We smoke because we're unhappy, because of the war and because we're poor.' The doctor's legs were shaking, as often happens to Vietnamese when they talk about politics. 'Are you going to see the Communists?' When I said I would like to but it was hard to arrange, the doctor lowered his voice and said that the real enemy were not the Communists but the Americans.

A navy colonel, whose brothers and sisters were all in Europe, spoke lovingly of his fishing-rods and the big bream up-river. He offered to take me fishing but could not stick to his offer because upstream it was not safe, while in Hue all the fish had been killed off by hand-grenades. A literary man regretted the time when you could take a walk to the source of the Perfume River: 'There were iguanas, sometimes elephants and always fish, like trout, as many as you could catch. It was a place for lovers and poets, but it's fifteen years now since it was safe to go there or to the Hill of Clouds on the way to Danang.' His friend pointed over the river towards the Citadel. 'Do you remember, only five years ago, how it used to be all red with flamboyants? Now they've cut down most of the trees and those that remain don't produce any flowers.' A civil servant complained that all people's ideas had been turned upside down. 'A cyclo-driver makes more now than an engineer. We say that the Perfume River flows upstream.' A helicopter pilot, who had been flying combat missions that day, spoke lovingly of Cambodia, where he had been before that country was dragged into the war in 1970. 'Before the fall of Sihanouk, it was the last paradise, the last paradise.' Even Jacques Sanlaville, a normally sanguine type, grew wistful about his native Burgundy: 'There's marvellous cheese, great slices of fresh bread and as much red wine as you can drink.'

The older people in Hue spoke French but most of those in their twenties and thirties had learned some English. A naval lieutenant, whose legs shook incessantly as he spoke, listened to BBC broadcasts twice a day, and quizzed me on British affairs:

'Could you tell me, sir, why your leader Edward Heath is not married? Wouldn't you agree, sir, that Southern Rhodesia has the only civilised government in Africa?' A still more earnest young man gave me a card introducing himself as Hue Chapter Treasurer of the Vietnam Junior Chamber of Commerce. In turn I gave him a yellowing card of the *New Statesman*, for which I occasionally wrote. He looked at it and then looked up, with an expression of eagerness and delight. 'Are you a Christian, sir?' he said, and before I could answer went on: 'I'm a Gideon, sir. That is the Gideon sign on my tie. You will have seen our Gideon Bibles in all the best hotels of Saigon – in the Caravelle, the Majestic and the Continental. Unfortunately, sir, our hotels here in Hue aren't good enough, but I can assure you, sir, that when you come back to Hue in a year, you'll find a Gideon Bible in your hotel room.' He must have sensed my bewilderment for he took another look at the visiting card and read out loud 'Richard West. *New Statesman*', before saying sadly: 'I'm sorry, sir, when I looked at the card first time I thought it said "Richard West. New Testament".' I, too, in turn, felt disappointed, and somehow ashamed.

From Hue, in December 1971, I went to Ban Me Thuot in the Highland province of Darlac, where four years earlier I had ridden on elephant back and spent happy days in the Montagnard villages. Since then, the Communists had taken over much of the western Highlands, and tens of thousands of Montagnards were forcibly 'relocated' and their land given to carpet-bagging Vietnamese. An American missionary, Phil Young, told me: 'Sometimes the Vietnamese gave them sufficient warning in advance. Sometimes they just arrived by chopper and told them to be ready to leave in two or three hours' time. Then they destroyed the houses, killed the livestock and poisoned the crops.' Relocation brought misery to the Montagnards. Deprived of their rice fields, their livestock, poultry and game, they could not stomach the foreign food they were offered in the resettlement camps. Accustomed to cool, wooden long-houses, they were hot and miserable in tin-roofed, concrete huts. Forbidden their sacrifices, their rice-wine feasts and their gongs, they became morose and begged from the Vietnamese to buy cheap alcohol.

The Vietnamese in the Highlands increased from 20,000 in 1954 to more than half a million in the 1970s. In Darlac Province the 100,000 Vietnamese now outnumbered the Montagnards, whose land had been taken and who now had to do labouring jobs, such as constructing refugee camps for themselves. The pillage was badly disguised by a pretentious show of affection for the Montagnards on the part of President Thieu. In 1971 he made a highly publicised visit to Pleiku, donning a Montagnard costume and greeting carefully chosen chiefs. It had been arranged that a buffalo should be sacrificed in his honour and its blood poured over his feet in traditional fashion, but on the day his advisers warned that this might offend American TV viewers, so the buffalo was pre-killed and Thieu's feet were anointed with red wine.

The Americans I had met in Ban Me Thuot in 1967 were fond of the Montagnards and wanted to cherish their way of life. By 1971, even the US aid officials cared little about their plight. The first two I approached refused to talk to me, but I tracked down a third in the bar of a cheap Chinese hotel. He was ready to talk when he heard that I too liked Kipling, his favourite poet, although he ignored Kipling's appeal to America to 'take up the white man's burden' in the Philippines. This aid man was only too eager to let this burden drop. 'The Montagnards in these camps are eating the bark off the trees,' he told me. 'Of course they've always eaten bark but we should give them better bark before putting them onto something more nutritious. Instead we give them a few thousand pounds of bulgur flour and cooking oil and we think how generous we've been. It's like the American Indians. But do you really care what happens to these people? Aren't you really only interested in yourself, your family?' He bought two more beers, recited *Mandalay*, then nodded towards a bar girl who was sitting on my left. 'She's lovely, really beautiful, isn't she? It's kind of sad to think that in a year or so she may be marched through the street with her head shaved.'

The Special Forces, who once befriended the Montagnards, had long since left Vietnam, indeed they were almost gone by the time the film *The Green Beret* was shown in the country. Its star was the great Western actor John Wayne, now paunchy and slow on his feet but no less pugnacious in his sardonic snarl, and no less majestic as the most famous Hollywood frontiersman. Moreover as a political conservative, Wayne threw his conviction as well as his talent into the role of a Green Beret. To help with publicity after the film was made, Wayne went to Vietnam to be photographed with the troops in the field. Shots were heard from the VC (or perhaps from a public relations man) and after the picture session, Wayne gave each of the soldiers present a cigarette case inscribed with his signature and the words 'F— Communism'.

Sadly for Wayne, the script and production were awful. The location scenes were shot in the United States, and no attempt was made to give authenticity to the setting, so that the Vietnamese parts were performed by Chinese, Filipinos and even Japanese. The women wore Chinese *cheong-sams* instead of the Vietnamese *ao dai*. Rickshaw men rather than cyclo-drivers scurried around Danang. This caricature of a country so well known to television viewers in the United States suggested a flight from reality. The political propaganda was so crude that a VC colonel was seen to ride in a chauffeur-driven limousine to his mansion in the jungle, where he and his girlfriend sat down to a champagne and caviar supper.

Early in 1969 I happened to meet a civilian in the United Services Organisation (USO), which handled the distribution of films to the troops. I asked how the audiences had enjoyed *The Green Beret*, which had then been in the country several weeks. 'They love it,' he said. 'It's the biggest success we've ever had. They see it for laughs, you realise. There's one infantry unit just north of here where they've asked to see it three or four times. The bit they really love is where the helicopter is hit and bursts into flames at 3,000 feet and after that Wayne just steps out of the wreckage.'

I too laughed at the film, but I grieved as well. I had grown up loving American films, above all the Western, with its formalised plot, its simple contrast of good and evil, its exaltation of courage, humour, chivalry and respect for women and children. If there was one Western hero rivalling Gary Cooper in *The Westerner*, it was the young John Wayne in *Stagecoach*, the greatest film ever made. John Wayne in his screen persona, and so I have heard in his everyday life, was rough, hard-drinking, dominant of women, proud, patriotic and hard on his subordinates, but always keeping his temper, his humour and decency. Like Gary Cooper and several lesser Western stars such as Ronald Reagan, the future President, even the rough-hewn Wayne was somehow a gentleman. Somehow I felt that the old America died with the Green Berets, and the film Wayne made about them.

Another casualty of the Vietnam War was the comedian Bob Hope who suffered there an injury to his pride, his professional reputation and perhaps even his faith in America. The spectacle was especially poignant for those such as me who were brought up on Bob Hope jokes and thought of him as the king of American comics. In his radio programmes during the 1940s, Hope specialised in the kind of dirty joke that now sounds infantile, but seemed to us prurient schoolboys the very limit in daring and wit. Hope's reputation increased with the 'Road' series of films, of which many were genuinely and enduringly hilarious. The character played by Hope in these films was the All-American Man turned inside out, the coward pretending to be the cowboy hero, the he-man who never gets his woman, the weakling posing as Gary Cooper or John Wayne. What might be described as the Texan ethos has never been better mocked than in one great scene from *The Road to Utopia*, in which Hope and Bing Crosby are dudes seeking their fortune in the Alaskan gold rush. Mistaken for dangerous gunmen, they act out their parts by swaggering into a miners' bar where Hope first reassures the customers that they are 'not in a killing mood today – only a wounding mood', then inadvertently orders a lemonade instead of a whisky. Seeing the incredulity on the barman's face, he adds with a snarl: 'In a dirty glass.' This genre of humour embraced the New York Jewish jokes of comics like Woody Allen, a former writer of gags for Hope and still an admirer.

Although English-born, Hope had become a super American patriot, a life-long Republican, a friend of Presidents, a multimillionaire and impassioned anti-Communist. Each Christmas season since 1942, Hope had taken a troupe of performers abroad to entertain the GIs in places ranging from Germany to Korea, from, Guantánamo naval base, Cuba, to the strategic air force base in Greenland. In 1965, Hope went for the first time to Vietnam, where the risk of mortar attacks from the never far-distant enemy added an extra anxiety to the routine hardship of road-shows. The Christmas Hope concerts were filmed and edited for a television show, so in a sense these tours had a professional nature, but there was no doubt of Hope's sympathy and respect for the young, lonely and fearful soldiers. And yet on Christmas Day 1971, he was given the raspberry.

The sad fact was that Hope, the GI's friend, had become a part of the military establishment. This dawned on me in 1968 when a newspaper thought it had got permission for me to accompany the comedian on his Christmas tour. I went to Bangkok, from where he would fly each day to Vietnam, and booked myself into the Erawan Hotel, whose downstairs part was soon overrun by the Bob Hope troupe of starlets, musicians, public relations people and two sombre Jews to write the jokes. On the fourth floor, there was a military 'Bob Hope Room' staffed by a colonel, seven junior officers, several sergeants 'and of course a sergeant-major to make sure things get done'. 'It's really like a Corps Joint Command in a very exciting operation,' the colonel told me. 'Mr Hope is really a very wonderful person.' After a few days I realised that I would never get on the Bob Hope plane. The press in Vietnam was the responsibility of JUSPAO and the plane and its passengers came under MACVEE. However, when the plane returned, it became the responsibility of MACTHAI.

It was not until Christmas Day 1971 that I saw what turned out to be the last Bob Hope show in Vietnam. It was held just east of Saigon at Long Binh, where the Americans had their largest military installation outside the United States as well as the largest military jail, unlovingly known as the 'LBJ' after former President Johnson. The few reporters who boarded the military bus to Long Binh were given a purple identification pass showing Bob Hope's face and the inscription 'Operation Jingle Bells'. We were also promised packets of 'Christmas Candy, compliments of the US Navy', but this had run out when it came to my turn. Spirits were low on the journey, since we had all been to parties the evening before, and Long Binh motorway was a *via dolorosa* of truck depots, tyre dumps, rusting water tanks, hovel complexes, barbed-wire hedgerows and petrol stations of every oil company known to capitalism. On arrival at Long Binh we were shown into a room decorated with air force plaques – 'Golden Hawkies, we cover the sky' – and posters explaining the perils of heroin. Before going out to the stadium we were given quarts of Foremost Fruit Cup, then turkey sandwiches with bones as big as a sheep's.

The show started at 1.30. It had been due to start at one but most of the 10,000 GIs in the audience had taken their seats as early as ten o'clock. After two hours of waiting under a shattering dry-season sun, the mood of the crowd was restless and quarrelsome. The private soldiers hissed and yelled abuse at the officers, wives and distinguished guests who took the comfortable fold-up chairs in front of the stage. Any army is given a certain licence on Christmas Day; but this was not any army. The remaining 160,000 US troops, compared to the half million five years earlier, were no longer interested in what was left of the war. In the Long Binh area there had been rumours current of fake charges intended to frame political radicals, as well as a drug raid on an outpost called 'Whisky Mountain'. The radicals were still further annoyed by Saigon's refusal to give a visa to the actress Jane Fonda, who wanted to tour the country with an anti-war play.

Some of the radical soldiers had set up a picket outside the stadium carrying signs like 'Peace Not Hope' and 'Where is Jane Fonda?' Inside the stadium, protesters exploited the old tradition that film of the crowd would appear on TV and people could greet their folks at home with signs such as 'Hello, El Paso'. This year there were more and larger signs saying 'Help Keep Whisky Mountain Clean', 'Merry Christmas Nixon, Wish You Were Here' and 'We're Fonda, Hope.' Whenever a camera turned on the crowd, it met with a salutation of two-finger signs, black clenched fists, or white arms stretched high for peace.

The Bob Hope troupe this year included a line of chorus girls, a singer, a pair of roller-skaters and the actress Martha Ray. It should have included the reigning Miss World but the holder that year, a hot-tempered Brazilian, had fallen out with the contest promoters and had to be replaced with 'Miss World USA', a small-town Texan girl. There was a black women's singing trio and Vida Blue, a black Californian baseball player who also served as a straight man to Hope. The musicians did not attempt the latest rock music and sounded old-fashioned, even to me.

Bob Hope's jokes, like the starlets, were meant to remind the soldiers that they were red-blooded, virile, heterosexual, hundred per cent Americans, whose only desire was to get back home and bed a big-busted American girl. But Americans in 1971 were already starting to doubt their own sexuality. There was a chilly, even embarrassed silence at two Hope jokes about male effeminacy. The same silence greeted Hope's jokes about women's lib, as it then was called. One of Hope's jokes inflamed the crowd. The joke, as I noted it, was: 'You're off the front page back home. The Vietnam War is now tucked away between Lil Abner and Chuckle a Day.' It was like a dig in the broken ribs. With one joke, Hope had confirmed the two worst grievances of his audience: that people back home did not support them, and worse, that news of the war had been played down to help Nixon win re-election. After this joke, Hope was constantly heckled with shouts such as 'Where's Jane Fonda?' Black militants rushed forward to shake their fists at the television cameras. Even a group of military policemen climbed onto the stage in front of Hope to unfurl their banner: 'Pigs for Peace'.

Towards the end of the show, when a general came on stage to thank Hope and to give him a 'Ho Chi Minh bicycle', scores of soldiers stood up and walked from the stadium. Clearly rattled, Hope shouted back at the hecklers: 'In my heart, you're the guys that are against the war because you're the guys that are helping to end it. You've all listened to the garbage of the other cats... What have they ever done for the world? They talk a lot about the My Lai massacre but that's a load of nothing because they forget the good that we've done helping little kids and building orphanages...' The actress Martha Ray joined in the attack on the opponents of the war: 'Those characters you hear and read about, they couldn't shine your boots and don't you forget that!' This brought applause from the loyalists in the audience but the black sergeant next to me said: 'Get most of these kids back home and they'd be doing the same thing they're clapping against.' That evening, after the show, I thought once more of the saying that had been current for more than a year and was reproduced on a banner outside Long Binh: 'The Vietnam War Is A Bob Hope Joke.'

3

Cambodia, Laos and Thailand: 1972–3

At the end of 1971 I wrote from Vietnam a number of articles for the *New Statesman* which duly appeared with an even larger than usual amount of misprints and garbles. The critical tone of the articles greatly upset JUSPAO, the American propaganda machine, which wrote round to its representatives in Hue, Ban Me Thuot and other places where I had been, to obtain denials of my reports. Although I did not hear about this till very much later, a senior official of the American Embassy in London wrote to Richard Crossman, then the editor of the *New Statesman*, saying among other things that since I had spelt the name Ban Me Thuot incorrectly, I clearly cannot have gone there but instead had based my reports on Communist documents. Since Richard Crossman did not show me the letter, or even mention that he received it, my failure to reply to it was no doubt taken as an admission of guilt. The American Embassy appears to have passed on to the Embassy of South Vietnam its view that I was a Communist agent. As a result I was barred from getting a visa for more than a year.

I was therefore absent from South Vietnam during that shameful year when Richard Nixon sold out his former ally in order to get America out of the war and win re-election as President. In the course of 1972, the United States withdrew its remaining combat troops from South Vietnam, while Kissinger and his opposite number, Le Duc Tho, discussed the terms for an eventual ceasefire. Since Nixon no longer had his country's mandate for the deployment of troops in South-east Asia, his only bargaining counter against Hanoi was the threat to extend the bombing to centres of population, as well as supposedly 'military' targets. However, Nixon knew that the bombing of cities carried the risk of intervention by Communist Russia or China. Moreover, if he failed in 'bombing North Vietnam to the conference table', the American public might elect a Democrat ready to make peace on terms still more unfavourable to the South Vietnamese. Only when Nixon had been re-elected did he feel safe to authorise the bombing of Hanoi at Christmas 1972. By the terms of the ceasefire reached at the start of January 1973, North Vietnam agreed to release its American prisoners of war, and in return was allowed to keep its army in all those parts of the South that it held by right of conquest. As a reward for this squalid betrayal of South Vietnam, Kissinger and Le Duc Tho were jointly awarded the Nobel Peace Prize.

Since 1972 was the only year during a decade in which I did not visit South Vietnam, I shall take this as an approximate point in time from which to examine the neighbouring countries of Indo-China, also threatened by Communism. Although the Cold War had started in 1945 in Europe, along the 'Iron Curtain' stretching from Stettin to Trieste, it quickly had spread to the other end of the Europe–Asia land mass. The Chinese Communist leader Mao Zedong finally drove his nationalist rivals out of the country in 1949. The Vietnamese Communist leader Ho Chi Minh, who came to power in the north of the country in 1945, began another round of his war of revolt in 1946, when the French landed at Haiphong to regain their colony. Communist-led uprisings began in the newly independent Philippines. In 1948 the Malayan Communist leader Chin Peng, an ethnic Chinese like most of his party's members, ordered attacks on the British tin mines and rubber plantations, to start a revolt that came to be known as 'the Emergency'; the insurance companies would not have paid on death or damage in 'war'.

In June 1950, North Korea invaded the South and later received the support of Communist Chinese armies. As the war in Korea became a stalemate, the French were losing ground to the Vietnamese Communists, whom the Americans came to regard as the biggest threat in the region, especially after the French defeat at Dien Bien Phu in 1954 led to a peace agreement and the division of Vietnam. In that same year, Thailand became the headquarters of a regional anti-Communist league, the Southeast Asia Treaty Organisation, or SEATO, whose other members were Britain, France, the Philippines and Pakistan, which then included an eastern wing, now Bangladesh. In that same year, 1954, President Dwight D. Eisenhower coined or popularised a famous metaphor on what might follow a Communist victory in Vietnam: 'You have a row of dominoes set up, you knock over the first one, and what will happen to the last one is the certainty that it will go over very quickly.' Two years later, in 1956, the then Senator John F. Kennedy told the 'Friends of Vietnam' that 'Burma, Thailand, Japan, the Philippines and obviously Laos and Cambodia are among those whose security would be threatened if the red tide of Communism flowed into Vietnam'.

Those such as Kennedy, who feared for the future of Southeast Asia, put their trust in dynamic social reforms as well as counter-insurgency to beat the Communists at their own game. One of the chief proponents of this policy was a former advertising executive and wartime OSS officer, Colonel Edward G. Lansdale, who helped the Philippines government to contain the Communist rebels, then went on to be an adviser to President Diem of South Vietnam. Lansdale's fondness for Madison Avenue gimmickry, and his artless good will, may have contributed to the portrait of Alden Pyle in Graham Greene's *The Quiet American*, published in 1955. Lansdale appeared in a much more favourable light in a novel published in 1958 by William J. Lederer and Eugene Burdick, entitled *The Ugly American*, an implied riposte to Greene. Here Lansdale becomes Colonel Edwin Hillendale, the US adviser in 'Sarkhan, a small country out towards Burma and Thailand', in which he captures the hearts and minds of the people by moving among the peasants and playing on his mouth organ. Later, Hollywood made a film of *The Ugly American*, with Marlon Brando taking the part of Hillendale, and Kukrit Pramoj, an eminent Thai politician and author, acting the role of the 'Sarkhan' Prime Minister.

When President Kennedy took office in 1961, he tried to put into action the principles taught by *The Ugly American*. He gave new powers to the Special Forces, or Green Berets, to practise their style of counter-insurgency. He set up the Peace Corps and the Alliance for Progress in Latin America, to combat the poverty and corruption he saw as the causes of Communism. Throughout the 1960s and early 1970s, the United States was fighting both an actual war in South Vietnam and an ideological war in Southeast Asia to win the hearts and minds of the people away from Communism. Belief in the Domino Theory was not confined to American politicians. The leaders of most South-east Asian countries, especially Lee Kuan Yew, the long-time Prime Minister of Singapore, were convinced that the triumph of Communism in South Vietnam would lead to its triumph throughout the whole region. I travelled widely to see the side effects of the Vietnam War, especially upon the neighbouring states of Cambodia, Laos and Thailand.

When I had first been in Cambodia, in 1963, Prince Norodom Sihanouk was raging against the Americans, who in turn called him mad, and prophesied that the country would soon be bankrupt and under the rule of Communist China. Returning in 1968, I saw with delight that, contrary to the predictions of five years earlier, Cambodia was not only peaceful but prosperous. There were excellent new roads, railways, a deep-water port and hospitals, as well as schools that yielded a literacy rate of ninety per cent. The economy, without US aid or advice, had survived every prophecy of disaster. French and Chinese businessmen had increased their investment; indeed in the first three years since the expulsion of the Americans, there had been record balance-of-payments surpluses. Statistics showed a drop in the rice sold to the state purchasing boards, so that some economists feared that production was dropping. In fact the peasants were getting a better price by selling their crop to the Communist Vietnamese who used Cambodia as a supply base. Since the rice was paid for with US dollars, bought on the black market in Saigon, Cambodia got a bonus in hard-currency earnings.

In foreign affairs, Sihanouk still maintained his 'bad neighbour' policy towards Thailand and South Vietnam. Referring to a border dispute with Laos in May 1968, the Prince declared: 'We shall not surrender so much as a tree or an ant that bites us, provided that ant is Cambodian.' Nor had he allowed the Communists to gain undue influence. When the Chinese Embassy tried to send Red Guards through Phnom Penh they were threatened with instant expulsion. The police arrested, imprisoned and sometimes expelled Communist suspects; I once saw them making a search in Phnom Penh of everybody of Chinese or Vietnamese appearance. Sihanouk imprisoned and threatened to kill the native Communists, whom he himself dubbed the 'Khmer Rouge'.

However, the favourite enemy was the United States. There was a grisly piece of sculpture beside the river in Phnom Penh, composed of bits of the wreckage of an American warplane, a helicopter and armoured cars that had strayed into Cambodian territory. When a ship carrying beer to the American troops in Can Tho lost its way and sailed up the wrong stream and into Cambodia, Prince Sihanouk at first wanted to ransom the two US soldiers aboard, in return for two US bulldozers, but later relented and freed them, though keeping the beer. It was later revealed that in 1968 or 1969, American B-52 planes began to bomb Vietnamese Communists inside Cambodia. Later Sihanouk pretended that he had not known about this – a highly unlikely tale to anyone who has been within thirty miles of a B-52 strike. Critics of the United States even suggested that this aggression explained the subsequent viciousness of the Khmer Rouge guerrillas. I suspect that Sihanouk knew and approved of these raids on the Vietnamese intruders.

The quirks and about-turns of Cambodian foreign affairs

reflected the man who took all decisions in public life. During that visit in 1968, I changed from a critic to a devoted and lifelong admirer of Sihanouk. I liked the way that he busied himself with all aspects of life in Cambodia. In the film industry, he was the top director, producer, scriptwriter, cameraman and star. A composer and saxophonist, he frequently went to the microphone at diplomatic receptions. A poster of him in football shorts called him 'the father of the country's sport'. He loved to be photographed planting rice with the peasants or hurling gifts of cloth to them from his helicopter. He relished state visits, especially from women like Jackie Kennedy and Princess Margaret; he also liked parties, religious feasts and any ceremony that required his talents as a showman. He laughed a great deal, made shrill speeches, fussed over the guests and flattered the ladies. The monthly magazine *Kambudja* (editor: Prince Norodom Sihanouk) used to give much space to these state occasions.

The Prince distrusted foreign powers but he was always ready to learn from them and adapt what was useful in their cultures. France had given her language, which the Cambodians speak much better than do the Vietnamese, her sense of style and her *bonne cuisine*, which the Prince enjoyed so much that he kept having to go for cures. During these visits to Grasse or Vichy, the Phnom Penh papers carried respectful new items such as: 'This week Prince Norodom Sihanouk lost two kilos.' The Prince disapproved of Communist China, but during a state visit he was much impressed by the absence of night-clubs. On his return to Phnom Penh he nationalised the dance halls – and was furious when an American magazine said that his mother had taken over the brothel business. The Prince even borrowed one British idea. After a general election in 1966, Sihanouk discovered that there were too many wrong (i.e. pro-American) members of parliament. As head of state he could have simply dismissed the new government and installed himself as Prime Minister but instead he announced that the country would have a 'Loyal Opposition'. The Opposition was formed and started to publish a daily *Bulletin of the Counter-Government*, under the editorship of Prince Norodom

Sihanouk. Savage articles accused the regime of graft, sloth and incompetence until the Prime Minister had to resign and was replaced by – Prince Norodom Sihanouk. However, the new Prime Minister continued to edit the *Bulletin of the Counter-Government.*

Those aspects of Cambodian life that foreigners found mysterious, even absurd, were nevertheless true to the country's tradition and culture. Buddha himself taught that the truth, the Middle Way, was sometimes arrived at through paradox and confusion. Prince Sihanouk was often attacked because Cambodia would not admit the 'hippies' or 'travelling people', who then were roaming through Asia. An article in the *Bulletin of the Counter-Government* justified this ban. The writer explained that Cambodians sympathised with the hippy dislike of modern Western society. They too were in revolt against industrialism, violence and hypocrisy; so far so good. But in Cambodia, the article went on: 'The advance of science has not yet destroyed the foundation of our culture, which remains firm. The visiting hippies would have more to learn from us than to teach us. And in order to learn they should modify their behaviour out of respect for our culture and thought.'

At the end of an article singing the praises of Sihanouk, I wrote what later I came to see as sadly prophetic words:

> The Chinese, if they wanted to, could take over Cambodia in a week. So possibly could the Americans, the Thais and even Vietnam. It would not matter much in the balance of world power. Yet for anyone who has been to Cambodia, its loss would be a disaster. Of course it is rather corrupt and monarchical, and a little authoritarian. It is a country for escapists from things like student power, the space race, sociological surveys, debates on the Permissive Society, Mao's Thoughts, *Time* magazine (which is banned), the 'white heat of technology', traffic and war. 'I have seen the future – and it works!' said one journalist after visiting Lenin's Russia. Well I have seen the past – and it works!

I was in Brodard's Café in Saigon on 18 March 1970, when

someone told me the news of a *coup d'état* in Phnom Penh and the overthrow of Sihanouk.

A few days later the local Khmer Rouge and the Vietnamese Communists joined in an insurrection, whereupon the South Vietnamese and American armies crossed into Cambodia, hoping to find and destroy the Vietcong bases and stores. When I first went to Cambodia under its new regime, in June 1970, the Communists had already taken half the country and ringed Phnom Penh. An attack on the city was imminent, so I read in a paper given to me on the plane. There was no sign of the war in Phnom Penh but plentiful signs of political change since Sihanouk's downfall. The Americans had arrived in force as military advisers, intelligence agents, liaison officers with the Lon Nol regime, and propagandists on its behalf. Within twenty minutes of my arrival, I fell into conversation with a thin American, wearing the white shirt and black tie uniform of the CIA in those parts; he blandly informed me that he was handing out carbines. In the Monorom Hotel bar I noticed two crew-cut Americans hob-nobbing with two Soviet 'journalists', who had arrived to counter the influence of the rival Chinese Communists.

It was sad to hear Western journalists and diplomats gloating over the downfall of Sihanouk: he had been too domineering, and people were frightened of him; he had forced university graduates to go out and teach in the villages rather than stay in Phnom Penh; he had not managed to check the endemic dysentery that gave Cambodia its high infant mortality rate. These Westerners echoed the whines of the Phnom Penh bourgeoisie, the kind who spoke English and French and got a hearing. The same people later enriched themselves by black-marketeering and stealing from the Americans during the five-year siege of the city.

During the first weeks after the *coup d'état*, Cambodian troops were permitted and even encouraged to plunder and murder hundreds of ethnic Vietnamese, most of them fishermen on the Tonle Sap, the lake between Phnom Penh and Angkor. The corpses were thrown in the river and floated downstream into Vietnam, where they were photographed and shown in the Saigon newspapers. The Lon Nol government staged rallies at which the crowd applauded the burning of monster effigies of the Vietnamese conical hat. Lon Nol himself was very dark-skinned and liked to be known as Black Papa, to exploit dislike of the lighter-skinned neighbours. He reminded his people of the legend of how Vietnamese invaders once had buried three Cambodians up to their necks, then built a fire between them, using the heads as cooking stones.

Lon Nol's attempt to win popularity at the expense of the Vietnamese was triply foolish. It alienated a large able minority, driving them into the ranks of their Communist fellow-countrymen. It alienated the Saigon government which was his principal backer. It alienated many Cambodians who had lived in harmony with the Vietnamese and the Chinese under the rule of Prince Sihanouk. Oddly enough, this pogrom against the Vietnamese was explained away and even justified by many American and British journalists who would have denounced such 'racism' at home.

In December 1973, almost exactly ten years since I had first come to Cambodia, the one-time paradise had disappeared from the earth. Three years of American bombing and Khmer Rouge terror attacks had driven two million people out of the countryside and the smaller towns to Phnom Penh. The capital itself was receiving mortar, rocket and terrorist bomb attacks; not many, but not many are needed to make a city unpleasant. I stayed at the Hotel de la Poste by the river, and each night was continually woken by small-arms fire, probably sentries shooting at clumps of weed that might conceal a submerged attacker. One night the noise increased in volume and went on for many minutes but it was not till later I heard that there had indeed been some kind of commando raid by water.

As in Saigon, it was the poor who suffered most from the war; no food in the orphanages, no drugs in the hospitals, and rice selling at ten times its pre-war price. Even the Phnom Penh bourgeoisie now regretted the Sihanouk days, so that the French word I heard most often was *avant*, 'before'. '*Avant, monsieur, on mangeait bien. Avant il y avait la paix.*' However, the war had been profitable to the rascally generals and ministers who dealt in rice, drugs and arms. President Lon Nol was said to have banked over $80 million, so he was not much disturbed when his wife was apprehended at Paris airport with only $140,000 hidden in two teddy bears.

During this visit in 1973, I started to see that war was changing Cambodia into a strange and sinister country, quite different from anywhere else in Indo-China. The old charm and insouciance were still apparent but there were intimations of horror and savagery. Many soldiers appeared to regard the war as a game. Passing one government building, I noticed a sentry shooting at birds in the trees. When his colleague, a young woman soldier saw me watching, she burst into giggles and ducked out of sight, so that only the top of her rifle was visible over the sandbags. The commander-in-chief of the army was a Filipino dance band musician who treated the war as show business. Another senior general had suffered a serious scalp wound when he had placed an apple on his head and invited a colleague to shoot it off, in William Tell fashion. The army was troubled by astral events, particularly an eclipse of the sun, which the troops regarded as a giant toad, and attacked with millions of shots. Another aspect of the Cambodian character made itself known in the much publicised photograph of a smiling government soldier clutching in each hand the severed head of an enemy.

Slowly the journalists came to suspect that the Khmer Rouge might turn out to be very much nastier than the Vietnamese Communists. Almost from the start of the insurrection in 1970, refugees from the countryside had told how the Khmer Rouge crucified and tortured to death their class and political enemies. At first such stories were written off as propaganda. It was still the accepted liberal view that all Cambodia's troubles were to be blamed on American B-52 raids. Some of the doubts concerning the Khmer Rouge were allayed in 1973 when the exiled Prince Sihanouk appeared to give the insurgents his approval. He was the man who before the war had jailed and threatened to kill the

Communists, as well as giving them the opprobrious title of Khmer Rouge. For the first few years after his overthrow, Sihanouk did not align himself with the Communist insurgency, but when the new regime insulted his family and his reputation, even having his statue dipped in pig manure, Sihanouk lost his temper. In 1973, he made the arduous journey from North Vietnam along the Ho Chi Minh Trail through Laos to join the Khmer Rouge in the jungles of north-east Cambodia. This endorsement by Sihanouk swung public opinion behind the Khmer Rouge. If many Cambodians now were reassured, so too were many foreigners.

However, the Western journalists had particular reason to fear the Khmer Rouge. In Phnom Penh as in Saigon, the brave or ambitious reporters and still more the cameramen and photographers ventured in search of the war down one of the highways leading out of the city. In this murderous game of Grandmother's Footsteps, the players normally ended up at one of the roadblocks manned by government soldiers; however, they sometimes strayed into territory held by the other side. In Vietnam, the Communists usually left civilians alone or, if they intercepted a journalist, let him go free. In Cambodia on the other hand, many journalists vanished, among them Sean Flynn, the son of the Hollywood actor Errol, the man who had supplied opium to M. Ottavj. None was ever seen or heard of again. They were all certainly murdered by the Cambodian Communists.

After the fall of Phnom Penh in April 1975, and the mass expulsion of its inhabitants into the 'Killing Fields', the whole world understood the murderous character of the Khmer Rouge. One man who suspected this as early as 1973 was James Fenton, a young English poet who had gone to Indo-China as a writer for the *New Statesman*. He had stayed for a while at the Royale Hotel, Saigon, and travelled around the Vietnamese countryside, but later spent most of his time in Cambodia. Although when I had known him in London, James belonged to one of the Trotskyist groups, he was not an ideologue and his sacred book was Byron's *Don Juan* rather than any political tract. By the end of

1973, James was a well-known figure in Phnom Penh, seen riding around on a motor-bike, with his driver in front of him, and interpreter crouching behind him. With his poet's intuition, James had a good understanding of national character, and claimed to be able to grasp the difference between Cambodian and Vietnamese jokes. Although he loved the Khmers, James sensed the dark, demonic side of their nature. It was he who lent me the booklet *1200 Khmer-English Phrases* by Som-Vicheth and San-Sarun, which did not teach me the language but gave me an insight into the national psyche. Here are some of the phrases, selected almost at random but given in sequence:

> Don't make goo-goo eyes at me. She cast sheep's eyes at me. My eye! Go away, brazen-face! No one loves you. He died of love. He died for his Nation. Don't make faces at me! Don't purse your lips at me! Behold my bosom naked to you. No necking and crop allowed. He is a muff. This country is rife with foreign spies. Why rustle? For God's sake go away! My hair stands on end with terror. Your book is the best seller. Your sneers and jeers are hard to bear. You thickhead. I am thirstless of power. I used to travel England from end to end. He is surnamed a hunter of girls. What a swell you are! Bad boy you break wind very badly (with too bad smell). She exclaimed 'I won't'. You are a bad hat. Don't hiss at me! You are quite lousy (slang). Vagina (pussy). War is a rude reminder. She is a poisonous snake. Unfasten your clothes. Don't violate my virginity. This guy is a local dude. The independence of the country is at stake. The fighting remains a stalemate. Don't splash me.

A British diplomat and friend of Graham Greene who had served twenty years in Indo-China, much of the time in Laos, decided one day to write his memoirs. He smoked a few pipes of opium, drank some whisky and sat down at the typewriter, only to find that he could not remember a thing. My acquaintance with Laos lasted only eight years and I cannot have spent more than a few months there altogether, but I find much the same difficulty as the diplomat. Crossing the Mekong was for me like crossing the Lethe, the river of forgetfulness. For example I cannot remember my first visit, in spring 1967, although there are entrance and exit stamps in my passport of the time. I never wrote any articles there or made any notes, except as an *aide-mémoire* to remind me which room I had taken in which hotel. One day my eye was caught by a *Bangkok Post* headline, 'Reds Launch Big Drive In Laos', and it took me at least five seconds to realise that this was the country in which I was standing.

Only one journalist, Estelle Holt, ever understood Laos and she was fired by her news agency because the true reports she filed were not as acceptable as the fiction filed by everyone else. How could one explain a country where three armies, Right, Left and Neutralist, were locked in vague battle along the misty valleys; where the main industry, opium-growing, was backed by the CIA; where the capital could be shelled by its own police in an attack on the army (or maybe the other way round); where the peace talks began at a fancy-dress ball in which the American Ambassador was attired as Sinbad the Sailor? The war was not so funny for others in Laos, especially the hill tribes, whose land was constantly bombed and whose people were driven to refugee camps to be labelled as 'Ethnic Meo' or 'Ethnic Yao'. In the evening on the terrace of the Million Elephants Hotel, I watched the crimson trails of the B-52 bombers from Thailand, crossing high over the Mekong to pound some target up in the north.

For visitors such as myself, Vientiane offered escape from reality. In May 1968, I flew there from Saigon, after the fighting described in the previous chapter. The day before I had had to fling myself on the tarmac of Le Loi Street as a rocket went overhead and exploded in Nguyen Hue. But in Vientiane they were celebrating their New Year by firing enormous toy rockets over the Mekong. The tubes of wood and paper were about forty feet long and decorated with bright pictures of dragons, tigers and elephants. They made an agreeable swoosh on firing, and there were cheers from the crowd if one landed anywhere near the Thai bank of the river.

On that visit I stayed at the Constellation Hotel, whose

Corsican-Vietnamese owner was also a prominent businessman. It was the time of the student riots in Paris but I could not understand at first why M. Cavalleri kept asking my view on whether de Gaulle would fall from power. Then he took me into his office and showed me the pile of francs and cheques he had bought cheap from those who feared a devaluation. Cavalleri's dealings were watched with fascination by one of the permanent guests, an Air America pilot who had retired there and wanted to start a Vientiane Stock Exchange. 'Don't you think Vientiane's an ideal place?' he kept asking. Another guest that time was an expatriate Englishman who used to swim in the Mekong, fully dressed, and then dry out in the sun. He lectured me on his two favourite authors, William Butler Yeats and Adolf Hitler.

Although Laos was then at war, it was still in theory at peace, under a treaty drawn up in 1962 and afterwards broken by the Americans. In theory the government still included Communist ministers; they did not take up their posts, but their front organisation the Pathet Lao maintained a compound in Vientiane. Their representative, Colonel Sot, was said to be quite a character so I paid him a visit to hear his usual speech, which always ended in Voltaire's phrase '*Il faut cultiver notre jardin*'. This maxim of Candide's was particularly inappropriate since Colonel Sot's own garden had gone to seed and was now almost jungle. The Pathet Lao compound was close to the US Embassy, and also to an anti-Embassy, run by a radical Boston psychiatrist, the owner of Vientiane's first psychedelic night-club. It had an exotic kaleidoscope which fascinated the small son of a Vietnamese lady with whom I was then friendly. She boasted of living in Vientiane's industrial quarter, but this seemed to consist of one factory, powered by an outboard motor, and making rubber shoes.

Early in 1973 I came to Laos from Singapore on the railway that terminates at Nong Khai, on the Thailand bank of the Mekong. Vientiane was awaiting a visit from the American Vice-President Spiro Agnew but it was hardly agog with excitement. There was more gossip concerning a Russian spy who had wrapped his car round a tree, an incident summarised by the *Bangkok Post* as

'Drunk Diplomat Fired'. Agnew's visit coincided with the news that Nixon was a candidate for the Nobel Peace Prize and caused the same derision. Both men were engaged in betraying Laos as they had sold out South Vietnam.

The duplicity of the United States was a cause of special bitterness to my friend Peter Kemp, who had seen what had happened in Laos in 1945, and spent much time there and in South Vietnam during the 1960s and early 1970s. Peter had fought three years on the Franco side in the Spanish Civil War, then with the Partisans in Albania, and finally Poland, where, having escaped the Germans, he was jailed and nearly murdered by the Russians. On his release, Kemp volunteered to drop into Thailand to join the resistance against the Japanese. After Japan's surrender he stayed on to maintain civil order at Nakhon Phanom, across the Mekong from Thakkek in Laos. He soon heard that the French people there who had previously been interned by the Japanese were now under a far worse threat from the Vietminh, or Communists from the Vietnamese ethnic minority in Laos. Kemp was joined at Nakhon Phanom by two Free French officers, Lieutenant François Klotz and Lieutenant Edith Fournier, his wireless operator, who intended to take possession of Thakkek. When Kemp and Klotz crossed the river on 7 September they found the French community close to despair. Eighteen women and fourteen children, whose menfolk had almost all been massacred by the Vietnamese, were now themselves in fear for their lives: 'They show us their knives and make gestures of cutting our throats,' Kemp was told. Driving north he managed to stop a battle in which 150 Vietminh with four machine-guns were laying siege to a group of French and Laotians.

In Laos, as in North Vietnam, the American OSS were backing the Communist Vietnamese against the French and their British ally. An OSS agent, Major Banks, instructed the French at Vientiane to 'cease their aggression' against the Vietminh. The French commander at Thakkek complained to Kemp: 'He [Banks] spoke to me as I would not dream of speaking to a servant – in front of my own soldiers and the Annamites, all of whom understand

French. He called me a pirate...' This attitude of the OSS to the French was soon to result in a murder.

One day in September, Kemp and Klotz decided to cross the river to take some medicine to the French civilians in Thakkek. Major Banks had instructed Klotz not to go but the Frenchman, a veteran of the Maquis, answered: 'I can certainly go to Thakkek if I wish. I am a French officer and Thakkek belongs to France.' He boarded the yacht with Kemp and one of the OSS men, Lieutenant Reese. At Thakkek they jumped ashore and climbed the bank to the road where they heard a high-pitched command from the Vietminh Lieutenant Tu, telling his men to train their guns on the visitors. Then Tu uttered his ultimatum: 'The British and American officers may go free. They are our allies. The Frenchman is under arrest and will come with us. The French declared war on us yesterday in Saigon.' Kemp protested, but the American Reese had joined the Vietnamese and was leaning against a house on the other side of the street. 'I guess we're neutral,' he said, ostentatiously refusing to come to the help of the Frenchman.

With or without the help of Reese, Kemp determined to get Klotz to safety. 'Monsieur Tu,' he said, addressing the Vietnamese commander, 'since our presence here is unwelcome to you, my friend and I are returning to Siam.' He put an arm around Klotz and together they turned to go to the ramp leading down to the boat. 'No,' screamed Tu, 'you may go but he stays here!' Kemp heard the rattle of rifle bolts and orders shouted in Vietnamese. Only a few yards lay between them and the launch under its dirty awning. The Vietminh fired a burst of shots, apparently in the air. Kemp was now walking almost behind Klotz to give him maximum protection. Kemp heard another burst of shots then 'a figure ran up on my left, thrust his rifle under my arm into Klotz's back, fired once and then disappeared'. Klotz staggered and let out a terrible despairing gasp. 'Oh, Peter,' he whispered. 'Oh, Peter.' He was dead by the time he was in the boat.

Back in Nakhon Phanom, Kemp had to break the news to Edith Fournier, the wireless operator. As the tears rolled down her cheeks, she muttered: '*C'est la deuxième fois, mon Dieu.* It's the second time!' On her last mission in occupied France, her chief had been grabbed and murdered by the Gestapo. Later, Kemp asked Edith to help him break the news to the French refugees and nuns at the hospital. The crowd stared anxiously at Kemp's grim face and blood-stained shirt, then broke into sobs when he told them what had occurred. Grief turned to anger when he told them about the 'neutrality' of the OSS man Reese.

The cemetery lay in the part of Nakhon Phanom occupied by the Vietnamese, who have settled in north-east Thailand as well as in Laos and Cambodia. Time and again in the next few weeks, the Vietminh supporters desecrated Klotz's grave by stealing the cross. Kemp was amazed by the hatred felt for the French by the Vietnamese, a feeling not shared by the Laotians.

The savagery of the Vietminh in 1945 helps to explain if not to excuse the later cruelty of the French to the Vietnamese. Even the chivalrous Kemp now came to detest the Communist Vietnamese as much as he liked the Thais and Laotians. After Klotz's funeral, Kemp walked back by the Mekong: 'Gazing at those hateful hills above Thakkek, which only yesterday I had thought so beautiful, I felt Edith's tight grip on my arm. '*Nous le vengerons*,' she whispered, 'we shall avenge him.'

Kemp built up a small flotilla of river boats armed with machine-guns to ferry arms and supplies to the French in Laos, who now were guerrillas fighting the Vietminh. During the rest of 1945, Kemp was engaged in a number of bloody naval battles, hundreds of miles upstream from the Mekong Delta. The Vietminh put a price on Kemp's head and he was several times shot at in Thailand, once during a dinner party, making him spill his Indo-Chinese rum over his newly washed khaki drill slacks. In turn Kemp planned to get his revenge on the Vietnamese Tu and his superior Le Hoq Minh, who both frequently crossed the river to Thailand. Once, when he heard that Le was to pass through Nakhon Phanom the following evening, Kemp cabled to Bangkok asking permission to go ahead with his plan of dealing with his opponent and throwing the body into the Mekong. To his disappointment, Kemp received a one-word reply in old-fashioned cable language: UNOFFBUMP ('Don't Bump Off').

Before he could get his revenge on his Vietminh enemies, Kemp was given the job of liberating the island of Bali in what were the Dutch East Indies and now were becoming Indonesia. He later became ill, retired from the army and turned to journalism and authorship in order to satisfy his love of adventure. He was in Hungary during the uprising of 1956, as the *Tablet* correspondent, then went to the Congo and other African countries in turmoil. From the mid-1960s he frequently went to Vietnam for the *News of the World*. When the Americans left in 1972 and Fleet Street lost interest in the Vietnam War, Peter obtained a Churchill scholarship to go to Thailand and Laos. Although he never got over the murder of Klotz, Peter had long forgotten his anger against the Americans and the Vietnamese. He admired the regime in Saigon, which was where I first met him.

The Laotians and the inhabitants of north-east Thailand, who are almost identical in their language and customs, continued to dislike the Vietnamese minority. Moreover the French in Laos were much more popular than the Americans; so perhaps Klotz and others had not died wholly in vain. However, by December 1973 it was evident that the Communist Vietnamese and their local auxiliaries, the Pathet Lao, were soon going to seize this enchanting country. At Vientiane airport I saw two Soviet transport planes unloading trucks, and a platoon of Pathet Lao troops wearing baggy, grasshopper-green fatigues, and pastry-cook caps. The increasing Communist presence was noticeable at the Constellation Hotel, which now had a tourist poster of Lake Baikal – 'the blue gem of Siberia'. After the fall of the Soviet Union we learned that Lake Baikal was the most polluted water in the world.

On this trip, I at last summoned the energy to fly to Luang Prabang, the royal capital, 250 miles up the River Mekong but only 150 miles by plane. The Pathet Lao territory began about fifteen miles away and there were bombings and shootings occasionally in the town. Most of Luang Prabang lies on a spit of land between the Mekong and one of its tributaries, which here flow between heavily wooded hills. From either side of the central street, you looked down on powerful brown streams, dotted with long-boats and fishing buoys and, in the shallows, women washing clothes and children playing with old lorry tyres. The wooden houses were well built, and the carvings and gold leaf on the many pagodas were richer than I had seen in any Buddhist country. As early as four in the morning I woke to the beat of pagoda drums and then to the boom of the gongs, which is somehow more soothing than sleep itself. At this time of the year it was very cold in the early morning so that the trishaw drivers outside the market wore leather jackets and caps, and stamped their feet as they waited. There was a smell of wood-smoke, and morning mist that gave way by nine to a pure blue sky. The only people I did not like in Luang Prabang were the children with catapults who menaced the pilgrims climbing the hill to the king's pagoda.

'Luang Prabang is the last paradise on earth,' said a café acquaintance. 'The people,' he went on, 'are peaceful, polite and friendly, even after all they've been through. But it's changed a bit from the time you could leave your house unlocked or leave your motor-bike in the street if you were too drunk to drive. I've really enjoyed it here.' I asked him where he was from and he said: 'I am Cambodian from Phnom Penh, but I've been working here ten years. Every year I've gone back to Phnom Penh for a holiday and I used to enjoy a whole fortnight. But now I can't stand more than three days. Our flat is full of relatives from the countryside who are refugees and have lost everything and are very unhappy because so many are dead. They cry all the time. It makes me very depressed. Ah yes, *monsieur*, Cambodia was a paradise once but now one has to come to Luang Prabang. It is the last paradise left.' But not for long.

In the early 1970s, as the Communists were coming ever closer to power in South Vietnam, Cambodia and Laos, many foreigners feared that Thailand also would fall to the domino effect. Since a *coup d'état* in 1932 ended the absolute power of the Chakri kings, the government of Thailand had alternated between the rule by demagogic politicians and brutal, corrupt military leaders. Millions of people were fleeing the poverty of the arid north-east, the men to work in Bangkok or the Middle East, the women too often entering prostitution, for instance at Pattaya, the beach resort for American soldiers on 'rest and recreation' leave from Vietnam. As in Malaysia, Indonesia and the Philippines, the Chinese in Thailand were a troublesome and unpopular minority; in Bangkok itself they almost outnumbered the Thais. There were many Chinese radicals in the guerrilla bands in northern Thailand and in the extreme south, close to Malaysia.

Foreigners such as myself were inclined to think of Thailand as an American satellite, aping some of the worst features of Californian life. We deplored the bars and the go-go dancers of Patpong Road, the bowling alleys and hamburger joints, and the faculty of Public Relations at one of the Bangkok universities. The north-east provided the US Air Force with bases from which to bombard Cambodia, Laos and North Vietnam, also attracting the usual whores, touts and other camp followers. Udon struck me in 1968 as far more unpleasant and violent than towns in the countries on the receiving end of its B-52 bombers. Some of the Vietnamese at Udon told me that they supported Ho Chi Minh. Thailand sent two divisions of troops to fight for South Vietnam, and in 1970 thought of invading Cambodia. The Vietnam War resulted in economic and social advances in Thailand. Between 1960 and 1970, the proportion of people in agriculture fell from 74 per cent to 63 per cent; meanwhile twice as many Thais were attending school and universities. The population of Bangkok had doubled since I first went there in 1963, and most of the former canals were filled and paved over. Since it was rapidly changing from a delightful into a hellish city, I now felt happy to leave Bangkok for Saigon.

Many years later, when I began to know Thailand better, I came to see that my earlier judgements were wrong. Things like motorways and skyscrapers, which I regarded as American, were just as typical of Japan or Taiwan. Thailand quickly adopted foreign fashions but just as quickly discarded them. The poverty of the north-east did not make it a breeding ground for Communism. The Chinese merged quite amicably into the Thai way of life. These and many other matters in Thailand became more clear to me in the 1980s, when I spent many months in Thailand, and particularly when I read the English translations of three delightful novels, concerning the Chakri court, the north-east and the Bangkok Chinese.

The first of these novels, *Four Reigns*, was written in 1950 by Kukrit Pramoj, the scholar, journalist, wit, connoisseur of the arts, and politician, who played the role of the 'Sarkhan' Prime Minister in the film of *The Ugly American*. He afterwards talked of the experience:

> I was important cast... Marlon Brando had his own dressing room which was a trailer with everything inside, air-conditioning, gin flowing from the tap. I had the same thing, identical and Marlon insisted on that... I'm born a one-movie actor. You see, Hollywood calls a person like me a type actor. You are only called when they need another Oriental Prime Minister.

Even to the *farang*, or Westerners, in Thailand, Kukrit was a renowned jester, although often there was a serious message under the banter. He once gave this advice to a conference of foreign travel agents on how to behave in Thailand:

> There are certain institutions which a Thai respects... They are his religion, which is mostly Buddhist, his king and his parents. If you say to a Thai that his politicians are rotten he will kiss you on both cheeks. If you tell him that he is a crook, he will deny it with great good humour and will not take offence. If you call his wife a bitch he will agree with you completely and ask you to have a drink to that. But as for those three institutions which I have already mentioned, I would advise you to leave well alone... since according to police statistics, the percentage of premeditated murders in this country is very low; most murders are committed in sudden passion.

It was not till 1989, when I read *Four Reigns*, that I, for one, realised that Kukrit was also a world-class writer, equipped with imagination, humour, narrative skill, and keen understanding of human nature.

Like the best epic novels, *Four Reigns* is enjoyable at many levels. It is on the surface a saga of aristocratic life, centred on one woman, Ploi, from her childhood during the 1880s down to her death in 1946. It is a pageant of Thailand's history during a period when the Chakri dynasty changed from absolute monarchs, the 'Lords of Life', into constitutional rulers, having to arbitrate between squabbling politicians and generals. This was also a time of social change and Westernisation. Although Kukrit never preaches, or even intrudes a personal view, *Four Reigns* is clearly meant to explain and extol to a new generation of Thais the customs and faith of their ancestors. His heroine, Ploi, embodies the Thai ideal of respect and honour to king, religion and parents. Westerners may regard this as old-fashioned or even reactionary. So it is. Almost all Thais look to tradition rather than new-fangled isms and ideologies. They do not partake of our Western obsession and grievance on matters like class, race, sexual orientation, human rights and social justice. What we call individualism they regard as selfishness. The family is paramount, which is why Thai women especially love *Four Reigns*.

The first of the four reigns referred to in Kukrit's title is that of King Rama V (1868–1910), who abolished serfdom, encouraged education and medical services, sent his children to study in England, Prussia and Russia, and during his leisure moments amused himself with cooking, astronomy, clocks and the motor car. He also had seventy-seven children by ninety-two wives. The last fact helps to explain the peculiar nature of Thailand's family system, the character of its aristocracy, and, in modern times, the insouciant attitude of the Thais toward prostitution. The system of royal polygamy during the nineteenth century meant that the nobles sought to advance themselves by getting their daughters married to, and made pregnant by, the king. The Thai aristocracy, and therefore the court, the civil service, the army and the judiciary were all in effect an extended royal family. Kukrit himself is a *rajawongse*, a title loosely translated as prince, but in fact meaning a king's great-grandson. Whereas in England the old Norman nobility seldom married into a royal family, which tended to come from Wales, Scotland, Holland or Germany, in Thailand people were aristocrats by virtue of royal blood.

As we learn at the start of *Four Reigns*, the humbler members of Thailand's aristocracy also practised polygamy. The story opens a hundred years ago, when Ploi as a girl of ten is taken to serve a royal princess in the Inner Court of the Bangkok royal palace. Ploi's mother has left her place as junior wife to a kind-hearted but ineffectual nobleman. The relationship between senior and junior wives, and half-brothers and half-sisters, adds complication but richness to Kukrit's story. Having walked out on her husband, Ploi's mother also stays for a time in the Inner Court before going to work as a moneylender; for Thai women, then as now, were often engaged in business, either in competition or partnership with Chinese merchants. When Ploi's mother returns to court to say she is getting married again, she brings her daughter the charming gift of a basket of miniature foods, like brown, crispy fish the size of a little finger, and salted eggs, not of chicken or duck but the tiny rice bird. Children and food are the main Thai loves.

Although Ploi had suffered at home from the spite of a half-sister, she is at first lonely and shy in the all-female world of the Inner Court. She studies the etiquette and the arts of a Thai lady, including the preparation of betel nuts, the making of scented water, the care of clothes, and the rules on what colours go with which days of the week: 'Both bean colour and iron colour are correct for your Wednesday *palai*. And this is for Thursday: green *palai* with bird's blood red . . .' Many Thai women still follow these rules on colour; also on which day to visit the hairdresser.

When Ploi reaches puberty, she goes home for the ceremony of removing the topknot. Her father, a sad and rather Chekhovian aristocrat, complains of the servant problem:

Not like when you grandfather was alive. Those days there were hundreds and hundreds of people living in the house under his care. There were his clerks, his oarsmen, his labour corps, his musicians and women dancers ... a whole troupe of them, and relatives and hangers-on, drifting in and out all over the place ... you should have seen the cauldrons we had for the cooking rice, rows of them, like in a regular barracks.

Ploi marries a rich and handsome Thai Chinese in the civil service, whose son by a previous mistress she gladly accepts and comes to love as much as her own children. Her attitude to her husband is very Thai: 'We live together and it's natural that we love each other. But over and above this, I feel infinitely grateful to you. I'm in your debt. I owe you everything.' When her husband grows despondent, she asks if he wants a junior wife, and of course is relieved when he says no.

When Rama V dies, he is succeeded by a new kind of king, an English-educated dandy, a lover of country sports and theatre, happier in the company of his own sex. Rama VI proves reluctant to marry even one wife. Ploi's husband nevertheless adapts to the latest court fashions such as collecting ivory boxes and walking sticks, dressing in pink, and having his jackets sent to be laundered in Singapore. Ploi is obliged to abandon betel and scale her teeth, making them white again.

Ploi sadly agrees to let her sons go to Europe for education, as Kukrit did himself. The boy who goes to Paris picks up left-wing views and later takes part in the *coup d'état* of 1932, ending the absolute monarchy. The weak, Old Etonian king then abdicates and a right-wing general takes over the country, changing its name from Siam to Thailand. The Japanese occupy Thailand in the war; Ploi is bombed out; then the British replace the Japanese, and the youngsters along the canal bank shout 'Okay' and 'Thank you' instead of '*Bansai*' and '*Arigato*'. At the end of the war, the young king Ananda comes back from Switzerland, to the intense joy of the Thais. Then on 9 June 1946, the most calamitous day in almost two centuries, Ananda is found shot dead in his room in the palace. Ploi, the heroine of *Four Reigns*, drops dead from shock and grief.

Here Kukrit ends his novel abruptly, and also prudently for the death of Ananda is even today a delicate subject. The mildly left-wing prime minister at the time announced that the king had shot himself by accident, which remains a just possible explanation. The right-wing generals who had been compromised by their pro-Japanese attitude in the war accused the Left of having murdered the king, and in 1947 launched a *coup d'état* to install the first in a series of army dictatorships. Three palace servants were charged with regicide and eventually executed. The lawyers for the defence were not allowed to suggest that the king might have committed suicide. Although the present King Phomibol is loved and revered in Thailand, the death of his elder brother was a disaster from which the country has never quite recovered.

During the decades of military rule that followed the *coup d'état* of 1947, Kukrit the novelist and his elder brother, Seni Pramoj, were prominent in the democratic opposition. While Seni was a leading jurist and university lecturer, Kukrit became a prolific and influential journalist and newspaper proprietor. One of Kukrit's pet campaigns was the need to pump some of the wealth of Bangkok into the countryside, especially into the poor north-east. Legend says that this region, the Isan, has always suffered from poor soil, scrub vegetation and frequent drought, but Kukrit and others also blamed the timber concessions given to Danish businessmen at the turn of the century. Although the north-east was a cause of shame and embarrassment to the richer parts of Thailand, it did not become the hotbed of Communism that so many Westerners feared. For one thing the Isan farmers normally own their land and have not suffered the scourge of rack-renting and usury. The emigration has meant a flow of money from Bangkok back to the land. The Isan people are not really Thai but Laotian and share with the people over the Mekong a hearty dislike of Communism and of the Vietnamese, the traders and artisans of the region. The Isan people revere the Buddhist religion and their king, who in turn has devoted years in this region to projects like irrigation.

The many *farang* who have wondered why the Isan people are not more bitter and angry should read Kampoon Boontawee's *A Child of the Northeast*, translated and with an introduction by Susan Fulop Kepner. The story covers a year in the life of a boy of about eight, named Koon, during the economic depression of the 1930s, when north-east Thailand suffered outstandingly. It is a genre of autobiography that lends itself to political posturing and self-pity, but *A Child of the Northeast* is overwhelmingly joyful, tender, and funny, without ever turning to sentimentality. I have seldom read such a cheerful as well as convincing account of childhood. Anyone who has been a child in the country will understand the excitement of Koon as he learns to set the dogs on a mongoose, to snare a chameleon with a noose, or to bring it down with a blowpipe; to pluck the cicada on the wing, and to grope in the mud for a catfish without getting spiked by the fins.

During the drought at the start of the book, Koon says that he hates the sky, and for this he is caned by his schoolmaster, an aged monk who makes him repeat: 'From this day on I will never blame the sky because the sky never punished anybody.' At the end of the book, when the rains have come and the baskets are full of rice and fish, Koon 'knew that there would be other years when the sun would blaze in a cloudless sky, and when the rain would not fall, other years when the earth would crack, and the rice grow low in the silos . . . and he knew too that he would meet these years, and he would survive, because he was a child of the Northeast'.

In her introduction, Susan Kepner remarks that when a film was made of *A Child of the Northeast*, some Westerners were bewildered to see Koon's father smiling and laughing:

> This was a man who was supposed to be desperately worried about the survival of his family . . . Why was he laughing all the time? Thais perceived him as resolute, courageous – and a man so brave that he could laugh in the face of famine.

The excellent Susan Kepner has also translated and written an introduction to Botan's *Letters from Thailand*, which deals in fictional form with the life of the Chinese minority. Of all the countries of South-east Asia where Chinese have settled over the last four centuries, it is only in Thailand and to a lesser extent the Philippines that they have been accepted and even assimilated. The Muslim states of Malaysia and Indonesia maintain harsh, discriminatory laws. Vietnam, after 1975, was to drive out most of it Chinese population.

The Thai kings, from as long ago as the fifteenth century, welcomed Chinese traders and sometimes offered them posts in government service. From early on it was noticed that Thai women favoured a Chinese husband as being more prudent, industrious, and above all more faithful. In the nineteenth century the Thai kings earned as much as forty per cent of the national revenue by farming out to the Chinese traders a state monopoly on gambling, lotteries, alcohol and opium, all of them vices strictly forbidden to ethnic Thais. By the start of this century, Bangkok was a largely Chinese city and so remained until about twenty years ago when a huge migration developed from northeast Thailand.

The Chakri dynasty itself has Chinese blood and has always looked favourably on the Chinese community, with the exception of Rama VI, the fop who had learned from his British friends a fear of the 'Yellow Peril', and may have written the pamphlet on the Chinese that came out in 1914 called 'The Jews of the East'. Most of the Thai aristocracy, including Kukrit Pramoj, have some Chinese ancestry. The main threat to the Chinese came from the right-wing generals, often of humbler stock, who came to power in the 1930s after the overthrow of the absolute monarchy. Sinophobia probably underlay the decision to change the name of the country for international use, from Siam to Thailand. The first is a geographical expression. The word transcribed as *thai* means 'free' but sounds very similar to *Tai* or *T'ai*, the name of the major ethnic group. Many people would like to return to 'Siam' because they think that 'Thailand' discriminates against the Laotian or Isan people, and still more against the ethnically separate Chinese and Malays. It could be said that calling Siam 'Thailand' is something like calling all Britain 'England'.

In spite of occasional bouts of harassment, the Chinese in Thailand went on running the commerce, banking, manufacture and service industries. At any tourist hotel in Bangkok, the chambermaid will be Thai, but the manager, the reception clerks and the headwaiter will all be Chinese. In the bars of Patpong Road, the strippers and live-show girls will almost certainly come from north-east Thailand, but the woman cashier will be Chinese.

The last big wave of immigration from south-east China, just up the coast from Hong Kong, occurred during the four years of famine and civil war between the defeat of Japan and the Communist takeover in 1949. One of these immigrants, Tan Suang U, is the hero and narrator of Botan's novel *Letters from Thailand*, in which he describes to his mother at home his trials and adventures in Bangkok. The young and rather pig-headed migrant sets off for Thailand, full of confidence that he and his children will marry and live among fellow Chinese, maintaining their Chinese habits of thrift and industry, while reaping the benefit of a fertile country whose own inhabitants have not the wit or the will to make money.

The deft and at times hilarious comedy of these letters lies in the slow but relentless erosion of Tan Suang U's principles, under the balmy influence of a sunnier, lazier land. While still on the boat from China, Tan Suang U is given a few tips about Thailand: Never reveal that you have not been to school, since the Thais have more respect for diplomas than skill, and like to see a bit of paper. Showing this you can get a job without being able to count past five. With the elder Chinese, this does not matter so much, but the younger ones who have grown up in Thailand have started to think like Thais. He is warned not to let slip that his mother worked as a servant, for 'Thailand is full of people who would rather steal than be servants'.

The industrious Tan Suang U finds a job in a trading store and soon marries the boss's daughter, but gradually he discovers that his wife, his sister-in-law, his children and friends are drifting away from the old Chinese virtues toward the Thai spirit of *mai pen rai*, 'it doesn't matter'. The children start wanting to take Sundays off, as the Thais do, then even Saturdays as well. His wife and her sister take a fancy to every expensive novelty such as cars, television, and Western fashions. 'I have to laugh,' Tan Suang U writes to his mother, 'for not so long ago we were talking about footbinding and how barbaric it was. The shoes they are wearing today must have nearly the same effect . . . with the heels three, four or even five inches high.'

The letters are full of complaints about the Thais, especially their laziness and drunkenness:

> They steal and gamble and lie with each other's wives . . . We're superstitious, they say, because our superstitions are different from theirs. They speak as if they were gods, to know that burial is wrong and a funeral pyre the only release of a spirit.

The Thais call Tan Suang U a *jek*, the opprobrious word for a Chinese, but Thai women are happy enough to get a Chinese son-in-law: 'Good for you, daughter! Marry a *jek* and you'll eat pork every day; you won't eat dried fish and chase ducks round a pond all your life, like your poor mother.'

When his wife suggests using contraception, Tan Suang U tells her to stop talking filth. Children are strength, he says, to which his wife replies with a Thai proverb that one child equals seven years of poverty. 'Sure,' says Tan Suang U, 'if you raise a child the way the Thais do. Treat him like a little God. Give him everything he wants. If a child is twenty and hasn't even begun to work – like some I've seen here – then one child is a lifetime of poverty, not seven years. But my children will be raised to work, and study, and grow up able to look after themselves.'

In this too he is disappointed. His only son takes to drink and goes off to live with a prostitute from the north-east, while his favourite daughter becomes engaged to a poor Thai school-teacher, to whom Tan Suang U is most ungracious. The young man seeks to explain that Thais love and respect their parents just as the Chinese do, but show their feelings in different ways: 'You see, Thai parents let their sons depend on them. The Chinese and the *farang* don't understand why Thai parents encourage that, but they do it because they see dependence as a form of love.' Eventually Tan Suang U relents and goes to live with his daughter and Thai son-in-law. He ends up saying about his children: 'I could not shelter them from the thousands of daily experiences which made them another people, another race. There are so many of our people here, yet the Thais have won.'

When *Letters from Thailand* first appeared, it aroused much anger both from the Thais and Chinese. On second reading, most people came to acknowledge the truth of the satire, and anyway could not resist the humour and good nature with which it was written. The Thai Ministry of Education later made *Letters from Thailand* a set book for the teaching of social studies, and wisely so, for a good novel is worth a shelf of sociological tracts.

4

Vietnam Without the Americans: 1973–4

In August 1973, I enjoyed three separate pieces of fortune that got me back to Saigon for a four-month stay. An airline gave me a free return ticket to Singapore; the Vietnam Embassy gave me a visa; and Richard Ingrams commissioned a book for his *Private Eye* publishing house. This was to be the first of three long sojourns in South Vietnam between the departure of the Americans and the victory of the Communists. Early in 1973, Henry Kissinger and his opposite number Le Duc Tho had cobbled together a most dishonourable Peace Treaty. The United States had agreed to withdraw its troops and stop the bombing of North Vietnam, in return for which the North Vietnamese were allowed to set up a chain of military installations in the South with hundreds of tanks and a dozen airstrips, including one at the Khe Sanh base where the US Marines had fought so gallantly and to so little purpose during the Tet Offensive of 1968. The last US troops left early in 1973, along with most of the counter-insurgency experts, spies, economists, engineers and agricultural advisers.

With the Americans gone, and now obsessed with the Watergate scandal, Vietnam was no longer news and most of the journalists and the cameramen had left to cover the fresh horrors of Africa, the Middle East or Northern Ireland. A New York publisher said of my subsequent book about this period: 'Hell!

He writes as if the war was still going on!' The Army of South Vietnam (ARVIN) was still losing hundreds of dead each week. Much of the fighting was now much closer to Saigon, making the city noisier and more alarming. The former US military briefings, the 'five o'clock follies', had been replaced by ARVIN briefings; but few foreign reporters ever attended them.

As usual I stayed at the Royale Hotel, whose ancient proprietor M. Ottavj was now very frail and barely able to walk. He no longer went to his opium den but instead had the pipes prepared in his room by a silent woman he called *'la boyesse'*. Occasionally I accepted his invitation to join him in a pipe or two, and to hear again the stories I knew so well about Corsica, Africa, Syria and Cambodia, and then his reminiscences of the unending Vietnam wars. He gave me his gloomy view of world affairs, especially the trouble caused by *'Hitler et compagnie'*, *'Nixon et compagnie'* and more recently *'Brezhnev et compagnie'*. To explain the departure of the Americans, he said that Nostradamus had predicted for late in the twentieth century, the defeat of a great world power by a small nation. *'C'est le Vietnam, Monsieur Oo-est.'*

The Royale Hotel was a haunt of the few foreign journalists left in Saigon, most of whom were British and Australian. The earnest pundits and paramilitary war correspondents had left the field to a less famous and even Bohemian type. There were old-timers such as Peter Kemp, a veteran of Spain, Albania, Poland and Laos before he began a second career as a journalist. On the other extreme in age and political views was James Fenton. There was Jon Swain who had reached Vietnam by way of the Foreign Legion, and another adventurous Englishman, Stuart Dalby, who had come to Saigon after losing all his money on the Hong Kong Stock Exchange. Once the distinguished author David Cornwell came to Saigon to do research for one of the thrillers he writes under the name of John Le Carré. He invited Dalby, Swain and myself to a Sunday bouillabaisse lunch at the best French restaurant in Saigon, treating us lavishly to its real Chablis and pear liqueur. At about six o'clock he asked us what he imagined to be an all-important question: how did we fiddle our expenses?

We gaped at him, for none of us had an expense account, let alone one large enough to eat at this restaurant.

Even those journalists who had a retainer or 'string' from a European paper or radio station were seldom encouraged to file from Saigon. The American press and public did not want to hear about the country they had abandoned. Some of the Vietnamese, in their turn, were bitter against the Americans, as I discovered on 2 November 1973, when I attended a Mass at Saigon Cathedral, marking the tenth anniversary of the death of President Diem. I had long been interested in the argument over the *coup d'état* against Diem, his brother Nhu and his lovely but frightening sister-in-law Madame Nhu. For some years before and after his downfall, Diem was abhorrent to liberals in the United States. He was considered a Catholic bigot, a recluse who would not listen to counsel except from his brother, the still more tyrannical chief of police, and Madame Nhu, who was said to have gloated over the 'barbecued' Buddhist monks at the An Quang Pagoda. For his first two years in office, President Kennedy would not change his policy of support for Diem. He was a fellow Catholic, and may have had an affinity with these rich aristocrats from Hue who ran Vietnam as a family business.

At the Mass in Saigon Cathedral ten years later, there were bus-loads of mourners, supplemented by youth groups in smocks and cross-garters rather like Morris men, who banged their sticks in the funeral dance. I was handed a statement in English to say that the service was not intended to rekindle hatred. 'Were he living this day,' the statement continued, 'President Diem's magnanimity would not have tolerated such an undertaking.' There was little magnanimity in the severe professor who organised the Mass. At every question I asked, he hissed with rage that I, a foreigner, dared to question the popular love for Diem. When I asked if Buddhists were taking part in the tribute, he said that, yes, there would be a service at one of the Buddhist pagodas. The An Quang Pagoda? Yes, the An Quang Pagoda had sent them a telegram of condolence. In turn, the professor asked me what was the role of America in the *coup d'état* against Diem. In vain I tried to explain to him, for the third time, that I was not an American.

From the cathedral I walked to the main Catholic cemetery, where a Mass was to be said in front of Diem's tomb, an ugly grey plastic slab. It was a morning of activity at the cemetery, for Diem's anniversary falls on All Souls' Day, when Catholics honour the dead. A memorial service had just been held by the French *anciens combattants*, not least of them M. Ottavj, the secretary of the War Honours Committee. As the Diem supporters proceeded between the graves, they passed M. Ottavj going away in his black suit and tie, with his heavy stick and his no less heavy tread. In front of Diem's tomb there was a VIP area barricaded by barbed wire of the latest kind – rather like rose thorns – on which I managed to cut my finger. Speeches were made by a politician, the mayor of Saigon and lastly a priest, who also conducted another service as blue smoke shot from the tomb to mark the departed spirit. There was something odd in this ceremony for a man who was still widely unpopular in Vietnam, not least with M. Ottavj, for Diem and his puritanical sister-in-law had outlawed the opium pipe, along with such pleasures as dancing, boxing, adultery and beauty contests.

It was even odder, the following day, to go to a Communist press briefing at Tan Son Nhut airport. By the terms of the ceasefire agreement, the People's Revolutionary Government (PRG) had stationed a team of observers in the territory ruled by the Republic of South Vietnam. The site of the camp may have been chosen to keep the Communists apart from the people of Saigon, or perhaps to discourage rocket attacks on the airport. The industrious PRG had decorated their camp with lawns surrounded by stone borders and ornamental vases. They had even dug their own vegetable plot.

The PRG Saturday press conference started at nine in the morning and went on till twelve, providing time to rebut all the allegations made at the daily ARVIN conferences: 'Last week the Saigon American puppet government committed 743 ceasefire violations, bringing the total to 32,463 ceasefire violations, and 682 land-grabbing operations, bringing the total to 49,583 land-grabbing operations.' There was one moment of interest when the spokesman, a colonel, was asked if it was true that the PRG forces had blown up a train. 'Yes,' came the reply, 'the train of the Saigon American puppet regime had entered the territory of the PRG and, after careful consideration, we decided to destroy it.'

The spokesmen at these conferences were all from the PRG, that is local Southern Communists, but North Vietnam also sent a liaison officer, a young and intelligent-looking man who was sitting next to me at the table. He was obviously even more bored than I was at having to hear this catalogue of 'ceasefire violations' and 'land-grabbing operations', for when I started to read a book, he started to read one too. I asked in a whisper what his book was about, and he whispered back 'patriotic poems'. He looked over at my book, *Right Ho, Jeeves*, but did not question me on its contents. He asked me about the Mass for Diem on the previous day, and in turn I asked how he and the other North Vietnamese managed to get back to Hanoi. 'By American Air Force planes,' he said with a chuckle, 'the very same planes that were bombing us.' He asked me about the rice situation in Saigon and said: 'The Saigon regime is fighting two wars – the Vietcong War and the Rice War.' Although I could see that the PRG colonel was glaring at us for whispering during the conference, the man from Hanoi went on to his next joke: 'Poor Nixon. He has both Watergate and Vietnamisation gate.' Such ideological jokes were not as good as P. G. Wodehouse; however when next I met this man from Hanoi, more than fifteen years later, he turned out to have a good sense of humour.

The 'rice war' to which the man from Hanoi alluded was one of the economic problems facing South Vietnam. The United States withdrawal at the beginning of 1973 had meant that 300,000 Vietnamese were out of a job within days, followed by gradual dismissals throughout the year. As the cost of living rose by about five per cent each month, so earnings fell, causing poverty and starvation. A Saigon car dealer reported in August

1973 that sales were coming at one a month, compared to one hundred a month in the previous August. Professional and executive men, who had earned 100,000 piastres a month when working for the Americans, were reduced to jobs at less than a tenth that salary. One morning I looked from the Royale Hotel at a huge crowd of young women in front of the offices of the National TV company of Japan, which had made big profits during 'the time of the Americans'. Each month National interviewed 400 applicants for about twenty jobs, paying 7,000 piastres a month. Most of these applicants had once worked for the Americans at about 15,000 piastres, when the piastre had double the purchasing power.

The Vietnamese could accept the loss of luxuries such as television sets, scooters, cigarettes and sweets, but they could not bear the swift and amazing increase in the price of rice, which doubled in 1973. Rice was not only their staple food but part of their civilisation, with ritual and magic importance. The very word for rice is the word for food. By late 1973, the cost of rice was an inescapable part of all conversation, taking precedence over the war. The magnitude of the problem was explained to me by one man: 'I have a salary of 8,000 piastres a month. The rice I need for my wife and eight children costs 20,000 piastres.' To get even a half ration of rice, the poor Vietnamese had to stop buying clothes, medicine, meat, fish or vegetables, other than seasoning such as chilli. The newspapers often carried stories of heads of families who had killed themselves because of their inability to provide.

Nobody understood why rice was dear. An expert at the American Embassy told me that most of the crop had been sold to the Communists, who then resold it cheap for propaganda purposes. However another American expert at Can Tho, the principal town in the Mekong Delta, said that far from there being a shortage of rice, there was a bumper harvest, that 95 per cent of the quota was reaching Saigon, where there was now a danger of surplus and much of the wet rice was rotting. When I asked what was the cause of the high price of rice, he answered: 'The American Embassy in Saigon.'

There was one other theory, to which I subscribed at the time, that the government and the senior generals were now getting from rice the money they no longer gained from the heroin business formerly run by the CIA. Like many people, I had been influenced by Alfred W. McCoy's recently published book *The Politics of Heroin in South-east Asia*, based on dozens of interviews as well as a mass of documents. In his introductory chapters, McCoy explains how the French had turned opium into the basis of the colonial economy. Only six months after annexing Saigon, in 1862, they imposed a franchise on opium brought into Indo-China from India, taxed at ten per cent of its value. The Opium Monopoly was later reformed and expanded so that by 1918 there were 1,512 government dens and 3,098 retail shops. Thanks to opium giving a third of its revenue, Indo-China started to turn a profit. Between the world wars, when other colonial powers tried to suppress this social evil, the French actually raised Indo-China's revenue from the opium tax.

The legal traffic in opium was abolished in 1946, but a clandestine traffic continued, and it was this that French intelligence agents first took over and then expanded in order to finance rival groups to the Vietminh, such as the Catholics, the Cao Dai sect and the Binh Xuyen river pirates. The opium for this 'Operation X' was supplied from Laos and north-west Vietnam, where the French had built up a mercenary force from the Meo and other Montagnard tribes. This arrangement was doubly ingenious since the Meo were paid for growing the opium poppies, while down in the South the mercenaries also got rich from refining and selling the finished drug. The middlemen in this operation were Corsican gangsters in Vientiane, who shipped the drug to Saigon on French military planes.

After the French departed in 1955, President Diem at first tried to suppress the opium traffic but he too found that he needed its earnings to finance his mercenaries and his secret police, whose operations depended on hundreds of thousands of paid informers. From 1956, there was an ever-increasing opium traffic from Laos to Saigon, first on charter planes owned by the Corsicans and later by courtesy of the Vietnamese Air Force. After the fall of Diem in 1963, the secret police system built up by him and his brother soon collapsed, for want of the drug money to pay informers. Communist agitators flourished even in Saigon.

In the 1960s the CIA restarted the 'Operation X' set up by the French almost twenty years earlier, and once again with the same double purpose: to give encouragement to the Meo in Laos as well as financing the anti-Communists in Saigon. Since there was no longer a widespread habit of opium-smoking in South Vietnam, the CIA turned to the manufacture and sale of heroin. This far more dangerous drug was sold at first to the US troops, then to the Vietnamese and finally to the international gangs for export to Europe or the United States. The borderland between Laos, Thailand and Burma, or 'Golden Triangle', became the world's principal source of heroin.

McCoy's book was published before the Americans left Vietnam, and did not explore what happened later. However, it seems clear that from 1973, the Saigon government and its senior generals badly needed another source of cash. In IV Corps, the Mekong Delta region, the military put the squeeze on rice merchants, who in turn put the squeeze on the peasant growers, who in turn passed on the cost to eaters of rice. The ravages of the 'rice war' were seen at their most depressing at Can Tho, the largest town in the Mekong Delta. This was how I described a visit in late 1973:

> Those Americans in Can Tho who once wanted to make the Mekong Delta a 'get-up-and-go, greedy society' have never returned to see the result of their labours. Certainly greed, or at least hunger, stares from the eyes of scores of tattered, whining beggars, many of them with missing limbs and all of them thin and sick. Rice, in the heart of the rice country, costs almost as much as in Saigon to those who do not live on their own farms.

Some of the Chinese are fat but there are few fat Vietnamese under the rank of major... I cannot record as fact but as an impression the overwhelming nastiness of Can Tho; the filth, stench, waste, ugliness and the misery of the faces. It is a town where you start each morning in certainty that not one single enjoyable thing will happen all day. After one horrible afternoon I locked myself in my hotel bedroom and tried to read but dropped off to sleep with the lights on. I woke from a nightmare to find that the hag who collected the laundry had brought in a girl whom she was forcibly pressing upon me, the girl's body on mine and the girl's mouth (with ulcerous gums) on my mouth. After explaining that I was not in the mood, I went for a much-needed drink to a riverside café, remarkable for the fact that its staff occasionally smiled. There was a very loud tape of rock music from the United States, which I had heard the night before but could bear to hear again. After some twenty minutes a commotion took place with the arrival of a young woman and two soldiers. All three were drugged and the girl promptly fell into unconsciousness. A legless beggar pushed himself to their table and started to tug at the trouser leg of one of the soldiers, who shouted a bit and stared round the café. The manager of the café told them to go, and then turning to me, whispered 'Heroin'. As this was going on, the tape started to play the rock version of Beethoven's finale to the Choral Symphony, with words roughly adapted from Schiller. While the two men staggered out of the café, holding their woman friend by the arms and legs, still followed by the legless beggar, the music rose into the blood-stirring magnificent theme which was Beethoven's message of joy to all mankind.

Although I saw and reported the squalor and poverty of Can Tho and Saigon itself, I do not seem to have spotted an apparent contradiction: that nobody looked for salvation to the Communists. The PRG denounced the 'Saigon American puppet regime' but did not offer a welcome alternative. There were North Vietnamese army units in northern parts of the Delta near the Cambodian border, but there were few indigenous Vietcong, except in the marshes of the Camau peninsula. The Vietcong were no longer safe in most of the villages, still less the towns. After the Communist conquest in 1975, the PRG admitted that in Can Tho their support amounted to well below one per cent of the adult population.

After a disagreeable stay in the Mekong Delta, I thought I would cheer myself up by going to see one of the legendary figures of South Vietnam, the Italian coffee planter Santilli (I never discovered his first name). Although his plantation was near Ban Me Thuot, with which I was now familiar, Santilli was not on the telephone and therefore hard to find. However, I had a letter of introduction from M. Ottavj, and somehow effected a meeting when next I went to Ban Me Thuot. The manager of the little hotel where I stayed informed me that Signor Santilli would meet me next morning at the agreeable café the *Souris Blanche*, or White Mouse.

Signor Santilli turned out to be a stocky, ruddy-faced man of about sixty with lively, brown eyes, a loud voice, still louder check shirt and a soft white hat on his head. He was teasing an old French priest in an argument interspersed with fake tantrums of fury: 'You should have a woman, *mon père*, it's ridiculous that you don't have a woman.' 'At my age?' retorted the priest, and started to sulk over his vermouth. It was like a scene from one of those old comic films about rustic life in Provence or Tuscany, *La Femme du Boulanger* perhaps, or the Don Camillo series. When I showed him Ottavj's letter, Santilli asked me to come out to lunch with him at his plantation.

The drive was noisy, for Signor Santilli was an Archangel Gabriel on the car horn, and it was also slow, for he kept stopping to talk with friends, doffing his hat to the men and ogling the women, especially the Montagnard girls. As we came to the coffee plantations he pointed out with bellows of indignation where Vietnamese had taken the land – 'not bought, *taken*, monsieur!' – until we came to his own wooden house, perched on stilts in a clearing. We drank aperitifs on the veranda looking down on a hillside of gum trees, bare and ghastly white, rising tall as a cathedral out of the underbrush, from which came spicy smells and the noise of crickets. His Montagnard wife and their several beautiful daughters served me and the other guests by far the largest meal I have ever consumed in the tropics. Parma ham was followed by pâté, spaghetti, steak, cheese, and papaya doused in cognac that supplemented the vermouth, red wine and champagne.

'The VC often come through here,' said Signor Santilli over the coffee, 'they were here last night, although only in small numbers. After Tet 1968 the Americans dropped a stick of napalm on my plantation, destroying twenty-two hectares, but what can you expect in a war?' Yet the plantation appeared a peaceful, even a happy place as we went for a walk in the afternoon. 'All my employees are Montagnards,' Signor Santilli said, 'and I pay them well on piece rate, so that they work as much as they want. They're very good people.' It was clear that the workers returned Santilli's affection, as well as the bawdy shouts and mock abuse that he roared at them in the Rhade tongue. It was December, the start of the coffee harvest, and as we moved through the dark bushes we came upon groups of Montagnard girls, picking and sorting the green from the red beans. My host made a pounce on several women who screamed, pretended to run away, laughed and in one case bared her behind in derision. Signor Santilli's attitude to the Montagnards was not founded on liberal ideology. Later that day, when we were once more on his veranda, drinking beer, I saw him get out a gramophone and a record. Soon the forest was sounding to the swell of Italian oratory: '*Italiani! L'Italia ha finalmente l'impero! L'impero fascista*!' It was Mussolini, on 9 May 1936, announcing the establishment of his Fascist empire, after the capture of Addis Ababa.

From the Highlands I went to Hue for the first time in two years. In April 1972, the Communists had launched an offensive south down the 'Street Without Joy' capturing Dong Ha and Quang Tri but failing to capture Hue, and also suffering heavy casualties. The courageous South Vietnamese Marines then counter-attacked and retook the rubble that was all that was left of Quang Tri. During this battle, thousands of people abandoned

Hue in fear of a massacre similar to that of 1968. 'It was like France in 1940,' said Jacques Sanlaville, who had managed to get his family to Danang but himself had remained to keep going the two institutions he loved – the Cercle Sportif and the power station.

As a result of the Peace Treaty early that year, the North Vietnamese at the end of 1973 had heavy artillery and at least one armoured division within easy range of Hue. An ARVIN officer told me casually that he had spent the day watching the North Vietnamese move up their troops by lorry. 'If they attack a third time,' he told me, 'just pack your bags.' Another ARVIN officer who had served seven years told me: 'I'm going abroad. I've done my duty. I can't go through it again.' Many no doubt felt the same way; yet as I observed at the time it was always unwise to exaggerate defeatism in South Vietnam. The Americans had made this error, sneering at ARVIN and so contributing to their depression; then the Americans gave up the struggle, yet ARVIN fought on. It was argued that the Northern Communists must prevail because they had fought so long and suffered so much, but the anti-Communist Vietnamese had fought as long and made comparable sacrifices. Fifty Vietnamese officers in the French Army volunteered to be dropped into Dien Bien Phu on the day before it was overrun in 1954. The North Vietnamese were ready to die because they belonged to a grim and oppressive state where life was unpleasant, just as the armies of Hitler and Stalin fought it out to the death. The South Vietnamese, who valued life rather than abstract ideology, fought in a spirit of sad and stoical resignation.

A comparison has been made with the fall of France in 1940, but even in France, where defeatism was widespread, there were hundreds of thousands ready to fight against all odds. In Hue, on this visit in 1973, I chanced to be reading *Pilote de Guerre* by Antoine de Saint-Exupéry, the poet who served in the air force until his death in 1944. During the German invasion of France he was pilot of a reconnaissance plane flying perilous and probably useless missions behind the enemy lines. One passage seemed most appropriate to the mood in Hue:

> Is my mind filled with the thought of the war of the Nazis against the West? Not at all. I think in terms of immediate details. I think of possible wounds. I think of the absurdity of flying over German-held Arras at two thousand feet; of the futility of the Intelligence we are asked to bring back; of the interminable time it takes to dress in these clothes that remind me of men made ready for the executioner. And I think of my gloves. Where the devil are my gloves? I can no longer see the cathedral in which I live. I am dressing for the service of a dead god.

Whereas Hue had always remained a Vietnamese city, Danang in the 1960s became an American military base, so that nowhere was I more surprised by the American absence. Gone were the dumps on the quayside, the lorries and jeeps, the pimps and prostitutes and the black market stalls, from one of which I had hurriedly purchased a US uniform, only to find when I was wearing it in the field that the patches of what I had thought was dirt, was the dried (but now melting) blood of the previous owner. At one roadside stall, dealing mostly in plastic Buddhas, I found some of those three-sided plaques of marble or wood that Americans like to inscribe with their name, and place on their desk or mantelpiece: 'Albert C. Tucker USAF', 'Dave Hook. Vietnam 1970–71', 'Rock and Jessie. Always', 'Danang. Rocket City 1969–70'. The people who had commissioned these objects must have died, forgotten them or sold them back to the stall holders who now purveyed them as souvenirs of the departed ally. The very few Americans who were left in Danang would sometimes come up and say hello and ask what I was doing in town.

The Marine Press Centre was long since closed, so that the insults to European journalists were now handed out by Vietnamese rather than US colonels. In a restaurant one lunch-time I noticed that I was being glared at by a colonel in the Rangers, who at last came over and said, 'I remember you,' as he probably did, for I had brushed with him already. He demanded, rudely, to see my ARVIN press card, and after some fruitless efforts to pick a quarrel, went back to his table and an annoyingly pretty woman. Before going, he sneered: 'You journalists make good money in this country.' I kept silent and thought about those cheques from the *Listener* and the *New Statesman*.

Danang, although still not a pleasant city, was so much pleasanter than before as to be almost unrecognisable. The rubbish was collected, the pavements had been repaired, and blue paint applied to government buildings. The shops were clean, there were two floating restaurants on the river, and elegant new cafés. Some of the credit for all these improvements was due to the foreign oil companies, vying for the chance to drill off-shore tests. A Vietnamese who had opened the Salon Danube restaurant, furnished with suits of armour, found objects and local impressionist paintings, also providing good French food, was confident of the future: 'This year, it's true, there are not so many Americans, but soon they will be back – drilling for oil. At the moment, most of the oil men are in Saigon, but there's lots of oil up here, near Hue, and the drilling will have to be done from Danang, as it's the safest base.'

On this visit I spent several hours at the Danang Museum of artefacts from the age of the Chams, the race conquered and almost destroyed by the Vietnamese about six hundred years ago. To judge by their statues and miniature temples, the Chams were akin by culture and race to the Khmers, who built Angkor in Cambodia. The Danang Museum had been shut during the 1960s; however, I had a quick peek thanks to the US Marines, who were guarding it as part of their civic action programme. Since then, I noted with sorrow, a few more statues had lost their heads. The curator blamed this on rocket attacks but I suspected the work of art thieves. However, no harm had come to the Goddess Tara from Duong Binh, a thick-lipped, ugly, imperious woman with big breasts and a full belly bulging under her tight-waisted sarong. Nor had harm come to the Buddha from Dong

Duong, in Quang Ngai, whose stern and autocratic face contrasts with the gentler Buddhas of Angkor. He is seated with wide legs apart and hands on knees, and round the base of the statue there is a bas-relief frieze showing Amforas, or dancing girls. But whereas at Angkor these girls are full face and smiling, here they are leaning on one arm with downcast stare, like a melancholy *vahine* in a Gauguin painting. All these works date from the fifth and sixth century AD.

Some Vietnamese felt guilt for having destroyed the earlier civilisation, and blamed the continuing war on the 'Curse of the Chams'. I had also heard that some of the thirty thousand Chams remaining in Vietnam were found in a village near Phan Thiet, south of the seaside resort of Nha Trang, where there is also a large Cham temple. Late in 1973, I set off in search of the Chams with a New York photographer named Sarah Webb Barrell, a tall, blonde and very attractive woman who had already broken many hearts in Saigon and Phnom Penh. The men she rejected spread the story that 'Sarah Dum-Dum' had worked as a New York hooker to buy her cameras and ticket to Saigon, but I always regarded her as an old-fashioned romantic and Bohemian, like so many attracted to Indo-China.

Sarah and I flew first to Nha Trang, then rode in a motor trishaw down to Phan Thiet in a part of the country that journalists never visited, perhaps because it was always peaceful. We checked into a vile hotel and slept on different sides of a low partition, for there was only the one room available. Sarah was always faithful to her current lover, at that time a pugnacious Australian. The next day we took a taxi out to the Cham village near the sea. The elders received us graciously, they talked of their pride at having served in the French Army and how much they wished that the French had remained. While they were telling us of their grievances against the Vietnamese, we suddenly heard loud shouts of rage and one of terror. We ran across and found a group of the villagers poking their guns into a cowering creature, our taxi driver. The elders made the men release their victim, who clung to us for protection and begged us to leave the village.

We asked the elders what the driver had done to deserve this savage treatment. 'He is Vietnamese,' was the simple reply.

Sarah took pictures and I took notes for an article that I think was never published. We drove on another trishaw back to Nha Trang and went for a swim in the sea. That evening in the courtyard of the Fregate Hotel, we ate a long and delicious dinner of local oysters and lobsters with two or three bottles of wine, and told each other our troubles, and just as quickly forgot them. Sarah had the unusual gift in a sexually very alluring woman of being friendly without being a tease. She was also very funny. Apart from its chaste conclusion, this was one of the happiest days I spent in Vietnam.

On the plane back to Saigon next day, I sat next to a businessman who boasted of being the only Vietnamese graduate of the London School of Economics, an institution he hated because of its left-wing bias. Back in Saigon, the happiness of the trip to Nha Trang soon wore off. I spent two days visiting heroin clinics with Rowly Carter, an old South African friend. When the curfew descended after an evening of drink, I made my way to the rooftop bar with a licence till one in the morning. I ordered a beer, looked round at the bar girls (who knew me of old as a 'cheap Charlie' who would not buy them a drink) and prepared to brood for a half hour alone. A new girl appeared and started a conversation: 'I spend one year at college. I know many English words that other bar girls they no know. Do you know word 'castration', to rip the flesh from the body? I have a very nice apartment. Maybe you come there for fornication and copulation?' No, not tonight, I said, I was feeling too tired and anyway (joking) I was getting too old for that kind of thing. 'Oh, yes,' she replied in her little American voice, 'you old, but I think you very sexy senior citizen.' I thought it was time to leave Vietnam for ever.

A day or two after Christmas 1973, M. Ottavj asked me into his dingy office but seemed uncertain of what he wanted to say. For the first time since I had known him he was embarrassed. At last he said: 'Monsieur West, I know you will be very depressed by this news but on 1 January I am to be made a Chevalier of the Légion d'Honneur.' Of course he was really pleased but perhaps he knew he was near the end of his life. He had grown gloomy of late and more than usually superstitious. He was alarmed by a box of Laotian matches called '999' that he had seen upside down and taken for '666', the number of the Beast in Revelation. He thought that 1974 might see the beginning of war between the planets, with Earth coming under attack from '*Jupiter et compagnie*'.

On New Year's Day 1974, M. Ottavj gave a small dinner to celebrate the award of the Légion d'Honneur. He brought out his best wines, his treasured photographs, and the programme of music by Edna Barrett's all-woman band in the Majestic Hotel in the 1930s. Once again I thought of the all-woman band in Conrad's novel *Victory*, and of the concept of victory which was the leitmotif and also part of the title of my second book on Vietnam. At the dinner on New Year's Day I was facing a plaque to the *Vieilles Tiges* (Old Joysticks), the French Air Force old comrade association, which once had held its reunions here. Around the plaque there were pictures of four air force heroes, including Antoine de Saint-Exupéry. Two of his greatest books, *Vol de Nuit* and *Pilote de Guerre*, take victory as their theme. It is the last word of *Vol de Nuit* and the constant refrain of *Pilote de Guerre*, on the fall of France: 'Defeat... Victory... Terms I do not know what to make of. One victory exalts, another corrupts. One defeat kills, another brings life. Tell me what seed is lodged in your victory or your defeat, and I will tell you its future.' Those words exactly described the mood of South Vietnam between the departure of the Americans and the final Communist onslaught.

Heyst, in Conrad's *Victory*, is defeated because he rejects life and love. For Saint-Exupéry, victory comes from acceptance of life and duty to others. In *Terre des Hommes*, describing the Spanish Civil War and his crash in the Sahara during the Paris–Saigon air race, Saint-Exupéry writes:

> To come to man's estate it is not necessary to get oneself killed

round Madrid, or to fly mail planes or to struggle along in the snow out of respect for the dignity of life ... It is only when we become conscious of our part in life, however modest, that we shall be happy. Only then will we be able to live in peace and die in peace, for only this lends meaning to death and life.

I thought of this when I heard a few weeks later, back in London, that M. Ottajv had died at Tet.

When *Victory in Vietnam* went off to the printers in April 1974, I sadly reflected that this was the end of my ten-year connection with Indo-China. Vietnam had dropped entirely out of the news. The London magazines were no longer sending people to write on exotic places; at any rate they were no longer sending me. The *New Statesman* and *Private Eye* were now my only sources of income; my travels confined to Holborn and Soho. Moreover I now had a wife. Then in May, I got a telephone call from Tony de Lotbiniere of the BBC who asked me to lunch, said he had liked my earlier book on Vietnam, and asked me to make a television documentary, *Personal View*. By the beginning of July 1974, I was back in Saigon.

While making plans for the film before Tony de Lotbiniere and the crew arrived, I stayed at the Royale Hotel, though it was now very forlorn without M. Ottavj. The last British journalist, Stuart Dalby, had left for Phnom Penh; the food was worse and the rats more daring. As soon as Tony de Lotbiniere and the crew arrived I took the excuse to join them in the Continental Hotel. For the first time in more than eight years in Saigon, I had the chance to enjoy a bath, a telephone and room service, as well as the money for Chinese lunches in Cholon, and Corsican dinners with real French wine in Nguyen Hue Street. It was also a chance to study at close quarters one of the two hotels that are part of Saigon's history. The Continental began in 1862 as an officers' mess, later rebuilt as the present three-storey edifice over an open-air terrace café in 1880. The sentimental novelist Louis Roubaud gave the hotel this accolade in *Christiane de Saigon*, published in 1931:

From six to eight before dinner at the corner of the Place du Théâtre and the admirable Rue Catinat, the Continental – bordering the pavement – is at once a club, a salon, a stock exchange and a station. Elsewhere there are real clubs and salons but it is here you get the gossip and the business deals, romances, the news from Europe and Asia. I know old Frenchmen in Indo-China who have never been to Hue, Phnom Penh or Hanoi but there is not a white man from Tonkin, Cambodia, Laos or even China and Japan who is not bound to know Saigon and through Saigon, the Continental.

The story of *Christiane de Saigon* is based on the uproar during the late 1920s after a puritanical governor tried to expel the white prostitutes. Then, in 1930, the French had something graver to worry about, as Ho Chi Minh started an insurrection that led to police repression, army massacres (one of them close to My Lai in Quang Ngai Province), a number of guillotinings, and the establishment of an Asian Devil's Island at Poulu Condor, off Cap St Jacques. Among the French journalists who arrived to report on the revolution was one Andrée Viollis, a left-wing lady whose *L'Indo-Chine S.O.S.* was published in 1932. She stayed at the Continental but she was told by a Vietnamese radical: 'Excuse us for not coming to your hotel but the *boys* are almost all spies. If they saw us with you, we'd risk being arrested.'

After the Second World War the Continental became a target for Vietminh and other terrorists. The British writer Norman Lewis checked into his room one morning in 1950, walked to the window and found himself flung backwards by a colossal explosion. Then looking down onto the Place du Théâtre, he saw dozens of dead and wounded bodies, and two survivors clutching each other's shoulders for support, and lurching about like Greek bouzouki dancers. In his novel *The Quiet American*, Graham Greene blames this atrocity on Alden Pyle, the CIA agent hoping to build a 'Third Force' between the French and the Communists.

In Greene's novel, the Continental terrace was also a haunt of the loud American journalists, gloating over each French defeat.

When I was first in Saigon in 1966, the 'Continental Shelf' as it now was called was the haunt of a new breed of journalists, many of them in combat fatigues or safari suits. It was there that I met the young British photographer Tim Page, wearing bandages after the first of the many wounds he suffered over the years. He is now one of the few survivors of that zany gang of reporters and cameramen who rode to the war on motor-bikes, frequently high on marijuana, rock music and danger.

The Corsican-Vietnamese proprietor of the Continental, Philippe Franchini, was a successful painter, although the one exhibition I saw was too macabre for my taste. The paintings, etchings and montages – *Terres d'amour, nuits de mort* – included studies of parted vaginas, impaled corpses, pink baby dolls behind prison bars, and a naked, whimpering girl with her bottom stuck in the air, a work that was marked as sold to the deputy manager of the rival Caravelle Hotel across the road. I never saw any of M. Franchini's films, one of which was said to have been banned at the first Paris Film Festival, but he firmly denied to me that he had once wanted to make a film of fifty Japanese eating spaghetti. He used to say that the Continental had the worst food, the rudest staff and the ugliest prostitutes in the East. In fact the staff were polite, especially the wizened old waiter who shooed off the beggars and cigarette girls.

During the early 1970s, as the Americans were getting ready to leave, the Continental terrace suffered a curious change of clientele. There had always been one or two men in drag, but now it became what the world was starting to call a gay bar. The gents was apt to be full of twittering Vietnamese men, discussing their boyfriends and fiddling with their make-up. On one occasion, the homosexual set were present in force when the Shriners, a semi-Masonic body, were holding their annual dinner at the Continental. The epicene boys, with eye-shadow and fluttering hands, gazed adoringly at the huge American engineers in unaccustomed suits, and fezzes adorned with the names of eastern cities like Cairo, Baghdad and Mecca. The homosexual phase in Saigon may have been partly attributable to the presence for so many years of half a million Americans buying the Vietnamese women and mocking the pride and virility of the local men.

When I went to stay at the Continental in 1974, the terrace café was quieter and rather forlorn. There were few foreign journalists, or Americans of any kind, except for one drunk who had been there eight years. The front tables were occupied by Poles and Hungarians from the International Control Commission, the body intended to safeguard the Peace Treaty. Back in 1966, some of the Poles had lived in the Royale Hotel, and used to trade their vodka for our whisky, as well as going to dine with us at their favourite French Foreign Legion restaurant. The new lot of East Europeans seemed to be less friendly. Their presence had the effect of discouraging the homosexuals and bringing back the female prostitutes, although they were reckoned as 'cheap Charlies' compared to the former Americans.

The Continental was also a useful starting point for our documentary film on how life continued in South Vietnam after thirty years of war. As in the previous documentary for Richard Taylor, I was filmed on the terrace, giving a talk this time on the foul-tasting '33' beer. Because the Vietcong always took a tax on the transport of beer, the Americans spread the rumour that it would give you leprosy, while the Communists (so the story went) claimed it as an antidote to defoliation sickness. The topic of beer was really just an excuse for me to drink it and calm my nerves. We also filmed at the zoo, the French cemetery and the Saigon race-track.

Tony de Lotbiniere was touched by the very idea of the Tourist Board of South Vietnam, especially its efforts to sell Saigon as 'a city with a certain smile'. We decided to make our film in some of the tourist centres like Dalat, the hill station, Nha Trang, the seaside town, and Hue, on the Perfume River. We went first to Hue in order to join a coach trip advertised by the Tourist Board, to visit the battlefields on the 'Street Without Joy', now known as the 'Highway of Horrors'. This was a part of the country I knew from 1966, when I went with the US Marines to Quang Tri, Dong Ha and Con Thien. In 1968 and again in 1972, the

North Vietnamese had stormed down this highway to attack Hue. The 'Street Without Joy' runs about six miles from the South China Sea, skirting a desolate tract of sand-dunes, marshes and reed-beds. The few inhabitants of this region have always been poor, fierce and rebellious. From 1947 onwards, the French regarded this as the most dangerous part of Vietnam, a place of ambush, mines and booby-traps. In 1953 the historian Bernard Fall witnessed a sea-borne attack called Operation Camargue, after which French and Moroccan troops combed the dunes and swamps:

> Hundreds of infantrymen swarmed out with mine detectors or simply long metal rods, thumping their rifle butts on the ground to detect suspicious hollow areas... Every now and then one member of this human rake would scream as he stepped on a caltrap – a small wooden plank studded with seven-inch-long barbed steel arrowheads which could pierce a foot even through the thick soles of a jungle boot.

In July 1954, when France made peace after defeat at Dien Bien Phu, the Communist Regiment 95 emerged from the dunes and marshes along the 'Street Without Joy', holding their weapons and marching in broad daylight along Route 1 to the North. When the Communists rose in the South in the early 1960s, the same Regiment 95 began attacks on ARVIN along the 'Street Without Joy'. From 1965 it became a place of torment to the United States Marines. A few days after I met him in Saigon in 1967, Bernard Fall returned to the 'Street Without Joy', stepped on a land-mine and was killed. Now, in August 1974, we were travelling there on a coach trip.

The pretty young tourist guide shrieked into her megaphone: 'Ladies and gentlemen, this is what we call the Highway of Horrors, the site of one of the bloodiest battles of the Vietnam War. Almost two years have gone by, and the army has cleared most of the debris of war. Ladies and gentlemen, you may pick up anything from the place as a souvenir of the Highway of Horrors in Vietnam.' Each time we stopped, by a broken bridge, a burntout Communist tank or a ruined basilica, our guide repeated her invitation to pick up a souvenir – whether a cartridge case, a shell fragment or a piece of bone, I did not gather. One of the few other tourists, an American girl in a Vietnamese conical hat, took photographs of her husband beside an upturned cross, and posing in triumph upon a tank. During these pauses we felt on our skins the hot, dusty wind from the sand-dunes that always tormented troops on the 'Street Without Joy'. Helicopters provided an escort all the way to Quang Tri.

The Ben Hai river, just north of the ruined town, was now the frontier within Vietnam. On our bank there floated the orange and yellow flag of the South; across the water we saw the enormous red and blue flag with a yellow star of the North. Both sides bellowed across at each other through highly amplified megaphones, also blaring out martial music. A leaflet of the Tourist Board said that sometimes 'North Vietnamese female psychological agents gambol along the river's bank'. Sadly we did not see this. Sometimes the South resorted to pantomime, so we learnt from the same leaflet:

> A few weeks ago, the North Communists boasted that once in a while they eat canned food for a change. It was a mockery directed against our soldiers who they think are living mainly on canned food. As a reply to such an insult, our soldiers asked them to look carefully for twenty minutes at a hill on this side of the river. Our soldiers then raised up a twenty-metre pole with clusters of live ducks quacking and dangling from the top of the pole, meaning that 'on this side we have plenty of fresh meat to eat'.

The same Tourist Board leaflet quoted the words of General Bui The Lan, Commander-in-Chief of Marines at Quang Tri: 'If we can continue chaffing and calling names at each other in this kind of "saliva or cold war", perhaps we can keep away from the "hot one".' Alas, General Bui and his gallant Marines would go down fighting next year.

Back in Hue we filmed at length on the Perfume River, in the gardens of the Imperial Palace, and in the aristocratic south-east suburb. The houses there are built in a Sino-Vietnamese style, with three or four steps leading up to a stone veranda supporting a tiled roof, usually ornamented with dragons. The cool, airy rooms have low tables that also serve as beds, many lacquer vases and gilt Buddhist shrines. Our guide Doan, the beautiful wife of a Vietnamese broadcaster, introduced us to some of the elderly people who had survived the war and the Communist massacre of 1968. We met a sister-in-law of the last emperor, Bao Dai, a shrewd man often unfairly labelled a playboy. We filmed an old man tending his flowers and another lighting a candle in front of his shrine. Once, in this drowsy afternoon, a gong sounded, an old dog woke, yapped briefly and went back to sleep. As so often in Indo-China, I found myself thinking of Tsarist Russia as described by Chekhov and Turgenev. There was the same sadness and apprehension, the same grace in coping with loss and disappointment. Here, as in the Russian plays and novels, the servants and other retainers no longer stood in awe of their masters and mistresses but sat about on the steps, chatting, smoking and eating snacks. The long war had reduced them all to the same state of futility.

By great good fortune I happened to find, at the Cercle Sportif, Vietnam's most famous poet and composer, Trinh Cong Son, whom I had first met in Saigon in the 1960s and then here in Hue in 1973. He was sitting with a beer at a table beside the river, writing one of the songs that were and remain the most popular music in Vietnam and are also very attractive to Western ears. When I asked if he had a song we could use in our film, he not only agreed but provided us with a singer, a girl of about nineteen with a beautiful, serious face, dressed in a yellow *ao dai* with a brooch at the neck. She sang to her own guitar accompaniment, standing beneath a tree in the palace gardens, a song of such beauty and sorrow that it has haunted me ever since. It tells of a woman crossing the bridge on the Perfume River. Her husband has just been killed in the war, and her heart is empty because she has no one to love.

In the subsequent film, which I have just been watching again on the video tape, the camera moves from the singer to the bridge at sunset, showing a spooning couple on a bench, a motor sampan chugging upstream, and a young woman walking across the metal span, who raises her hand to steady her conical hat as a breeze tugs at the gown of her *ao dai*. I can remember how, even when we were filming these shots, the singer and her song represented all that I wanted to say about South Vietnam. Even now, twenty years later, when hearing that music and seeing the lovely, unsmiling face of the girl in her yellow *ao dai* in the palace gardens, I know that the film was not made in vain.

From Hue we flew to Dalat and stayed in the Palace Hotel. The immense public rooms were as usual empty. The silver duck press was still on display, as were the stuffed stoats and deer; also the real deer in a miniature zoo. Down at the artificial lake the fishermen still left the ends of their rods in the water, a practice condemned by all the angling books. I did an 'into camera' explaining how dull I had always found Dalat, and how dullness was not always a bad thing. We met a Vietnamese who asked where we came from and then said: 'I could not live in London. Too scary! Because of the IRA.'

We went to see an English missionary I had met the previous year. A big, burly young man in a tweed jacket, David Heath used to be a policeman in Leicestershire and hunted with the Quorn. He agreed to be filmed addressing a congregation of Montagnards in a nearby village. This is what he said to them:

> This afternoon I would like to tell you how I came to be here in this village. It was eight years ago, as a policeman in Leicestershire, that I first trusted the Lord Jesus Christ as my saviour. I lived the life of most young people in England. I went about and had a good time. I had lots of friends and lots of money. But I didn't know real peace in my heart. You people have known much of suffering. You have had to move your village many times and you

know that unless you have peace in your heart, there is much suffering in life. I had to trust the Lord Jesus Christ with my life... I had to confess that, yes, I was what the Bible calls a sinner and I needed the forgiveness that Jesus Christ could give when he died on the cross at Calvary.

In our subsequent film we touched on the plight of the Montagnards, now overwhelmed by immigrant Vietnamese. I did an interview with a Montagnard youth whose cowboy jacket and stetson hat proclaimed his fondness for the Americans, the last friends and champions of his people. He said that his dream in life was to visit Disneyland but it was hard to earn any money under the Vietnamese oppression. 'They are taking our land,' he said. 'We are working by hand and they have all kinds of bulldozers and tractors.' On this last trip to the Highlands under the old Vietnam, I regretted that I had not spent more time with the Montagnards while they still retained their ancestral ways. Back in the 1960s it had been possible to examine what was a truly prehistoric society. They were some of the last survivors of what Rousseau called the Noble Savage, and in a way they confirmed Rousseau's belief in primal innocence. They had spears and crossbows for fighting but do not seem to have taken war seriously. They enjoyed rice wine and their women went naked, at least to the waist. However, they lived in terror of evil spirits, which they placated by slow and painful animal sacrifice. The Montagnard Adam and Eve were no longer in Eden. Oddly enough I never met any anthropologists at work among the Montagnards. They were ignored by journalists as being only a marginal story. Some of the missionaries got to know the Montagnards but they were trying to alter, rather than study, their ways.

From Dalat we went down to the sea by minibus, for this was one part of the country that was safe. I remember with joy the view from the edge of the escarpment. We actually reached the coast at Cam Ranh Bay, the former French naval base from which Japan launched its attack on Malaya in 1941. In the 1960s,

Cam Ranh Bay was not only a vast naval and air base but in effect an American town, so safe from enemy infiltration that Presidents Johnson and Nixon went there on visits. The thousands of Vietnamese who worked there were not allowed to live in the camp, and even the prostitutes came in a mobile brothel and left when their work was finished. Now, in 1974, Cam Ranh Bay was only a junk heap of tyres, chassis, metal plate, barbed wire, ammunition casing and similar rusting *matériel*.

At Nha Trang we stayed at the Fregate Hotel and filmed the life of the beach. When the film appeared, viewers were startled to see the Vietnamese in bathing suits, kicking a football or turning somersaults on the sand. We also discovered two of the local oyster pickers, an elderly blind man and his youngest son, who worked in a creek. We filmed them, up-ending themselves like ducks in the muddy water, and popping up after a minute or two with their hands full of shells. After his work the old man drank a prodigious amount of the local absinthe and broke into song, apparently on the dangers of taking a second wife. Wordsworth might have written a poem about *The Blind Oyster Gatherer*.

We met one of the few GIs who had stayed in the country, a kindly black named Willis, who cared for his women and their many children. The majority of the bar girls were not so lucky, lounging mournfully on the beach with their half-caste brood. 'That's my souvenir, do you want him?' one of them called to me, indicating her son, a wizened autistic creature. However, I think that most of these girls would not have adapted to life in the United States. Philip Jones Griffiths told me once of meeting a bar girl who actually did get married and now was preparing to join her husband in Dallas. Before she left, she wanted to get an elaborate body tattoo. Philip tried to dissuade her without success until he came up with the clinching argument: 'In Dallas only the cyclo-drivers have tattoos.' In the commentary to the TV film I hear myself saying that 'most Vietnamese are tolerant of the bar girls and their half-caste children'. This may have been true of the old regime, but the Communist rulers of South Vietnam proved harsh to the bar girls and to their mixed-race children, especially to those of black fathers, such as the good-hearted Willis.

While doing research for the film before Tony de Lotbiniere and the crew arrived, I heard reports of a twenty-two-year-old English girl, Liz Thomas, who lived in a slum street in Cholon, devoting herself to helping prostitutes, prisoners, orphan children and drug addicts. The British Embassy had not even heard rumours of her existence. One of the British journalists, Jon Swain, said he had seen her, but feared meeting some old acquaintance among the fallen women. He imagined hearing an accusation along the lines of: 'You number ten cheap Charlie. You give me baby-san. Look same-same you.' At last I tracked down Liz through an American, Dick Hughes, who ran a hostel for shoe-shine boys, and then a Vietnamese Roman Catholic priest, Father Hoang, who looked after child strays and drug addicts. Father Hoang promised to bring Liz to the Royale Hotel the following evening.

Somehow I had expected that Liz would be earnest, priggish and very impatient with everybody who did not share her obsessive interests. I could not have been more wrong. She was tall, with a splendid figure, long golden hair and blue eyes, set in a face full of laughter. She ordered and drank with enjoyment a large gin and tonic. As I wrote in my diary later that evening: 'Liz is great fun to be with. Father Hoang had been cheerful when I met him before but now he was almost giggly. In civilian clothes, with spectacles on his plump face, he could have been a reporter out on the spree.'

Liz was wearing the simple blouse, the baggy black pantaloons and flip-flop sandals of any poor Vietnamese woman. As she told me her story, I found myself trying to place her accent and manner of speech. Surely not Eastbourne where her family lived, nor London where she had trained as a nurse, and then I understood it was Vietnamese pidgin: 'Even he come here, I no say to him I go to see one girl . . .' She spoke enough Vietnamese to get along, but she was really most fluent in bar girl's English. Only later, when Liz had talked for hours in interview to the camera, did she revert to her natural idiom.

From the age of fourteen Liz had wanted to come as a nurse to Vietnam, and with that in mind had trained at the Middlesex Hospital. Shortly before she qualified at the age of twenty, she took out the telephone book and made a list of the agencies that might have workers in Vietnam: 'They all said I was too young but finally it was a children's organisation that paid my ticket [the Ockendon Venture]. They said they only took me for my persistence.'

Liz had worked at first at an orphanage subsidised by the Ockendon Venture. She said that the nurses chained the handicapped children into their beds at night; they gave the babies a bottle propped on a pillow so that it often rolled away, they left the babies on tables from which they fell and injured themselves. Liz said that the older children used to amuse themselves by catching a rat, drenching it in petrol and then setting fire to it. Later I went with her to this orphanage, now in the care of the Cao Dai religious sect. She said conditions were better, but they were still very grim, and incomparably worse than in the orphanages I had seen back in 1966. Now, in the summer of 1974, Liz was employed at the hospital run by the Seventh Day Adventists and she was not very happy: 'They don't allow smoking and I get through three packets a day. One day, some of the drug addicts they get in some beer and ask me to drink some, so I do. Next day one boy is high on heroin, he ask the doctor why he is held when I drink beer and smoke in the toilet.'

As we were talking in the Royale Hotel, a shoe-shine boy entered, looking for custom, and to his dismay saw Father Hoang who called him over and made him kneel. It looked like a confession until Father Hoang took the boy's arms and showed us the needle marks. He spoke to the boy, no doubt reproachfully but in gentle tones. Afterwards he explained that the marks were recent, from injecting opium. How did he get the money? I asked. 'Some Americans give them huge tips,' Liz replied, four or five thousand piastres, then worth three or four pounds. During that summer of 1974 and again during the following April, Liz was to prove a guide to the lowest depths of the Saigon underworld, as Virgil had been to Dante in the *Inferno*.

Before making a film about Liz, I took Tony de Lotbiniere and the camera crew to the drug clinics I knew from the previous year. At Mac Tin, the Catholic clinic, we filmed the boys peering from behind the bars and showed the hands reaching out from a punishment cell, a kind of cupboard. I noticed a warder stroking the leg of a good-looking boy addict. The other clinic, across the Saigon River, was run by a Dr Quang Phuoc who told me he started his 'school', as he called it, because he loved children (*J'aime les gosses*). The previous year I had noted the fondness of Dr Phuoc for marching and drill:

> We went to a shed by the vegetable garden to find some fifty very young boys parading in ranks in front of a prefect of twelve [these were all heroin addicts it should be recalled], who ordered them about in a voice grown prematurely hoarse. 'One, two, three, four' and the class started to mark time, clump, clump, clump, clump, the short bandy legs rising and falling, the bare feet turned outwards, slapping the concrete. The prefect started to sing and the boys joined in *Clementine*, but I did not enjoy the music, nor the sight of those shifty and sullen faces. After marking time for a while, the boys were marched off in columns around the room, singing their national anthem.

This year, 1974, Dr Quang Phuoc was doing so well that he had built a smart entrance hall on the front of the clinic. The courtyard behind was as grim as ever. We filmed a boy locked in a small, metal punishment cage, and behind him, some thirty or forty boys in their teens or even their early twenties, shuffling round with their legs bent at the knees and their arms akimbo, a painful exercise under a blazing sun. They did this shuffle around the courtyard to the tune first of *Jingle Bells* and then *Silent Night*. I saw on a table in one of the classrooms a bamboo cane, much flattened and splintered by use, suggesting that this clinic was run by the methods of Wackford Squeers.

The boys in these clinics were the lucky few whose parents could pay for some kind of treatment. The less fortunate lived in the prisons or in the Saigon streets. With Liz Thomas I went where I had not dared to go on my own, to the infamous Le Lai quarter near the market, the lowest circle of Saigon hell. Murderers, thieves, the insane, army deserters and prostitutes gathered here to buy and sell drugs. Men, women and children openly 'shot up' into their wrists, which Vietnamese prefer, or when the wrists were too covered with scabs and sores, into the ankles or other joints. Some of the many amputees would get a friend to inject the drug into their head. We filmed a boy of about thirteen whose arms and legs were covered in festering sores. The misery in his eyes was heart-rending, and still is twenty years later on video tape.

Soon after meeting her, I visited Liz Thomas's house in Tran Binh Trong lane in the Cholon Chinatown, though most of her neighbours were ethnic Vietnamese. The lane was paved and some of the houses were concrete and new, to replace those destroyed in the two offensives of 1968. Compared to some Saigon streets it was not a slum, yet some of the houses held many families. Liz's own house, No. 333, held twenty-two people, most of them prostitutes and their children or younger brothers and sisters. The front half, with its sofa and chairs for visitors, served as a dormitory at night. The back had a kitchen and cupboards.

When Liz went there first, she set about scrubbing the floor to show she intended to live like the rest of the lane. As I could see, she now had an easy and friendly relationship with the local food-stall holders, a cyclo-driver, a Chinese herbal physician, the father and daughter who taught the local school, the electricians, plumbers and pastry makers. All of them clearly liked and wanted to help Liz, as she in turn often treated their minor ailments. Liz's household always included a dog for the children to pet. They were so upset when their last dog called Nixon died that they started to dig a grave at the end of the lane to give him a proper burial. However, the gendarmes at the police station opposite thought they were planting a bomb or doing some other mischief, and called off the interment, so Nixon ended up in a plot of waste land. 'Poor old Nixon, he was just full of worms,' said Liz, apparently quite unconscious of the political implications.

Although Liz tried to dissuade the girls from going back into prostitution, she did not try to reform them or change other people's lives. Although she probably had a religious belief, she did not talk about it, and once said with vehemence that she could never be a social worker. Most of the women had been on drugs and went into prostitution to pay for the habit. They had started out selling flowers, cigarettes or peanuts, then drifted onto the game. Many were still really children, like Mai, a great friend of Liz whether she stayed in the home or went back to her beat beside the Continental Hotel. When I saw her first she was peeling vegetables and I noticed the scabs and scars on her wrists; Mai was also recovering from a bad case of venereal disease, Liz told me. Yet she was dogged, hard working and good with the children.

It was always the plight of the children that drove Liz Thomas to work in Saigon. She started to visit the Central Prison where scores of the waifs were herded together off the streets. They had little to eat, and burnt their clothes to boil up the drugs they injected even in custody. She got to know the governor of the prison, an army colonel who said he was very unhappy in his job, and gave permission for Liz and the girls from her home to bring in food for the young detainees. When I asked how she had won him over, Liz simpered and said, 'I think he think I am *dep* [Vietnamese for pretty].'

Some of the children in prison were as young as five. One boy that Liz befriended died there from tuberculosis, after being wrongly diagnosed as a drug addict. She and Father Hoang decided to give him a funeral. A home movie shows a carpenter banging nails into the little coffin, which then is borne on the shoulders of four of the street children out to a burial place in the fields. It was the rainy season, so Liz and the other mourners are shown wading up to the knees through fetid swamp, and then bailing the water out of the grave. The film shows the coffin lowered into the ground and covered in mud as Liz weeps at the side of Father Hoang.

Even while we were making the film, Tony de Lotbiniere knew that Liz had afforded us a rare, even extraordinary insight into the darker side of Saigon. However, he thought that her childish voice and strange intonation would not come over on film. As soon as he saw the rushes back in London, Tony changed his mind and declared that Liz was a television natural, one of those people who come across better on film than in real life. He asked me if I would go back again next year to make an entire film about Liz Thomas. At that time, September 1974, we could not guess how soon this would have to be done.

5

The Fall of South Vietnam: 1975

It had been my hope that October 1974 would see the appearance both of my new book, *Victory in Vietnam*, and Tony de Lotbiniere's documentary, 'The War That Never Ended'. However, the book was withdrawn on the eve of publication because of a curious legal suit, and the film was delayed till the following year to make room for a series on European history. By early 1975 I began to fear that the book and the film might come out too late, for South Vietnam would no longer exist. Early that year James Fenton made an extensive tour through the Highlands, accompanied by a French photographer who spoke Vietnamese and was also a Communist. James sent a report to the *New Statesman* saying that North Vietnamese troops were roaming almost at will through the former II Corps region, and seemed to be making ready for an attack. Although the *New Statesman* did not publish the article till it was out of date, I saw the original telex and felt alarm. The Communists had already taken one or two district towns about sixty miles north of Saigon, and close to the rubber plantation where Gerald Scarfe and I had gone to report on the war in 1966.

In February I was asked by the BBC to join in a radio talk with Sir Robert Thompson, a counter-insurgency expert who had made his name in Malaya, and for years had been an adviser to Nixon and Thieu. The BBC had no doubt hoped for an angry confrontation, but as it turned out Sir Robert and I agreed with each other, or rather I agreed with him, for his views were based on far greater knowledge, especially of military matters. In conversation after the programme Sir Robert said that the one remaining hope for the South was to bomb Hanoi, and that only the raids of Christmas 1972 had made the North agree to the Peace Treaty. He said the South Vietnamese had no longer the means or the will to continue resistance. I recall his exact words: 'They are going under.'

The Appeal Court lifted the ban on *Victory in Vietnam*; one of the three judges was kind enough to say he had found the book interesting. The television film we had made the previous summer appeared on 4 March 1975, the very day that the Communists launched their final offensive, striking first at the town of Ban Me Thuot that I knew so well. Now I was faced with the job of getting commissions and raising the money to go to Saigon. For the freelance, writing mostly for weekly papers and constantly under threat from various tax collectors, this is a problem that gets worse year by year. Faced with a major story, such as the fall of Saigon, the national papers, TV and radio stations all send out staff reporters, and do not want historical and reflective articles. 'Mounting these expeditions,' I wrote in my journal when I had reached Saigon, 'is rather like mounting one of those merchant ventures in the Elizabethan times. You get the commission for pepper or cinnamon. You hire the ship and recruit a crew. You get the permission from the Queen to loot many Spanish galleons ... And then the wind changes, or sickness breaks out, or the Queen wants to appease the Spaniards and changes her mind ...'

On this occasion I had the rare good fortune to raise £250 from a colour magazine whose editor was away on holiday. A Sunday newspaper promised me £100, the *New Statesman* rather less, and I got an offer to send reports to the *Irish Times* and Irish Radio. Moreover if Tony de Lotbiniere could raise a camera crew to film Liz Thomas, the BBC would pay for my Saigon expenses, as well as a fee for doing the interviews and the commentary.

Then political problems arose once more. The American Embassy had not liked our previous film, 'The War That Never Ended', and told the BBC that I personally would not be welcome in the United States. A Mr Bach at the South Vietnamese Embassy had also remarked that the film was anti-American. I decided not to get a visa in London but hoped to get one at Saigon airport. Then I got a message to ring Mr Bach.

When I called Mr Bach, the following conversation ensued:

'Mr West, I think you like the people of South Vietnam but you do not like the government of the United States.'

'In view of what is happening now, I don't imagine that *you* would like the American government either.'

'For that reason I think I will give you a visa.'

When I went to the Embassy in Victoria Street in Kensington, I found Mr Bach was bitter against the United States and the world in general, for what he saw as indifference to the plight of his country. He seemed in part resigned to the coming catastrophe but he clung to hope still: 'If we can resist all these years, we must be a race of heroes. The general commanding Hue has sworn to defend the city or die,' he told me. But when I left Mr Bach and bought an *Evening Standard*, I read that the people of Hue had begun an evacuation. Later the general gave up the city, a sad failure of nerve in a soldier of proven courage.

Having obtained a visa, I picked up the money that had been promised to me in cash, and with this bought a return ticket to Bangkok from one of the bucket-shop travel agencies. At Bangkok I heard I had missed my onward connection, and learned that the later Air Vietnam flights had been cancelled. 'I began to fear (or perhaps, secretly, to hope) that I would not get to Saigon,' my journal records. It also records that on that evening in Bangkok I gave a commentary to the BBC on that day's downfall of President Lon Nol of Cambodia, 'a broadcast fuddled by jet fatigue, beer and ignorance'. The next afternoon, 31 March 1975, I got on an Air Vietnam flight to Saigon. The beautiful air hostess started to show us the life jacket procedure then stopped, laughed and gave a kind of despairing shrug as if to say, 'Why should we bother about a crash in the sea when there are so many other dangers?' I booked into the Continental, 'a grotty little room over the kitchen', and went straight to bed. From here on, I shall tell the story in part through extracts from my journal, in part with retrospect.

1 April. It seems that I was fortunate in my dark little room over the kitchens. Those guests with corridor rooms at the front of the hotel are now woken punctually at seven by government loudspeaker vans blaring political exhortations, 'Cheer up, do not lose heart, we still have our Constitution and our Courts of Justice', and still more hideous patriotic songs such as 'Vietnam, Vietnam, the sound of a cradle rocking a baby', played at a volume that would drive little Patrick [our baby] into a fit of howling.

I was not really fortunate in my choice of a room. Back in London in May, I went into hospital with a fever and a swollen knee. Later I heard that two other English journalists who had stayed in nearby rooms at the Continental contracted the same symptoms, diagnosed as a mosquito-borne disease, rather similar to elephantiasis, though without the horrific side-effects. One man spent six months in the Tropical Diseases Hospital before he was pensioned off by his newspaper.

These first days are spent on what I like to think of as orientation. I pick up the gossip from old friends and try to understand what is happening. Most have come back from Danang, where the atmosphere at the airport is gruesomely illustrated by photographs of an ARVIN soldier's legs hanging out of a Boeing wheel compartment. Today several people tried to get on a plane to Nha Trang but by 3 p.m. we heard that Nha Trang too was '*fini*'. Qui Nhon too is encircled but it seems that Communists troops are not pressing to capture the city. Why should they? It will be theirs soon enough.

Strange stories abound. Air Marshal Ky is making a bid for power and has joined the Anti-Corruption League! The workers of the Save the Children Fund in Danang arrived back heavily armed against looters and panickers. The French Michelin company has already dispatched some of its Vietnamese employees to negotiate with the Communists on maintaining their rubber plantations. And why not? It is the fashion now for the great multinational companies to work in harmony with the Communist states. Exit visas are now said to be selling at £3,000, and rich people are trying to buy small boats at Vung Tau.

I went into the British Embassy for a press conference given by Colonel G. G. Strong, a beak-nosed spectacled man, an intellectual of the Wingate type, rather than one of your hearty pukka officers. He is far removed from an earlier military attaché who pointed to an area on the map (from which I had just returned) and proclaimed: 'Just there, Victor Charlie is getting a damned good kick up the arse.'

Anyway, Strong says that Binh Dinh Province is cut off. Tay Ninh is irrelevant. VEENAF [the South Vietnamese Air Force] have lost 200 planes. An NVA artillery division is advancing on Saigon and, in general, the South Vietnamese could only have won if they'd fought the North on their own ground... However, he did advance the cheerful notion (I had even advanced it once myself) that the Vietnamese, as Buddhists, always allow their enemies an escape route. We shall see.

As it turned out, Colonel Strong was right. The Northerners did not force the Southerners into a last ditch battle. They did not go for a kill. Moreover they spared Saigon from artillery bombardment. The next day's journal entry begins with talk of some of the military politicians whose names are now almost forgotten. I do not seem to have taken them seriously at the time.

2 April. Increasingly wild rumours over possible government changes. Will Kiem take over from Thieu or bring in Ky or 'Big Minh'? It seems preposterous that they should care, until you remember that Goering and Himmler battled for power in the bunker. The cowards like me hope it will go to Tran Van Don, an ancient, who has met with the PRG in Paris and might be accepted in an interim government.

Meanwhile, troops have appeared guarding the avenue outside

Thieu's Palace, and most of the police now carry carbines. One journalist [Martin Woollacott of the *Guardian*] thinks that President Ford wants a government of national unity, and if the Communists then advance on Saigon, he will unleash B-52s on them. This show of force, so the argument goes, will salve the hurt of Americans at having lost their first war. I can't see that the Americans would gain self-respect by this last hideous blood-letting.

Wrote an article for the *New Statesman* – not an easy job for I was feeling ill and jumpy and miserable – more the result of jet fatigue than anything else.

The Times correspondent... has hired a bar girl as his interpreter. I like to think of a story beginning: 'In a formal interview with *The Times* in Saigon yesterday, the President of the Republic of Vietnam, General Nguyen Van Thieu, expressed his concern over United States policy to his country: 'Mr Kissinger, he Number Ten Cheap Charlie! Why he shit me?'

3 April. One of the drollest sights I saw today was a small child selling lottery tickets. The booksellers are still here but one of them has only one book, *The Ugly American*. He practically shoves it in your face.

An Australian journalist down from the north describes an evacuation by plane. It was one of those planes that let down a ramp at the back. A mother was lying on the ramp and holding on to the end of it as well as to her two small children. 'You could just see the children's heads sticking out over the end. Then the ARVIN rushed on, trampling all over them...'

I had lunch with a Canadian pilot who flies a DC8 into Phnom Penh about four times a day. It was his day off. He had just been robbed of $20 by the girl he slept with the night before. Should he report this to the police? I advised against. The police would only shake him down. He says that a lot of the pilots run gems and stones, and that he too had tried to set up a trade in 'household products', whatever these are. He says that if the time comes his DC8 will be able to accommodate 800 people, standing up. I think I'd rather stay and be massacred.

More reports that in Danang twenty Frenchmen were killed by ARVIN, but I gather this is an exaggeration of the reports that troops fired wantonly into the Centre Culturel where the French were sheltering...

Passing Air France, I saw the woebegone figure of Sanlaville, my old friend from Hue. He was red-eyed and unshaven because he had left his family in Danang. How could I reassure him that they were probably all right? 'Do you remember that last bottle of whisky?' he asked me, gripping me with his two-fingered hand – the result of an old VC ambush. I wish I had a bottle to give him now... Curfew extended to nine o'clock, by order of the loudspeaker vans.

Earlier that day, 3 April, I went to see Liz Thomas, feeling rather ashamed about not having answered some letters she sent me. Last July she had told me she wanted to be a front-line nurse. Now she had become one. A week or so earlier, she had made four trips taking medicine to Tay Ninh near the Cambodian border. It is on this road that Fowler and Pyle are nearly killed in Greene's novel *The Quiet American*. Liz had an even more harrowing experience. Later she told the story to camera. This was how I noted it down on 3 April:

I didn't tell anyone I was going. I was in a bus behind a convoy of TNT and shells. Outside Tay Ninh, the rockets started coming and then soldiers shouted 'get out!' I was much nearer the other side than the soldiers were. One rocket killed four children – one little boy had the top of his head blown off. There were only four ARVIN soldiers there and they weren't fighting back. One of them was paralysed by fright and couldn't move his legs. Afterwards I had to spend an hour in a bunker and I just stayed like this (in an attitude of prayer). I saw four dead VC. They just left them out there in the road, although the ARVIN always carry their own dead away...

Sometimes when I go into the country, I do my hair in a bun and wear a headdress and Vietnamese clothes. I even put boot polish on my face.

This last remark was typical of Liz's naivety and charm. No

amount of disguise could have turned this big blonde girl into a Vietnamese peasant. She still had not told the British Embassy she was in Vietnam – 'I don't want them to worry' – and anyway she was planning to stay on under the Communists. 'I couldn't leave my girls,' she said, and yet she believed the atrocity stories about the Communists. 'They kill the half-caste children,' she said, 'in Danang they took one child and cut its head off.' While we were talking, Liz had a visit from two Vietnamese women who worked for a Catholic charity. They were middle class, and their apprehension contrasted with the sanguine mood in Liz's lane. Like most Vietnamese, they looked to foreigners such as myself for the reassurance we could not give. They had left it too late to get out by air and the city was now almost encircled. 'We can only go to the Delta – and then what?'

My old friend Murray Sayle arrived on 4 April, his huge body and Roman beak as ever symbolic of strength and assurance. Whereas most of the journalists talked only of day-to-day incidents, Murray as usual related the war in Indo-China to Gibbon's *Decline and Fall of the Roman Empire*, the military theories of Clausewitz and Ludendorff, the Habsburg Empire, Sun Yat Sen, and above all the Forty-seven Samurai of Japan. We had gone to an outdoor restaurant where Murray ordered a Chinese noodle soup and a bowl of red peppers. As he ate and expounded his theories, Murray continued to scoop red peppers into his soup bowl until it resembled a pond of scarlet lilies. The sight attracted a crowd of children who wondered, as I did, how he could swallow this fiery brew without once calling for water.

Since by now I had stopped expecting the BBC to send a camera crew, I decided to write a piece on Liz Thomas for one of the colour magazines. To this end I enlisted the help of Jean-Claude Labbé, the French photographer who had been with James Fenton during their earlier tour of the Highlands. Although an amusing chap, Jean-Claude was a Communist of the deepest red, an admirer of Stalin and the Albanian despot Enver Hoxha. He also suffered a nervous tic, almost St Vitus's dance, that caused him to wave his arms around in what boxers call the haymaker style. How he could hold a camera still, I never could figure.

When we got to Liz's lane, Jean-Claude took some pictures, then made a speech to the locals in Vietnamese on how they should welcome the forthcoming regime. He stopped when we explained that a police station was only fifty yards away. Liz told us that two of the boys from Father Hoang's hostel had come here asking for money: 'They are unhappy because Father Hoang is away, and they regard him like a natural father. Now they want money to go to the cinema, to see John Wayne in *The Green Beret*.' When Jean-Claude heard this, he started to shout and flail his arms around but Liz told him simply: 'I like the boys too much to refuse. When they come back, I'm going to give them money for the cinema and for cigarettes too.' At this Jean-Claude got even angrier: 'Give them the money now you've promised them, but you shouldn't let them see that shit, that American propaganda!'

When Jean-Claude started to lecture her on what she should tell her household about the coming change of regime, Liz said she distrusted and feared the Communists. 'I suppose you believe the Communists are like this,' said Jean-Claude, gripping a finger between his teeth like a pirate holding a cutlass. 'Yes,' said Liz calmly, and Jean-Claude was jubilant at his own superior wisdom. Then he tried to reassure her: 'The People's Revolutionary Government will not harm you because they will ask about you from people in the street and they will say you are a good person. Radio Vietnam [i.e. Hanoi] has said that foreigners will be allowed to stay if they behave. But before that you may be harmed by the ARVIN. You may be raped.' Poor Liz, the idea must have crossed her mind already, without this brutal warning. As it turned out, she came unscathed through the fall of Saigon and the subsequent PRG takeover. The following day was very harrowing. The previous evening a US Galaxy aircraft that had just brought in sixteen pieces of heavy artillery left with a cargo of two hundred Vietnamese children, then crashed at the end of the runway, killing the lot. Fortunately, one of the girls at Liz's house called Lien – her dark beauty spoilt by gold front teeth – had refused to let her two half-caste children get on the plane. The little daughter, according to Liz, was 'more loved than any other child in the street because she is very skinny and because of her golden hair'. Over lunch at the Continental, Liz told me stories of Saigon life that depressed me almost as much as the news of the crash:

> Some of my boys and girls cut slashes all down their arms. It's the mark Bui Doi, meaning 'Dust of Life', because these boys and girls go from place to place [*Dust of Life* was the title of Liz's subsequent book]. Three of the girls in my home cut themselves with the big kitchen knife . . . some of our boys were taken into the police station and beaten. One of them has no legs so he can't defend himself but he got angry and threw a bowl of hot soup at the warder. The police tied him up by his hands and then beat him with his crutches, breaking both his arms. At the detention centre they put their hands face upwards on the table and then beat them on the palms . . . In the Saigon hospital where I'm doing some shifts as a nurse, I saw them bringing in a young man who was in a drugged sleep. They kicked him to see if he was alive and he stirred. After that they put him onto a bed with an old man who had been dead for days and was stinking, so that when the boy came out of his sleep and put out his hand he would feel the cold body beside him. Do you wonder people take drugs?

Over lunch Liz herself voiced a question that had been nagging me: 'I often wonder why I stay here. It's to look after my girls but also I want to see what will happen. When I go back to England, I feel strange. Even when I went to Bangkok, I felt like crying because everyone was so well fed and had so many clothes.' Liz grieved over the poverty and suffering and yet in a way she loved Saigon, with its vitality, bustle and camaraderie. She liked going to weddings, wakes and even the horse races. She liked beer and cigarettes in the noisy outdoor cafés. According to some of the girls in her home, Liz also fancied certain young men. She was not a missionary or a moralist. It was just because she was not a saint but a fallible human being that Liz was so lovable.

After the first week, when I was over my jet fatigue and the sense of strangeness, I found the situation more depressing than exciting. I spent many afternoons in the cinema, watching French B movies. I especially liked the southern comic Louis Funes, and still more the lugubrious Norman whose name I have now forgotten. These films made no intellectual demands. In fact they were almost unintelligible because of the screeching sound-track and a screen obscured by subtitles in Vietnamese, Chinese and English. The last was a kind of eastern Franglais. In one crime thriller, Jean-Paul Belmondo asked his girlfriend to pass the toast over a subtitle: 'I am envious of grilled bread.'

7 April. Another day of blue skies and intense heat... Everyone seems to be much more cheerful. The black market rate for the dollar has dropped almost as sharply as it rose last week. People are smiling more. The government has announced the recapture of Nha Trang, a town it never lost. I got a telegram from Dick Cawston of the BBC to say that the documentary on Liz Thomas has been abandoned since the crew are not coming.

Murray Sayle told me his theory about the collapse of South Vietnam. I wrote it down after a lunch with him, and in retrospect it seems accurate. Perhaps it is worth recording as proof that some of the journalists such as Murray and James Fenton understood what was happening better than did the generals:

After the fall of Phuoc Binh, Thieu began to blackmail the US government into giving him more support. Meanwhile he made contingency plans to evacuate the MR I [I Corps]. Then the Governor of MR II, for reasons of internal politics, ordered 23 Division from Ban Me Thuot north to Pleiku, leaving the town to the Regional Forces.

The Montagnards took their chance to revolt, and the NVA took their chance to attack the 23rd Division, as it was hurrying back to the defence of Ban Me Thuot. As the Highlands crumbled,

Thieu hurriedly brought forward his plans to evacuate MR I, therefore losing both regions without much fight.

Murray and I and most of the other Western observers failed to understand that the North Vietnamese in 1975 had an overwhelming advantage over the Southerners in infantry, tanks and artillery. The NVA General Van Tien Dung, who led the attack on Ban Me Thuot and later pursued the terrified refugees down to the coast, stated after the war: 'Because we had concentrated most of our forces in the main zone of the campaign, we had the advantage over the enemy in that area. In infantry we had 5.5 soldiers to the enemy's one; in tanks and armour we had 1.2 to the enemy's one; in heavy artillery we had 2.1 to the enemy's one.'

We Western observers did not learn till after the war that the mastermind of the final offensive was Le Duc Tho, the opposite number to Kissinger at the earlier Paris peace talks, and with him the joint recipient of the Nobel Peace Prize. In his *Vietnam: A History*, Stanley Karnow recounts how after their Highland victory, Van Tien Dung and his men had made their headquarters at Loc Ninh, north of Saigon: 'On April 7, as Dung and his comrades were conducting a planning session, they heard the roar of a motor-cycle outside. The rider was a tall figure in a blue shirt and khaki pants, a black leather bag slung over his shoulder. Le Duc Tho had arrived from Hanoi to monitor the final phase, entitled the Ho Chi Minh Campaign . . . The offensive against Saigon was to be launched no later than the last week of April.'

8 April. At about 8.25, three jets streak low overhead, one of them breaking the sound barrier. Surely this isn't the right time of day for a *coup d'état*? Outside in the corridor, one of the *boys* [servants] is imitating the sound of bullets, 'rat-a-tat-tat'. All this has interrupted my reading of Kipling. A little later I came out into the corridor to find Colin Smith of the *Observer* discussing the incident with the *Chicago Tribune* man. They judged it was VEENAF [the

South Vietnamese Air Force] showing off, followed by ARVIN shooting at one of their own planes.

This is what I wrote in my journal a few minutes later. A proper journalist would have rushed out to see what was happening but it seems that I went back to the Kipling poems, and then started to write some thoughts in my journal. A later entry records:

9.45. While I was wasting time on these philosophical musings, everyone else had gone out to find that the noise I had heard was indeed semi-serious. The planes were attacking the President's Palace. What I had thought was a sonic boom, or booms, was the sound of bombs. And what I had thought was small-arms fire was anti-aircraft fire. It came only after the third or fourth plane, presumably because the gunners were caught off guard . . . When I left the hotel about fifteen minutes after the attack, Tu Do Street was unnaturally crammed because Pasteur, Cong Ly and other streets near to the Palace were closed and the side approaches sealed with barbed wire or solid barricades. I walked up as far as the Cathedral and stood among the crowd of sightseers. After all, even in Vietnam it's not every day that the Palace gets bombed, although such bombings were common during the anarchy from 1963–5.

The traffic in Tu Do was going in both directions, very slowly. There were truckloads of soldiers looking tense and important, but probably going nowhere in particular; a motor-cycle pulling a cart piled high with bananas and on top of them an immensely old woman; a long-haired American on an 'Easy Rider' bike which may look elegant on a freeway but looks preposterous in a traffic jam.

It seems to have taken me two hours to discover what really happened.

10.20. Soon after the bomb attack, the loudspeaker vans announced a twenty-four-hour curfew – the first I can remember here – and the crowds dispersed quickly. I met Jon Swain who had been up to Reuters, which looks diagonally onto the Palace, and said there was nothing to see. The attack had been the work of one man, a secret Communist, who flew on north to one of the airfields held by the Communists. 'It's typical of the Americans,' Jon remarked, 'they've been training VEENAF for ten years but now the pilots can't hit a palace, even when it's not moving.' Apparently no human beings were hurt, though rumour persisted that one of the bombs had killed a pet baby elephant.

That morning, 9 April, Jon Swain told me he was about to go to Phnom Penh. 'You'll get killed,' I warned him. He very nearly was. Because of the curfew, we spent the afternoon at the top of the skyscraper Caravelle Hotel, commanding a view of the city and its surroundings. A radio reporter played the tape of an interview with a US adviser to a Cambodian army unit that recently ate its quartermaster: 'They took the heart, the liver and best of all apparently the hams and calves of the legs, which they cooked before eating...'

9 April. Went into Reuters to write an article for the *New Statesman*, beginning with a comparison of Harold Wilson and President Thieu, and ending with an attack on the orphan airlift [a joint operation between the Ockendon Venture and a London newspaper]. Almost by chance I discovered a cable from Tony de Lotbiniere, saying that he did indeed plan to come over with a two-man volunteer crew. I answered (maybe rashly) that the situation made filming still possible and encouraged him to arrive on Saturday. After writing my article, I then wandered about the town in a desultory way and had rather too much to drink.

Because there was no more room at the Continental, I booked Tony de Lotbiniere and the crew, as well as myself, at the Majestic by the Saigon River. My journal suggests I was turning against the Continental:

10 April. It has now been joined by a frightful American, drug-infested person called Dr Hunter Thompson who appears at breakfast in shorts, and takes photographs of people who do not want them taken... In the evening I talked to Jean-Claude Labbé and an American friend of his who is writing a thesis on United States aggression. We had a long argument on whether one should read authors like Kipling and Malraux if one doesn't agree with their political views. They said one should read nothing but Marx, Mao, Che and stretching a point, Macheotti, who is apparently rather in vogue in French leftist circles... Jean-Claude kept getting excited and trying to pick arguments with Americans at the next table... Having sent yet another reassuring telex to Tony de Lotbiniere, I was rather taken aback to learn that all the *Washington Post* had been told to evacuate instantly, as were *Newsweek* the following day. 'They're just trying to tell us they know something we don't know' was the jeering response.

Earlier in the day I had gone to the Mini Rex cinema to see *Murphy's War*. Afterwards I read a thriller called *Rosebud*, about the Black September gang... Its story, flavoured by coincidence, bogus technological skill and sexual glamour, seemed more credible than the blundering tragedy here... My reading was interrupted by David P, Liz Thomas's half-brother, who had come here to try to persuade her to leave. He had heard on Capitol Radio that the Communists had started to shell Saigon.

11 April. Came down at breakfast to hear at 9 a.m. the much awaited policy statement by President Ford. He was not as alarming about Vietnam as expected. He devoted more seriousness to the Middle East and even such tuppeny-halfpenny places as Ecuador... The amazing Dr Hunter Thompson appeared at breakfast again in shorts, holding a bottle of beer and a camera. I met him later that morning. Some friends were taking him to what he thought was the seaside but in fact was the scene of a heavy battle. When I explained this to him, he worried that he was insufficiently drugged, so I gave him some tranquillisers which he gulped down with his beer. Having at first taken against him, I found him rather engaging; and at least he had come to Vietnam, unlike so many American writers against the war.

12 April. I spent the morning in the familiar, unpleasant job of renewing my visa at the Immigration Office, though even at this late hour the clerks were efficient, polite and did not demand a bribe. I chatted with an Indian who had previously fled from Pakistan in 1947, and then from North Vietnam in 1954. He said that from his experience this government had another six weeks. Or perhaps this was wishful thinking, as he had not managed to sell his store. There was a very angry American who had earlier been imprisoned here for his part in a driving accident. He had come *back* to Saigon from Africa only a few days earlier. He kept muttering that he might be put back in prison. The Immigration officers were all draft dodgers, while the US Embassy was staffed by Communists and foreigners.

Everyone is curious about the mysterious disappearance of most of the city's cyclo-drivers, who have apparently been arrested on suspicion of VC sympathies. Probably this is one more example of the government coming to swallow its own propaganda, or rather the propaganda put about by the Americans when they were here. Scores of times I was assured that all cyclo-drivers, bar girls and Frenchmen were Communist agents... The disappearance of the cyclo-drivers has encouraged the taxi drivers to charge still more extortionate rates from the dwindling number of foreigners, estimated at 6,000 Americans and hundreds of Europeans, Japanese and Koreans.

13 April. I moved to the Majestic, whose staff are not very able, but eager to please. Because the Tourist Board has an office upstairs, the lounge is adorned with colourful posters of Hue and Ban Me Thuot, both now lost to the Communists... The view of the river is pleasant except that it looks straight into the trajectory of any shells from the east, and we are only fifty yards from a military target, two naval vessels... I did a broadcast for Irish Radio who asked me what plan I had for evacuation and I said 'none', then I realised that Mary's [my wife's] family might be listening, so I took the question again and I said I was thinking seriously about it.

Tony de Lotbiniere and his two-man crew were at the Majestic when I returned, bearing a copy of the *New Statesman*, and also a message from Mary saying she is not worried as she thinks all the scare has been dreamed up by journalists. Much as I distrust journalists, it seems to me that this time most of the scare has been caused by the advancing Communists ... Continual noise of artillery tonight from over the river.

14 April. Since I am doubtful whether Saigon can hold out for very long, I got the TV team to work at a brutally early hour, regardless of their jet fatigue. We went down to Liz's street and immediately started filming some of the neighbours. We met a family who had invited Liz to Tet to share a chicken and a bottle of Vietnamese whisky between fifteen people. Next to them was an elderly man with a whispy beard and a book on palmistry. Liz said of him: 'He comes over when the children are sick and treats them and tells them what to do. And sometimes if he sees my light on when I am working late, he comes over and tells me to rest.' We filmed the baker next door who was teaching the girls to make little biscuits. Liz said that the man on the other side of her house 'only comes at the weekend with his girlfriend'. I had never thought of this lane as a place for a love nest.

I saw Father Hoang who has just returned from a trip to the United States. Several relatives had advised him to stay away. He speaks of the Silence Party and is evidently reconciled to the Communists as the price of peace. He was pleased that the bishops of Hue, Danang, Kontum and Dalat had all elected to stay. He feels that the refugee problem would not have been so bad if other priests had set an example.

I met Mark Frankland. He talks of the general now in charge of the defence of Saigon, who has a penchant for young girls. The Vietnamese joke: 'Like Napoleon he wants to be with a woman when he takes his military decisions. Unfortunately, the resemblance to Napoleon ends there.'

Liz came round to the Majestic and talked into tape. I did my 'into camera' on the Majestic roof, without any stage fright this time. It was a pleasant change having a two-man, volunteer crew. The regular BBC crews in those days spent their time fiddling their overtime and expenses, even staging strikes. This cameraman and sound man were splendid, although it must have been daunting to go to the East for the first time into a city under siege. And with jet fatigue. But if they were nervous they did not show it. There was also a pleasant lack of restrictive practices, so that at Liz's house I did the electrician's job of holding the extra lights in place.

> At lunch I met some reporters who said that a man had disembowelled himself in front of the National Assembly. Apparently many troops have killed themselves from shame, especially sergeants.
> 15 *April.* It is kite time, in the hot April wind. The children are swimming in the pool under the statue outside, and at dawn on the waterfront, people still do their exercises. The day had begun being woken by some kind of bang. It turned out to have been an ammunition dump.

We wanted to go to the seaside resort of Vung Tau, where Liz sometimes worked in a home for children. As we were leaving, one of the wheels fell off the car. We were grateful this had not happened on the way back, in one of the stretches of road controlled by the Communists.

> 16 *April.* This being the day for writing my *New Statesman* piece, I called at the Continental breakfast garden in order to hear the gossip... It appears that the wave of panic last week was based on the opinions of Dr Hunter Thompson... The American who has been flying refugees from the north [of South Vietnam] has now himself left town in one of his planes. He turned up at the airport with an AK-47 assault rifle... The American radio station carries a number of very mysterious messages such as: 'Miss Moon, otherwise known as Miss Moon, please report to Colonel Lamping.' Everyone wants to know the code for evacuation. In Phnom Penh it was playing *Jingle Bells*... Phnom Penh is expected to fall today. All the journalists predict a bloodbath there but a peaceful changeover here.
> 17 *April.* Before we went off to Vung Tau, Father Hoang gave me a private, indignant message about the BBC Vietnamese Service, above all one journalist whom he accused of exaggerating the

badness of the situation. 'Every evening people listen and they feel panic . . .' But what could the BBC have said of the military situation? The South is losing the war.

On the way to Vung Tau, we passed the depots and shacks of American times, and the advertising hoardings for rubber tyres, petrol, tinned milk, apple juice, Bastos toothpaste (a black man's face with a big white smile) and Mytox insecticide. At vital bridges the blockposts were deserted. The sentries had taken off their boots and helmets, and they were dozing or chatting in the shade . . . At Vung Tau we filmed at a children's home and met a few more fallen women. Almost all the refugees had gone, and the little town seemed to be almost deserted. We ate fish at a restaurant on the sea-front run by a Vietnamese who had once worked as a chef on a French liner. Vung Tau was the first and last sight of this country for Frenchmen in those days of the ship. From there the ships went up river to Saigon. [Two days after our visit, Vung Tau fell to the Communists.] This evening we heard that Phnom Penh had fallen, with both sides embracing in the streets. So much for all the fears of blood-letting and cannibalism.

18 April. I went down to Immigration and met a pleasant American accountant, who praised the courtesy and efficiency of the Vietnamese officials in processing the leaving permits. He told me: 'I had six stamps and the sergeant here said I needed a seventh to show I had paid property tax. I explained that, as a foreigner, I wasn't allowed to own property. He said that sounded reasonable and took me to see the major who gave me clearance. It helped that I spoke French.' He said there were thousands of Vietnamese who thought that because they had even talked to an American in the last fifteen years, they were going to be shot. Many Americans are trying to get out their mistresses, even though they have wives at home. Marriages are proceeding apace at the US Embassy.

Conversation increasingly turns to the subject which all of us are considering. When do you get out? Or do you get out? How much risk do you take? In Phnom Penh, seeing the journalists going as far as they could 'down the road', I thought of the children's game Grandmother's Footsteps. Now in Saigon, I thought of the Conrad novel *Lord Jim*.

Suppose like Lord Jim you jump into the lifeboat, and then the ship does not sink. Few people are wholly honest about their intentions. I have heard journalists say they will leave and then come back 'when things get more interesting', as if they were not pretty 'interesting' already... Nick Wheeler says he proposes to stay, but like the rest of us, is afraid of the last few days when ARVIN go wild. Since most of my prophecies go wrong, maybe ARVIN will behave with impeccable discipline and the NVA will arrive, drunk, raping and slaughtering.

Among the journalists in Saigon was the famous war reporter Max Hastings who later distinguished himself in the Falklands campaign by almost single-handedly capturing Port Stanley. I bumped into him on the Continental terrace and was surprised when he said he was going to fly back to England for one of his children's birthdays. He did actually go back for a day or two, then flew back to Saigon under siege. Like Murray Sayle, Max was a figure of great curiosity to the Vietnamese because of his huge size and forceful monologue. Quite a crowd gathered to hear him jest about a Welsh friend of ours, let us call him Owen.

> My wife's always complaining that my journalist friends are a lot of drunken oafs who can't be invited to dinner. So I said, not so, some are very respectable and proper people. Who for example? Well, Owen for example. So she asked me to invite him one evening, seven-thirty for eight. And would you believe it, bloody Owen staggers in at half past nine and falls asleep on the sofa.

The Vietnamese were spellbound by this anecdote.

> *19 April.* Yesterday evening we met Mai, the girl we had filmed last summer at Liz's house. She upbraided me for not having recognised her a few weeks ago when she greeted me in the street. It was hardly surprising as she was back on the game, and dressed that way. I remembered her as a crop-haired, plain girl in the dress of a coolie, peeling potatoes on her haunches. And now here she was in the finery of a prostitute – long hair, make-up, bell-bottom trousers and rather a smart blouse, with long sleeves to hide the

injection marks. When I asked her why she had left the home, she said that Liz had taken up with a man and this had created ill-feeling. Liz gave another explanation. She said that the atmosphere of the home was overcharged.

In the Majestic Hotel, the sad, nice receptionist with the pock-marked face saw me holding a copy of Yeats, and said, 'You like poetry?' but this was only a lead-up to the usual request for reassurance: 'We have lost our country, do you think we shall lose our lives?' She said she was going to cut her hair short and take off her nail varnish before the Communists came.

My journal then expresses the rage I felt against those in the West who were gloating over the Communist victory, a rage I would later express in my last *New Statesman* article from the old South Vietnam. By now I was writing daily reports for the *Irish Times* and making frequent broadcasts for Irish Radio, as well as working hard on the film, so my journal became rather scrappy.

20 April. The Continental terrace was full of rumours that all the journalists in Phnom Penh were dead. Ten minutes later, we heard they were safe in the French Embassy. Apparently the American Radio call sign for evacuation is, 'the temperature is rising to 105 degrees', followed by the playing of 'White Christmas' . . . There are rumours of seven American ships in the Saigon River . . . That the Green Berets will be brought back . . . The Germans are said to have gone, but the British have issued invitations to a cocktail party for Tuesday week . . . The Australians and New Zealanders are quarrelling over an airstrip and have threatened to bomb each other.

'*21 April.* An historic day for Vietnam,' says my journal pompously. In fact this was only the resignation of President Thieu, an announcement greeted with ironic cheers . . . We spent the day in Liz's street, which went on functioning just as normal. We filmed a class in the little school, with its very well-behaved children. Throughout this crisis I noticed how life went on normally and efficiently. The letters I sent arrived in England, and only ten days before the fall of Saigon I heard from my wife that the Inland Revenue back home was threatening court action. The police and Immigration kept their discipline. Everything was much more orderly than in the time of the Americans. When I pointed this out in my final *New Statesman* article, a typical *New Statesman* reader's letter compared this to Mussolini making the trains run on time.

That evening I met Mark Frankland in Tu Do Street. He told me that the matriarch of the family in Hue who had entertained us over the years was now in Saigon. She had put her future under the Communists in stark terms: 'I shall say goodbye to the children and then I shall swallow cyanide.' In fact she survived, but she and her family suffered badly under the new regime, many of them spending years in prison or concentration camp.

22 April. Outside the cathedral I watched an ecumenical meeting: Roman Catholics, Buddhists and other sects, like the Cao Dai. Among the press in attendance were two men in a camera crew who spoke with pronounced Belfast accents. They turned out to be brothers employed by a US network. I remarked on the oddity of their coming so far from Northern Ireland to film an ecumenical meeting, then asked if they were Protestants or Catholics. Neither, they said. They were Jews... Back at the Majestic at 4.45 there was the sound of another huge explosion. The waiter grabbed a customer by the shoulders. The pock-marked receptionist came over to me and said, 'I am very afraid but now that I see you I am better.' Such is the fame of the BBC. A girl at the next table used the explosion as a pretext to come over and talk, and then to try to sell me some bad jade rings... Ate dinner at the Corsican restaurant in Nguyen Hue, round the corner from the Royale Hotel... The proprietor said to me, '*On attend les roquettes cette nuit.*' [We can expect some rockets tonight.]

This was the final entry in my journal.

The Lord Jim problem of whether to stay or leave was solved for me by Tony de Lotbiniere. He and the crew were leaving for

Bangkok and then returning to London to make the film. If I went back with them I would get the full credits and a fee for writing the script. If I stayed, I would only be paid for research. This was a choice between making a small profit and making a big loss on the expedition. We booked our tickets and said goodbye to Liz who was suffering from a fever but was still resolved to remain. In the morning I went to the Reuters office and sent that final article to the *New Statesman*. We had agreed to have lunch on the opening day of a new restaurant run by refugees from the north, who saw the irony of the situation but faced it with typically Vietnamese courage, stoicism and black humour.

One sentence of Tolstoy's *War and Peace* describes better than I can do in a chapter the atmosphere of Saigon in April 1975: 'Like a criminal being led to the gallows, who knows that in a minute he will die yet stares about him and straightens his cap sitting awry on his head, so Moscow automatically carried on with the routine of daily life, though aware that the hour of destruction was at hand, when all the conventional conditions of existence will be torn asunder.'

Although I was shocked and saddened by the impending tragedy, the end of South Vietnam had at least purged from my mind a great deal of ideological humbug. In a bitter article for the *New Statesman*, most of whose readers supported the Communist Vietnamese, I wrote many things that I should have written many years earlier:

> It is not true to portray South Vietnam as a fascist regime overthrown by a revolutionary movement. Even at this eleventh hour opposition movements have some right of protest, while Saigon's press is less timid than London's in its exposure of rascals in office. The Vietcong, or indigenous Southern Communists, now play only a tiny part in the war; the Saigon proletariat, which ignored two calls for an uprising in 1968, seems more apathetic than revolutionary. What began as guerrilla war has turned into an old-fashioned conventional invasion of the South by the North, which has an immense advantage in tanks, artillery and divisions... It

is distasteful, here in Saigon, to read the gloating tone of some foreign newspapers over the fate of anti-Communists here. Such a tone is acceptable from members of the Communist Party (not Trotskyists, whose group here was exterminated by Ho Chi Minh), from those without property, mortgage or motor-car; from those who do not wish to visit a foreign, non-Communist country. The gloating is unacceptable from the rich radical chic who are even now doubtless planning to hire a refugee South Vietnamese au pair girl.

6

Thailand, the Refugees and a Guided Tour of Vietnam: 1975–80

On leaving Saigon in the last week of April 1975, I spent a night in Bangkok, then took the train to Vientiane in Laos. It was there on 30 April, while having a drink with my old friend Rowly Carter, that I heard of the fall of Saigon. Thus I had been in Vietnam when Cambodia fell; I was in Laos when Vietnam fell; and Laos itself was already more or less Communist. Troops of the Communist Pathet Lao, in apple-green uniforms and pastry-cook caps, patrolled the market-place and the bank of the River Mekong. The foreigners were already leaving, the Corsican gold-smugglers, the soldiers and airmen of fortune, the drug-fuddled proprietors of vegetarian restaurants and psychedelic night-clubs. Life still had its dream-like charm, but already there were intimations of nightmare. The Kingdom of the Million Elephants was slowly becoming Communist Laos, a title as incongruous as the People's Republic of Shangri-La. It was the hottest time of the year in Laos; the mosquito-borne illness that I had caught in Saigon gave me a swollen knee and a fever; all things contributed to a sense of loss and sadness.

The Communisation of Laos, coming on top of the fall of Cambodia and South Vietnam, was causing alarm in Bangkok where I stayed a few days before returning to England. Those diplomats and journalists who had always subscribed to the Domino Theory once propounded by Eisenhower and Kennedy now expected to see it take effect. There was something like panic in the American business community, with some executives sending their wives and families back to the United States. Fear even affected the neighbouring countries, especially Singapore, whose Prime Minister Lee Kuan Yew predicted that Communist Vietnam would conquer the whole of South-east Asia. Some of the more thoughtful revellers in Patpong Road may have wondered whether Bangkok was about to suffer the fate and punishment of Pompeii or Sodom and Gomorrah.

The Domino Theory proved to be false and soon it was the Communists who were on the defensive in South-east Asia. Much of the credit for this should go to Thailand's daring and far-sighted Prime Minister in 1975, the scholar and novelist Kukrit Pramoj. Thailand had been in a nervous condition since October 1973, when the people of Bangkok rose in a vast demonstration in favour of more democracy. As usual the riots were followed by army repression, but this time the demonstrators had made their point. The King supported the popular wish for freedom and soon afterwards chose as Prime Minister Seni Pramoj, the elder brother of Kukrit, who had first held the position thirty years earlier. Then in March 1975, after much political wrangling, Kukrit took up in earnest the role of an Asian Prime Minister that he had first played opposite Marlon Brando in *The Ugly American*.

Kukrit, whose name means 'bold supernatural power', was born in 1911, the fifth child of a royal prince of Persian as well as Thai and Chinese ancestry. After an education at Trent College and Queen's College, Oxford, Kukrit went back to Thailand and took a job in the Finance Ministry. He served in the army and saw action during a border war against the French in 1940, then went into banking. After the Second World War, when his brother Seni became Prime Minister, Kukrit also went into politics, founding his own party and later his own very successful newspaper, *Siam Rath*, for which he wrote not just squibs and satires but serialisations of his novels such as *Four Reigns*. He also became renowned as a connoisseur of art, a director of Thai dancing and theatre, above all as a wit, a kind of Bangkok Dr Johnson. Once when invited to dinner at a house near Silom Road, my host told me not to bother with streets names, which taxi drivers ignore, but simply to ask for Soi Kukrit, 'Kukrit Lane'.

Kukrit's appointment as premier came as a major sensation, presaging all sorts of excitement. He did not disappoint these expectations. Kukrit wanted to safeguard the freedoms won by the demonstrators in 1973, to pump some of the wealth of Bangkok into the countryside, especially the poor north-east, and above all to reconsider Thailand's foreign policy, now that Cambodia, Laos and South Vietnam were turning Communist. Kukrit's domestic policies were similar to those pursued by his brother Seni before and after his own premiership. His foreign policy was both more radical and more drastic, involving a change of alliance from the United States to Communist China. His policy was based on the belief that the United States was no longer able or willing to fight, and that only China could now stand up to the threat from Vietnam.

In an interview in 1976, Kukrit spelled out the fears underlying his foreign policy:

Do you think Vietnam will go on aiding insurgencies?
It will go on. It will go on aiding insurgencies in this country and others in South-east Asia. That's normal work – that's routine.
What did Thailand learn from the Vietnam experience?
We have learned that Uncle Sam is impotent.
In these circumstances, or in any conflict?
Impotent in the full sense of the word. I don't know – ask the doctor.
Impotent or just tired?
I think impotent.

Since the Thais felt threatened by Vietnam and no longer believed that the United States could defend them, they looked to a new ally, Communist China. Soon after taking office in March 1975, Kukrit told the United States that Thailand would not renew the lease for the air force bases. In June 1975, Kukrit went to Beijing.

With Chou En-lai, Kukrit worked out Thailand's new partnership with China in an alliance against Vietnam and its backer the Soviet Union. This also entailed support for the Cambodian Communists, or Khmer Rouge, the most anti-Vietnamese of all the people of South-east Asia. In return for supporting China, Thailand received the latest Chinese weapons as well as a promise to stop backing local insurgencies. In seeking advice on how to defeat Thailand's Communists, Kukrit went to the world's most famous guerrilla fighter, Mao Zedong, who, in one of the strangest examples of poacher turned gamekeeper, offered these maxims:

> First of all, don't issue any propaganda against them to tell the people they are bad. They won't listen to you . . .
>
> Secondly, don't kill them all because they like being heroes . . . They'll come to get killed. They like to be killed.
>
> Thirdly, don't send any soldiers against them because you'll be wasting time and a lot of money. The Communists are in the jungle. If you send soldiers against them they will just run away.
>
> Finally, the only thing to get rid of your Communists, the only way to defeat them, is to see that your people are happy. See that they are well fed, that they have work to do, that they are satisfied with their work and their station. Then the Communists cannot do anything.

This last piece of advice from Chairman Mao on how to prevent Communist revolution is oddly similar to the theories advanced in the film *The Ugly American*.

Kukrit's alliance with China aroused opposition, particularly in the army and the police force. Although foreigners put this down to ideological opposition to Communism, it probably had as much to do with ethnic rivalry between the rural Thais and the Bangkok Chinese, such as Kukrit. In August 1975, a mob of policemen wearing civilian clothes invaded Kukrit's house, looting or smashing his priceless collection of Thai antiques. The police and military funded a scurrilous and successful campaign to defeat Kukrit in his own constituency in the election he called for April 1976. Once more Seni Pramoj came back to replace his younger brother as Prime Minister.

In spite of the opposition to Kukrit personally, most Thais came to support his new foreign policy of alliance with China against Vietnam. This national solidarity grew stronger during the late 1970s as Thailand was inundated by refugees from Communist Indo-China. Hundreds of thousands of Laotians crossed the River Mekong to join their kinsmen in the Isan. From 1976 onwards, up to a million anti-Communists fled Vietnam, almost all by boat, and most of them ending up on the south-east coast of Thailand. For three and a half years few people managed to flee Cambodia, now transformed into one vast concentration camp, and most foreigners could not credit the stories they told of the 'Killing Fields'. Then in December 1978, Communist Vietnam finally lost patience with the armed incursions it had endured from its savage neighbour, and launched a lightning blitzkrieg into Cambodia, expelling the Khmer Rouge and giving the chance for hundreds of thousands of starving Cambodians to make their escape to Thailand.

It was in 1979-80, after the overthrow of the Khmer Rouge, that I once more travelled to South-east Asia to meet the Laotian, Vietnamese and Cambodian refugees living in Thailand. The least publicised of the refugees and the least unfortunate were the hundreds of thousands of people from Laos who had boated or swum across the Mekong to safety. Near Nong Khai, the railhead on the Thailand side of the river, there was a camp with 47,000 inhabitants, or nearly as many as those remaining in Vientiane. The camp was really a town of wooden or reed houses, with meat and vegetable markets, photo shops, chemists, barbers and even a dental surgery. The inmates were free to go into Nong Khai and to take jobs there, and since this part of the country was short of population, the newcomers were not resented. Most of the refugees at Nong Khai were ethnic Laotians, almost indistinguishable from the people of the Isan. Problems arose with the tribespeople, most of them Meo or Mnong, who tended to settle up in the hill country of north-west Thailand. Under pressure from the US Drug Enforcement Agency, the Thai government stopped these refugees growing their usual crop, the opium poppy, and taught them instead to plant cabbages and potatoes. However, these vegetables took up much more land than the opium poppy, resulting in soil erosion spreading down the hillsides and devastating many valleys, especially in the province around Chiangmai.

The refugees from Laos, both tribespeople and ethnic Laotians, blamed the misery of their country on the alien Vietnamese. An American diplomat I met in north-east Thailand told me that 'Laos is about as much a part of Vietnam as Lithuania is of the Soviet Union'. I wonder whether he or any Americans then in South-east Asia recalled the role of the OSS in 1945, in backing the Vietminh against the French and Laotians. It was in Nong Khai that OSS agents from Vientiane first came into head-on collision with British officers such as David Smiley and Peter Kemp, who took the side of the French, Laotians and Thais.

Now in 1979, the Americans were unpopular with the government of anti-Communist Thailand, as of the governments of Communist Laos, Vietnam and Cambodia. The enormous bomber base at Udon was once more a sleepy market town. The only Americans that I met there were airmen who had retired with their meek and lissom local wives, now grown portly and termagant. ' "Why you drink so much? Why you no got job? Why we no got a new automobile?" that's all we hear,' I was told by two of the men who used to service the B-52s. When I stayed at Udon in 1968, some of the Vietnamese minority were vocal in their support for Ho Chi Minh and the Communists. Now in 1979, the Bangkok government was trying to arrange the deportation of 30,000 Vietnamese from the Udon region. To encourage them to leave, the Thais had issued an order in June 1979, stating the twenty-seven occupations open to Vietnamese, such as bicycle repairs, laundry, vehicle body assembly and optical work, but not the two occupations of engine and radio repair in which the Vietnamese had a virtual monopoly. The Bangkok government was exploiting a deep racial antipathy to the Vietnamese, a fear and hatred running much deeper than that felt for the Chinese or *jek*. In popular legend throughout the Isan, or north-east Thailand, the Vietnamese are accused of usury, the eating of unclean food, child murder and witchcraft. The Hollywood film of *Rambo: First Blood Part II*, which shows Sylvester Stallone slaughtering dozens of Vietnamese with gun, knife, crossbow and bare hands, was an all-time box-office hit in Communist China but still more in Thailand.

The Thai Army publicised the good treatment shown to the refugees from Laos, in order to steer attention from what was happening to the refugees from Vietnam and Cambodia. I saw an example of this publicity in 1979 when Princess Anne, the President of the Save the Children Fund, went to visit a camp near Ubon close to the borders of Laos and Cambodia. The road to the airport was blocked more than an hour before the Princess's arrival, and when I had managed to talk my way past the guards, I saw dozens of heavily armed, steel-helmeted soldiers crouched in menacing posture round the runway.

When Princess Anne came down the steps of the plane she was introduced to a bevy of generals and colonels, then driven off in an armoured procession of fifteen vehicles. I had never seen such a cavalcade for the Queen of England, nor one so well protected. The roads wherever we went had been cleared of traffic, and armed sentries guarded the crossings with all side-roads. It turned out that the Save the Children Fund paid the wages of two doctors and three nurses employed at the camp, but did not contribute toward the refugees' food, clothing or shelter. The inmates of the camp had not endured any danger or hardship other than paying a fee of £40 to the Thai Army to 'intercept' them on this side of the River Mekong. The object of the preposterous military operation was to emphasise the danger from Vietnam, and to draw attention away from the bad treatment of Boat People and refugees from Cambodia.

The most publicised of the refugees in Thailand were those

who had come by boat from Vietnam to the south-east coast around Songkhla, or Sangora as it was called by the Europeans, a town that was gaining a sinister reputation. Even two or three blocks from the waterfront, your nose tells you that Songkhla is a fishing port, the Grimsby or Peterhead of Thailand. You notice that most of the fishermen are not Thais or Chinese but dark-skinned Malays. You do not notice that Songkhla is a nest of pirates, as avaricious and cruel as any who plundered the Spanish Main. In his novel *The Rescue*, set in this part of the world, Joseph Conrad describes how an English yacht is wrecked on the 'shore of refuge', a bitter joke, for the people who live there are warrior Malays with spears and muskets, who plunder the ships coming too near their savage kingdom. The pirates of Songkhla had never enjoyed such easy pickings as when the Boat People started to come after 1975.

In 1979, when the Boat People were arriving in very large numbers, a US official in Songkhla told me: 'They couldn't have come to a worse shore in the world. It's the current that brings them, since some of them tried to head eastward to get to the Philippines.' He said that although Thai naval vessels and planes kept constant patrol, most Boat People were discovered first by fishermen:

> The refugees are robbed, raped or rescued, or all three, according to how negotiations go. Most of them have some money, an old ten-dollar bill in a shoe or a trouser cuff. The Vietnamese government shakes them down but some arrive with nothing, and that's what the fishermen can't believe. Sometimes the refugees come in naked. They jump out as soon as they land, and fall flat on their faces with exhaustion . . . and then they burn the boat to stop the Thais towing them out to sea again.

At the time I was there in 1979, a senior Songkhla official announced the arrest of three hundred fishermen, not for robbing or killing the Boat People but for helping them to get ashore. 'Too many people have boat licences,' he added grumpily, 'especially since the Gulf of Siam is almost fished out.' A foreigner explained to me: 'It's very hard on the immigration officials. If they're hard on the refugees, they get the outside world coming down on them. If they're lenient they get their own ministry coming down on them. The atmosphere has soured badly during the last few months.' When the Thai government came down hard on the pirates, this made things worse for the Vietnamese, since the robbers then tended to kill them to stop their mouths. As late as March 1989, three Songkhla fishermen were charged with having sunk a boat and broken the arms and legs of the Vietnamese with cutlasses so that they could not swim to shore, and so that the blood would attract sharks.

According to *The Nation*, about 150 Vietnamese were massacred in an attack in June 1989. The sole survivor, a seventeen-year-old girl called Phom Hong Cuc, said that eight Thai fishermen rammed their two trawlers into the boat, sinking it and drowning everyone but herself and fourteen other women. They were taken onto the trawlers and raped by the fishermen for a week. On the eighth day, as the trawlers were coming near land, the fishermen threw the women into the sea, and all but Cuc were drowned. She survived by holding on to an oil drum, thrown by a fishing vessel that spotted her but would not pick her up. After two days in the water, she was rescued by another fishing boat that took her to Songkhla.

After the publication of Cuc's story, a spokesman for the Thai Supreme Command, Lieutenant-General Naruedol Detoradiyuth, denied that pirates were preying on Vietnamese in the Gulf of Siam. He said these attacks took place outside Thai waters. 'There are no pirates in Thai waters,' he told *The Nation*. General Naruedol also said that the Vietnamese who survived pirate attacks tended to exaggerate their ordeals in order to gain sympathy. He added that stories of piracy harmed Thailand's image. As for Cuc, she was held in custody awaiting deportation to Vietnam. 'The fact that she was raped does not make her a political refugee,' an official explained.

By the late 1980s the outside world had forgotten about the

Boat People, except for those who went to Hong Kong. Ten years earlier, the plight of these refugees from Vietnam caused anguish and guilty conscience. The Thais said that the Vietnamese were swamping their country, preparatory to an invasion. The West blamed the Thais for turning away the Boat People, and the Thais turned round and said: 'Why don't you pick them up by ship and let them settle in your countries?' To make matters more complicated, most of the Boat People were ethnic Chinese from Cholon or from the towns in the Mekong Delta. This prompted the Western friends of Hanoi to suggest that most of the Boat People were war profiteers, dope dealers and brothel keepers, the same smear aimed at the Jews under Hitler. In fact there was at the same time an even greater exodus from North Vietnam of Chinese fishermen, dockers and miners, all of them heading for Communist China. The exodus grew after the brief invasion of Vietnam by China early in 1979.

Most of the Boat People came in part for financial reasons; they wanted to better themselves as well as to live in a free society. Moreover I thought at the time and still think now that the West was hypocritical in condemning Vietnam for the exodus of Boat People. The regime did not try to prevent escapers by setting up the equivalent of an Iron Curtain. Although the coast guards occasionally shot at Boat People, they normally allowed them or even obliged them to leave. They also allowed them to take some possessions and valuables. Compare this with Solzhenitsyn's account of how Stalin starved and tortured his victims to make them give up their gold.

Although Vietnam in 1979 was a poor and beleaguered country, fighting the Chinese as well as Cambodian Communists, it still appeared to the neighbouring countries of South-east Asia, and to the United States, as a menacing super-power. The American Consul in Songkhla told me:

> I have a theory. I offer it to you that Vietnam is not really a nation, it's an army. Fighting is the thing they really like and are really good at. Do you know why the Chinese didn't put any planes

up over Vietnam in January? They'd have been shot down. The Vietnamese have the latest MIGs and the Chinese planes are twenty years old. The Chinese got a rude surprise trying to invade Vietnam. And those Americans who want to play the Chinese card are on a loser. China isn't an ace, it isn't even a face card. It's nearer a deuce. Vietnam is the card to play in this part of the world, as the Russians know. When Vietnam went into Cambodia there were Americans who said they'd bitten off more than they could chew. They took down their maps – Americans in this part of the world love maps – and they pointed to the River Mekong. No army could cross the Mekong, they said. It took the Vietnamese an afternoon to cross the Mekong. All it needed was lots and lots of bamboo . . . And this sending out of refugees was a stroke of genius. They couldn't have thought of anything that would so destabilise South-east Asia and other Western powers.

Belief that the Boat People came to Thailand as part of some fiendish plot by the Hanoi government could not survive a visit to their camp near Songkhla. The faces that stared out from behind the wire expressed only desperation and fear – that they might be put out to sea again. The Thai immigration officials would not allow me to enter the camp, for which I was rather grateful. If you talk to such sad people, you raise false hopes of escape from their plight.

Some Americans blamed the Vietnamese for the host of refugees who had fled Cambodia after the overthrow of the Khmer Rouge. The main camp at Khao-i-Dang, near the Thai frontier town of Aranyaprathet, was now the largest Cambodian city, with more than 200,000 people living in huts and tents, and cared for by the United Nations. Most of the new arrivals were near to death from disease and starvation. Most of the children appeared to be in a state of shock; they could not write or read or even apparently speak their own language properly. I met one little girl of ten who, when she was given a crayon and paper, drew only corpses and skulls. There was not even the anger and indignation one normally finds among refugees: just apathy and despair. A nearby camp run by the Khmer Rouge in exile was still more depressing. There the faces showed nothing but hatred; even the children were scowling zombies. The Khmer Rouge, with the support of the Thai Army, ran their camps as military training centres, drilling the men to fight and the women to carry supplies through the minefields into Cambodia. Even in Thailand the Khmer Rouge exercised powers of life and death over their followers, often locking offenders into a metal punishment box, to bake in the sun. There were also in Thailand two other Cambodian armies, hostile both to the Khmer Rouge and the Vietnamese, one of them owing allegiance to my hero Prince Norodom Sihanouk. The Vietnamese Army did not venture to go into Thailand in 'hot pursuit' of its foe, but sometimes shelled the neighbourhood of the camps, maiming and killing Thai civilians as well as Khmers.

The Vietnamese invasion and conquest of Cambodia puzzled both left- and right-wing commentators. To the Right it meant the end of the long-cherished Domino Theory, once advanced by Eisenhower, Kennedy and more surprisingly Graham Greene, in an article for *Paris-Match*, 12 July 1952. According to this the 'red tide' of Communism would flow from China through Vietnam into Laos, Cambodia, Thailand and then all South-east Asia. Now, four years after the fall of Saigon, the dominoes seemed to be falling in reverse with Vietnam under attack from the Cambodian and Chinese Communists. The Right had always warned of the monolithic character of 'international Communism', frequently with the adjective 'godless' tacked on the front. The Right had explained away Russia's quarrel with Yugoslavia and then with China as ruses to fool the West. Now in 1979, the Right could not explain away the fact that different Communist countries were actually fighting each other.

The overthrow of the Khmer Rouge, and the revelation of their atrocities, dealt a blow to the Left throughout the world. The evils of Nazism had been exposed after the Second World War when journalists and cameramen entered camps like Belsen and Auschwitz. No outside observers had witnessed what happened at Kolyma, Vorkuta and other camps of the Soviet Gulag Archipelago. When Malcolm Muggeridge saw and tried to report the mass deportations and murders in the Ukraine, even his own newspaper would not believe him. At the start of the Khmer Rouge terror in April 1975, Jon Swain and other reporters gave some indication of what was to follow. A French Roman Catholic priest, François Ponchaud, told in his book *Cambodia Year Zero* how Pol Pot and his men were murdering up to a third of the population. But still many people could not or would not believe him. For example, Richard Gott of the *Guardian* described Pol Pot's Cambodia as an 'interesting social experiment'. One British admirer of the Khmer Rouge, the sociologist Malcolm Caldwell, finally went to Phnom Penh and was murdered by his Khmer Rouge hosts in the government rest-house, perhaps because he had seen too much. Yet by and large the international Left simply ignored Cambodia until the Vietnamese invasion.

From 1979 onwards, the Left tried to argue, first, that the Khmer Rouge were not really Communists and, second, that their brutality was the result of US aggression, especially the B-52 raids that started in 1969. Neither argument really stands up. The Khmer Rouge leaders such as Pol Pot and Ieng Sary had joined the Communist Party as students in Paris in the 1950s, worshipping at the feet of a long line of terrorists from Robespierre to Stalin. After Stalin's death, the Cambodian Communists found a new hero in Mao Zedong, who had just embarked on the murder of tens of millions of Chinese 'class enemies'. The Khmer Rouge in 1979 were not alone in the admiration of Stalin, whose portrait hung in the Hanoi politburo at least until 1982. When the Vietnamese Communists took power in the North of the country in 1954, they were truly Stalinist in their liquidation of landlords, kulaks and the bourgeoisie. Later they saw that this was an 'error', and most of the Vietnamese leadership had become more pragmatic, but it was not till 1986 that they moved towards the abandonment of Marxist-Leninist theory.

Like Lenin and his Bolsheviks in Russia, the Khmer Rouge set out to smash all memory of the old Cambodia. Families were deliberately split and the members given new names. The ancient music and songs were abolished, the Buddhist temples destroyed and the monks murdered. The Khmer Rouge smashed statues of Buddha, used them as clothes-racks or wheel blocks, and urinated on them; all this took place in a country even more Buddhist than Thailand. The Khmer Rouge banned from the language the subtle and intricate forms of address to show respect for age, social position, family ties and religion. All adults had to be called 'mum' and 'dad' by the young 'cadres', itself a bastard word from the French for 'framework'. Those to be shot or clubbed to death were 'sent to the higher organisation'. This assault on the language explains why the young refugees were scarcely able to speak. The Khmer Rouge were not just Communists; they belonged to the purest revolutionary line from Rousseau and Robespierre to Lenin, Trotsky, Stalin and Mao Zedong.

The tendency to blame the United States for the atrocities of the Khmer Rouge began in 1979 with a book by the British journalist William Shawcross called *Sideshow: Kissinger, Nixon and the Destruction of Cambodia*. This was not an apologia for the Khmer Rouge or any kind of Communists, for unlike some of the people who later used his book for their own purposes, Shawcross had known Cambodia during the war and had studied with horror the writing of Father Ponchaud. The argument of the book was that Nixon and Kissinger, by secretly authorising B-52 raids as early as 1969, had dragged Cambodia into the Vietnam War, had helped to get rid of Sihanouk, and incidentally deceived their colleagues, the press and Congress. Shawcross accepted Sihanouk's statement that he had not known of the bombing raids against the Vietnamese Communists inside Cambodia. In arguing that these bombing attacks on Vietnamese sanctuaries inside Cambodia were wrong and illegal, Shawcross suggested that they were also unecessary. He dismissed the idea that the Vietnamese depended on safe havens across the border. ' "No guerrilla war in history was ever won without sanctuaries" was a favourite phrase,' he wrote scornfully.

Although an admirer of Sihanouk, I simply cannot believe that he did not know of the B-52 raids on his eastern provinces. Even if these were taking place in remote and almost uninhabited jungle, the noise and reverberation must have been sensed for miles around. Since Sihanouk feared and distrusted the North Vietnamese almost as much as he did the South Vietnamese, he may have welcomed American raids on these uninvited guests. Moreover, in spite of the lies and deception practised by Nixon and Kissinger, one has to accept that in purely military terms the raids were useful. 'No guerrilla war in history was ever won without sanctuaries' may have been a catch-phrase and cliché, but it was largely true. In other South-east Asian countries such as the Philippines and Malaysia, the Communists never succeeded because there was no neighbouring country to give them shelter and get supplies. Ironically, by the time of publication of Shawcross's book, the Vietnamese Army was itself faced with the problem of Khmer guerrillas using Thailand as a sanctuary. The Bangkok newspapers reported the Vietnamese shelling of 'safe havens' inside Thailand, as well as the build-up of troops for a 'hot pursuit'.

Some left-wing readers of William Shawcross carried his argument one stage further, suggesting that the American B-52 raids not only dragged Cambodia into the war but turned its inhabitants into homicidal monsters. The idea that American bombing somehow caused the atrocities of the Khmer Rouge cropped up in the powerful film *The Killing Fields*, photographed by Chris Menges, the cameraman who had worked with Richard Taylor and me in making a documentary on a Mekong Delta village, in 1969. The protagonists of *The Killing Fields* are the *New York Times* correspondent Sydney Schanberg and Dith Pran, his Khmer interpreter and legman, with supporting roles for other reporters such as Jon Swain.

The film blames American air raids for driving the population out of the countryside and for inflaming the wrath of the Khmer Rouge. When the actor playing Schanberg is criticised for not having predicted the Khmer Rouge atrocities, he pleads in his defence that he could not have known the effect of the US bombing. After *The Killing Fields*, it was left-wing orthodoxy to put the blame for the Khmer Rouge killings on the United States, and also on Thailand, still portrayed as America's puppet. The Left failed to understand that Thailand had long since renounced its US alliance in favour of Communist China.

There are flaws in the argument that American B-52 raids caused the savagery of the Khmer Rouge. In the first place America ended its bombing missions early in 1973 but it was not till 1974 that the Khmer Rouge took over the leadership of the Communist struggle from North Vietnam. When the raids started in secret in 1969 and during the early 1970s most of the bombs were aimed at Vietnamese troops coming along the Ho Chi Minh Trail. Although later some air raids missed their target and fell on villages or even towns, the survivors did not respond by joining the Khmer Rouge but by fleeing to Phnom Penh, which was itself under frequent attack from Khmer Rouge rockets and mortars. Perhaps because I had been in Phnom Penh under siege, I cannot resist the impression that these attacks on a crowded city probably did at least as much damage as B-52 raids out in the jungle.

The theory that bombing caused the savagery of the Khmer Rouge fails to explain why far worse bombing did not have the same effect on the Vietnamese Communists, who suffered for thirty years from high- and low-level air attacks, napalm strikes and artillery bombardment. In Operation Canyon, in sixteen days of 1969, at least 750,000 pounds of bombs were dropped on the river island of Go No, measuring five by two miles. The Vietnamese troops and civilians were tough to survive this bombardment yet nevertheless came out of the war as normal human beings, not monsters.

If *The Killing Fields* encouraged the view that America was to blame for the tragedy of Cambodia, it incidentally produced the most telling rebuttal. This came in a book written not by a journalist such as Sydney Schanberg or by his interpreter Dith Pran but by the highly intelligent man who played the part of Dith Pran in the film. This was Haing S. Ngor, a doctor of partly Chinese descent who had himself toiled in the Killing Fields, suffered torture, and witnessed the torture and murder of many others, including the disembowelment of a pregnant woman. On his escape from Cambodia in 1979, Haing S. Ngor risked death from land-mines and murderous bandits, and even after he reached the safety of Thailand, he nearly became one of the many refugees forced back into Cambodia by the Thai Army.

Yet Haing S. Ngor's book *Surviving the Killing Fields* rejects the political message of the film in which he had played the leading role. Whereas the film projected onto Cambodia all sorts of Western guilt and neurosis, the book regards the tragedy through Eastern eyes. Ngor thinks that the US bombing did little to boost the popularity of the Khmer Rouge, blaming this largely on Prince Norodom Sihanouk. Although Ngor first welcomed the Vietnamese invasion, he came to resent their occupation. He blames the madness and cruelty of the Khmer Rouge on the character of his people, with its obsessive lust for revenge. He admires and is grateful to Thailand, the country that first gave him refuge, and the United States where he went to live.

Like most Cambodians, Haing S. Ngor had greatly respected Sihanouk as a ruler. The Prince appealed to the pride of the dark-skinned, ethnic Khmers by telling them over and over again how lucky they were to be Cambodians; yet he also protected the rights of the paler-skinned Chinese and Vietnamese. 'When he spoke to us in his loud, high-pitched voice, shouting and gesturing wildly, eyes bulging with excitement, we listened with respect.' After the *coup d'état* in 1970, Sihanouk should have retired to his villa in France, Ngor now thinks, but the new regime's campaign of vilification hurt Sihanouk's pride. He went on Beijing Radio to announce the setting up of a government in exile, and called on the people to liberate their country. When Sihanouk, in 1973, actually came down the Ho Chi Minh Trail to visit the 'liberated zone', he seemed to be endorsing the Khmer Rouge: 'Compared to Lon Nol, who was despised even by those who worked for him, Sihanouk was highly respected. Even if Sihanouk was only a figurehead for the Khmer Rouge, it was hard to believe that the cause he represented was cruel or bad.'

Western liberals, stricken with guilt about their real or imagined 'racism', are unwilling to see that Asian people also dislike each other because of appearance or skin colour. Haing S. Ngor believes that much of the trouble in Cambodia springs from 'an old, old grudge against the Vietnamese', founded in part on dislike of their paler skins. He examines the harm done to Cambodia by France, the colonial power, the United States, China and Vietnam, then concludes: 'But sad to say the country that is most at fault for destroying Cambodia is Cambodia itself.' He attributes this to *kum*.

> *Kum* is a Cambodian word for a particularly Cambodian mentality of revenge – to be precise a long-standing grudge leading to revenge much more damaging than the original injury. If I hit you with my fist and you wait five years and then shoot me in the back on a dark night, that is *kum* . . . it is the infection that gnaws at our national soul.

During the sixteen years since my first visit there in 1963, Cambodia had changed from a paradise on earth into a hell of *kum* and hatred.

In March 1980 when I had just returned from a stay in Thailand, I received a telephone call from Peter Crookston, the editor of the *Observer* Colour Magazine. Would I like to go on the first conducted tour of South Vietnam under its Communist rulers? Peter had seen the advertisement in one of the tourist pages and booked two places for a reporter and photographer. Of course I accepted, as did Tim Page, the much battered photographer, whom I had first met on the Continental terrace in 1966, when he was swathed in bandages after his first or second wound. Several years later, Tim was almost killed by a land-mine explosion. After many years of convalescence and semi-retirement in California, Tim was now fit and raring to go back to Southeast Asia. Already he was becoming a cult figure, as one of the few survivors of the drugs-and-danger or hippy school of reporters from Indo-China. He later figured large in Michael Herr's book

Dispatches, in Coppola's film *Apocalypse Now*, and finally in a television serial about his life. With Tim around, it promised to be a lively tour.

Besides Tim Page and myself, our pioneer tourist party comprised a Reuters reporter from Bangkok, a man from the BBC Vietnamese service, and two genuine holidaymakers, as well as our courier, a mysterious Scottish businessman. After a night in Bangkok we caught the weekly Air France flight to Saigon, or Ho Chi Minh City as I would never learn to call it. The first surprise came at Tan Son Nhut airport, as we were taxiing to the arrival building. We passed scores of military planes, bombers, fighters and C130 transports, but all of them rusting, dismembered and falling to bits. This put paid to the theory that after the fall of Saigon, Communist Vietnam was the world's third largest air power. Without the spare parts that could only come from the US manufacturers, most of these planes were useless. Our little party toured in what had been advertised as an 'air-conditioned Mercedes', but the air-conditioning did not work, and the engine worked only spasmodically.

The Health, Immigration and Customs staff appeared to be soldiers, including the beautiful peach-skinned girl with a yellow star in her cap. The officials were friendlier than they used to be, but then they had little to do; few people wanted to come to Ho Chi Minh City, though millions wanted to leave it. We drove from the airport through streets virtually free of cars and scooters. Chickens strutted along the empty boulevards and children played football outside the former Brinks Building, one of the US Army recreation centres. The old French quarter was busy as ever but social life now went on at outdoor cafés and stalls. There was a huge open market outside the former Parliament building for selling the cigarettes and other valuables mailed by relatives outside the country.

We tourists stayed at the Caravelle Hotel, now renamed Doc Lap, or Independence. Most of the guests were officers from Hanoi, or advisers from East Europe and Cuba, the latter no doubt advising the Vietnamese on how to go bankrupt. The food was as bad as ever, the rats in the rooftop garden as brazen as ever, squealing, scuffling and even taking a dip in the goldfish bowl. Since the rats sometimes nipped people's ankles, I wished I had had a rabies inoculation, as well as the one against the bubonic plague.

Soon after checking into the Caravelle I crossed the road to the more familiar Continental, now an officers' mess for the North Vietnamese. The terrace café was open for business but now it was fenced off, deterring the vendors of paintings, crossbows, ship's bells (made out of shell casing) and books such as *The Ugly American*. However, the child vendors of cigarettes were still allowed on the terrace and still competed among themselves, and still abused the regular patrons for any shift of loyalty. 'Why you buy from her? You number ten thousand.' Even the same old waiter was there to shoo the children away with his stick, although he was much too kind to whack them in earnest. He remembered me and greeted me but I cannot say it was good to be back. The other guests were dejected, and drunk on the now nationalised '33' beer. I remembered the 'into camera' I did on this brew. Later I heard that the Vietnamese had sent a shipload of '33' to the Soviet Union, as part of their payment for aid, but the Russians had sent it back again as undrinkable. The person who told me the story showed me the massive crates of beer stacked in Nguyen Hue Street.

'The swifts are twittering in the dusk,' I wrote in my journal, sitting on the Continental terrace. 'The fans clank slowly round but fail to disturb the damp, rancid heat of April. The sad-looking young men open another bottle of beer, and talk, their legs twitching in agitation, a nervous habit of Vietnamese. A child who has slipped past the custodian of the terrace empties a packet of nuts on my table. "Why you no buy?" ' I was joined by Tim Page, the incorrigible. Within an hour of coming to Saigon, he announced his intention of buying some marijuana, ignoring my nervous complaint that this was illegal and might get us all into trouble. In the first café he entered, he bought a packet, almost a sack, of powerful grass and rolled it up into large cheroots, smoking these happily for the rest of the week, to the utter indifference of our hosts.

In England, when you return after many years to a town you once knew well, you find that most familiar buildings have been destroyed, or 'redeveloped' for ring-roads, shopping precincts or high-rise blocks. Saigon was melancholy in a different way; the buildings were still there but had changed their nature and purpose. As I walked round, I had the sensation, common in dreams, that everything was familiar but not quite right. The Royale Hotel had become a factory making Communist flags and cardboard articles. The French patisserie in the same street was still in business but it was nationalised; looking in, I saw the staff engaged in a session of Marxist self-criticism. The cyclo-drivers were now from the former 'bourgeoisie' and often spoke good English or French. On one trip the driver behind my back lectured me on the rival merits of Camus and Jean-Paul Sartre.

Nearby I entered a bar that used to be run by a Corsican and a Vietnamese. The Corsicans had gone but some of the customers were French textile advisers, jolly and boisterous, with one hand clutching a Cholon Pernod, the other a bar girl's thigh. The Vietnamese co-proprietor still remained and remembered me. Indeed he became quite eloquent over the old days: 'In those days there was air-conditioning, not just fans, and you could take a girl into your hotel bedroom. It was *une belle époque* . . .' I tried to remind him that during that *belle époque* there was a war going on, with many dead or wounded. But it was no use. Another old acquaintance entered, a man of about my age I had met on a plane returning from Nha Trang seven years earlier. He had told me ironically that he was the only Vietnamese graduate of the London School of Economics. When I reminded him of this, he laughed and pointed around him, saying 'And look what it's done to this country.' Once he had been the local head of a large European corporation; now he was wearing flip-flop sandals, and rode a push-bike instead of a car. He was bitter, but then he was bitter before the fall of South Vietnam. He told me he could, if he wanted, leave for France but he hated that country for what he considered its betrayal. The French consul in Saigon was giving visas only to thieves and prostitutes. He despised the United States because it had lacked the courage and will to fight the Communists. 'Only Solzhenitsyn understands, from what I have read of him,' he told me.

Our tourist guide took us to see one of the few busy factories in the city, producing lacquer work. It was also a tourist attraction under the old South Vietnam but I never went there, not liking lacquer. However, I could not believe that in the old days the workers were as badly paid. They were getting only two dollars a month, in terms of what it could buy as well as on the exchange rate. Throughout this visit, the journalists in our group kept questioning people on what they earned, and sometimes we thought we must be confusing dollars with dongs, or days with months. We found that a brain surgeon was getting less than a pound a week. A packet of cigarettes cost a week's or even a month's wages.

Soon we came to see that wages in Vietnam were almost meaningless; the townspeople lived on what they were sent from overseas, and the country people lived off the land. The main point of taking a job was to qualify for a ration of rice and petrol at subsidised prices, rather than having to buy them on the free market. During my stay I met two Germans employed by a Swiss bank to examine the countries of South-east Asia and find which ones were worthy of credit. They said Vietnam was utterly hopeless. No firm or factory knew how to do its accounts. The only viable product was duck feathers, sold to a Hamburg firm of upholsterers. The two Germans said that Vietnam was better off than North Korea which now was literally bankrupt, since all its foreign exchange had been spent on press advertisements of the thoughts of the country's dictator, Kim Il Sung. When Kim ordered a telex to send out more of his thoughts and also appeals for cash, his creditors apprehended the machine.

Soon after our visit, Hanoi announced that thousands of 'unemployed' had been sent to the Soviet Union and other socialist countries under a contract by which half of their earnings went to repay Vietnam's national debt. I wrote at the time that these migrant workers were likely to fare even worse than the Vietnamese coolies sent to work for the French on the New Hebrides copra plantations, or even the convicts forced to work on building railways in Equatorial Africa. Eight years later the Hanoi newspapers claimed that the Soviet Union was ill-treating and underpaying the Vietnamese migrant workers.

In most Communist countries that I had visited, the official guides had done their best to blacken the character of the previous regime and to hide the defects of the present system. Perhaps because Tim Page and myself had known the country, we were not shown any propaganda against the old regime, nor even the small museum of American pornography that I had read about in the newspapers. They took us to see the old presidential palace, including the state rooms used by 'Mr Thieu' and his various carpets, tapestries and paintings – all rather hideous – a row of model boats (for 'Mr Thieu' was a naval man) and even a buffalo's head with the stuffing coming out. I could not understand why we were shown these things, which did not discredit the former regime except in matters of taste. We saw no torture equipment, dungeons or evidence of an orgy. Indeed I came to suspect that the palace might soon come to be used by the new regime in the North, as a kind of provincial headquarters. We saw Ho's picture upon the wall and one of his aphorisms: 'Vietnam is one nation. The river can go dry and the mountains be eroded but this truth cannot change.' True enough. But the Communist Northerners were not alone in wanting a united Vietnam. This was the dream of 'Mr Thieu' as well.

The decorations were going up for the fiftieth anniversary of the Communist insurrection in Saigon and the Mekong Delta in 1930, the events described by Andrée Viollis in her subsequent book *L'Indo-Chine S.O.S.* But we were shown no evidence that the Southerners launched an insurrection in 1975 or welcomed the Northern army. Instead our guides wanted to take us to see the network of tunnels at Cu Chi in the 'Iron Triangle' where thousands of Communist troops lived underground in the 1960s.

I backed out of this visit, preferring to wander about Saigon. Since virtually all the troops at Cu Chi belonged to the army of North Vietnam, a trip to the tunnels seemed only to rub home the truth that the Southerners lived under an alien occupation.

Although dollars were now an accepted currency, our tourist guides insisted we buy a token number of dongs at the old Banque de l'Indochine, a magnificent glass-roofed building down by the river. I think we were taken there just to see the display of photographs lining the walls. These were all from the war the previous year against Communist China, snap after gruesome snap of Chinese corpses with gory wounds and gaping faces, stretched out in ditches, in rivers or on the roadside. Our tourist guides wanted to show us that the Vietnamese detested not just the Chinese invaders but the minority Hoa. They took us to Cholon and put us down in front of a fine Chinese pagoda whose portals held up the carving of an immense open boat on which the founders had come from Canton in the nineteenth century. This blatant reference to the plight of the Boat People enraged an elderly lady standing on the pagoda steps. She screamed abuse at our guides and then explained more calmly to us that two of her sons had died in trying to escape the country. By the time of this tourist visit in April 1980, much of the population of Cholon had left as Boat People; those who remained had insufficient thalers of gold to buy a passage, or maybe had left the decision too late, for by then the Vietnamese government was not abetting departure. During the visit, I talked to some of the Chinese traders in Tu Do, where they and some Indians still sold paintings, lacquer and porcelain elephants. I heard their lamentations: 'I would be in Hong Kong but I did not have the thalers... Can I give you the name of a nephew in the United States? Only my daughter is alive, in Canada... My brother and nephew were drowned...'

Western apologists for the Hanoi government tried to suggest that the Chinese leaving Saigon as Boat People were former black marketeers, drug dealers, brothel keepers and similar undesirables. However, a book on the Chinese minority, *The Hoa in*

Vietnam Dossier, brought out in 1978 by the Foreign Languages Publishing House in Hanoi, makes it clear that the state-sponsored Sinophobia was more concerned with the Chinese in North rather than South Vietnam. Whereas the Cholon Hoa were hoping to get to capitalist America, the northern Hoa were heading back to their still Communist motherland. The book makes only a passing reference to the Chinese war profiteers of the former Saigon regime:

> Some were given the title of 'king'. Thus Ma Hy was the 'Rice King', Ly Long Than and Lam Hue Mo 'Iron and Steel Kings', Dao Mau 'Glutamate King'; Ly Hoa 'Gasolene King' etc. . . . After the liberation of southern Vietnam and the setting up of the socialist system there, a number of capitalists of Chinese origin worked against the revolution . . . By dishonest methods – scattering properties and hiding assets, tax evasion, speculation, hoarding, raising commodity prices . . . they cause serious problems to the economy.

However, *The Hoa in Vietnam Dossier* is much more concerned with Beijing's propaganda campaign, urging the Chinese in North Vietnam to flee the threat of a Sino-Vietnamese war and persecution:

> It stresses the ordeal of the young Hoa who will eventually be forced to fight in the ranks of the Vietnamese against the great Chinese Army . . . Young megalomaniacs are taught that the twenty-first century is to be the Chinese century . . . This psychological warfare started with a campaign of rumours about a Soviet fleet entering Camranh Bay . . . another about a new Vietnamese army mustering along the border. The Hoa in Hanoi were informed of an exodus of the Hoa from Haiphong, the Hoa in Mong Cai of the persecution of those in Lao Cai and vice versa. The story was circulated of drops of blood falling from the sky in this or that locality . . . An offensive of promises started. Before young people were dangled prospects of a fine future; before old folk those of final rest in the ancestral land; before intellectuals

mirific opportunities for training and studies in Paris, London, Tokyo or New York... before traders, the possibility of doing business in Hong Kong, Macao, Singapore.

Whether they fell for this propaganda or just as probably feared persecution, tens of thousands of Hoa crossed the border to China. The authors of *The Hoa in Vietnam Dossier* tell of the desolation caused by the exodus of the Chinese:

Between Tien Yen and Mong Cai, over a distance of 80 kilometres, one travels through deserted towns and villages, past closed houses and courtyards overgrown with grass. On the front doors of whitewashed cottages, the square pieces of red paper bearing Chinese ideograms have begun to be covered with spider's webs... There is a visible shortage of hands for the forthcoming harvests of rice and peanuts... With the Hoa lumbermen gone, not enough props are being cut for the pits in Hon Gay and Cam Pha collieries. With the Hoa fishermen gone, it is the common people's daily food ration that suffers.

The authors of *The Hoa in Vietnam Dossier* blame Beijing for exploiting the Hoa minority, just as 'exactly forty years ago, the Germans in Sudetenland supplied Hitler with a pretext to annex Czechoslovakia cynically'. However, the reader detects an undercurrent of racial malice, for instance in the account of a trial at Mong Cai in October 1975: 'The nine accused, all Hoa, belonged to a network of traders in women slaves, which, between 1973 and 1975, had sold to China forty Vietnamese women, at the price of 300 to 400 yuan each, about the price of a cow-buffalo.'

This Sinophobia did not endear the Hanoi government to the Vietnamese of Saigon, one of whom asked me: 'Why don't the Americans and the Chinese join in giving us our freedom back?' The persecution of the Hoa was matched by the cruel treatment of women with children by Americans. They would accost us tourists at night, when the police were unlikely to notice them: 'My husband, he go through Vietnamese marriage. Now he no send money . . . He live Dallas, Texas . . . He live Seattle.' They told us their children were not accepted at school, or badly bullied. A few years later, all mixed-race children were expelled. The Communist authorities may have condemned these by-products of foreign intervention; however, the mass of the Saigon population seemed to have fallen in love with all things American.

During the time of the Americans and during the time when they stood alone, the South Vietnamese had always resisted most manifestations of United States culture, from *Playboy* to *Time* magazine, from Hollywood to the Woodstock festival. Now, five years after the Communist victory, Saigon shuddered and boomed to the omnipresent, incessant and bellowing uproar of old Western pop music, on tapes and records dating back to American intervention. From the foyer as from the restaurant of the Caravelle Hotel, from every café in Tu Do Street and even at dances patronised by the Russians, my brain was beaten about by the sound of *Proud Mary*, *Scarboro Fair* and *Let It Be*. The same sort of Vietnamese, often the very same people who used to curse America, now listened to ancient rock music and dreamed about California. The overwhelming majority of those who left as Boat People wanted to settle in Canada or the United States, few opting for France unless they had relatives there. The horrors of war were forgotten in the nostalgia for the American years, that *belle époque* as the barman called it. Another Vietnamese told me candidly: 'Yes, I know we used to prefer the French and despise the Americans. But now the Americans have gone we realise how much we liked them. And that's why I say the Americans really won the war. They won because we all want them back.'

Remarks such as this could not be written off as the whine of the dispossessed middle class. After the fall of Saigon, Liz Thomas stayed on for about six months in her alley in one of the poorer parts of the city, where most of the people had welcomed the Communists, if only because they wanted the war to end. Certainly none had much to lose from a social revolution. Yet when she returned to England, Liz Thomas told me that most of the street had grown disillusioned and now wanted America back. Of all the people of South Vietnam, the Saigonese demonstrated their feelings in the boldest and clearest way, by flatly refusing all efforts to move them into the countryside. They refused to budge from their charming, corrupt, unsocialist city.

Unlike the inhabitants of some other Communist countries, the South Vietnamese expressed their detestation of the regime. Even those who had endured 're-education courses' (the labour camps) or exile in the 'New Economic Zones' (known as 'monkey houses') were willing to talk of their experiences. People hated most of all the shameful sessions of 'Marxist self-criticism', imposed on employees of the state. One of our guides confessed that she had to endure the reproaches and even the anger of some of her acquaintances because she worked for 'them', the Northern Communists. The regime discouraged but did not actually close down remnants of private enterprise such as food stalls. There was even a high-class private restaurant, La Bibliothèque, run by a woman who once had stood as a 'Third Force' deputy in parliament. I enjoyed the French cuisine there, in a room surrounded by books including Tolstoy and Dostoevsky; however, I felt that La Bibliothèque carried the taint of collaboration.

Our tour programme took us to the seaside town of Vung Tau, where I had last been with Liz Thomas and the TV crew only two days before it fell to the Communists in April 1975. Five years earlier, our trip had to be postponed because the car broke down as we were setting off from Saigon. This time, our ancient Mercedes started to break down only after we left the city, so that we spent many hours waiting about in the countryside. However, it has to be said that the countryside had been improved. There was nothing now but fields and cottages where once there had been depots and dumps and maintenance shops, and above all barbed wire. After Bien Hoa, I saw that the rubber plantations now looked weeded and well kept, as they had not been during the war. Vung Tau itself had two well-furnished hotels. The new prosperity depended on Vung Tau's emergence as the base for Vietnam's off-shore oil industry.

As well as becoming an oil town, Vung Tau remained a fishing port and therefore a source of boats for people wanting to leave the country. We heard from Norwegian oil men that up till July 1979, the Vietnamese authorities permitted and even encouraged people to leave the country. On at least one occasion a freighter chartered from Singapore had docked at Vung Tau to take off hundreds of emigrants. Then in July 1979 a conference took place at Geneva at which the countries receiving the Boat People, especially Thailand and Malaysia, demanded that Vietnam halt the exodus. The police at Vung Tau clamped down on the issue of exit permits; informants were paid to report on sailings; above all the navy and coast guard were told to arrest the boats they had once let by. This change in policy soon resulted in horror. A boat full of refugees was rammed by a coast guard ship and crushed on an oil rig. Some of the refugees climbed to safety and into the hands of the Norwegian oil men. The coast guards threatened to open fire; the refugees were dropped back into the sea and there machine-gunned. A similar massacre took place two months later. A senior Norwegian told us this at a meeting arranged by the Vietnam Tourist Board.

These stories did not add to the charm of Vung Tau as a seaside resort. In contrast to Saigon, people there were fearful of talking to foreigners. Once, on the beach, a group of four men who had been telling me about the escapes and other matters, suddenly got to their feet and left me. The reason for this became evident with the appearance of two hatchet-faced men in dark glasses – obvious secret police. Vung Tau's once saucy entertainment was now reduced to a dance on Saturday night on the roof of the main hotel. A number of drab and sullen women were brought by bus from Saigon to dance with the oil men who were the only other customers. As soon as the music started, the price of drinks doubled or tripled. A Russian kindly offered to share his private bottle of peach brandy. The high point of the evening came when a Yorkshire oil man did a quite passable Elvis Presley imitation.

Our tourist programme took us to Dalat in the Highlands, a welcome change from the gruelling April heat. One of the cars broke down in the mountains, and this time we were surprised to see that out guides and drivers were anxious, if not afraid. They said it was 'not safe' at night in the Highlands, a frank admission of discontent among the Montagnards. We later heard that the Montagnard guerrilla movement, FULRO, which had flourished during the early 1960s, had once more attracted supporters. Our guides would not allow us to visit a Montagnard village, nor even to get a closer look at the statue of a gigantic chicken that we had seen in the distance from the road. I never discovered its significance.

The Hanoi government blamed Beijing for the discontent of the Montagnards, as I learnt from *The Hoa in Vietnam Dossier*:

> Its agents are conducting secret zapping operations among the Tay, Nung Giay, Zao, Meo and other minorities, urging them to come and settle in China. By so doing they intend to deprive Vietnam of those Montagnards who have so effectively contributed to the defence of her frontiers, and worse still to forge them into a weapon to be turned against Hanoi... Here again Chinese propaganda makes use of the stick and the carrot, the stress being laid on the latter: a better life in China, with better thermos flasks, fabrics and coloured threads than in Vietnam, and the return to the fold of all the populations who have originally migrated from southern China.

When we finally reached Dalat, we booked in at the Palace Hotel, as sombre and empty as ever. However, I noticed that the duck press that disappeared during the early 1970s was back in its place in the dining room. Perhaps one day the staff would remember its purpose. We were apparently the first British tourists to visit Dalat since liberation in 1975, so we were met by representatives of the press and television as well as by dignitaries of the Dalat Tourist Board. These were elderly gentlemen from North Vietnam, who reminded me rather of British trades union officials at conferences in Blackpool or Scarborough. They smiled through their false teeth, nodded a great deal and made speeches on peace and Anglo-Vietnamese relations, then pressed us to drink a number of toasts in what they said was 'artichoke whisky', brewed in the cellars of the Palace Hotel.

Later I saw Dalat for the first time under the influence of artichoke whisky. It was just as dull as ever. The anglers lining the lake at the foot of the Palace steps as usual kept the ends of their rods in the water, a practice I disapproved. There were now more pony traps and fewer cars. The market showed that the neighbouring farms were still supplying plentiful strawberries, asparagus and of course artichokes. But there was never much to do in Dalat except feel cool. The cinema used to be popular; indeed when the Vietcong raided the town in 1966, they hoisted their flag over the poster of Rock Hudson. Now, the locals complained to us, the films were Russian, Hungarian and Romanian in the original languages. An interpreter stood at the back and explained what was happening: 'She is beginning to fall in love with him . . . He has been named a Hero of Socialist Labour . . .'

On the last day of the tour, we went on an outing to My Tho in the Mekong Delta, near the village where I had made a documentary film in 1969. Some Austrians I had met in Saigon who worked at Can Tho, the main town in the Delta, said they were not allowed to leave their hotel after six at night, and frequently heard gunfire. This may explain why we were not allowed off the main road nor encouraged to talk to people in My Tho itself. Our guide admitted implicitly that the Mekong Delta peasants had not taken kindly to Communism. He said that in North Vietnam in the 1950s, the government had made a 'mistake' by collectivising land, so it had not been attempted in the South. Life in the villages still revolved around the family, he assured us.

Our guide took us to My Tho's one tourist attraction, the Coconut Island just upstream in the River Mekong, and once the home of a weird Buddhist sect run by a monk who lived in a tree. We saw the statue of Christ and Buddha walking hand in hand, but not the pictures of Thieu and Ho Chi Minh that used to be a feature of this island of peace. The temple included nine totem-pole dragons, a model of the Apollo spacecraft and a cluster of fairy lights that used to glitter over the Mekong. We were told that the Coconut Monk himself had 'disappeared', a piece of news that greatly upset Tim Page, who had been a friend and indeed a disciple. After our trip to the island we were given lunch in a Buddhist temple, which Tim and I both regarded as sacrilegious. It is all right to smoke in a Buddhist temple – in Thailand you can buy cigars and cigarettes during the service – but eating was not right, especially since our meal included meat. Afterwards Tim and I exacted a tiny revenge on our blasphemous tour guides. When the usual crowd of children gathered to stare at us, we taught them to chant some phrases of English: 'Richard Nixon, Number One! Ho Chi Minh, Number Ten Thousand!' This made us feel better after a very depressing week.

7

Vietnam in Books and Film

After that visit in 1980, I had no wish to see South Vietnam until it was given a tolerable government, as started to happen in 1986. However, during the 1980s I travelled often to South-east Asia, especially Thailand, Hong Kong, Singapore, Malaysia, India and the Philippines. I also made a first, brief but enthralling trip to Communist China. Everywhere that I travelled I got an impression of optimism and confidence, so different from the misery I had seen in South Vietnam. I also began to sense that South-east Asia was taking over the leadership of the world from Europe and North America. Once I went to Malaysia to write on the grievance of the ethnic Chinese students who no longer received a subsidy to study in Britain; the local universities were reserved for ethnic Malays. What struck me most was that all the young Chinese who had managed to get a degree in law, accountancy or medicine, immediately started to earn about double the money of similar young men and women in England, and four or five times the money of ageing freelance writers such as myself. Moreover they did not suffer the penal taxation that falls on even the poorest people in Britain. Largely because of low government spending and therefore low taxation, Malaysia, Singapore and Hong Kong were rapidly growing more prosperous than their former colonial ruler.

My belief that the mantle of greatness had passed from the

Europeans and their American cousins to South-east Asia became still stronger on visits to the United States. The moral decline that began in the 1960s and did such damage in South Vietnam now seemed to have turned into utter depravity. Books, magazines, Hollywood films and television were fouled by crude and often violent obscenity. For most of the poor and especially the blacks, the family was a dying institution. There was a craze for mad and hysterical witch-hunts and trials for imagined 'child abuse', the prosecutions for which increased from 300 in 1963 to more than 3 million thirty years later. Heroin and cocaine abuse, which had virtually been stamped out in 1920, when Prohibition was introduced for drugs as well as for alcohol, had now reached epidemic proportions. The United States government, rather than cracking down on its own drug abusers, tried to put the blame on the growers of coca leaves and opium poppies in Latin America and South-east Asia. The prevalence of intravenous drug injection, as well as the legalisation of homosexual acts, produced an AIDS epidemic, first in the United States and then all over the world, especially hitting Thailand.

The feminist movement, coming on top of drugs and sexual licence, still further reduced the morale and fighting capabilities of the US armed forces. Once, in 1983, I was in Honduras when the United States was holding army manoeuvres intended to cow the Marxist regime in Nicaragua, or even to pave the way for invasion. In Tegucigalpa I spent a few evenings in one of the new 'GI bars' like those I remembered from Saigon. The proprietor was an ex-Marine who had served in Vietnam and afterwards fought as a mercenary, or 'soldier of fortune', in various countries in Africa. Most of the customers were young American soldiers taking part in the exercises, and some of them were women. These girls were not just clerks or drivers but combat soldiers steeled in the toughest of infantry training schools. These American women soldiers were homesick and miserable. One of them told me that most evenings she stayed in her tent and polished her boots; she showed me a photograph of her husband and two children, the boy with freckles, the girl with a brace on her teeth. Another, single GIess told me how much she missed her parents back in New Hampshire. A third wept, literally into her beer. The only happy women GIs I saw were two lesbians walking arm in arm down a street of Tegucigalpa. The recruitment and training of women as combat troops was started at the insistence of feminists, who then changed their minds and said it degraded women to teach them to kill.

Both in Central America and the United States, people I met seemed unable to come to terms with the Vietnam War. In Honduras, El Salvador and Nicaragua, the North Americans were obsessed with the danger of the region becoming 'another Vietnam'. In the United States, both those who had supported and those who had argued against the Vietnam War were now agreed it had been a disaster. Supporters blamed the politicians for having obliged them to fight with 'one hand tied behind the back', and then of having betrayed the United States, though not apparently South Vietnam. Former opponents of the war now blamed it for all the defects of the country, from racial hatred to drug abuse, crime and suicide. Vietnam veterans especially blamed their experiences for failures in marriage, careers and physical or mental health.

From the late 1970s, I read as much as I could of the histories, memoirs and novels about Vietnam, and I saw most of the Hollywood films on the war and how it affected American people. In the chapter that follows, I first describe three books that seem to me to put the war in perspective and offer real insight into its meaning. Then I look at Barbara Tuchman's *The March of Folly: From Troy to Vietnam*, the most ambitious and far-reaching attack on the US involvement, as seen from the liberal viewpoint. Then, turning to the cinema, I examine the anti-war works of Oliver Stone and others before discussing *Apocalypse Now*, the one film of genius to have emerged from Vietnam. Finally I discuss the films, novels and investigative books arising from the persistent belief that more than two thousand MIA, or American Missing in Action, were held by the Communists after the end of the war.

Stanley Karnow, the author of *Vietnam: A History*, also masterminded an excellent twelve-part television documentary series for the American Public Broadcasting Service. Karnow had studied in France and become an authority on China before his first visit to Vietnam in 1959. He went back in 1965 to cover the first few years of America's intervention, then settled in Washington to cover the Nixon administration. He knew virtually all the important politicians and military men in Saigon and Washington, and after the war he interviewed most of their former opponents in Hanoi and Ho Chi Minh City. His neutral attitude to the war is summed up by his account of meeting Daniel Ellsberg, a former official who leaked the 'Pentagon Papers' to the *New York Times*, the principal voice of opposition to Nixon:

> When our paths first crossed in 1966 in Saigon, where he belonged to a special counter-insurgency team headed by Edward Lansdale, he was a fervent believer in the war who hotly disputed my lack of enthusiasm. Four years later, when we met again in Cambridge, Massachusetts, he had become an ardent foe of the war who seemed to be disappointed by my detachment from it.

My one encounter with Stanley Karnow has left me with a respect amounting to awe for his knowledge of South-east Asian affairs. This was on 7 February 1986, when Ferdinand Marcos, the President of the Philippines, had rigged a general election in order to cling on to power. Over lunch in the charming Spanish colonial town of Vigan, Karnow and I were joined by excited local people who asked what he thought would be the result. Without hesitation, and speaking hours before the polling booths were due to be closed, Karnow said that Marcos would claim to have won with 54.4 per cent of the votes. A few days later I opened the paper to find that Marcos had claimed this exact figure of 54.4 per cent. Although I do not suggest that in *Vietnam: A History* Karnow writes with the same Olympian knowledge, I do respect his authority.

For one thing, Karnow understands the importance of the historic division of Vietnam between North and South. The

French saw it as three regions: Tonkin in the north, Annam in the middle and Cochin-China in the south. In fact the division split Annam at roughly the place where North and South Vietnam were divided till 1975. Graham Greene also saw the distinction. In an article for *Paris-Match* in 1952, he wrote that the people of Cochin-China 'differ much more from the Tonkinese than they do from the Siamese . . . If one sees Cochin-China in colours of green and gold, one sees Tonkin only in brown and black . . . In Tonkin the population is physically more solid than in the south, the climate harsher, the clothing coarser, the women less pretty and gambling is forbidden.'

What Greene understood with his novelist's intuition, Karnow explains from history. In the sixteenth century, when families such as the Mac and the Trinh were competing for power in the north, a third clan, the Nguyen, broke away to form their own fiefdom in central Vietnam, then pushed south to conquer the Mekong Delta, still under the feeble rule of Cambodia. Karnow goes on:

> Civil strife continued in Vietnam for two centuries, as the Trinh and the Nguyen fought each other. Just as the Geneva accords of 1954 divided Vietnam at the seventeenth parallel, so the earlier rivals eventually agreed to a partition along roughly the same line. They also conceded to an expedient truce, each hoping to fight one another again once it had regained strength.
>
> The Nguyen leader of the late eighteenth century turned to France to bolster his cause. His appeal, carried to Versailles by Pigneau de Béhaine, set the scene for French intervention . . . The war between North and South Vietnam after 1954 largely expressed regional animosities only newly overlaid with an ideological veneer. And the same tensions continued after 1975 as southerners, Communists among them, balked at northern domination.

Vietnam was once more divided in 1945, after the Japanese capitulation. The North came under the Chinese Nationalists, aided by the American OSS who wanted to hand power to Ho Chi Minh and the Communists. The South came under the British Asian commander, Lord Louis Mountbatten, who gave the order to hand the territory back to the French. On 21 September 1945, the British in Saigon released from internment and armed about 1,400 French troops, most of them Legionnaires, who went on the rampage, starting with an attack on the Vietminh and going on to a general massacre of *les jaunes*. The Vietminh ordered a general strike for 24 September. 'If any one date marks the start of the first Indo-China war, it might be that date,' Karnow remarks.

Why did the British Labour government want to hand Indo-China back to its former colonial ruler? And why did the French and later the Chinese Communists go along with this policy? The second difficult question is tackled by Karnow. The French Communist leader Maurice Thorez stated in 1945 that he did not intend to 'liquidate the French position in Indo-China', and two years later, as deputy prime minister in a Socialist government, Thorez countersigned a directive for military action against the Vietminh. The Vietminh in turn distrusted the French less than they did the Chinese, whatever their ideology. In 1946, Ho Chi Minh was ready to have the French come back in order to kick out the Chinese Nationalists. He told dissenting comrades: 'You fools. Don't you remember your history? The last time the Chinese came here they stayed a thousand years. The French are foreigners. They are weak. Colonialism is dying. The white man is finished in Asia. But if the Chinese stay now, they will never go. As for me, I prefer to sniff French shit for five years than eat Chinese shit for the rest of my life.'

Ho found the Chinese Communists no more friendly than the Nationalists. At the Geneva conference on Indo-China in 1954, the Chinese delegate Chou En-lai stopped Ho Chi Minh from getting control of South Vietnam, Laos and Cambodia. China believed that a French presence in these three regions would help to prevent American intervention. Besides, so Karnow says:

Chinese foreign policy throughout the centuries had been to fragment South-east Asia in order to influence its states, and Chou subscribed to that tradition. A divided Vietnam suited the Chinese better than a unified neighbour, particularly one that had quarrelled with China for two thousand years. Similarly, China's security would be served by restraining Vietnamese ambitions to Laos and Cambodia.

Karnow's fascinating account of Chinese–Vietnamese rivalry in the 1950s is based on hitherto classified French foreign policy documents, now revealed in François Joyaux's *La Chine et le règlement du premier conflit d'Indochine*.

Although Stanley Karnow does not set out to be a revisionist or debunking historian, he challenges many received opinions about what happened. Contrary to what was believed at the time, the Vietnam War was not expensive in money. By the middle of 1967, it was absorbing only about three per cent of America's gross national product, compared to forty-eight per cent for the Second World War and twelve per cent for the Korean War, at their peaks. It is interesting to learn from a poll of Vietnam veterans that seventy-one per cent said they were 'glad to have gone', seventy-four per cent said they enjoyed their tour there, and sixty-six per cent expressed a willingness to serve again. Another surprise in the book concerns the Phoenix Programme, run by the CIA, which involved murdering Communists in the villages. Journalists such as myself had tended to write off the Phoenix Programme as self-defeating because we believed it killed non-political peasants as well as a few Vietcong. But Vietcong survivors after 1975 told Karnow that Phoenix had been 'very dangerous', had 'created tremendous difficulties', 'was devious and cruel' and caused the 'loss of thousands of our cadres'.

Another received idea in Saigon under the old regime was the great venality of the South Vietnamese politicians and generals. Yet as Karnow remarks in a casual aside:

Judging from their destinies, though, numbers of senior Vietnamese were either too honest or too incompetent to enrich themselves. General Tran Van Don arrived nearly penniless in the United States in 1975; [Nguyen Cao] Ky opened a modest liquor store in California despite his alleged gains, while Bui Diem, the ambassador to Washington, ended up running a Jewish delicatessen there.

Returning to Vietnam in 1981, Karnow discovered 'a land not only ravaged by a generation of almost uninterrupted conflict, but governed by an inept and repressive regime incompetent to cope with the challenge of recovery'. Moreover the new regime was as venal as the old.

Much the same conclusion is reached by the German television journalist Peter Scholl-Latour in his unforgettable *Eyewitness Vietnam*, the English translation of *Der Tod in Reisfeld: Dreissig Jahre Krieg in Indochine*. Like Stanley Karnow, Herr Scholl-Latour was educated in Paris, and brings to his journalistic work a knowledge of the literature, art, religion and history of European and Asian civilisation. He exemplifies Dr Johnson's dictum: 'As the Spanish proverb says. "He who would bring home the wealth of the Indies must carry the wealth of the Indies with him." So it is in travelling: a man must carry knowledge with him if he would bring home knowledge.' Herr Scholl-Latour has done just that. He has written an outstandingly wise and often poignant book on his Indo-China experiences that started in 1946 when he first arrived as a Legionnaire on a troop-ship.

Herr Scholl-Latour has observed all three Vietnam wars: the French against the Vietminh; the North against the South Vietnamese (supported from 1965 to 1972 by America); and Communist Vietnam against Communist China and Cambodia. He admired the fighting qualities of the French and the South Vietnamese but not of the Americans:

> Some GIs wore badges on their shirts that said: 'I'm not scared of Hell any more – I've been through Vietnam'. In most cases this was an idle boast. On average one in twenty American soldiers, at

most, actually had contact with the enemy. Every soldier wounded in action was transported by helicopter, without delay to operating theatres equipped with the very latest equipment. Compared with this, the conditions the French had to fight in during their war in Indo-China were appalling.

Early in 1979, Scholl-Latour noted ironically that the Vietnamese were fighting against guerrillas in Cambodia, in the same way as America fought in Vietnam. They would occupy a district, take control of the major roads, then crush any resistance with napalm, bombs and artillery. They were combating 'a rude band of highly mobile, self-sufficient jungle fighters who were using Vietcong tactics to challenge General Dung's mechanised divisions'. He visited both sides during and after the brief Sino-Vietnamese War of 1979, and praised China's good treatment of prisoners:

> The Bo Doi [Vietnamese] were almost certainly better off under their Chinese captors than they would have been in the two preceding wars. The prisoners of war taken by the French had not had an easy time of it. Rations behind the barbed wire had been meagre, and methods of interrogation brutal. The Americans had taken very few prisoners in their military operations against the Vietcong. Anyone who was lucky enough to survive was handed over to the South Vietnamese military authorities, which inevitably meant systematic ill-treatment and torture.

Scholl-Latour challenges many received ideas about Vietnamese politics and religion, especially concerning events in the early 1960s. He acknowledges that the then President Diem's Catholic bigotry had alienated many Buddhists; however, he says that the Communists had indeed managed to infiltrate the pagodas and used the monks for political propaganda. Moreover he says that Buddhism was only a fringe religion in Vietnam, 'the last refuge of the poor and oppressed' among a people under the stronger influence of Confucianism and Christianity. However, he says, these subtleties were lost on the American journalists, who flocked to Saigon in the early 1960s.

> They had set up camp in an air-conditioned bar on the top floor of the Caravelle, a modern hotel rumoured to be owned by the Catholic Church. It did not take the Americans long to reach a unanimous verdict on the political situation in Saigon. Diem the dictator had to go, leaving the true representatives of the people, the Buddhists, to save the day and point the way to peace and democracy. It was up to them, and them alone, to steer a middle course between the clerical fascism of 'The Incorruptible' and the left-wing Communism of the Liberation Front.

Under the influence of these correspondents, the American government turned on Diem and engineered his overthrow, but not his murder. The US advisers gave Diem the option of fleeing, says Scholl-Latour, but being a man of some pride and dignity he turned down the offer and so chose death instead.

> Diem may have been stiff-necked and intransigent, but he was a patriot and a man of integrity. The Americans let him down, and their policy in Vietnam never recovered from the odium of that crime. Henceforth it was forever to be branded with the mark of Cain.

Those liberals in Europe and the United States who complain of the alleged ill-treatment of Roman Catholics in Northern Ireland remain indifferent to the undoubted persecution of Roman Catholics in Communist Vietnam. Here again, Peter Scholl-Latour offers a welcome corrective. In Hanoi, in August 1976, he got permission to film the service on the Feast of the Assumption in St Joseph's Cathedral. After describing the men in the congregation, devout and defiant, and women whose faces bore the marks of recent suffering, Scholl-Latour writes:

> It was the children who moved me most, though. They followed every detail of the service with grave expressions, intent on the

actions of the priest. They were making the greatest sacrifice of all. As Catholics they would never be allowed to wear the red neckerchief of the Young Pioneers, for example. And in later life they would be barred from all positions of responsibility and excluded from worthwhile careers ... I knelt down in a pew at the side and crossed myself. Here in Hanoi I could listen to the Christians of Vietnam using the traditional Latin mass, calling to God *de profundis*, from the depths of their misery and rejection.

Quare me repulisti et quare tristis incedo, dum affligit me inimicus. Nobody would have denied the congregation of St Joseph's belonged to the oppressed and silent church, but for me, as they knelt there in the flickering light of the candles, they were the true *ecclesia triumphans*. As a child I used to recite the 'Te Deum', a line of which now came to mind: '*Martyrum candidatus exercitus . . .*' 'the shining army of martyrs'.

Although Scholl-Latour knows Vietnam longest and best of the countries of Indo-China, he also writes beautifully on Laos and Cambodia. He comes up with the odd but somehow appropriate piece of information that the last monarch of Laos, King Savang Vatthana, was a devotee of Proust and could even recite by heart whole chapters of *A la Recherche du Temps Perdu*. One can only hope that the knowledge helped to relieve the misery of the concentration camp in which the King was done to death by the Communists after 1975. Scholl-Latour also adds to our stock of knowledge about Prince Norodom Sihanouk of Cambodia. Apparently, in the 1960s Sihanouk wrote and put on plays including a one-act drama, *The Ideal Husband*, concerning a king who discards his favourite wife because she torments her cat by pulling its tail. Nor did I know that Sihanouk occasionally signed himself, tongue in cheek, as foreign correspondent for *Le Canard Enchaîné*, the French satirical magazine. Had I known this, I could have approached him as a colleague, for I was the South-east Asia correspondent of *Private Eye*.

Towards the end of *Eyewitness Vietnam*, Herr Scholl-Latour describes a dinner hosted by Sihanouk and his wife Monique, in their exile in Beijing in March 1979. The Prince gave an enlightening analysis of the character of the Khmer Rouge, then led his guests to a viewing room to see one of his films – a travelogue of Cambodia in the 1960s.

> The prince and his wife were not the only ones to feel sad at the sight of these scenes. Everyone in the cinema felt overcome by a deep sense of melancholy. As we watched, pre-war Phnom Penh came to life once more, with its bustling markets, its modern university, its cheerful inhabitants, its beautiful temple-dancers. Then the strains of a sentimental ballad were heard. 'That's my tribute to Monique. I wrote it myself,' whispered Sihanouk.

A third book that gave me fresh and valuable insights into the Vietnam War was *Cruel April: The Fall of Saigon* by the French political commentator Olivier Todd. Unlike most historians of that final invasion, Todd writes in sympathy with the losing side, an attitude still more surprising from one on the left in politics. Todd covered the Vietnam War from 1965 to 1973 for the socialist weekly *Nouvel Observateur*, the French equivalent of the *New Statesman* to which he also contributed. The preface to the French edition of *Cruel April* gives us to understand that for most of that period, M. Todd was sympathetic to the Vietcong, or Southern guerrillas, and even to some extent the regime in Hanoi. Then in 1973, after the US withdrawal, Todd made his way to the desolate part of the Mekong Delta still controlled by the Provisional Revolutionary Government (PRG), the remnants of the Southern Communists. He travelled with the fine American journalist Ron Moreau, who speaks Vietnamese and knows the country backwards. The experience was shattering:

> My views of the war changed radically. The uneasiness I'd felt during my visit to North Vietnam the previous year precipitated out as if chemically. I came back convinced that I'd been wrong. With a few faint reservations in the *Nouvel Observateur* I had defended what had seemed a movement of national liberation and the last stage of an anti-colonialist battle; I discovered, a bit late,

that the PRG in the South was the secular and ideological arm of the Communist government in Hanoi. Had I been to some extent a victim of what Jean-François Revel calls 'the totalitarian temptation'?

Although he does not appear to have gone back to South Vietnam after 1973, Todd appreciates that it was gaining strength as a country, economically and politically. If it had held on till the off-shore oil came on tap, South Vietnam could have bought the armaments needed to match the military build-up of the North. Noting that, in 1975, Saigon had branches of eighteen Vietnamese and fourteen foreign banks, Todd drily comments: 'Ministries of foreign affairs often keep embassies in foreign countries for show; banks never.'

American liberals never understood that the Saigon regime was becoming both more efficient and more accepted. As late as February 1975, a group of US Congressmen went to South Vietnam to lecture the government on its 'human rights violations', a cant phrase even then growing in popularity. The Congressmen would not accept the explanation given by Tran Van Lan, the President of the Saigon Senate: 'Our country was practically born in the war. It has never had a chance to practise true democracy... Whatever our system's faults, at least it allows for possible change.' Endorsing this argument, Todd goes on to say: 'The quasi-dictatorship of the right, as opposed to dictatorships of the left, can alter... During the fall of Saigon, Solzhenitsyn shocked the left by saying that one was freer under Franco than in the Soviet Union. And yet it was true.'

The success of the Northern invasion in 1975 was due to their overwhelming superiority in infantry, tanks and artillery. Their commander Van Tien Dung said that in the central Highlands they had 5.5 soldiers for every one of the Southern army. When the North tried to take Hue in 1972, they were driven back by a smaller Southern army and lost a whole division. When the North struck again in 1975, they captured Hue only because of their two to one superiority in numbers. Olivier Todd praises the courage of

ARVIN, against all odds. When the North attacked Phuoc Long, the outnumbered defenders fought literally to the death, losing 5,400 officers and men, or half a division. When the Southerners would not withdraw from Xuan Loc, the invaders rained down nearly 10,000 shells on the town in a single day. This went unnoticed in the American liberal newspapers. As South Vietnam entered its death agony, opinion polls in America showed that eighty per cent were against meeting even its basic needs in petrol and ammunition.

Although the invading Communists called on the population to rise up against their government, in no place did this happen. There were virtually no defections from ARVIN, the Southern army. Most of the population either fled or greeted the invaders with sullen dread. The leader of a PRG group in a suburb of Can Tho, in the Mekong Delta, admitted that in her district of 19,000 people 'the revolutionary core consisted of only fifteen patriots'.

Looking back at my own journals and articles written in Saigon in April 1975, I find that my strongest feelings were admiration for the indomitable South Vietnamese, and rage at those in the West who were indifferent to their plight. That same anger inspires Olivier Todd:

> Richard Nixon has written that Vietnam was a tragedy for the Americans. No doubt, but it was first – and still is – a tragedy for the Vietnamese. When Saigon was about to fall, Ambassador Graham Martin said that it would not be 'all that pleasant to be an American in Saigon'. It was most difficult of all to be South Vietnamese. For the astonishing Vietnamese people that war is still a festering wound, a poison still toxic.

In a preface to the English edition, written after the end of Communism in most of the countries of Eastern Europe, Todd offers this admonition to the United States:

> Americans, notwithstanding My Lai and other abominations, should not feel ashamed of their effort in Vietnam. The United

States probably should not have gone in alone, and the war should have been conducted differently, but Americans must not allow Hanoi to work on an American guilt complex. Had the South Vietnamese and the Americans won the war, the anti-Communist revolution would have spread to North Vietnam in 1989 or 1990. Cambodia might have been spared the Khmer Rouge bloodbath. A united Vietnam would be developing politically and economically.

Todd urges the United States to start rethinking its attitudes to the Vietnam War.

Unhappily, with a very few exceptions such as the excellent Stanley Karnow, most American writers on Vietnam have stuck by the dogmatic opinions they held at the time of the US involvement. The 'hawks', as they used to be called, who had favoured pursuing the war, if necessary by even crueller bombing of North Vietnam, continued to feel betrayed by pusillanimous politicians and left-wing journalists. The 'doves', as they used to be called, who made up the overwhelming majority in the press and the universities, established the standard view of the Vietnam War as a crime and disaster. Both hawks and doves were agreed on one thing: they thought of Vietnam only in terms of the US involvement from 1965 to 1972. Unlike Stanley Karnow, Olivier Todd, and Peter Scholl-Latour, most American writers on South Vietnam have ignored what happened there between the end of 1972 and the fall of Saigon in April 1975. They have not woken up to the fact that by the end, the overwhelming majority of the Southerners were anti-Communist and indeed pro-American. They have clung to the slogans and misconceptions of twenty or thirty years ago. Some of the most successful books on Vietnam have been written by two of those correspondents, caricatured by Scholl-Latour, who stayed in the Caravelle in the early 1960s, and backed the Buddhists against the Diem regime.

Apart from the three already mentioned, most writers on Vietnam have succumbed to the old temptation to think that because something happened it must have been bound to happen; that South Vietnam was doomed to be Communist. The leading proponent of this theory was not, as one might imagine, some Marxist professor or fashionable journalist, but one of America's finest historians, Barbara Tuchman, the author of internationally famous books such as *The Guns of August, Stilwell and the American Experience in China*, and *A Distant Mirror*, a study of Europe in the fourteenth century. Barbara Tuchman's witty and elegant style, her two Pulitzer prizes, her interests ranging through many countries and ages, not least her authorship of a book about China, all lent authority to *The March of Folly: From Troy to Vietnam*, on 'the pursuit by governments of policies contrary to their own interests'.

Barbara Tuchman identifies four types of misgovernment: tyranny or oppression; excessive ambition, such as Japan's bid for an Asian empire; incompetence or decadence, such as the late Roman Empire; and folly or perversity, which she defines as 'the pursuit of policy contrary to the self-interest of the constituency or state involved'. Self-interest is 'whatever conduces to the welfare or advantage of the body being governed; folly is a policy that in these terms is counter-productive'. To be classed as folly according to Barbara Tuchman, the policy has to meet three further criteria. It must have been perceived as counter-productive in its own time, not merely by hindsight; a feasible alternative course of action must have been available; the policy in question must be that of a group, not an individual ruler, and should persist beyond any one political lifetime. The four examples of folly she chooses appear in the chapter headings: 'Prototype: The Trojans take the Wooden Horse within their walls'; 'The Renaissance Popes provoke the Protestant Secession: 1470–1530'; 'The British lose America'; and 'America betrays herself in Vietnam'.

The acceptance by Troy of the Wooden Horse was a single instance of folly, not a continuous policy, which is why Barbara Tuchman calls the story a prototype. She retells in sprightly fashion how Laocoön warned the Trojans not to accept the horse because he feared the Greeks, even bearing gifts; how two serpents rose from the sea and strangled him and his sons; how

Cassandra, having the gift of prophecy but the curse of not being believed, warned the Trojans against the horse 'that has your destruction within it'; how she too was slaughtered by the triumphant Greeks.

According to Barbara Tuchman: 'The existence of the legend can tell us only one thing: that Laocoön was fatally punished for perceiving the truth and warning of it.' From this we are meant to deduce that Laocoön and Cassandra would have warned the United States against the intervention in Vietnam. However, the legend tells us another thing, equally relevant to Vietnam, that we should not trust those who mean to destroy us. The Trojans were weary of war and therefore persuaded themselves that the Greeks too had peaceful intentions, thus allowing themselves to be tricked by the wily Odysseus. So, in the 1930s, after the horrors of the First World War, the British longed to believe in the peaceful intentions of Adolf Hitler, and would not heed the warnings of Winston Churchill, the Laocoön and Cassandra of the twentieth century. Again, after the Second World War, there were many in the West who longed to believe in the peaceful intentions of 'Uncle Joe' Stalin, and branded Churchill a warmonger for talking about an Iron Curtain in Europe. However, this time the Western governments listened to Churchill and set up the North Atlantic Treaty Organisation, so keeping the peace until the dissolution of Communism in Europe.

And so, during the Vietnam War, the hawks warned the doves not to believe in the peaceful intentions of North Vietnam and its wily Odysseus, Ho Chi Minh. However by 1972, the Americans were so weary of war that they allowed themselves to believe in the fraudulent Paris Peace Treaty. Nixon and Kissinger even allowed the North to station its tanks, artillery and several divisions of infantry inside South Vietnam, a Trojan Horse if ever there was one.

Having established at Troy her prototype of political folly, Tuchman moves from pre-history to the six Renaissance popes whose avarice and depravity encouraged the rise of Protestantism in northern Europe. She retells with gusto many scandalous and salacious stories, such as how Pope Alexander VI and his children, Cesare and Lucrezia Borgia, watched fifty naked women pick up chestnuts, not with their fingers. While reminding us that the Renaissance popes committed all the deadly sins, Barbara Tuchman fails to prove them guilty of folly, or 'the pursuit of policy contrary to the self-interest of the constituency or state involved'. The Renaissance popes were much too selfish to bother about the interests of the papacy. Although for a time they held secular power in Rome and its hinterland, this was always subordinate to their spiritual duty as Vicar of Christ; and none of the six popes in question gave a hoot for Christ's injunction to St Peter. The purity of the faith meant nothing to men who could hold a bullfight in St Peter's Square, or take their children to 'live shows' such as you see in the Patpong Road in Bangkok. Wickedness, rather than folly, was their undoing. Their only tenuous link with the Vietnam War was in having begun in Renaissance Rome the same onslaught on sexual morality that did such damage to the United States in the 'Sixties Revolution'.

Barbara Tuchman's next example of folly, the failure of England to hold its North American colonies, does conform to the terms of her definition. The policy was condemned at the time by statesmen as wise as Pitt the Elder, Charles James Fox and Edmund Burke. Alternative courses of action were always available, and the policy was pursued by a group of statesmen, not by an individual ruler, although George III played a predominant role. However, Tuchman's argument rests on a doubtful premise: 'Britain's self-interest as regards her empire on the American continent in the 18th century was clearly to maintain her sovereignty, and for every reason of trade, peace and profit, to maintain it with the goodwill and by the voluntary desire of the colonists.'

The economic benefits that Britain received from trade with the North American continent were small compared with those from the East Indian spice trade and West Indian sugar plantations. Wealth from the tropical colonies furnished the capital for the coal mines and canals of the Industrial Revolution. Nor did the independence of the United States damage Britain's trade.

Tobacco from the Virginia plantations continued to fill the pipes and later the cigarettes of British smokers. The Lancashire mills received their raw cotton from Alabama and Mississippi as freely and cheaply as if these states had remained in the king's possession.

Most of the early British settlers had been to some extent rebels before they left, such as English religious dissenters, Ulster Presbyterians escaping the penal laws, and many thousands of convicts sent as indentured labourers to Virginia. Even if they had stayed loyal to England throughout the eighteenth century, the Americans would have wanted their independence when their numbers were swollen by immigrants from other countries of Europe, not to mention the Catholic Irish after the Famine. It may have been well for Britain to break with the colonies sooner rather than later, and without real enmity. Apart from a fracas in 1812, the United States and Britain were to remain friends and allies throughout two centuries and two world wars.

In Troy, Renaissance Rome and eighteenth-century England, Barbara Tuchman finds early examples of what she regards as the folly of US involvement in Vietnam. Moreover she says that American statesmen were still more culpable than their Trojan, papal and British predecessors because they were better informed: 'Ignorance was not a factor in the American endeavour in Vietnam, pursued through five presidencies, although it was to become an excuse. Ignorance of country and culture there may have been, but not ignorance of the contra-indications, even the barriers, to achieving the objectives of American policy.' The arrogance of that condemnation is all the more irritating since Barbara Tuchman's two hundred pages of commentary on the Vietnam War are stuffed with false assumptions, unproven popular legends and plain errors of fact.

Tuchman's hostility to the Vietnam War is based on three dubious premises: that the United States did not need to resist Communism in South-east Asia; that Ho Chi Minh and the North Vietnamese leadership were Indo-Chinese nationalists rather than Communists; and that South Vietnam had neither the means nor the will to remain independent. In a chapter headed 'Self-Hypnosis: 1946–54', Tuchman approves the response of the West to the Iron Curtain in Europe, but not its response to the Communist takeover of China. 'Hysteria over the "loss" of China took hold of America,' Tuchman avers, 'and rabid spokesmen of the China Lobby in Congress and the business world became the loudest voices in political life.' In 1950, Senator Joe McCarthy started his anti-Communist witch-hunt, and 'North Korea, a Soviet client, invaded South Korea, an American client', whereupon Truman ordered a military response. Tuchman then refers to the spies who gave the Soviet Union the knowledge to make nuclear weapons: 'During these abject years the Rosenbergs were tried for treason, convicted in 1951, and when President Eisenhower refused to commute a death sentence that would make orphans of two children, were subsequently executed.'

Thus, in the eyes of people like Barbara Tuchman, the murder of countless millions of Chinese by Mao Zedong is somehow balanced out by the hysteria of the China Lobby, McCarthy's persecution of Hollywood actors, and the refusal of clemency to admitted traitors. No moral distinction is made between the two 'client' states of Korea. Even writing in 1984, Tuchman does not seem to have grasped the stupendous cruelty of the Communist bloc in the period she describes, 1946–54. According to Solzhenitsyn, prisoners in the Gulag Archipelago hoped and prayed that the war in Korea would escalate into nuclear conflict and the destruction of Soviet power, whatever the cost in human lives.

Focusing attention on divided Vietnam in 1955, Tuchman discerns the Southern President Diem as a US puppet, the Northern President Ho Chi Minh as an Indo-China patriot. She suggests that the US government backed Diem only from fear of the redoubtable Cardinal Francis Spellman, the champion of the Vietnamese Catholics. Tuchman quotes with derision the cardinal's lamentation over the plight of the Roman Catholic refugees from the North and of those who remained under the Hanoi regime: 'Alas! for the newly betrayed millions of Indo-Chinese who must now learn the awful facts of slavery from their Communist masters, in repetition of the agonies and infamies inflicted upon the hapless victims of Red Russia's bestial tyranny.' Such language may sound strong to an East Coast liberal but not to anyone who has lived in a Communist country.

Barbara Tuchman even hints that America is to blame for the excesses of North Vietnam, and that the State Department in 1945–6 could have turned Ho Chi Minh into a Tito for Indo-China:

> In Indo-China, choice of the alternative would have required imagination, which is never a long suit with governments, and willingness to take the risk of supporting a Communist when Communism was still seen as a solid block. Tito was then its only splinter, and the possibility of another deviation was not envisaged.

But Tito did not appear as a 'splinter' till June 1948, when the Yugoslav Communist Party was thrown out of the Cominform at a meeting in Bucharest. In the period 1945–6, to which Barbara Tuchman quite specifically refers, Tito was seen by the State Department as more rabid a Communist than Stalin himself, threatening world war over his claim to Trieste, shooting down two US airplanes and jailing the Catholic Archbishop Alojzije Stepinac. Moreover Ho Chi Minh's Indo-China was no more of a nation-state than Tito's Yugoslavia, both of them later breaking up into quarrelling fragments.

Barbara Tuchman sums up her argument on the Vietnam War: 'The folly consisted not in pursuit of a goal in ignorance of the obstacles but in persistence in the pursuit despite accumulating evidence that the goal was unattainable . . .' Like many supporters as well as opponents of the war, Tuchman seems to forget its original, limited goal: to save South Vietnam from conquest by Communism and to establish a government acceptable to the people and capable of defending itself. The goal was not just attainable; it was actually attained. Like so many American liberals, Tuchman formed her opinion of South Vietnam in the early

1960s, and failed to notice the changes during the next ten years. In her ignorance, she grandly proclaims: 'The viability of a non-Communist South Vietnam, for which America had wrecked Indo-China and betrayed herself, inspired confidence in no one unless in Nixon and Kissinger, who convinced themselves that the West could still retrieve the situation if necessary.' She scorns Vietnamisation and the idea 'that floods of matériel would somehow accomplish what had not been accomplished over the past twenty-five years, the creation of a motivated fighting force able to preserve a viable non-Communist state, at least for an "acceptable interval" '.

Her remarks about the South Vietnamese are patronising as well as insulting: 'Americans were always talking about freedom from Communism, when the freedom that the mass of Vietnamese wanted was freedom from their exploiters, both French and indigenous. The assumption that humanity at large shared the democratic western idea of freedom was an American delusion.' Reading that, after a visit to South Vietnam suffering under its Communist tyrants, I felt enraged against Barbara Tuchman and her smug, pampered kind. Now that Communism has disappeared from Europe and lingers on in Vietnam only in a benign and relaxed form, I think of Barbara Tuchman's book with sorrow rather than anger. It should have been called *The March of Folly: From Troy to New York*.

The American experience in Vietnam has not yet produced a major novel, certainly not a *War and Peace*, nor anything as memorable as Crane's *Red Badge of Courage*, or Hemingway's *Farewell to Arms* and *For Whom the Bell Tolls*. This is variously attributed to the shameful character of the war, the lack of good writers, above all the nature of military service. Most Americans saw little of Vietnam outside their zone of operations, and met few Vietnamese except bar girls. Their experience was confined to army life with its long stretches of boredom, interrupted by terror. Even Tolstoy's *War and Peace* would not be remembered if it was limited to the scenes of military life. In Hemingway's fine novels, set in France and Italy in the First World War, and in Spain in the 1930s, the hero is American but he becomes involved with Europe and a European woman. Indeed when we think of *For Whom the Bell Tolls*, the characters that spring to mind are not the American protagonist, but Pilar and her band of gipsy guerrillas.

Even a very good novel on the Vietnam War, Tim O'Brien's *Going After Cacciato*, is confined in its scope to the members of one platoon in one small stretch of the coastal plain, and might have been written of any war, in any country. Indeed the story about the attempt to bring back a deserter, Cacciato, soon turns into a long dream of escape, in which the platoon drifts across Asia in the direction of Paris. So the subconscious mind tries to cope, in sleep, with the fears and anxiety of a soldier's waking life. In another book of short stories, loosely related to Vietnam, Mr O'Brien writes mostly of how the war affected people in the United States.

Another acclaimed book on the Vietnam War, Michael Herr's *Dispatches*, is almost entirely concerned with the Americans. It is not really fiction so much as imaginative reportage, and it was much praised by other 'New Journalists' such as Tom Wolfe and Dr Hunter Thompson ('*Dispatches* puts all of us in the shade'). And Michael Herr is a fine descriptive writer:

> When the rain stopped and the ponchos came off there was a smell that I thought was going to make me sick: rot, sump, tannery, open grave, dumpfire – awful, you'd walk into pockets of Old Spice that made it even worse.

His descriptions of getting about Vietnam by helicopter are almost as terrifying as the real thing. But the lean writing is larded with rhetoric: 'You ... might as well say that Vietnam was where the Trail of Tears was headed all along, the turn-around point where it would touch and come back to form a continuing perimeter; might just as well lay it on the proto-Gringos who found the New England woods too raw and empty for their peace and filled them with their own imported devils.' Like many of the 'New

Journalists', the narrator, Herr, speaks in the same tone of voice, using the same racy slang and obscenities, as the GIs he meets. There is no contrast.

Herr celebrated the 'war freaks', the amateur journalists who rode out by helicopter or motor-bike to the sound of rock music and firing, constantly high on drugs and danger: 'As long as we could have choppers like taxis it took real exhaustion or depression near shock or a dozen pipes of opium to keep us apparently quiet, we'd still be running around inside our skins like something was after us, ha ha, La Vida Loca.' It was *Dispatches* that first made Tim Page famous. 'In Saigon I always went to sleep stoned,' writes Herr, which is maybe why Saigon seemed to him 'like sitting inside the folding petals of a poisonous flower, the poison history, f—ed in its root no matter how far back you wanted to run your trace'. Saigon and the Vietnamese people did not intrude into Herr's private world.

The impressionistic, even phantasmagoric prose of Herr and the other 'New Journalists' merges readily into the visual world of Hollywood, now also trying to come to terms with the Vietnam experience. But like the writers, the film makers tended to see the war only in terms of how it affected Americans, both in Vietnam and back home. This was apparent in one of the most successful and also imaginative of the Vietnam films that started to pour out of Hollywood in the late 1970s, Michael Cimino's *The Deer Hunter*. The first and, to my mind, the better half of the film introduces a group of young men from an *émigré* Russian community in a Pennsylvania steel town, on the eve of their going to serve in Vietnam. They attend a wedding party, go on a hunting expedition and afterwards drink in a bar with an overhead fan, that all of a sudden changes into the strident roar of a US helicopter attacking a Vietnamese village. The friends are taken prisoner by the Communists, held in a bamboo cage sunk up to their necks in a river, and are forced to play Russian roulette as their captors bet on the outcome. They escape but are still in Saigon in April 1975, with one of them playing Russian roulette in a gambling hell run by a villainous Frenchman – another familiar figure of popular Vietnam fiction. At the end of the film the physically maimed or psychologically shattered survivors join in a wake for the one who died, singing 'God Bless America'. The critics could not agree whether this was a genuine or ironic expression of patriotism.

The equivocal and enigmatic style of Cimino's *The Deer Hunter* is not to be found in the Vietnam films of Oliver Stone, who actually fought in the jungle near the Cambodian border in 1967. He wears his liberal-left sentiments on his sleeve. In his first film, *Salvador*, Stone had the bright idea of introducing to Central America two of the pot-smoking, insouciant Vietnam journalists now popularised by Michael Herr in *Dispatches*. As the American author Robert Stone observed in an article in *The New York Review of Books* (17 February 1994):

> The only thing really novel about *Salvador* was its timeliness. Its mildly druggy, anti-establishment buddy team . . . provided yuppie audiences the shock of recognizing the likes of Hunter Thompson. Scenes in which the hippies get to flake off 'establishment' journalists and too-handsome US military-industrial zombies took everyone back to the glory days of the Sixties. In them, Stone was displaying a sure instinct for the spirit every Hollywood director has tried to summon forth – the little kid inside every moviegoer who likes to bounce up and down in the seat and clap.

Oliver Stone's first Vietnam film, *Platoon*, was remarkable for its photographic realism. Whereas other directors had done their location shots in the outer suburbs of Bangkok, or even in the United States, Stone made his film in a part of the Philippines similar to the jungle he knew in Vietnam. He trained his young actors to live under the same conditions he had endured, suffering heat, rain, insects and the weight of heavy equipment. As a physical evocation of one part of Vietnam, *Platoon* is outstanding. As a commentary on the politics and morality of the war, *Platoon* is at best sententious, at worst abhorrent.

The screenplay, written by Stone himself, gives very much

more than a simple account of men on patrol in the jungle. The platoon at one point enter a village, batter an old man's head in, shoot several people and rape some women. Two men are murdered by fellow American soldiers, and as a result of all the carnage, very few of the whole platoon are alive at the end of the film. In moments of relaxation, over their joints of marijuana, the soldiers indulge in homespun political talk. 'They're poor, they're the unwanted,' says Clive, the Oliver Stone figure, talking about his fellow soldiers, 'yet they're fighting for our society and our freedom.' This maudlin expression of middle-class guilt is echoed by one of the kindly and noble black men in the platoon: 'The poor's always being f—ed around by the rich.' The good sergeant, the one who appeared on the posters as in a crucifixion scene, gives his view of America's place in the world: 'We're going to lose this war. We've been kicking other people's asses so long, I figure it's time we got ours kicked.' The officer, who has understandably lost control of this mob, finally gives up trying: 'I don't give a shit. I don't give a flying f— any more.'

Scenes of violence alternate with expressions of mawkish self-pity, sometimes to the accompaniment of Samuel Barber's *Adagio*. The few survivors embrace, and falter for words to describe the ghastliness of what they have seen, and reflect that from henceforth they will be men apart. The Oliver Stone figure mumbles portentous phrases about the enemy within. None of them seems to have the reserves of fortitude, humour and faith that keep a soldier going in any war; so instead they rely on hashish. In British army parlance, the whole platoon are an absolute shower.

The film is expressly set in 1967, in jungle resembling the Parrot's Beak region near the Cambodian border. The soldiers appear to be wearing the flash of the 25th 'Tropic Lightning' Division in which Stone served. Not having been in the Parrot's Beak and having, I think, only once encountered the 'Tropic Lightning' Division, I cannot comment on the authenticity of *Platoon*. However, from what I saw of other American units in other sectors in 1967, I do suggest that the film is anachronistic. Later on in the 1960s, and still more in the 1970s, much of the

US Army was a drug-crazed, murderous rabble, egged on by Black Power activists and middle-class white radicals. But in 1967, most of the army was made up of regular soldiers and volunteers, who certainly did not think of themselves as 'the poor, the unwanted . . . being f—ed by the rich'. Incidentally, the film lends credence to the belief, first voiced by Martin Luther King, that young blacks in Vietnam 'fight and die in extraordinarily high proportions relative to the rest of the population'. The military historian Guenther Lewy has found that in 1973, blacks of military age represented 13.5 per cent of the total population; the proportion of black army servicemen in Vietnam was never higher than 12.5 per cent. However, Lewy says that blacks formed more than half the population of Long Binh Jail, the military stockade.

Because of its technical brilliance and its excitement, *Platoon* reinforced some other misconceptions about Vietnam. This was not a uniquely horrible war. Most of the men who went to Vietnam saw little or no combat, and certainly not the butchery of civilians, for most of this was carried out from the air or by long-distance artillery. Even those unlucky enough to serve in the jungle – most of Vietnam is open country – did not suffer the misery of the Allied soldiers in Burma and Papua New Guinea during the Second World War, or the British in Malaya in the Emergency. The Americans went on patrol for at most a few days at a stretch; they had ample food and medicine; the wounded were taken away by helicopter. Neither in hardship nor in casualties can Vietnam be compared with either world war.

Oliver Stone's second film on the Vietnam War, *Born on the 4th of July*, is based on the true story of Ron Kovic, a young man paralysed from the waist down by a wound received in action. We first see Kovic, played by Tom Cruise, as a high school student on Long Island with his devoutly Roman Catholic family. Just to remind us that this takes place as long ago as the 1960s, Kovic's mother berates him for reading *Playboy* – 'I want you to go to confession, right away, do you hear?' Young Kovic hears a recruitment address for the Marine Corps – 'Don't forget, a good

Marine is a thinking Marine' – and lectures his friends on the menace of Communism, only ninety miles away in Cuba: 'Our dads got to go to World War Two. This is our chance to do something ... You heard what President Kennedy said, "There's not going to be an America unless there are people prepared to make sacrifices".'

Kovic joins the Marines and has a shocking experience near the Cua Viet River in October 1967. 'Do you see those rifles?' a sergeant yells, pointing towards a village, and some of the squad open fire, but later find they have killed only women and children. 'We didn't do this, did we? Jesus Christ! Mother-f—er! We wasted them!' In another engagement, in January 1968, Kovic is hit in the chest and spine, becoming paralysed from the waist down.

Back in the United States, Kovic's physiotherapist turns out to be a Black Power propagandist. His college friends are sympathetic but nevertheless remind him, 'You bought that Communist bullshit.' His younger brother opposes the war and tells him, 'You served our country and look at you.' His girlfriend is an anti-war protester. But Kovic still believes in what he has done, and turns up in his wheelchair as the star of the local 4th of July celebrations in 1969. The following year, he goes with his girlfriend to an anti-war demonstration but stays outside in his wheelchair. Nevertheless he is bludgeoned by state troopers.

At this point Kovic cracks. He gets drunk and shouts at his mother: 'F— you! It's all a lie. There's no God! God is as dead as my legs! F— you, Mom!' Now full of booze, drugs and self-pity he joins a group of Vietnam cripples in Mexico, where we see him apparently having sex with a local prostitute. He and another wheelchair victim leave town in a taxi but for some reason are dumped on a desolate stretch of highway. There they confront each other, wheelchair to wheelchair, screaming repeatedly at each other 'F— you! F— you!' Towards the end of the film, Kovic goes to the Republican convention in Miami to demonstrate with other cripples against the Vietnam War: 'One, two, three, four, we don't want your f—ing war.' He even makes a speech at an anti-war rally: 'We were tricked into going to fight against a poor, peasant people who have been fighting for their independence for a thousand years.'

My response to this film was at first incredulity, then derision and finally laughter. By trying so hard to exploit our pity, Stone arouses our ridicule instead, especially during the scene of the two men cursing each other in Mexico. Among the cheap and obnoxious tricks of *Born on the 4th of July* is its titillating treatment of sex among the severely wounded. Most young men in combat fear a wound in the genitals almost more than one that removes a limb or causes paralysis to other parts of the body. The tragedy of a wounded soldier unable to have a child by the woman he loves is the theme of Hemingway's novel *The Sun Also Rises*, and it appears in one or two Hollywood films about World War Two, notably *The Best Years of Our Lives*. In those days the subject was treated with delicacy and compassion. However, in the Hollywood of the Permissive Society, when almost every film had scenes of naked simulated sex, directors decided that impotence was not good box-office. In *Coming Home*, one of the first anti-war movies, made in 1973, the wheelchair veteran not only recovers his sexual potency, but is shown romping naked in bed with Jane Fonda, his nurse.

More than any other film I have seen, *Born on the 4th of July* made me think that the United States has become a degenerate nation, spoilt, self-indulgent and wallowing in self-pity. They are all Freud's children now, I reflected. In fact the film's most memorable line sums up Freud's teaching: 'F— you, Mom!'

Of all the films about Vietnam, by far the most powerful is Francis Coppola's *Apocalypse Now*. For me it had a peculiar poignancy since it seems to be based partly on incidents that I had witnessed and written about in my first two books on Vietnam. Moreover the central character of the film and even part of the script is taken from Conrad's immortal *Heart of Darkness*, one of the three stories I took with me on my first journey to South-east Asia, and one that has haunted me all my life. Conrad's tale of a journey up the Congo in search of Kurtz, the philanthropist turned murderer, is a metaphor of the savagery lying below the surface of civilisation. I had written about *Heart of Darkness* in several books about Africa and even in one about England, for Conrad emphasised that 'this also has been one of the dark places of the earth'.

Apocalypse Now opens with the old but arresting juxtaposition of helicopter rotor blades, whacking across the jungle, and the ceiling fan of a room in a dingy Saigon hotel. Here Willard, an officer in a state of nervous exhaustion, is waiting for his disgrace or another assignment. He is called to the Special Forces base at Nha Trang, and ordered to go in search of the Green Beret Colonel Walter E. Kurtz, who has absconded from the US Army and now runs a bloodthirsty private kingdom, across the border in Cambodia. He is ordered to kill, or 'terminate with extreme prejudice', the errant Kurtz.

Instead of taking a helicopter, Willard elects to make a journey up-river, with all the risks entailed of attacks from the shore. Not only does Willard travel by boat, like Conrad's narrator Marlow in *Heart of Darkness*, but he starts at the very mouth of the river, witnessing a US air attack on a fishing village, with helicopters coming in low to the sound of Wagner's *Ride of the Valkyrie*. As cinema, this is stupendous and also introduces the unforgettable gung-ho Colonel Kilgore, whose helicopter carries the motto 'Death from Above'. He urges his men to surf and water-ski during the battle, and when it is over exclaims: 'I love the smell of napalm in the morning.'

The lugubrious Willard sets off up-river on a small naval vessel whose crew are high on alcohol, drugs and rock music. The Chief or skipper, who never appears to leave the wheel, is a serious-minded black who alone imposes some order on anarchy. They pass an island, illuminated at night like the Coconut Island at My Tho, where American girls are doing an entertainment for the troops, as in a Bob Hope show. Further up-river, the boat is attacked from the shore, first by arrows then gunfire, again conforming to Conrad's *Heart of Darkness*. The sailors stop a sampan and during a search of its contents, suddenly open fire on and kill all the occupants, a chilling and all too believable sequence. At last they reach Kurtz's private domain of terror and murder among the ruins of a Cambodian temple. The only other European there is a photo-journalist, closely resembling Tim Page, who seems to be part of Kurtz's savage court. At this point the film rather loses direction; in fact Coppola tried it with two different endings. It mostly consists of Marlon Brando, as Kurtz, reciting some of the ominous parts of *Heart of Darkness*, such as his verdict on the Congolese, 'Exterminate all the brutes!' and his dying words, 'The horror! The horror!'

Some of the incidents in *Apocalypse Now* bear a resemblance to scenes already described in this book. 'Colonel Kurtz' and 'Colonel Kilgore' could have belonged to the Special Forces team on Phu Quoc island who relaxed from their work of massacring peasants by water-skiing among the sampans. The journey up-river on a navy vessel resembles the trip from Danang to Hue described by both Murray Sayle and myself.

Many sequences of *Apocalypse Now* are taken from photographs by Philip Jones Griffiths who provided the illustrations for my second book on Vietnam, as well as producing his own magnificent *Vietnam Inc.* His pictures include the water-skiing on Phu Quoc island. The sequence from the film in which the vainglorious Colonel Kilgore leaves his visiting card on the Vietcong dead is taken from Philip's photograph of an officer doing just that. The scene in *Apocalypse Now* of a roped line of prisoners walking along a sea-shore is copied precisely from one of Philip's photographs. One sequence in the film borrows not only Philip's photograph but his caption. An American officer finds a dying Communist who has fought with a cooking bowl strapped over a stomach wound. On hearing that his South Vietnamese captors refuse to give the wounded man anything more than river water to drink, the American pushes them aside and says: 'Any soldier who can fight three days with his insides hanging out can drink from my canteen any time.' These scenes from *Apocalypse Now* reminded me of Dorothy Parker's quip, when told that Hollywood was under investigation for making films allegedly sympathetic to Communism: 'The only ism that Hollywood understands is plagiarism.'

Apocalypse Now was further proof of the power of Conrad's *Heart of Darkness*, which Orson Welles had also wanted to make into a film. As early as 1925, T. S. Eliot quoted the words 'Mistah Kurtz – he dead', on the title-page of his poem 'The Hollow Men'. The French novelist André Gide was so obsessed by Conrad and in particular *Heart of Darkness* that he made an arduous journey through French Equatorial Africa, afterwards writing *Voyage au Congo* and *Le Retour du Chad*. Another Conradian, Graham Greene, went up the Congo by steamer to write *A Burnt-Out Case*, which if it does not deal with a madman like Kurtz, certainly exercises what Conrad called 'the fascination of the abomination'. More recently V. S. Naipaul went up the Congo to Stanleyville which becomes 'our town' in his masterly novel *A Bend in the River*. One of the characters is like Kurtz at first, an academic who hopes to bring enlightenment to the Congolese; another, like the later Kurtz, is an ivory trader. The steamer is once again attacked from the shore, and the Africans are terrorised not by Belgian slave-drivers but by their own independent government and its beer-swilling mercenaries.

When I first went to the Congo in 1964, I found that the journalists there read *Heart of Darkness* as therapy. 'Ten minutes of it before breakfast and I can face the day,' one of them told me. Even the independent Congo was not as bad as Conrad's description of shackled criminals, rotting hippo meat, and the row of impaled heads outside Kurtz's stockade. The journalists saw Kurtz as the prototype of those well-meaning philanthropists who had put their trust in independence for Africa, and then went mad when they saw the result of their dream. A few years later, when I was writing a history of the exploration and colonisation of French Equatorial Africa, I found that Conrad's Kurtz was not an exaggeration of the rapacity of the white men. To get their quota of rubber, the French officials burnt down villages and chased recalcitrant villagers into the bush, and even attacked them with hand-grenades. Men who refused to carry a thirty-kilo load for fifteen miles of forced porterage were subjected to fines, imprisonment and fifty cuts of a heavy whip. Two French officials, both of them learned anthropologists like Kurtz, were accused of cooking a woman alive in an oven, blowing up people with dynamite and forcing a servant to drink soup boiled from a victim's head.

In *Heart of Darkness*, the narrator Marlow begins his Congo tale to a party of friends on a yacht moored at the mouth of the Thames, where he muses on the resemblance between the two rivers that open up their respective countries. Although England now had a mighty empire and sent her ships to all parts of the world, this had seemed as savage as the Congo to Roman officials, eighteen centuries earlier. Conrad understood a hundred years ago what is only too evident now, that England would not forever remain a rich and imperial nation; her light was 'like a running blaze on a plain, like a flash of lightning in the clouds ... But darkness was here yesterday.'

Although *Heart of Darkness* is magnificent as a metaphor of Africa, or even of England, it fails when applied to South-east Asia. A journey up the Congo passed through the realm of savage men, but a journey up the Mekong led to the ancient civilisations of Angkor and Luang Prabang. Even Colonel Kurtz in *Apocalypse Now* resides in a ruined temple. The Europeans who sailed up the rivers of South-east Asia during the seventeenth, eighteenth and nineteenth centuries were merchants or interlopers rather than men like Conrad's Kurtz, with a philanthropic mission. Conrad described such a Far Eastern adventurer in Lord Jim, a character said to be based on 'Rajah' Brook of Sarawak, in Borneo. But the Malay people who come to regard Jim as their *tuan*, or lord, are not portrayed as savages like the Congolese in *Heart of Darkness*.

The one man who tried to become a Lord Jim or Rajah Brook for French Indo-China ended up as a drunk and opium addict, unable to pay his bill at the Continental Hotel. This was Marie David de Mayréna, who first came to Cochin-China in 1862, as a junior officer in a regiment of the Spahi, or native cavalry corps for French North Africa. Twenty years later, Mayréna returned to Saigon as a freelance journalist, and also went in for gun-running to pay for his opium and absinthe habits. His mistress, Anahia, who claimed to be a princess of the Cham royal house, filled Mayréna's head with stories about the Moi or Montagnard people who lived in the Highlands, hunted tigers with crossbows, and wore decorations of gold. On the strength of Anahia's information, Mayréna wrote an article in *Le Saigonnais* describing the fabulous wealth of this highland region of 'Attopeu'.

The French Governor-General Constans studied the article with interest, for he had heard that the Germans were planning to launch an expedition from Siam (the present Thailand) into this uncharted 'Attopeu', perhaps in the hope of annexing it to their empire. This was the age of the 'Scramble for Africa' and other unclaimed parts of the earth. In 1888, Governor-General Constans asked Mayréna to go to 'Attopeu' to try and set up a French protectorate. Although this was not an official expedition, Mayréna was to be paid expenses and given the promise that in the event of success he would hold the concession to all the mines of 'Attopeu' as well as 'the honour of calling himself the Chief of the Moi Confederation'. The word *moi*, meaning foreigner or barbarian, was used by the Vietnamese to describe the Montagnards.

Mayréna and one of his drinking companions planned to begin their expedition from Qui Nhon, on the coast, where they would also take command of a party of native troops. At this point Anahia, the self-styled Cham princess, was forced to admit she was really a Vietnamese and had no intention of risking her life among the savages of the interior. However, the Frenchmen went on without her, and thanks to the help of a Christian missionary, met some of the Montagnard chieftains, who were ready to sign a treaty giving protection from the Siamese.

Since there was no gold or any other source of wealth in 'Attopeu', Mayréna returned from his expedition with nothing but a worthless treaty. However, at the end of 1888, the manager of the Continental Hotel, Saigon, a Monsieur Laval, was roused from his siesta by an excited porter who said that a European, dressed in a scarlet uniform and describing himself as the King of the Sedangs, was downstairs with his courtiers, demanding accommodation. Laval arrived to find that the king was the well-known charlatan Mayréna, but nevertheless gave him a suite, and credit at the bar. The end of the story is told by the hotel's recent proprietor Philippe Franchini, in his delightful memoir *Continental Saigon*:

> Alas, when, several days later, Mayréna moved out of the hotel, nothing was left to Laval as payment for his services, except for a decoration, that of the National Order of the Kingdom of the Sedangs, which the king gave him before departure ... Without knowing it, this very dubious prince had inaugurated at the Continental a tradition that was to continue up to the final day: that of unpaid bills.

Mayréna later became involved with a Swedish woman spy in Bangkok, was thrown out of French Indo-China and committed suicide in Singapore by injecting himself with curare.

8

Thailand, Vietnam and the Missing in Action: 1988

It was in 1985 that the film *Rambo: First Blood Part II* introduced the rest of the world to America's mounting obsession with 'MIA', the Missing in Action thought to be held in captivity in Indo-China. Ten years after the end of the Vietnam War, the film's muscle-bound hero, played by Sylvester Stallone, is freed from the prison where he is held by an ungrateful government, and offered a pardon if he will go back to the jungle of Indo-China and photograph the Americans said to be held in a secret camp. Rambo locates the camp, and contrary to his orders frees one of the prisoners. His superiors then abort the mission, leaving him to what they believe is certain death; the trip had been undertaken to try to prove to the US public that there were no MIA. Rambo is captured by the Vietnamese and tortured by them and their Soviet mentors, but he escapes, massacres hundreds of Communists and brings out many Americans in a hijacked helicopter. Back in Thailand, Rambo confronts the duplicitous colonel who sent him on this mission, and tries to convey in words and grimaces that he and his buddies could have won the Vietnam War if they had not been betrayed by their own cowardly government. The film earned more than $100 million in the United States alone, and broke box-office records in Thailand and Communist China, where hatred of Vietnam amounts to a national frenzy.

By the late 1980s, belief that more than 2,000 MIA were held in Indo-China was not confined to Hollywood and the sensational press. It was shared by the great majority of the US public, by politicians like Ronald Reagan and military men like General William Westmoreland, the former Commander-in-Chief in Vietnam. The MIA obsession was both a cause and effect of America's failure to come to terms with the Vietnam experience. It reinforced the stereotype of the Vietnamese as a race of satanic cruelty, and it fuelled desire for revenge. As Rambo himself asked, sardonically, at the start of his mission: 'Do we get to win this time?' The MIA issue became the principal obstacle to a peace agreement and normal relations between the United States and Vietnam; it reinforced the hard-line Communists in the Hanoi politburo; it undermined efforts to end the war in Cambodia. Nixon and Kissinger in their retirement were now the most powerful men in the China Lobby, the voice of the Beijing Communists urging the United States to take a tough line against the Hanoi Communists. Thus had the Domino Theory come full circle.

About eighty per cent of the 2,273 MIA were fliers, shot down in bombing raids over North Vietnam or on secret missions to Laos, where the CIA used to run an army of tribespeople, financed by opium. Since the United States never declared war on North Vietnam, and Laos was a supposedly neutral country, captured Americans there had only a dubious claim to be POWs, under the rules of the Geneva Convention. This was especially true of Laos, where most American fliers wore civilian clothes. In the land battles fought in South Vietnam, both the Communists and the Americans normally shot their prisoners. As the Communist Vietnamese repeatedly pointed out, they themselves had 300,000 men listed as MIA.

A National League of Families of the Prisoners and Missing in South-east Asia was founded in 1966 in San Diego, California, a naval base and the home of many pilots flying from aircraft carriers. As more men were captured, the League moved to Washington, DC, where it became a channel of anti-Communist propaganda, making much of the fact that the North Vietnamese had failed to provide a list of the prisoners whom they were torturing in the 'Hanoi Hilton'. The League became a lobby for President Nixon's policy of withdrawing from Vietnam in exchange for American prisoners. At the Paris Peace Accord of January 1973, the United States in effect agreed that in return for the prisoners, the North could retain all the territory captured in South Vietnam. For the sake of getting back 750 servicemen, none of whom where genuine POWs, the Americans betrayed the Saigon government they had once resolved to defend.

So eager was Nixon to clinch this deal, that he wrote a private letter to Hanoi pledging a post-war reconstruction grant of $3.25 billion 'without any political consideration'. Soon afterwards, Nixon fell from power over the Watergate scandal, whereupon the United States felt free to renege on the promises made to its North Vietnamese foe, as to its South Vietnamese friend. Nixon and his successors gained no political benefit from this shabby business. The relatives of the nearly 750 POWs freed in the summer of 1973 dropped out of the National League of Families. The relatives of the MIA understandably did not want to accept that their menfolk were dead, as the US government now suggested, and so began to allege a Washington cover-up.

The search for the MIA began in earnest in 1978, when the American Department of Defense published fifteen volumes of intelligence documents called the 'Uncorrelated Information Relating to Missing Airmen in South-east Asia'. Each of these 700-page documents contains declassified reports of men taken prisoner and seen in captivity during and shortly after the war. They contain interrogation reports of defecting Communist soldiers, captured documents, serial photographs and information from spies. The British author Nigel Cawthorne writes in *The Bamboo Cage: The Full Story of the American Servicemen Still Held Hostage in South-east Asia* (London, 1991) that the documents show:

> Prisoners were moving around a lot, so it is not possible simply to

add up the numbers held at different places. Estimates can be wildly off, informants may be lying. But 200 here, 400 there and 600 at the other place in North Vietnam, and twenty here, forty there, sixty at the other place in South Vietnam do add up – even if they are all inflated by a factor of four.

Yet even if all the 2,273 men listed as MIA were taken alive and held for a time during the 1960s and early 1970s, we still do not know how many of them, if any, were alive in 1973, the time of the Paris Peace Accord. The bomber crews captured in North Vietnam were kept as bargaining counters and used for propaganda purposes, since several cracked under torture and made statements denouncing the war. Apart from the bomber crews, captured Americans served no purpose. It is safe to assume that most American servicemen captured in South Vietnam were soon afterwards shot, or later died of disease and privation. The one man I had known who later survived some years of captivity in the bush was Mike Benge, a civilian working near Ban Me Thuot, who was also exceptionally fit and accustomed to living rough in the countryside. The same reservations apply to reports of the MIA coming from Boat People and other refugees from Indo-China during the late 1970s. Many claimed to have seen captive Americans, while one, a Laotian, may have mentioned the names of two listed MIA. More often the scent ran cold. One refugee claimed to have copied the names of forty-nine Americans held in Saigon itself, but had lost the list when his boat was attacked by pirates. Some refugees probably thought that having seen an MIA would help them to get to America.

Interest in the MIA was revived in 1979 when Hanoi released a US Marine, Bobby Garwood, captured as long ago as 1965. Because he had learned Vietnamese and was given considerable freedom to move around, Garwood was viewed with suspicion by other American prisoners. He was discharged from the service and put under pressure not to discuss his years in captivity. Then journalists such as Monika Jensen-Stevenson and her husband William H. Stevenson, the authors of *Kiss the Boys Goodbye: How the United States Betrayed Its Own POWs in Vietnam* (London, 1991), interviewed Garwood and heard his claim of having seen US prisoners long after the 1973 'Operation Homecoming'. However, Garwood comes across as a weird if not untrustworthy witness.

Another person contributing to belief in the MIA was Jerry Mooney, an airman who had worked for twenty years as an analyst for the National Security Agency, the outfit responsible for codes, ciphers and communications intelligence. During the Vietnam War, Mooney was a master sergeant with NSA headquarters at Fort Meade, Maryland, analysing radio traffic and other electronic intelligence from South-east Asia. He retired in 1977 and went to pack shelves at a supermarket in Wolf Point, Montana. Then, in 1985, Mooney saw a television report on a pilot said to have died in an air crash in Laos. Remembering from his NSA work that the pilot and several others survived the crash, Mooney resolved to disclose some of the other evidence on the fate of the MIA. Intercepts of Communist Vietnamese radio messages do indeed show that some of the MIA survived a crash and were taken prisoners. They do not reveal what happened afterwards. Nigel Cawthorne is one of those who paid attention to Mooney's speculation:

> Mooney believes they [certain MIA] were given Vietnamese citizenship, tried as common criminals under Vietnamese law and held in inner compounds of civilian jails ... Mooney believes Armstrong would have been used as slave labour on the Ho Chi Minh Trail ... Money believes Hopper was probably killed during capture. There is slight hope that he had special knowledge which was revealed under interrogation – that is torture – and was sent into the Soviet Union.

The Stevensons in *Kiss the Boys Goodbye* call Mooney 'an artist at distilling intelligence ... Working from a small village in Vietnam, he could transcribe precise information via satellite to a US army unit anywhere in the world within sixty seconds.' Yet according to Cawthorne, Mooney had not worked from a small village in Vietnam but from Fort Meade.

Whatever his later flights of fancy, Mooney had known what was happening on the ground in Indo-China. Some of the other people cited in these books on the MIA are grotesque or sinister. There is Mooney's old colleague Charlie O. Stout, who, according to Cawthorne, 'opened the wrong mail one day and read that total abandonment of the remaining POWs was now the official policy. "Jerry, we've given up on them, we will never get them home," he told Mooney. He became withdrawn, paranoid and began to sit in a tree and get drunk a lot . . .' An IRA gun-runner, Sean O'Toolis, went to Vietnam in 1980 and claimed to have met an Irish American working in a gun factory. He spoke to him and then passed him a note in Gaelic. The Stevensons bring as a witness the legendary Victor Louis, a Soviet KGB agent and journalist, and a mine of misinformation in both roles. One man interviewed by Monika Jensen-Stevenson was 'the free-booting CIA agent Ed Wilson, who was later jailed for selling plastic explosives to Muammar Qudaffi'. The greater the public concern over the MIA, the less information or even rumour arrived at the body dealing with them, the Defense Intelligence Agency. According to Cawthorne: 'After the mass exodus from Indo-China in the late 1970s, reports have slowed to a trickle. Of the ninety-one unresolved live sighting reports the DIA were working on in 1986, only twelve came from the period 1982–85 and none had been received that year – 1986 – at all.'

The feebler the evidence that the MIA were alive, the more the United States believed it. The seizure of American hostages by Iran in 1979 encouraged the fear and suspicion that Vietnam was doing the same thing. The election the following year of Ronald Reagan as President of the United States gave new heart to those who believed in the justice of the Vietnam War, and found in the MIA an explanation of why things went wrong. During the 1980s, growing belief that the MIA were alive led to positive action to find them. A group of former intelligence officers, backed by private financiers and right-wing Congressmen, mounted an expedition to Laos in 1980 to check reports of a clandestine prison camp. The men who went on the mission claimed to have photographed 'Caucasians', but later the negatives were destroyed and one of the group died in mysterious circumstances in Bangkok. This was the germ of the film *Rambo: First Blood Part II*. One privately financed group, the American Defense Institute, offered a $2.4 million reward to any Laotian, Khmer or Vietnamese who came out with a live MIA; twenty-one Congressmen were among those pledging $100,000 or more. Leaflets advertising the offer were put into plastic bags with parcels of dollars and floated across the River Mekong to Laos.

In 1988, when I was writing a travel book about Thailand, a magazine commissioned an article on the MIA searchers, then streaming into Bangkok. An American journalist directed me to the bar in the Patpong Road that was much frequented by Vietnam veterans, fantasising over the past; but I could not take them seriously. On the advice of the journalist, I went to Nakhon Phanom, in north-east Thailand, from where some Americans recently crossed the River Mekong to rescue the MIA they believed were on the other bank. They were arrested and spent some time in jail at Thakkek, the town across the Mekong. This was the stretch of the river where Peter Kemp, with his Free French allies, conducted a naval war against the Vietnamese Communists in 1945, after his friend Lieutenant Klotz was murdered at Thakkek, while an American OSS officer looked on without protest. Now, by a curious twist of fate, American intelligence officers were trying to get to Thakkek to rescue their fellow countrymen from the Vietnamese Communists.

Those who believed that the MIA were alive came to Nakhon Phanom because there you could clearly see the 'Bamboo Curtain' dividing Thailand from Communist Indo-China. At dawn I sat on a bench by the river and watched the first pale yellow and rose of the skyline clearing the mist over the forests and knobbly foothills of the Annamite Chain. The boom of temple gongs and the metal twangling of loudspeaker music sounded from over the river. When the sun got up, wooden canoes with outboard motors

The Missing in Action: 1988

started to cross from the other shore, heading upstream to allow for the pull of the current. When the Laotians got to the Thai side they climbed up the steps from the jetty and greeted the customs and immigration, but there was no formal inspection. It was common knowledge along the Mekong that during the hours of darkness, trade flourished over the river, with rafts of cars and lorries crossing from Thailand, with timber and maybe opium going the other way. They are the same people on either side of the river. Vietnamese smugglers took millions of US cigarettes from Thailand to Laos and then into Communist China, to purchase bicycles, beer and apples to sell to the North Vietnamese, in exchange for rice. For years there had been continual coming and going between the Thais and the people of Communist Indo-China, yet nobody claimed to have seen or heard of American MIA. Why the Vietnamese would have wanted to hold American hostages, not only in Laos, but in a border town of Laos, was not a question that worried these American Scarlet Pimpernels.

Returning from Nakhon Phanom and other Mekong towns, I went to a Bangkok bookshop to sample some of the MIA fiction, now popular in the United States. Although the two thrillers I read were good of their kind and even exciting, they made me think that America could not come to terms with the Vietnam experience. The title of the first of these, *Thai Horse*, by William Diehl, refers to the heroin (horse) made from poppies grown in the Golden Triangle, where Thailand marches with Laos and Burma. A report has reached Washington that a US pilot, Murph Cody, listed as MIA in the 1960s, has fled with other Americans from a jungle prison and is now engaged in the drug traffic in Bangkok, smuggling heroin packed in the bodies of freshly killed babies. The embarrassment to the United States of Cody's reappearance would be all the worse since his father was once commander of US forces in Vietnam.

An evil intelligence officer, Sloan, picks Christian Hatcher to find Murph Cody, a classmate at the Annapolis Naval Academy. Like Rambo and most of the heroes of MIA fiction, Hatcher has fallen foul of the US establishment and lives partly outside the law. He was a cold-blooded assassin during the Vietnam War, then an art thief, and he has spent the last three years in a Central American dungeon, framed by Sloan. Hatcher is sprung from his tropical Alcatraz and flown to South-east Asia. In Hong Kong he becomes engaged in a feud with Triad gangsters, then goes off by boat up a tropical river in Communist China, fighting off pirates and searching for information about the vanished Cody. This episode not only brings in the theme of *Heart of Darkness* but offers an apt quotation from Conrad: 'Some men go skimming over the years of existence to sink gently into a placid grave, ignorant of life to the last, without ever having been made to see all it contains of perfidy, of violence and of terror.'

In *Thai Horse*, no one sinks gently into a placid grave, nor misses out on the terrors of life. Hatcher shoots, knifes or blows up much of the population of Hong Kong and Bangkok, and never despairs of finding the MIA, whatever the scoffers say. He ignores the Dutchman up-river in China who tells him: 'All you Yankees tink your friends are alive over dere.' He ignores the jibes of Sloan. 'This is MIA shit, Hatch ... I'll tell you what I don't think ... I don't think there's twenty-four hundred missing Americans doing time in Hanoi; or up there teaching the Vietnamese to play monopoly or any other damn thing. Maybe a few turncoats. The rest of them were probably tortured to death or shot or died of malnutrition or disease. These are the ones who weren't killed on the spot.' But Hatcher is right. His friend Murph Cody was seen as late as June 1974 in a moving Vietcong camp 'about twelve clicks south of Muang on the Laotian side of the Annamitique mountains'. Cody and his companions later escaped from the camp in Laos, went down-river through South Vietnam and made their way to Bangkok, where they now spend their time in a bar on the Patpong Road, subverting the heroin trade and behaving as good Americans. The evil Sloan dies in the mayhem that follows the blowing up of a junk on a Bangkok canal.

The other thriller I bought in Bangkok was Mike McQuay's *The MIA Ransom*, published in 1986. The impoverished Vietnamese Communists have assembled 2,045 MIA, held for as long as twenty years, and offer to free them for one million dollars a head, in gold. If the ransom is not paid in a week, the men will be put on trial and executed. The Americans include air force pilots, army men and a number of AWOLs, deserters, who chose to stay in Vietnam rather than go home to America and a court martial. The sinister Communist Colonel Tin welcomes 'our guests at Camp Friendship', near the former American Embassy in Saigon, then invites them to make appeals for their freedom in front of the cameras of French television. Villainous Frenchmen are part of the stock-in-trade of American popular fiction about Vietnam. The plight of the hostages splits public opinion in the United States. The 'MIA wives' want to pay off the ransom to get back their men; the university students whose parents opposed the war are now right-wingers who want to 'take out' Saigon with B-52 raids. The hawkish American government shows old TV films of Vietcong atrocities, in order to put over the message that 'Vietnamese duplicity and treachery is a horror to a culture as refined as ours – they live as jungle animals, understanding and respecting nothing save strength greater than their own'. The author McQuay presents both sides of the argument, although he appears to agree with the MIA wives that their men were betrayed by successive American governments breaking the terms of the Paris Peace Accord and refusing compensation to Vietnam. Even the torturer Colonel Tin is shown as a man of principle: 'The reason we kept our people for so many years was the fact that we hated to take blood money. We wanted to get on our feet our own way. But the Russians . . . Anyway I use this gold to buy a future for my people.' The US President in *The MIA Rescue* sends a fleet to Vietnam, while the CIA look for a man to open the arms caches around Saigon and give the hostages guns for a break-out.

The man they choose is Cassady: 'The CIA had bailed him out of a jail in Bien Hoa around Christmas of '67. He had wasted several civilians during a bar fight. When they took him out he thought they were arresting him for fragging some candy-assed second lieutenant the week before. Instead they told him they were aware of the incident but had heard he was a good point man (the leading man in a squad) and they had a job for him if he wanted it ... to sneak into heavily guarded VC strongholds and to assassinate tax collectors and other public figures, usually dismembering the bodies somehow to let them know who was responsible.'

The CIA hire Cassady, then take him off the assignment when they find he has 'wasted' a Soviet spy without permission. Cassady leaves on his own for South-east Asia, 'wastes' a CIA agent in Bangkok, then charters a helicopter to Vietnam: 'The way his blood pounded, Vietnam was yesterday. He thought of Kim, her naked body twitching on top of the sheets, the overhead fan beating like the chopper props. Everything had been larger than life, every second an eternity of living ... In the jungle he had learned to walk like the Vietnamese, learned to make a Vietnamese shadow.' By the time Cassady finds Kim, he has spent seventy-two hours without sleep, travelled across the globe, committed two murders and dismantled most of the Vietnamese fleet in the Saigon River. Next morning he murders Kim and another CIA man and then frees the American hostages, who escape down the river to safety. The United States walks tall again.

The flight from reality and the national self-delusion demonstrated by *Thai Horse* and *The MIA Ransom* disturbed me all the more since I read both books during a visit to Saigon in December 1988. Indeed my hotel room overlooked that stretch of the Saigon River where Cassady sabotages the Vietnamese Navy and brings the MIA to safety. The real Vietnam was so far removed from the MIA fantasies that I came to see America as a country gone mad. The obsession with treachery and betrayal, the racial hatred of Vietnamese, above all the longing for revenge – 'Do we get to win this time?' – recalled how Hitler came to power by inflaming German resentment after the First World War. The flight from reality of those who once had supported the war and now took comfort in dreams of revenge was no less dangerous than the delusion of those, like Barbara Tuchman and Oliver Stone, who believed that the war had been pointless and wicked. The folly of both the American 'hawks' and 'doves' was nowhere more evident that in Vietnam itself, where the Communists and their opponents had come to terms with the war and now thought only about the future.

After my last visit to Vietnam in 1980, when I had made up my mind that I would not go back till the country was given at least a tolerable government, I had to rely on the report of others. Friends like Gavin Young, who went back in 1985 for the tenth anniversary of the fall of Saigon, reported that it was still overwhelmingly harsh and depressing. Then in 1986, as the Soviet Union started to buzz with talk about *glasnost* and *perestroika*, an even more dramatic change occurred in the Hanoi politburo. A Southerner, Nguyen Van Linh, who had been disgraced in 1975 because he opposed the collectivisation of land and the nationalisation of industry, was appointed General Secretary of the Communist Party. Even before introducing the *Doi Moi* reforms, a local from of *perestroika*, Linh brought a new spirit of tolerance to the country, freeing many political prisoners, curbing the power of the secret police, and welcoming the return of the Overseas Vietnamese, or Viet Kieu, many of whom were former Boat People. He also opened the country to foreign businessmen, tourists and journalists. Reading about this, and hearing reports from recent visitors, I got the impression that Vietnam was becoming less like Cuba or Czechoslovakia, and more like Poland or even Yugoslavia. By 1988, when I was doing research for a book on Thailand, I found myself longing to get back to the neighbouring country I had not seen for eight years.

One day in Bangkok in December 1988, I chanced to hear that the Vietnamese were trying to gather a press party to cover their forthcoming troop withdrawal from Cambodia. Hanoi believed that the government it had established in Phnom Penh (described as puppets by the Khmer Rouge) was strong enough to resist the three rebel armies based in Thailand; moreover Hanoi hoped that this first withdrawal of troops would lead to an international settlement and the end of the war in Cambodia. The Vietnamese Embassy gave me a visa and sold me a ticket for next day's Air

Vietnam flight to Saigon; although I told them I represented the *Spectator*, the last of the weeklies that I had written for, in fact I had no commissions for articles. I simply longed to be back in Saigon.

At Bangkok airport, the journalists on the trip to Cambodia were making each other's flesh creep with stories about the Air Vietnam plane that crashed here a few weeks earlier, killing all on board. According to Jon Swain, fuel was very much cheaper in Thailand than in Vietnam, so the plane had departed Hanoi with only enough in the tank to get to its destination. Because of a storm over Bangkok, arriving planes were instructed to cruise around for a while and the Vietnamese aircraft simply ran out of fuel. My confidence in 'Air Death', as Jon jocosely called it, did not increase on boarding the Soviet four-propeller plane, with signs in Russian and Spanish but no ventilation or air-conditioning. During our long wait on the tarmac, the cabin became like one of those metal punishment boxes used by the Khmer Rouge.

When we took off I started to chat with some of the Overseas Vietnamese, or Viet Kieu, going home on business or holiday, armed with their foreign passports and money. One of them, Nguyen, who held a Canadian passport and worked in Hong Kong as a trade consultant, insisted on talking about himself as a Vietnamese:

> Eighty per cent of our trade is with Japan. They invest here in our seafood processing and our wood industry. There's a very good factory that makes flooring from rubber trees. When the tree has run out of sap it's turned into flooring. It's so good that you have to wait your turn to buy it. We can't get any yet, we have to wait in line. Taiwan does a lot of trade with us unofficially. Our economies are complementary. They have technology, we have raw materials and cheap labour.

Nguyen said that business dealings were easier for the actual foreigners than for the Viet Kieu, who might have to wait a long time for payment. However, like other Viet Kieu I was to meet,

Nguyen was both patriotic and critical of the United States government:

> The Americans should help Vietnam instead of helping our enemies, like the Khmer Rouge. Your Prime Minister Mrs Thatcher is the only Western politician who understands. She has said she will not support any government in Cambodia in which the Khmer Rouge have any part at all ... The Vietnamese really want to get out of Cambodia but we're afraid of China there. The Chinese really want to take over all Asia. Besides Red China, there's Singapore, Hong Kong and Taiwan. There are two million Chinese in Vietnam and even more in Thailand. I don't think it's right that there should be no other culture than Chinese ... I feel really happy when I come back to Vietnam. We Vietnamese can never really live abroad. I think there is great hope for Vietnam. We are a hard-working people, very serious, look at the US and Canada. The Vietnamese do very well there, not just as businessmen but as doctors, lawyers, accountants. And I think many of the Overseas Vietnamese would like to go back if things got better. We Vietnamese are very attached to our country, to the land itself.

Across the aisle of the plane was a young, very tall and probably part-European Vietnamese with hair in a pony-tail in the hippy style of the 1960s, and wearing a trendy rip in the knee of his jeans. He lived in Los Angeles and said that this was his third visit to Vietnam already that year, partly on holiday, partly on business. I suspect it was only on holiday, for during the next ten days in Saigon I met him several times with a lovely but never the same woman. Saigon was corrupt, this Californian said. The whores now assembled in a street near the old Cercle Sportif, doing their business in public after dark. The police were said to ignore them, and when the authorities put in street lights, these were immediately smashed. Everything was corrupt. You had to bribe to get electricity or a phone installed, or even to use the lift in a hospital. This last claim was confirmed to me by a British doctor I met who had gone to Vietnam to study the health system.

He also said that the main Saigon hospital had a special floor for the treatment of Party officials, the *nomenklatura*.

The Californian Vietnamese was shocked by the meagreness and the lack of national character in the luncheon boxes offered by Air Vietnam. This was the first but by no means the last time I witnessed Viet Kieu loudly and ostentatiously criticising the old country. As we taxied along the runway at Tan Son Nhut airport I noticed that there were no civil aircraft and not even the wrecks of military planes I saw in 1980. Out loud I remarked: 'It's strange to recall that this was once the busiest airport in the world, after Chicago.' I meant it was busy because of the war but the Californian misunderstood me. 'Yes, it really makes me mad,' he exclaimed, 'because at that time, 1975, we were really doing well. We were far in advance of Thailand. Now we're way behind.' He measured advance by the number of planes in the airport.

Having arrived with the journalists bound for Cambodia, I was taken straight from the airport to an official military briefing in the old town hall. On a podium at the end of the conference room, a general sat at a desk in front of a bust of Ho Chi Minh. Some forty foreign journalists were grilling him on the troop withdrawals, an American in particular implying that these were really replacements: 'General, if you withdraw 5,000 troops from Battambang Province, does that mean that the Vietnamese troops will be 5,000 fewer in number?' Although I suspect that the general understood English, he waited for the interpreter's translation before giving his answer.

As the questions failed to provoke the general, I brooded on earlier press briefings in Vietnam. The American Granger, in Greene's *The Quiet American*, set in the early 1950s, had baited the French: 'Is the Colonel seriously telling us that he's had the time to count the enemy dead and not his own?' In the JUSPAO conferences in the 1960s, the journalists pestered the US officers with questions about the 'hot pursuit' and incursions into Cambodia. Now once again in 1988, a young American journalist, Granger's grandson perhaps, was asking the Vietnamese Communist: 'General, there were reports in Bangkok of shelling along the border between Cambodia and Thailand. Were the Vietnamese involved in any way in this shelling?' It was the same old question of 'hot pursuit' of guerrillas into neutral territory, and the general waited for his interpreter before he phrased his careful reply: 'As you are well aware, the Vietnamese have withdrawn to thirty kilometres from the Thai border. You are also aware that we have not brought into Cambodia any 175 artillery [with a range of thirty kilometres].' This 'as you are well aware' was the Vietnamese equivalent of the American 'no comment', and meant the same thing, that the general was lying. I felt a tap on my shoulder and turned to see a grinning Jon Swain. 'It's the five o'clock follies!' he whispered.

Although amused by the irony of their altered situation, I sympathised with the Vietnamese over their struggle in Cambodia. It had never been true to say that the Khmer Rouge and the Vietnamese Communists were brothers and sisters under the skin. The Vietnamese could be cruel but they were not mass murderers or fanatics; I doubted if they were even serious Marxists any longer. The Khmer Rouge were monsters, plain and simple. Hanoi had launched an offensive early in 1989, only after the Khmer Rouge had massacred tens of thousands of ethnic Vietnamese and driven the rest into exile. During the past ten years of war in Cambodia, the Vietnamese Army had lost 55,000 men, or almost exactly the same number as the American dead in Vietnam. In Cambodia, the principal cause of death and wounds were landmines, of which there were said to be three million planted, most of them made of plastic and therefore hard to detect. These loathsome devices had become the favourite weapons of left-wing guerrillas from Mozambique to El Salvador, where they were nick-named 'limb-removers'. The Cambodian war had more than anything wrecked Vietnam's economy and hopes of revival. A Vietnamese diplomat explained this cost in homely terms: one artillery shell cost the same as the annual income of eight Vietnamese families. Most important of all, the war in Cambodia was one of the pretexts used by the United States for persisting in its hostility to Vietnam.

Whatever my views on Cambodia, I did not intend to join the hundred journalists going there for the troop withdrawal. This was a news story, and I did not work for a newspaper. Besides I wanted to spend the whole ten days in Saigon. So when the rest of the press party left next morning, taking my passport with them to Phnom Penh, I jumped ship. As I expected, this brought me a reprimand from the press representative of the Hanoi Foreign Office, a highly intelligent man named Nguyen Quang Di, whose face seemed to me oddly familiar. I told him the half truth that I had hoped to write on Cambodia for the *Spectator*, but had later heard they were running an article on the subject by William Shawcross. After a ticking-off, Nguyen Quang Di allowed me to stay in Saigon; he could hardly have expelled me without a passport.

After this first unpleasantness, Nguyen Quang Di turned out to be very amusing company, full of mischievous stories about the other foreign journalists, especially their alcoholic, narcotic and erotic habits. I dread to think what he had on me. He was quite impressed that I was a friend and one-time collaborator of Philip Jones Griffiths, a frequent visitor to the country under the Hanoi regime. After a few beers that evening, Nguyen Quang Di happened to mention that one of his first jobs as a fledgling diplomat had been to accompany Prince Sihanouk from Hanoi down the Ho Chi Minh Trail to join the Khmer guerrillas in 1973, at the height of the civil war. This return to his country was testimony to the Prince's courage but not his political wisdom, for many Cambodians thought it endorsed the Khmer Rouge. Like all Vietnamese of whatever political leanings, Nguyen Quang Di regarded Sihanouk with some exasperation, but with respect for his acumen and sheer durability. After the war, Di went to study at Canberra University, and when he was asked to choose a subject for his doctoral thesis, 'I chose the only subject I knew about, Prince Norodom Sihanouk.'

When I ventured to ask about his later career, Nguyen Quang Di told me that after his trip to Cambodia in 1973, he was sent to Saigon as the Hanoi representative to the PRG, or Southern

Communist, delegation at Tan Son Nhut airport, under the terms of the Paris Peace Accord. It was then that I suddenly realised why he had seemed familiar. Nguyen Quang Di was the young man sitting beside me during a press briefing who brought out a book to relieve the boredom and later exchanged some whispered conversation. For some reason, I did not remind Di of how he had studied patriotic poems as I was reading *Right Ho, Jeeves*. However, I said I had been at one of those Saturday briefings, and how bored I was by the list of 'ceasefire violations' and 'land-grabbing operations'. Nguyen Quan Di groaned at the memory: 'If you thought it was boring once, can you imagine what it was like for me having to sit through it each week?'

My stay in Saigon in 1988 was as pleasurable as my previous stay in 1980 had been depressing. Even though most people were still living in penury, the shops and the market stalls were crammed with every kind of food and drink, imported as well as locally made clothes, pharmaceutical goods, electronic gadgets, musical tapes and stereos. Only in Yugoslavia and in Shanghai had I seen another Communist city in which there was no shortage, queuing, black market or currency control. There were bicycles in abundance and almost as many scooters as in wartime Saigon, for petrol was cheap thanks to off-shore oil. The passers-by in the street looked better dressed, better fed and above all much happier than they did eight years earlier.

On my first evening, taking a stroll up Tu Do Street, I stopped at Brodard's café, near to the old Royale Hotel which had now changed again into a modish dress shop. In the old days, Brodard's was a haunt of francophone, anti-American intellectuals who drank black coffee and muttered derogatory things about 'Anglo-Saxons'. This time Brodard's was full of tipsy and laughing revellers. 'Come and join us,' someone called out in English, making room at a table with another man and two women. He was disappointed at first to hear I was British and not American but after a moment he rose to his feet, insisted that everyone do the same, then lifted his glass in a toast to Margaret Thatcher and, as an afterthought, Gorbachev. He and his friends ordered more Saigon beer, which is stronger but no less vile than when it was known as '33', and I replied with a toast to Vietnam. When I tried out my theory that Vietnamese people were never happy in emigration, the man who spoke English roared his agreement and then translated what I had said to the whole café. There were shouts of approval, clapping and one of the waiters came up and shook my hand and said, 'Whenever you speak, I listen.' It was all very flattering.

My new friends at Brodard's were uninhibited, not just by Vietnamese but by any standards. The man who spoke English started to tell me about his family on the coast: 'My wife believes in the revolution, all that shit. Sometimes I feel like killing myself because I can't support my five children. I can't go home. I hate my father-in-law and I feel ashamed of myself that I haven't got any money. I used to be rich and a playboy. This is my girlfriend.' He indicated a flashily dressed woman who 'used to be a singer before she was fired'. I asked what his wife as a Party member thought of his having a girlfriend. 'She's a Communist,' was his answer, 'but she's also a Vietnamese woman and she accepts that I have to have a number two wife or even a number three.' He introduced the other man, a plump, laughing chap with a sultry girlfriend: 'This my friend escaped from the North by boat as a child in 1954, and now his woman friend is the wife of a major in MI, you know Military Intelligence. Now she's living with my friend.'

The next morning, a Sunday, I got up at six to go to Mass at the red-brick cathedral at the top of Tu Do Street, and found it packed with four or five hundred people attending an earlier service. When they streamed out, another four or five hundred took their place. Although women predominated, the men took part in the service rather than hanging around outside, smoking and chatting, as happens in Ireland or Italy. The mood in the church was severe. A little girl in the pew in front kept turning to stare at me but looked away when I caught her eye. The peace consisted of one brief nod to the person beside you, without the embarrassing smiles, handshakes or even kisses you get in the West. When the collection bag went round, I noticed that scarcely anyone put in money, not even the valueless small-denomination notes. This struck me as sensible. The Church in rich countries like Germany and the United States should subsidise countries like Vietnam.

There was a mural over the altar of Saigon Cathedral showing a field of golden rice, green trees, an expanse of blue sky and above it the clouds on which were arrayed the shining army of saints, angels and martyrs, wearing traditional Vietnamese costume. The Catholics here have good reason to see themselves as martyrs comparable with the Christians under the Roman Empire. When the Communists took the North in 1954, nearly a million Catholics sailed to the South as refugees under a safe conduct obtained by foreign politicians such as Senator John F. Kennedy. When the Communists took the South in 1975, they once more persecuted the Church, so that even in 1988 there were many priests and two bishops in prison. However, the Roman Catholics of Saigon did not suffer their persecution meekly. On Sunday evenings, starting at six or seven, a concourse of scooter or bicycle riders, all of them honking their horns, paraded from Le Loi Street, down Tu Do to the embankment road, then right up Nguyen Hue, constantly honking their horns for hours on end. The young of Saigon had not yet coined their slogans but this was nonetheless a political demonstration, as the authorities knew and admitted. It was not a revolt of the starving masses, for most of the riders, with younger brothers and sisters sitting behind, were wealthy enough to afford a scooter and petrol. It was not a carnival, for the demonstrators looked solemn, even grim. In 1988, these demonstrations were only beginning, and yet I had the impression that the former victims of persecution, such as the Roman Catholics, were confident and unafraid.

One of the pleasantest features of Saigon in 1988 was the number of small shops selling things that I really wanted to buy.

For those who have neither the money nor taste for luxury brand name products, silk or sharkskin clothes and above all gold and jewellery, cities like Bangkok and Hong Kong are dull and dispiriting. So was Saigon when the main shopping attractions were lacquer work, glossy silk screens and china elephants. Now Tu Do and the neighbouring streets of the French quarter were stocked with artefacts from the homes of the Saigon bourgeoisie, especially opium pipes, 1920s rings, clocks, amulets, paper knives, money chests, candlesticks and the like. There were also some very attractive modern cotton goods, such as table-cloths, napkins and handkerchiefs, similar to the sort I had seen and admired in Communist China. I especially liked the many second-hand bookshops, also selling English and French translations of Vietnamese classics. At a shop near the old Royale Hotel I found for the first time an English translation of *Kim Van Kieu*, the epic tale of a woman who sacrifices her honour to save the family; and then, at the saleslady's suggestions, I bought a selection of works by the eighteenth-century poetess Ho Xuan Hong, now claimed by some as a proto-feminist. According to the translators, Ho had twice been married but each time as a junior wife, with all the humiliation that involved:

> To share a husband with another . . . what a life!
> The one sleeps under the covers, well snugged in, the other
>   freezes.
> By chance he comes across you in the dark, once or twice a
>   month . . . Nothing.
> You hang on hoping to get your share but the rice is poor and
>   underdone.
> You work like a drudge, save that you get no pay.
> Ah, had I known it would be like this,
> Willingly would I have stayed alone just as I was before.

Ho Xuan Hong's verse was erotic, and although most of the *double entendre* is lost in translation, the reader soon grasps the symbolic meaning attached to physical objects such as a fan, a swing or a feature of the landscape, for instance 'The Mountain Pass of Ba Doi':

> A gap, a pass and still another pass,
> Praise to the sculptor of this land of sweet suspense!
> At last the gate opens, crimson with a crested crown,
> A little rock hides there, dark under the moss.
> The pine branch shivers with the coming of the storm,
> Like pearls shines the dew on the leaves of the drenched willow.
> Wise men, people of great virtue . . . no one turns away,
> No one so finished, broken knees, feet collapsed, they still are
>   keen to climb.

One morning, when I was browsing in a bookshop in Le Loi Street, I was approached by a nervous man in his forties who wanted to practise his English. As a former officer in the army of South Vietnam, he was one of the new poor, and earned the family rice by teaching English and selling lottery tickets. The teacher suggested we go to a bookshop in Nguyen Thiep, just next to the one where I bought the poems of Ho Xuan Hong. As we walked he told me about the misery of life under Communism, a story I heard for the first time in Yugoslavia in the early 1950s, then in the other countries of Eastern Europe, in China, Cuba and latterly Nicaragua: 'I am desperate about money. You need it for everything. If you're sick, you have to pay at the hospital. There's no free health service. I work for my children, not for myself. I don't want them to grow up thieves, hooligans or beggars. There's so much crime now. Young people will kill for a bicycle. They hurry to get nowhere.'

As so often in Communist countries, I wanted to give this man some money but knew that he would not accept a direct offer. The problem was solved as soon as we entered the bookshop in Nguyen Thiep Street; perhaps he had planned it that way, for at once he went up to a couple of books on teaching English, clapping his hands with excitement and pleasure. It reminded me of one of my sons, then aged three or four, spying a red, double-decker bus in a toyshop window, and cooing with ecstatic pleasure. Of course I had bought the bus as I now bought the language primers. The teacher, now in a state of frenzy, asked as well for a world geography book, and money for blackboard and chalk, the whole thing costing less than a round of drinks in London. I felt ashamed for the teacher in his poverty, and ashamed of myself for so cheaply buying his gratitude. Added to this was the feeling that I had first expressed in print in April 1975, that we in the West had sold out the South Vietnamese.

After buying the books, we went for tea and lemonade to the café next door to meet a friend of the teacher, an older man who described himself as 'the barefoot civil servant'. In fact he was wearing those flip-flop sandals that the Australians call thongs. 'But what does it matter,' he said with regard to his footwear, 'I often walk through the paddy fields up to my knees in water, so I don't need shoes.' He worked near Can Tho in the Mekong Delta, interpreting for the crews of foreign ships that came upriver. 'We have to take a government job for four or five dollars a month, as well as a job to live on, otherwise they'd suspect us,' he told me. After 1975, he had done seven years in prison as a 'suspected CIA', apparently a general charge covering any previous contact with the Americans. Like so many Vietnamese, the barefoot civil servant was hoping to get to the United States. Before the fall of Saigon he had been legally adopted by an American civilian, a device to ensure his right of entry to the United States and eventual citizenship. He had not succeeded in escaping in 1975 and his 'father' had since died, but he was hopeful of getting permission to travel soon.

The barefoot civil servant understandably did not like the present regime but said that the peasants down in the Mekong Delta were better off than the Saigonese: 'They have to pay 35 per cent of their earnings to the state, and they sell rice to the state, but they own their land, and can sell ducks and pigs and chickens at a good price.' When I asked how people lived in the North he replied: 'They're poor but they're Party, so they eat chicken and smoke Triple Nickel ["555" cigarettes].' The teacher and the barefoot civil servant thought there were only two good politicians in the world, Margaret Thatcher and Gorbachev.

It was easy to see why men like these, who had served the old Saigon government, were hostile towards Hanoi. It was harder to understand the disillusionment of the former Southern Communists, the Vietcong who had fought so stubbornly against the Saigon regime and the Americans. Only now that a Southerner, Nguyen Van Linh, was General Secretary of the Party, had some of these Vietcong come in from the cold. Towards the end of this visit in 1988, I got a chance to meet one of these veteran Southern Communists, Tran Bach Dang, the head of the Saigon Party from 1965 to 1975, a period that included the Tet and May offensives as well as the fall of Saigon. Yet from 1975 until recently, Tran Bach Dang had been in disgrace. Steve Erlanger of the *New York Times* had arranged an interview and kindly allowed me to join in, along with the Foreign Office interpreter.

Dang lived in a good French mansion in Phan Le Binh Street, next to the former residence of the US Deputy Ambassador. He had stayed in the villa during the war when he was not living underground in one of the tunnels near Cu Chi. He entertained us in a gazebo in his garden among the trees, shrubs and vases. A cat was stalking about in pursuit of lizards, and at one point a small boy came up and put his arms round his grandpa's neck, with love and veneration. Dang has a fine aristocratic head, scarred but not deformed by wounds and the torture he suffered from the French. His family had been Chinese Mandarins and, like so many an English upper-class socialist, Dang was both an egalitarian and a bit of a snob. This was how he recounted his life story:

> I was born on 15 July 1926 in Rach Gia Kang, which I left in 1930 for Bien Hoa. I was educated there. At the age of fifteen, I came to Saigon and worked in a blacksmith's. In the evenings I learned French. I joined the Communist Party at the age of nineteen. I was born to a distinguished family, high-ranking Mandarins in the Hue Dynasty. My great-great-grandfather was in the

second of five ranks in the kingdom. He was Governor of South Central Vietnam. Another ancestor, Trinh Hoai Duc, was a famous author who wrote a classic novel on South Central Vietnam. He was head of a delegation to China. Another ancestor, Truong Gia Hoi, was deputy commander in a battle against the French in which Henri Rinel was killed. My grandfather did not become a Mandarin, in protest against the French presence. The younger brother of this grandfather used to recruit young people to study in Japan. This attitude of the Mandarin feudal intellectuals had an influence on me. They wrote in old Vietnamese characters.

My father had a brother-in-law who was a Marxist follower. He introduced me to the Communist Party. I became a member of the Party in 1945. On the night of 24–25 August 1945, we started an uprising of one million people and took over the Saigon Town Hall till 23 September. This was before General Gracey [the British commander] arrived. We tried to have negotiations with the British but this failed, so we started shooting. The day I entered the Town Hall was the proudest of my life.

I was the leader of a district in Cholon. We fought for a while in the city and then went south to a country area. My military group became a regiment . . . I was political commissar and later became a colonel. There were others of a similar background. In my regiment there were men from the Chu Quan power station, wide boys, robbers, pickpockets. The head of the regiment was covered in tattoos, a gang chief, but he could shoot better than I could. There was a Frenchman in my regiment, the armsmaster, and two Japanese.

Tran Bach Dang did not speak about his imprisonment and torture by the French, nor about the later struggle against the Diem regime, although he said that the day they took the decision to fight again, in 1960, was the 'second happiest' in his life. I wanted to hear of the shifts in his ideology and attitudes. How had he viewed such events as Khrushchev's denunciation of Stalin, the uprising in Hungary in 1956 and the crushing of Czechoslovakia twelve years later?

Tran Bach Dang replied that at the time the South Vietnamese

Communists took no interest in such events because they were too busy fighting their own war. When I asked about the differences between China and the Soviet Union, he at first answered the question in military terms. The experience of the Soviet Red Army in fighting the Germans bore no relevance to the war they were fighting in Vietnam. The Chinese sent military advisers but nobody paid them any attention. Then Tran Bach Dang described his impressions of China in 1969 when he had made a circuitous trip from Saigon to Hanoi to attend Ho Chi Minh's funeral:

> I went via Phnom Penh and Shanghai by Air France. The Cultural Revolution was at its height. My first impression of Shanghai was of a very sad city. Everywhere there were red flags and slogans in praise of Mao. In Canton I saw heads hanging from trees, the heads of victims of the Cultural Revolution. Unusual. On my way back from Hanoi to Saigon, I went through Hunan Province but I refused to see the home of Mao Zedong. I refused an invitation to Beijing. I could not stand all the noise. My not going to Beijing was intended to show that I disapproved of the Cultural Revolution and Mao's *Little Red Book*.

Having spoken of China, Tran Bach Dang went on to discuss his differences with the politburo after the liberation of Saigon in 1975: 'The ones who favoured a free system in South Vietnam were myself and the present General Secretary, Nguyen Van Linh. We were called revisionists but they could not hurt us. Comrade Linh and I had one advantage. We used to fight in this land so no crude measures could be taken against us. We persisted in our point of view. Comrade Linh and I were against industrial transformation and land collectivisation.' But are not these two things the basis of Marxist-Leninist teaching? I asked. Dang did not reply, so I asked him whether today's Vietnam was the kind of society he had hoped to create when he joined the Party in 1945. He replied:

> We were too naive. Life has proved to be very much more compli-

cated. We got our Marxist-Leninist theory from Stalin and Mao Zedong. It was simplified to a very great extent. Stalin said that only language has no class aspect. But we know that many human emotions have nothing to do with class: love, sexual relations, jealousy have no class aspect. Fortunately we had as our leader Ho Chi Minh, who had a very good understanding of human nature.'

When I asked him which of the world's Communist countries now had the best political system, Tran answered without hesitation: 'Hungary. They are going in the right direction, especially in agriculture.' This was only a few months before Hungary threw off the Communist system altogether. Although Tran did not enter Linh's government until the following year, 1989, it was clear that his views accorded with Hanoi's policy. Only a fortnight beforehand, hundreds of Mekong Delta peasants had marched on Saigon to protest against the theft of land by Party officials, whereupon General Secretary Linh flew down from Hanoi and reinstated the protesters, afterwards sacking hundreds of Party men. The quantity of food in the Saigon market proved that the farmers had an incentive to work. The abundance of ships on the Saigon River proved that Vietnam was once more busily trading, especially with Taiwan, Hong Kong, Singapore and Japan. Indeed I heard complaints that too much of the country's rice, chicken and ducks was going to Japan. An elderly Scot I met who represented a Singapore shipping company told me that as in Conrad's time, the Chinese were expert smugglers: 'They come here with trashy hi-fi and transistors, and come out with fine hardwood, teak and rosewood . . . They're expert at raping the country, these coastal Chinese.' He subscribed to the popular theory that Vietnam was going the way of Communist China, with Beijing and Hanoi stuck in a rigid, bureaucratic socialism, while Saigon, like Canton and Shanghai, reverted to capitalism. This was how it seemed in December 1988.

Just as in Europe at that time there were wiseacres who warned that *glasnost* and *perestroika* were tricks to deceive the West (as the Wooden Horse deceived the Trojans), so there were Far East hands who warned that *Doi Moi* was a feint in Vietnam's plan for the Soviet conquest of South-east Asia. Yet it was clear in 1988 that Vietnam no longer looked for aid and support to the Soviet Union. One evening at the Majestic Hotel a self-important European strode to the bar and asked in Vietnamese for a bottle of Russian Stolichnaya vodka. When this was handed to him, he took a suspicious look at the seal, opened the cap, sniffed, then started to scold the barman. 'Not okay?' I enquired. 'Not okay!' he confirmed, then stalked out of the café. The sheepish barman attempted to laugh this off and said that the man was a Soviet diplomat. 'The vodka's all right,' he went on to tell me, 'you were drinking it last night yourself.' 'Not out of that bottle,' I pointed out. He asked me to smell the vodka and then poured a measure for me to try. It tasted like turpentine. In a way I was glad to find that the Vietnamese retained their skill in manufacturing moonshine liquor, first absinthe for the colonial French, then Scotch and Bourbon for the Americans, now vodka for the Russians. A Viet Kieu told me that when he haggled over a bottle of genuine whisky, the market woman had offered him 50 cents rebate if he returned the bottle with label intact.

Although Gorbachev was popular both among anti-Communists and reformers within the Party, the Soviet Union as such had few friends left in Vietnam. The Saigonese habitually called the Russians 'Americans without dollars', or in the wartime slang 'cheap Charlies'. A Viet Kieu indicated a group in the hotel lobby: 'Look at them sitting with one bottle of beer between three people, eating the pickled cucumber they brought with them on the plane.' I heard but could not confirm that the Russians and other East Europeans tried to sell to the Vietnamese their inferior watches, clothes, and even the cutlery pinched from the airline. The Vietnamese had at first made souvenirs aimed at the Russian tourists. For instance among the paintings done on strips of bamboo, I noticed beside the 'Mona Lisa' a hideous reproduction of N. A. Yaroschenko's 'Portrait of an Unknown Woman'. This painting appears on the Penguin *Anna Karenina* and greatly annoyed me all the time I was reading the book because it is so unlike the Anna that Tolstoy describes and I imagine.

Even the Vietnamese Communists spoke coolly about the Soviet Union. An interpreter who had studied at Moscow University said she disliked the Russian crèche system 'which is depriving mothers and grandmothers of great happiness in looking after children'. (She would disapprove more strongly still of the treatment of mothers and grandmothers in Western Europe.) Vietnam's major grievance against the Soviet Union and other socialist countries in Europe concerned the exploitation of more than 200,000 Vietnamese migrant workers. Ten days before I arrived in Saigon, in December 1988, the Vietnamese army newspaper *Quan Doi Nhan Dan* claimed that these workers were poorly paid and still worse treated: 'We should reach agreement with these countries . . . not to send our labourers to dangerous places, such as contaminated areas, deep underground mines, or areas where the harsh weather conditions exceed the physical endurance of Vietnamese, and not to assign our labourers to work with their convicts under a system of forced labour.' Two years later an article in the same newspaper made explicit the accusation that Vietnamese had been sent to the site of the Chernobyl nuclear plant disaster.

This public attack on the Soviet Union strengthened me in believing that Communism was on its way out. The economy of the South was reverting fast to a market system. The population of South Vietnam, including most of the former Communists, was openly hostile to rule from Hanoi. The Soviet Union, the only major ally of Vietnam, was cutting supplies to the satellite states of Cuba, Afghanistan, Ethiopia and Angola, and seemed ready to ditch its former empire in Eastern Europe. China, the one major Communist state in Asia, loathed Vietnam and was backing the Khmer Rouge.

It seemed to me in 1988, and seems to me still, that the major obstacle to the liberation of Vietnam was the government of the United States. Unforgivingness and desire for revenge had forced Vietnam into a corner, and strengthened the hand of the diehard

Communists. Rather than giving encouragement to the reforming Communists, as they had done in Poland, Hungary and the Soviet Union, the Americans maintained an economic embargo, refused to have diplomatic relations, and even supported the murderous Khmer Rouge. The only justification for this spitefulness and folly was the supposed existence of some two thousand Missing in Action. The foreign policy of this once great nation was now under the guidance of Rambo.

9

From Hanoi to Saigon: 1990

During my visit in 1988 I came to believe that Vietnam might be the first country anywhere in the world to turn its back on Communism, sooner even than Poland or Hungary. The general public, at any rate in the South, was overwhelmingly hostile to Communism; the Party itself paid only lip service to Marxism; most important of all, the Soviet Union was too far away to suppress rebellion, as it had done in Hungary in 1956 and in Czechoslovakia twelve years later. However, during the fateful year of 1989, when the United States was backing Gorbachev in the Soviet Union and anti-Communist movements in other countries of Eastern Europe, it failed to support the reformists in Vietnam. On the contrary, by taking an ever tougher line on the MIA issue, President Reagan actively helped the Hanoi diehards to cling to their power and privileges. The suppression of the democracy movement in Beijing in May 1989 was only a minor set-back to the reformists in Hanoi. In Vietnam, as in China, the absence of parliamentary opposition did not impede the rapid liberalisation of economic and social life in the country. There were many who thought that in South-east Asia, greater freedom and better government did not depend on having a multi-party democracy in the Western style.

During that *annus mirabilis* of 1989, I spent some time in Thailand writing a travel book but I could not get a commission to go to Vietnam. Then in December I was approached by the *Independent* Magazine, which had printed my article on the MIA and sent me twice to Yugoslavia, another country near to my heart. The magazine had bought a set of photographs by a Frenchman depicting a journey by train from Hanoi to Saigon. Would I write the story to go with the pictures? The gloom of the past year's disappointment suddenly changed to sunlight.

In all the years of obsession with Vietnam, I had never had the occasion or even the wish to visit the North, a place I always imagined as drab, dour and infested with ideologues. Apart from Poland and Yugoslavia, where people were free to speak their minds, I had always hated going to Communist countries, and North Vietnam sounded one of the dreariest. Even into the 1980s, most of the Western visitors to Hanoi appeared to be either Marxist sympathisers or liberals, guilty about the Vietnam War. My latest impressions of North Vietnam had come from a curious, pro-Communist thriller, *The Last Man out of Saigon*, by a British Labour MP, Chris Mullin. The villain of Mullin's book, who later becomes its hero, is a CIA man masquerading as a journalist, MacShane, who flies to Saigon in April 1975 to set up a network of anti-Communist agents. He is arrested, thanks to the carelessness of the CIA, and in revenge betrays all his former colleagues. His captors not surprisingly treat him well and allow him to keep the copy of Noam Chomsky's *At War With Asia*, given him by his liberal girlfriend. As part of his re-education, MacShane is sent to work in a communal farm near Haiphong, the port of North Vietnam. Digging ditches, we learn, is 'not as demanding as it at first appeared', and the young farm women and children befriend MacShane and share with him their meals of rice and vegetables. After lunch, he takes 'a refreshing dip' in one of the fish-ponds, apparently not having discovered that these are also latrines. At this idyllic labour camp, MacShane falls in love with the local teacher, Miss Ha, and consummates the relationship on the floor of a disused Roman Catholic church. Small wonder that MacShane feels sad when he has to leave

Communist Vietnam, clutching his copy of Noam Chomsky, in which Miss Ha has inscribed: 'The human being is ever green.'

Perhaps because I was thinking of Chris Mullin's book, I was not in a cheerful mood when I got off the plan at Hanoi on a cold, wet February afternoon. During the long drive from the airport into town, I became still more depressed by the bleakness of the landscape and of the dull brick communal farms and factories. Nor did I see here the evidence of American bombing that later would change my feelings about the North. Although the Americans bombed the outskirts of Hanoi, including the principal railway station, they spared the city centre except during the Christmas raids of 1972. Even then the accuracy of the bomb-aiming devices meant that few civilians were killed when compared with Dresden or Tokyo in the Second World War.

If the Americans had spared Hanoi, so too had its Communist rulers. Far from decrying the French colonial architecture, the North Vietnamese admired and preserved it. I am told that the Hanoi newspapers often denounced Prime Minister Lee Kuan Yew of Singapore because he had replaced memorials of the British past with garish skyscrapers and shopping centres. Whereas Mao Zedong in China, and Kim Il Sung in North Korea had wanted to wipe out history, Ho Chi Minh and his followers treasured it. It is true that the mausoleum of Ho Chi Minh, with its goose-stepping sentries, brought to mind similar eye-sores in Beijing, Bucharest and East Berlin, but Ho himself had not ordered this monument. Nor did he have the usual vices of a dictator, such as a morbid fear of plots against him.

The Thong Nhat Hotel, where I stayed, was built by the French in 1907, and flourished till 1954 under the name of the Metropole. Unlike the Continental and the Majestic in Saigon, the Thong Nhat had declined both physically and in the morale of its staff. Designed with tall ceilings and tiled floors to mitigate the heat of summer, the rooms were bitterly cold at night in winter, especially for those with only tropical clothes. The journalists who were almost the only Western visitors dined at a seedy but cheerful café in a side-street, the Piano Bar, serving exquisite frogs, snails and similar Franco-Vietnamese delicacies. When I was there with Steve Erlanger of the *New York Times*, another American journalist and a rather mysterious Washington politician, the conversation kept coming back to the same baffling questions. Why did America support *perestroika* in the Soviet Union but not *Doi Moi* in Vietnam? Why did America back the hard-line Communists of Beijing against the reforming Communists of Hanoi? Why did America seem to condone the murderous Khmer Rouge? The answers to all three questions seemed to lie in the wounded pride and vindictiveness of Kissinger and Nixon; and in the belief that the MIA were alive.

After a few days in Hanoi I started to feel its melancholy charm. There were students everywhere, cycling through the drizzle over slippery streets, or strolling beside the lakes that feature in Hanoi poetry. In the little park behind the Thong Nhat Hotel, the spooning couples embraced under the trees in darkness, because they had no privacy in their homes. It reminded me of my own days as a student in Belgrade, where the housing problem forced young people to make love in parks, cemeteries, even in the sentry boxes behind the parliament building. I realised that I was now in danger of giving in to Commu-nostalgia, a hankering for the austere but strangely pure and romantic life of Eastern Europe during the fifties and sixties, for gipsy taverns in Sarajevo, for talk of Dostoevsky in the Bristol Hotel in Warsaw, for a village dance in Hungary, and for Prague in the spring of 1968.

Although charmed by Hanoi, I was nevertheless eager to start on the train journey south to Saigon. On the plane coming over from London to Bangkok, I read a report in one of the Sunday magazines by a journalist who had made the inaugural journey on one of Vietnam Railways' two luxury coaches, equipped with blue nylon curtains, a shower, a private kitchen and well-stocked bar, attended by beautiful train hostesses in *ao dai* and pantaloons. The writer added a sombre description of what it was like to ride in the other carriages, for the Vietnamese: 'It had to be the world's worst and poorest train, unlit, unheated, filthy and decrepit... passengers squatted on the floor with the children, belongings and livestock. The carriages gave off rancid smells of sweat and effluent . . .' Little did I realise that I would travel from Hanoi to Saigon, not in one of the carriages with the train hostesses and blue nylon curtains, but in 'the world's worst and poorest train'.

The day before I was due to leave, I met some officials of Vietnam Railways, elderly men in homburg hats who had started life fighting the French and later ran the railway under American air bombardment. In 1976 they got the system going again with Soviet diesels light enough to venture over the bomb-damaged bridges. The Saigon regime had left some equipment but there were no spare parts because of the US economic embargo. The most senior man in a homburg hat accepted my $90 fare from Hanoi to Saigon, then explained rather sheepishly that the first leg of the journey would be in 'normal' class and accommodation. However, if I came to the station at nine next morning, an hour before the time of departure, he could show me one of the luxury coaches on which I had hoped to travel. I did not take him up on this offer.

Next morning I left for the railway station with Duong Quang Thang, an intelligent and amusing Foreign Office guide, and Nick and Suzanne, a young English journalist couple I met on the plane from Bangkok. We got to the station with barely time for a cup of tea before boarding the train at its ultimate carriage. It was nothing like as frightful as what we would later endure. Right at the start of its southward journey, the train had been cleaned and the multitude of passengers were also new to their clothes. We were given the use of a six-couchette staff cabin, shared with the two 'captains' who took it in turns to command the train. Tatami mats eased the hardness of wooden boards, and so we were very well off compared with the people crammed into the other cabins, the freight and baggage compartments and even the passage between the carriages. The lavatory, consisting of two footrests on which to squat, had not yet been fouled, while gentlemen could relieve themselves through the open door at the end of the train that also served as an observation car.

One of the captains welcomed us and said we would reach the

city of Hue at seven next morning, an estimate that was only six hours out. A railway policeman, in red-collared uniform, warned us to keep the shutters closed at night because at a certain stage of the journey 'children sometimes throw stones'. He also warned us that on occasions these heavy shutters fell like a guillotine on people foolish enough to stick their heads through the window. Both warnings were later proved justified. We had brought a supply of bread, cheese, bananas, oranges, mineral water, vodka and one carton of cigarettes, which I had vaguely intended to hand out as goodwill offerings to our fellow passengers. After a look at the train I decided to start smoking again myself, and later I wished I had something stronger and more deadening to the senses than mere tobacco. Our guide Thang, who perhaps had a better idea than we of what the journey held in store, was also smoking heavily. Our spirits rose when a woman attendant brought in a meal of rice, chicken and pork with three or four bottles of Chinese beer, which is stronger and tastier than the local brew. Indeed I later heard that the ever ingenious Vietnamese had taken to selling the dreadful Hanoi beer in Chinese bottles.

When I asked Thang how Vietnam came to import beer from China although the two countries were still on such hostile terms, I heard an interesting lesson in economics. The trade with China was part of the new reforms, or *Doi Moi*, the Vietnamese form of *perestroika*. When the northern part of the country won independence from France in 1954, the Communists brought in collective farms, along with the usual murder, torture, and persecution of landlords, great and small. Although admitting to 'errors', the Party maintained the collective system till 1988, when peasants were given permission to sell most of their rice and others goods in the open market. To the amazement only of Marxist theorists, Vietnam changed in one year from a rice-importing and undernourished country, into the largest exporter of rice after Thailand and the United States. One million tons, mostly from South Vietnam, were exported overseas. Another half-million tons were unofficially sent overland from North Vietnam to Communist China, in return for such things as textiles, bicycles, beer and apples, a fruit the Vietnamese adore.

For hour after hour we clanked through the great chessboard of rice fields which is the Red River Delta. There was nothing to relieve the monotony and the bleakness of this region, so unlike the Mekong Delta of South Vietnam. The collective farms had been built in brick rather than mud and bamboo, and I saw only a few groves of coconut palm or fruit trees. Where were the pigs, chickens and ducks that abound in the Mekong Delta? Perhaps they would come with privatisation. Eventually we got to the Roman Catholic region that features in the beginning of *The Quiet American*. The sight of a gutted church brought home more starkly than ever the grossness of the American bombing. There are said to be twenty-two million bomb craters in Vietnam but almost all that you notice are in the North, where the US Air Force concentrated on roads, railways, bridges and economic targets, near what were called the 'population centroids', and sometimes on the towns themselves.

This railway, which runs for most of its course just next to the main road, Highway One, was singled out as a target. For mile after mile, the train passes a neat row of craters, frequent as telegraph poles. The fields alongside look like a huge golf course, covered in bunkers. The years of bombardment smashed every town and village along the track, including the city of Vinh. High-explosive bombs were supplemented by hideous anti-personnel weapons such as napalm and *fléchettes*. Like millions of people during the 1960s and 1970s, I thought the bombing was both a crime and a folly. How big a crime I did not till now understand. Even today, in this century that has seen the destruction by bombing of so many once great cities, the mind is numbed at the thought of the devastation unleashed on North Vietnam.

As darkness approached, we realised that there was no light in the cabin, but one of the captains before retiring to rest attached a bulb to two pieces of wire. Our spirits rose again and we brought out the vodka. Some of us even fought our way to the lavatory over the prostrate bodies and through the hammocks slung all along the corridor, as well as in the cabins and luggage compartments. Then we stretched out on pallets and tried to sleep. We stopped for about five hours at Vinh, because of mechanical failure we heard, and when the train started again it seldom attained a speed of more than twenty miles per hour. When it did so, the board on which I was lying bounced like a trampoline; but the motion was not unpleasant.

When I got up at dawn, I found we were getting close to the former Demilitarised Zone on the 17th parallel. This stretch of the coast is sandy and salt, so that only a few cattle were grazing among the recently planted tamarisk, pine and eucalyptus. Soon after crossing into the old South Vietnam, at Dong Ha, a place I remembered from 1966, the first stone slammed heavily into our carriage – *clang* – and looking out I saw the scowling face of the youth who had thrown it. An hour or so later we crossed the Ben Hai river and came to Quang Tri and the start of the Street Without Joy, or Highway of Horrors, down which I had passed with a television crew in 1974. We were told that the fusillades of stones and occasionally bullets that greet the 'Reunification Train' in southern Vietnam are at their fiercest here in the Street Without Joy. The inhabitants of this dismal salt-flat appear to hate the Communist North Vietnamese as bitterly as they hated the French and the Americans. Their attitude is that of the East End ruffians shown in an old *Punch* cartoon:

Who's 'im, Bill?
A stranger!
'Eave 'arf a brick at 'im.

The present regime is detested as much because it is northern as because it is Communist. The inhabitants of the Street Without Joy regard the Tonkinese rather as English border people regard the Scots.

Since the shutters had to be firmly closed against the assault by stones, the only way to get a look at the view was to stand at the back of the train where a passenger had slung his hammock across the open doorway. He slept on unperturbed by the danger of falling onto the track or getting hit by a stone. However, it seemed that this was the safest part of the train, because by the time it went by, the hostile forces had nothing left to hurl but abuse. It occurred to me that this was the first time anywhere in the world that I had seen people greet a train with hatred rather than waves and smiles. Looking out of the back of the train, I thought I could discern some of the tourist attractions I saw from the bus in 1974, such as the ruined basilica and the burnt-out tanks. It was a time to brood on all the battles fought here. Almost forty years had passed since Bernard Fall witnessed a French amphibious landing; twenty-three years since Fall himself was killed here; fifteen years since the Northerners struck once more down the Highway of Horrors, capturing Hue and then all the South.

At Hue station, our party of four were the only passengers to alight. The twenty or thirty embarking passengers would have to fight for room on what had been from Hanoi a jam-packed train. Gradually I was coming to understand that the Reunification Train was really a one-way service, taking Northerners to Saigon and back. It was scarcely used by Southerners at all.

The melancholy from which I had always suffered in Hue took hold of me once again on this visit. After the apprehension and suffering of the war years, most of the Hue people I knew were killed, imprisoned or driven abroad. The matriarch who said in 1975 that she would poison herself if the Communists won had failed to keep her vow and survived to see most of her family sent to the Vietnamese gulag. The woman who acted as my guide to Hue when making a television film in 1974 was abroad with her husband in the following year, when the city fell to the Communists, but her father-in-law was among those murdered. On the first evening in Hue I went to the old Cercle Sportif, which had been my headquarters on every previous visit. It was now a Labour Club, or to be more precise a video club; that evening they showed a rubbishy Kung Fu drama from Hong Kong, and a documentary on cycle racing. The hearty director said they had dances on certain nights of the week, 'It's a mini-disco, with tango, cha-cha-cha and slow'; he pronounced it *slough*.

The director of the former Cercle Sportif said that they still had tennis and swimming but no more billiards. He uttered the word with disapproval. Did Communists disapprove of billiards? The question had worried me since I heard a story about a Soviet television crew who were making a film on the life of Lenin, and tracked down an old woman in Zurich, who said she had been his landlady during the First World War. After extolling his virtues as a lodger, his cleanliness, sobriety and punctual payment of rent – all of which went down well with the television crew – the old lady said that Lenin's only hobby was billiards. The director was aghast. Lenin did not play billiards. The old lady persisted, then all of a sudden changed her mind: 'You're quite right. My memory's failing me. It wasn't Herr Lenin who played billiards. It was Herr Mussolini.'

The Huong Giang Hotel was quite unchanged from 1974 – I even remembered the bullet-hole by the staircase – but now in the lobby the staff had to hear a weekly lecture on Marxism, a chore to which they submitted with every sign of irritation and boredom. Even though Hue was said to have the most Stalinist Communist Party in South Vietnam, the populace did not conceal their enmity to the system. On the bank of the Perfume River, I came across a group of university students doing arms drill as part of their military training. Taking me for a Russian, they yelled out not 'hello!' but 'goodbye!' and just to make sure I had got the message, they added '*dosvidanya*!' Hue has always been xenophobic; not without reason. It was a hotbed of rebellion against the Chinese occupation. As Vietnam's capital in the nineteenth century, Hue led the resistance to French encroachment, and it was here that one of the Catholic missionaries met his death on the scaffold. When the French finally conquered Hue in 1885, they indulged in an orgy of killing and looting, worse in its way than the British sack of Peking in 1860. They burned the Vietnamese imperial library, with its ancient scrolls and manuscripts, and stole from the Palace everything down to the toothpicks and mosquito nets.

Back in 1968, I had taken a boat from Danang to Hue because it was dangerous on the mountain road; indeed my friend Sanlaville had lost two fingers in an ambush there. Now in 1990, our little party abandoned the train for a car in order to get a better view of the most spectacular sights in the country. At the start of the drive, while still in the outer suburbs of Hue, we stopped to see a Buddhist funeral cortège making its way to the temple. Because these people were not accustomed to Europeans and did not take us for Russians, they treated us with an amiable curiosity, the women admiring and touching Suzanne's fair skin, the boys tugging the hair on my forearms. It occurred to me that a whole generation had passed since the people of South Vietnam were used to the sight of hairy foreigners. Down at the coast at low tide, we came upon women searching for shellfish in the sand, who gave us a friendly welcome, and then on a group of girls carrying bundles of kale to spread on the rice fields. They asked if we in our country used green fertiliser. They could not have been more friendly.

At Lang Co there is one of the most magnificent beaches in the world, so I was not surprised to hear that the Club Mediterranee wanted to set up premises there. After all Vietnam has suffered, it surely deserves to be spared the international tourist trade that has wrecked so much of the coast of Thailand. There are even worse threats to the beauty of nature, as we discovered, climbing into the mountains round giddying, hairpin bends that must have been even more frightening in the days when they might conceal an ambush. A sign by the roadside warned of the danger of deforestation, but it had clearly come too late. Some of the mountains were already bald, or clipped to a stubble of tree stumps and weeds. Other mountains were only partly shorn of their forest cover, suggesting one of those Mohican haircuts. The felling of trees for sale to Japan and other industrialised countries did more damage to Vietnam's rain forest than all America's bombing and chemical defoliation. Everywhere in the country, I saw logs taken down to the coast by lorry and barge; on the road between Hue and Danang I saw the depressing consequence in these bare mountains. Already Vietnam was starting to suffer the ecological penalty of deforestation. Rain was irregular and, when it arrived in force, leached the top-soil from the now treeless hillsides. There were reports in 1990 that villages in the region of Dien Bien Phu, the scene of the French defeat in 1954, were flooded up to a depth of fifteen feet.

Except for Thailand, which had imposed though not entirely observed a ban on logging, deforestation was rampant throughout Indo-China. So many trees had gone in Laos that often the Mekong ran red with eroded top-soil; most of the felled timber came down by truck to Danang, where Laos maintained its own separate port. The Vietnamese-backed government of Cambodia was selling off timber to pay for armaments, as were the Khmer Rouge and the other resistance groups. Over in Burma, the Rangoon government had given concessions for teak and other magnificent hardwoods to Thai logging companies, the revenue going for weapons to fight the Karen rebels. The timber traffic was now more lucrative than the heroin traffic in South-east Asia and far more dangerous in its long-term result. At this rate the Mekong valley would soon be as dry as the Indus valley in Pakistan, which also once was a rain forest.

We arrived in Danang only a few weeks before the twenty-fifth anniversary of the landing by the United States Marines, an event that most Americans now regard as a prelude to disaster. The people of Danang, however, now looked on the United States with love and veneration. I noticed this first in its obverse form of hatred for all things Soviet. When I had come to Vietnam in 1980, people were too afraid to show any open hostility to the regime. In cosmopolitan Saigon, when I went there in 1988, people no longer assumed that all Europeans were Communists, and therefore objects of hatred. In Hue I had heard only the sarcasm of students. It was in Danang that I underwent for the first time the persecution by children that I had heard of from other journalists. Back in the 1960s, the Danang urchins would shout 'Hey you!' 'Number One!' or 'Okay Salem!' hoping to cadge a cigarette of that brand, but they were no more hostile than were we English children during the Second World War, asking the GIs: 'Got any gum, chum?' The Danang children, who started to yell at me '*Lien Xo*', or 'Soviet', were hostile to the point of menace, particularly when dozens joined in the chant and doggedly followed me down the street. An American photographer told me that once when he stayed at a town in the Mekong Delta, hundreds of children waited each morning outside his hotel to give him the '*Lien Xo*' treatment when he emerged. Occasionally this mobbing turns into violent assault. The same photographer and his official guide were eventually run out of town, in fear for their safety. Never during the war had I felt so hated as by these Danang children who thought I was Russian.

To get away from the children I entered the Danang Museum. Perhaps because the mobbing had unnerved me, I did not enjoy the Cham sculpture as much as during my last visit in 1973. I was standing in front of the Goddess Tara when two giggly girls of twenty or so approached and asked me where I was from. My answer both pleased and disappointed them. They were pleased that I did not come from a Communist country but disappointed that I was not an American. 'We all love America so much. East Germany and Czechoslovakia are very bad.' I tried to explain to them that both those countries were now free of the Communists, but they would not believe me.

On my second day in Danang I called at the local tourist bureau, one of whose tasks was to provide interpreters for Americans wanting to revisit the places where they had fought, twenty years earlier. Since legally Americans were not supposed to enter Vietnam, those who returned were almost invariably men who felt ashamed of the war and wanted to ask forgiveness from the Vietnamese. Few appeared to notice that the peasants and townspeople alike had greatly preferred the Americans to their present occupiers, the North Vietnamese. This was admitted to me by one of the guides at the Tourist Office, although he was very reluctant to talk about it. Moreover I soon discovered in

Danang the same phenomenon that appeared all over the country. The most pro-American and anti-North Vietnamese people were former Vietcong and their sympathisers. One of the people I met in Danang fitted precisely into this category. She was a highly intelligent, humorous woman in early middle age, who made no mention of politics until I happened to ask her if she had been in Danang at the time of 'liberation'. She laughed out loud at this, the official term for Northern military conquest, and then went on:

> I was in Danang at the time of 'liberation'. It was a day I thought would be sublime, strong, like a second incarnation. But it was nothing. The next day nothing had changed, and soon everything started to get worse. I had been hoping for liberation. As a schoolgirl I had taken part in demonstrations against the Americans. My father had been in prison many times because he supported the NLF [the National Liberation Front]. My uncle had been in the jungle, fighting, and lost a lung. I believed in the revolution.
>
> But the people who had fought so long and suffered so much were soon disappointed. No one was allowed to keep a private home. My father had a small business, selling petrol and cigarettes, but it was taken by the Party. There were NLF veterans who had fought for years, and then they were pensioned off and had to take jobs as security guards. Their humour and irony about the Party is a good lesson for us.
>
> The Northern soldiers who came to Danang thought they were born again. They'd never seen anywhere so rich. All the Northerners want a job in the South but they know nothing. You have a head of a foreign department who speaks no foreign language. In the North they think that if you get a job with foreigners you don't need to work. They think foreigners will accept anything, bad food, bad service. But the foreigners know what's happening. They know they're being cheated. That's why the Japanese won't come here.
>
> I'm annoyed with those Americans who come back here to see the places where they fought. Don't they realise the country people are worse off now than they were then? The people in the country-

side may have had their homes burnt two or three times – that was quite normal – but now they're worse off. There are people living on the edge of the Highlands who have only one day's supply of rice. I only wish the Americans had fought harder. Everyone here wants to live in Saigon. It's more open and easy, and you can live. Not on your salary, that's nothing, but through odd jobs, through friends. Or they want to go abroad. Our best people have left as Boat People. But at least we're not as badly off as they were in East Europe, in places like Romania and Bulgaria. We're better off than they were. We can speak freely. We can live.'

Another person in Danang compared the American military in the past with the Soviet Russians in Vietnam: 'The Americans used to appear in uniform but the Russians never. They say they are advisers and go out in the evenings in civilian clothes. At Cam Ranh Bay [the naval bases south of Nha Trang] the Americans used to guard the entrance in uniform. Now at the front gate it's the Vietnamese Navy in uniform, but at the second gate, the Russians in uniform. Inside it's a Russian city.' Later in 1990, the Soviet Union announced its intention of pulling out from the bases at Cam Ranh Bay and Danang, as part of its world-wide retrenchment. Vietnam, anxious not to lose the revenue on the bases, was keen to let them to the United States, providing another curious twist of history. However, this proposal, like so many others designed at reconciliation, was squashed because of America's mania about the MIA.

For the first time in many visits, I felt sorry to leave Danang on the second leg of the train journey to Saigon. There was still no sign of the luxury coaches but our carriage, which would have rated fourth class in Europe and most of Asia, was here reserved for the *nomenklatura*. Better still, we were actually next to a buffet car. At one end of this diner, two chefs were cooking over an open brazier. One of them left his work to come and sit at my table, smoke a cigarette and accept a beer. He asked me in sign language whether I wanted a woman and then, in English, whether I wanted ham and eggs. None of these things arrived. In turn I asked him and his colleagues about the bullet-hole in the perspex window opposite. They said it was caused by a stone, but no stone drills such a neat hole, the width of a middle finger.

We had boarded the train in the morning and hoped to arrive at Nha Trang in time for dinner, before spending the night in one of the beach hotels. The journey took us through Quang Ngai Province, the scene of the My Lai massacre, and then into Binh Dinh, where South Korea had sent its Tiger Division to join in the work of pacification. I have already described how I came upon a team of gunners practising Tae Kwon Do, when all of a sudden they rushed off – still in pyjamas – to fire off volleys of 105 howitzer shells in just the direction from which I had come. Many years later I read that the Vietnamese province chief had lodged a formal complain that the Tiger Division, as a preliminary to a raid on a village, had softened it up with a thousand shells. Whatever the South Koreans did in Vietnam was now forgiven. In 1989, the Vietnam Tourist Board sent a delegation to Seoul inviting 'former residents' to return and see the places where they had fought.

In this second or buffet-car stretch of the journey, the corridors were not jammed by hammocks and prostrate bodies, and so I got a chance to talk to our fellow passengers. One of them was a student of engineering at Karl Marx Stadt in East Germany, who was on his way back to what he called 'Ho Chi Minh Stadt'. Although he said he was no longer a Communist, he was clearly rather confused by the way that reunification in Germany had taken a different course from Vietnam, with the Communist East absorbed by the non-Communist West. Although I did not tell him as much, I thought that the same thing was going to happen in Vietnam, with the South taking over its Northern conquerors. By this stage of the journey I had grasped that virtually all the passengers on the train were going to Saigon to shop and to carry on 'business' as it was euphemistically called. Our guide Thang acknowledged that most Hanoi people who can afford to travel go only to one place, Saigon.

There were several eccentric Northerners in the buffet car. One tall young men wore nails extending half an inch from his fingers, 'for fun' he said, but probably to express his sexual inclinations. In the old Vietnam, as I believe in the old China, aristocratic young men would grow their nails long in order to show that they did no manual work, so the practice could not be popular in a workers' state. It was heartening to find that Hanoi was tolerant of unorthodox behaviour, unlike Cuba, which hounds and imprisons homosexuals.

One older man I met in the buffet car was a painter who offered to do my portrait. He loved his native Hanoi but greatly preferred the politics of pre-unification Saigon. He told me angrily: 'I detest this regime. My mother died of a cerebral haemorrhage because of her rage against the regime. She took a statue of Manitou and threw it out of her third-storey window. She was the only person I know who has thrown Manitou's bust out of a window.'

'Who is Manitou?' I asked.

'You must know who Manitou was, the Red Indian chief.'

'Yes I know. But whom do you call Manitou now?'

He leaned forward and mentioned a name I did not gather against the clatter of train wheels. Later I remembered from Longfellow's *The Song of Hiawatha*, the line about 'Gitche Manito, the mighty', so it was clearly a play on words with Ho Chi Minh. After a few more attacks on the government, which he said had killed off his father as well as his mother, the painter turned his wrath on me: 'Why do you keep saying yes, yes, yes? Why don't you say what you think about this regime?' Very pompously, I fear, I said I did not think it correct to discuss the politics of someone else's country. The artist went away in a huff.

Shortly before the buffet closed, there were two moments of drama. A very large rock clanged against the carriage. Then a shutter slammed down on the hand of a drunk at the next table. Both things were greeted with cries of *choi oi*, the Vietnamese wail of alarm. Two women train attendants bandaged the bleeding hand of the drunk.

What with the conversation and the occasional accidents in the buffet car, we did not observe that the train had managed to lose five hours on its scheduled itinerary, and did not arrive in Nha Trang until after midnight. Had we been sensible we would have stayed in our compartment and travelled all the way to Saigon, but we were feeling confident and wanted a day at the seaside. At Nha Trang station we telephoned the beach hotels but they were full or, more likely, could not be bothered to take us in at this time of night, so we slept in a dormitory at a railway hostel, for 50 piastres a head. The next day we inspected the Cham pagoda, swam in the sea and ate a delicious meal at one of the private restaurants in the town. We went to the station at half past five, feeling certain of finding one of the luxury tourist carriages for the final leg of our journey to Saigon.

The 5.30 that evening was not one of the tourist trains with luxury carriages, dining room, bar, showers and hostesses. It was not even one of the first-class trains for Vietnamese, such as we travelled on in the second leg of our journey. It was the 'popular' or 'economy' train from Hanoi to Saigon, now on the third day of its journey, It stank of excrement. It was jammed with a mass of people, some of them struggling to get on or off at Nha Trang. When we finally fought our way to the small compartment reserved for us, we found it deep in filth, luggage and people, what seemed to be dozens of people. A guard appeared – there were no police or 'captains' aboard this train – and managed to push out some of the squatters, with much cursing, shoving and yelling. Those we had evicted scowled and threatened us, while at least five people were left in the upper bunks. The corridor was a pandemonium. On the window-sill opposite our compartment, three villainous men with moustaches and gold-ringed fingers sat in a row and stared at us, like rapacious crows on a branch. 'Why don't we get off now, while we still have time?' I asked the others, but at that moment the train gave a jolt and began to move.

As the train clanked and lurched on its slow journey, the mood of our party lay between gloom and despair. When darkness fell, there was only a dim light in the corridor but reconnaissance showed that the lavatory, after a two-day journey, was intolerable. The only alternative was to get off the train at one of the halts in the countryside and then reboard, or perhaps even hitch-hike to Saigon. Later that evening the three crows and a fourth associate started a card game, half in the corridor, half in our compartment. Two of them tried to get on my bunk but I pushed them off, whereupon they got onto Thang's bunk. He was feeling too ill and alarmed to protest. The criminals helped themselves to our cigarettes and eyed the pockets in which they knew we kept our valuables. They kept flashing torches into our faces, hoping that we had fallen asleep.

Not daring to doze off, I lay on my bunk all night, smoking and sipping the Soviet brandy I bought in Nha Trang. I remembered Solzhenitsyn's account of how on the transport trains to the camps of the Gulag Archipelago, the criminal prisoners, known as *zeks*, would plunder those who were there for political reasons. Since Vietnam's rolling stock came from the Soviet Union, it occurred to me that this very carriage may once have served the Gulag. Thinking of Russia and trains made me think of *Anna Karenina*, which I had brought along to read in a luxury carriage sipping a cocktail prepared by a lovely hostess in *ao dai* and pantaloons . . . Don't fall asleep.

Joy cometh in the morning. As dawn broke we were only two hours away from Saigon. The villains ended their card game and got down to their business of contraband. One of them said he was bringing down rosewood, apparently stored in another part of the train. A buck-toothed man, who looked like a homicidal rabbit, told me to get off my bunk, which also served as a lid for a storage chest. From this he extracted a dozen or fifteen electric irons, which one of the others stowed in a sack. The purchaser paid for these with a thick bundle of dong notes, which the vendor tucked away in the pockets of his donkey jacket. We asked the smugglers about their trade. They said the electric irons were from East Germany, maybe stolen from a ship or brought over by tourists on a plane, for this was before complete German re-unification. The Poles, who were the champion smugglers in the old Communist Eastern Europe, conducted a regular commerce by air with Thailand, making their purchases from one particular street in Bangkok where the signs were in Polish. The Vietnamese smugglers run a chain of trading links reaching from Thailand through Laos and Communist China to Hanoi, the capital in a political sense, and then by rail to the real-life capital of the country, Saigon. Our little party got off the train in Saigon in a state of relief amounting to euphoria. The air was fresh, the sky blue and the cyclo-drivers entered into a chariot race to the river and the Majestic Hotel. After a day spent either in the shower getting rid of the grime from the journey, or making up for a night without sleep, I joined Thang, Nick and Suzanne for a wonderful dinner at Maxime's Chinese restaurant, with many bottles of good Bulgarian wine.

On the strength of some articles arising out of the train journey, I raised the money from different papers to go back to Southeast Asia for most of the summer of 1990, though I failed to make any profit after paying for my fare and expenses. Coming back to Saigon in July 1990, I found a change in the political climate since I had been there in February. There were rumours that the police had threatened or even arrested some of the more outspoken dissidents. Except for the Viet Kieu, people were now as cautious as previously they had been outspoken in conversation with foreigners. When someone approached me in the street and asked me to take a letter out of the country, I sensed immediately that he was an *agent provocateur*, so I refused his request and instead put my hand in my pocket and took out some money to give him. As I expected he shied away from the money and disappeared. Later I was told by a Foreign Office man that if I did interviews or talked to people I met in the street, the police would become suspicious. Perhaps the Foreign Office had not liked some of the things I wrote about Vietnam in February. But it seems there was also a quarrel between the Foreign Office, which favoured a policy of *glasnost*, and the Ministry of the Interior, which as in Eastern Europe during the dying days of Communism, was fearful of losing its power and privileges. Had I understood this better, I would not so rashly have set off to visit the Mekong Delta with Greg Davies, a Vietnam War veteran, now a *Time* photographer, and his Foreign Office interpreter.

The drive on the main road into the Delta was even more boring now than during the 1960s, since we were not permitted to turn off into the villages. At My Tho we inspected the statue of Ho Chi Minh, had a coffee and then continued to Can Tho. It was on the ferries crossing the Mekong and Bassac rivers that I first encountered the hatred that Greg Davies assured me was shown to all foreigners in the Delta. The young women vendors of rice and chicken passed us without even offering to sell us their goods, let alone smile. Scowling youngsters banged on the roof of the car and made threatening gestures. Greg Davies said there was frequent gunfire throughout the Delta and even political banditry. Travel by night in the Delta was as dangerous as it had been for the hero of Graham Greene's novel *The Quiet American*, set in the Vietnam of forty years earlier.

It was just getting dark when we arrived at Can Tho. After booking into a small but pleasant hotel, I had a shower and came down to the café for a beer with Greg Davies. Some ten minutes later, the Foreign Office guide returned with a local official and bad news for me: 'You cannot stay here. You must go back to Ho Chi Minh City immediately.' The police, or rather the local Ministry of the Interior, had said so. 'Can't I stay the night and go back in the morning?' I asked. 'No, if you don't leave now you will be arrested.' Here the local official tried to ease the embarrassment: 'You see you need a special permit to come to Can Tho. If I go to London, I need a permit to go to Liverpool, don't I?' It was Greg Davies who saved the day by suggesting it would not be safe to travel by night to Saigon. The logic of this appealed to the local officials, who did not want the responsibility of a dead foreigner. They agreed to let me stay the night provided I left at dawn the next day. After a stroll round Can Tho, I went back to the hotel, ate dinner and drowned my irritation in whisky. Next morning I made the long, dreary return trip to Saigon.

My journey to and from Can Tho had given me no opportunity to meet and talk with people as I had done on the train journey from Hanoi, and in Saigon itself. However, it gave me the clearest possible proof of the detestation felt for the Northern Communist regime. The very fact that journalists were not allowed to wander freely around the Delta, as they could under the old Saigon government, was evidence of acute social unrest. So was the hatred shown to foreigners such as Greg Davies and me, perceived as *Lien Xo*, or Soviet. This was the more remarkable since, in the 1960s, I never encountered any enmity from the Delta people, who must have taken me for American. Now, in retrospect, it is clear that most of us journalists misunderstood what was happening in the Mekong Delta. The misunderstanding went back to the early 1960s when Communist troops in the Delta were winning battles against the incompetent and venal generals of President Diem. The US military advisers in the field, notably Lieutenant-Colonel John Paul Vann, were outspokenly critical of the Saigon government and of the US military high command. They passed on their anxieties to American journalists such as Neil Sheehan and David Halberstam, who at that time were forming American attitudes on Vietnam. The idea that the Mekong Delta peasants supported the Vietcong against a corrupt and exploiting Saigon regime became the accepted wisdom for most of the later writers on Vietnam, re-emerging as late as 1989 in Sheehan's best-selling biography of Colonel Vann, *A Bright Shining Lie*. However, the journalists who had known the Mekong Delta in the early 1960s seldom went back there to see the changes that took place in the following decade. After the turmoil of the Diem regime and an interlude of struggle for power among rival generals, Nguyen Van Thieu emerged as a competent leader both of the government and the army. The Vietcong, or local Communists, in the Mekong Delta declined in effectiveness until they were virtually wiped out in the Tet and May offensives of 1968. The North Vietnamese Army could not operate among the Delta peasants, who looked on them as outsiders.

Land reform and improved methods of agriculture brought great prosperity to the Mekong Delta, as I observed when making a television documentary there in 1969. The Phoenix Programme of murdering Communists in the Delta villages further weakened the Vietcong as the survivors told Stanley Karnow in his research for *Vietnam: A History*. Moreover I later came to see that American efforts at pacification and civic action were far more successful than I and other journalists acknowledged at the time. This was brought home to me by one of the very best books on the Vietnam War, *Once a Warrior King* by David Donovan, the pseudonym of an officer who in 1969 had served as head of a CAP (Civic Action Programme) team in Kien Phuong Province, north of Can Tho and near the Cambodian border. Of all the American memoirs of the war, this is to me the most convincing, honest and in the end sad. It begins as a plain, factual account of a soldier's life in a CAP team but turns into a powerful and furious condemnation of those whom Donovan blames for the ultimate Communist victory. Although Donovan and his colleagues were in theory just advisers to the South Vietnamese, they in fact had authority both in military and civil affairs. There were no American units in the province, for which Donovan later came to be thankful, and only occasional air and artillery support. Again, this avoided needless civilian casualties from 'H & I', or 'harassment and interdiction' shelling. Donovan had to rely on ARVIN and on a mercenary force of Nungs, or ethnic Chinese, who were brave if brutal soldiers. He and his troops normally went on operations by boat or on foot.

Part of the book describes the arduous but on the whole successful struggle to keep the Communists out of the district and cut their lines of communication between the sanctuaries in Cambodia and the more populous parts of the Mekong Delta. Although he did not use the Phoenix Programme, Donovan does not disapprove of its methods: 'I wonder how much hollering there would be in Congress if those guys were sitting over here, never knowing when the local VC are going to blow up another school or another market . . . On each occasion, the suffering of the children, the depravity of the Vietcong, and my apparent inability to stop these murderous bastards, filled me with resentment, dejection and futility.'

Donovan and his team got on well with the villagers, though the women were arrant teases. Once at dinner, the host's daughter, standing behind and out of view of her father, first bared and then fondled her breasts to tantalise Donovan. On another occasion, a man asked Donovan if he would like to sleep with his sister-in-law, who was present and much enjoying the joke. Unhappily for the CAP team, these local women were also chaste. As well as this teasing, Donovan had to suffer the press. When a reporter arrives, asking tricky questions, Donovan tells him:

> I'm getting used to being the man in charge ... the village girls smile at me, the old folks ask me into their homes, people who come for help seem to believe that I can do anything ... Thirty thousand people live in this district. I feel responsible for their safety and welfare ... I know they aren't really my responsibility, but inside I feel they are. I'm going to do my best for them, not for Saigon or Washington, but for them.

This statement of principles, and indeed the whole book, was oddly reminiscent of something I could not place at first. Then it came to me. Donovan's memoirs are like those of a district officer in the British colonial service in for example Nigeria or Malaya. The Englishman also was not the absolute ruler of his district, having to act in harmony with the native chiefs and elders, but he felt the same pride in the trust and esteem of his people.

In an earlier chapter I mentioned Donovan's anger at the racial arrogance, brutality and indiscipline of many American troops in Vietnam in 1969. On his return home, anger against the army turned to bitterness against the American people. No sooner had he arrived at Atlanta airport than he began to feel the first symptoms of what would become a permanent dislocation: 'The ingratitude wasn't a problem with the army, it was a problem with the country. I felt my country didn't give a damn about me or the sacrifice I and thousands of others were making in their name. Much of the population openly took the side of the Vietnamese Communists, while complacent middle America offered no protest, no counterpart, only silence.' Donovan went to university in 1970, to find his fellow students shouting against American intervention in Cambodia.

Donovan was troubled by memories of Vietcong atrocities: 'I still cannot bear to be around injured children. I am haunted by the memories of the bloodied and mangled bodies we used to make such frantic but primitive efforts to save. It still hurts to recall their frightened faces, their pain and their lack of comprehension at what was happening to them . . . I think most veterans are pained at the obvious waste of our efforts and receive no comfort from the fact that every refuge around the South China Sea is littered with the evidence that we were right in the beginning. I don't mean that American methods were right, that is clearly not the case . . .' On 13 November 1982, when the American Army in Vietnam at last got its parade in Washington, Donovan saw a Vietnamese family looking helpless and lost in front of the Lincoln Memorial:

> I wanted to tell them that I and my kind had never called them slopes and had never thought of them as anything less than ourselves. I wanted so badly to let them know that I was David Donovan, that I had fought the Terror, that no one may know me but I was once a warrior king.

Americans like Donovan who are proud of having fought in Vietnam probably far outnumber those who regret having served there; moreover they are respected still by those they fought to protect. If Donovan could return to Kien Phuong Province, he would receive a hero's welcome.

After my brief trip to the Mekong Delta, I settled down to enjoy myself in Saigon, now without question my favourite city in the world. Since the Continental Hotel had been tarted up and its terrace café closed to the street, I had shifted my patronage to the cheaper, friendlier relic of French colonial days, the Majestic, overlooking the Saigon River, whose open café was now the centre of news and gossip. Before the Second World War, when most people came to Saigon by ocean liner or merchantman, the Bank of Indo-China and the Majestic appeared as symbols of French authority on the waterfront. The hotel stands on the corner between the embankment road and the elegant street which the French called Catinat, the South Vietnamese renamed Tu Do and the North Vietnamese renamed Dong Khoi, although it was commonly known by the second or even the first of these titles. The Majestic's graceful five storeys, in Second Empire style, have the high ceilings and tiled floors that mitigated the Saigon heat in the days before air-conditioning. The metal latticework in the open front of the café, the bamboo chairs and on the terrace the bushes clipped in the shape of deer, provide an odd but agreeable ambience.

The view from the Majestic over the Saigon River takes in the docks where, in 1911, the future Communist leader Ho Chi Minh signed on as a stoker and galley boy aboard a French freighter, the *Amiral Latouche Treville*. When the sun rises, directly across the river, a busy scene appears on the waterfront. The cyclo-drivers stretch their legs, eat a bowl of rice and urinate against the fence in front of the floating restaurant. The young people play badminton on one of the courts below the hotel, and the middle-aged do their laborious callisthenics, a kind of slow-motion physical jerks. One man bends down as though to tie up his shoelaces, then raises himself and stretches his arms sideways. Another lifts his arms slowly, with elbows bent, as though he were having his chest measurements taken, then drops his arms and begins again.

Those taking their exercise all face east, to where the sky is turning a pale pink over the warehouses, across the river. Before the Communists came, there used to be hoarding advertisements for cigarettes, Japanese TV sets and Hynos, the toothpaste whose trademark was an African with a gleaming white smile. The Hynos advertisement proved the power of suggestion, since before the French came, Vietnamese women prided themselves on their pale skins and carefully blackened teeth. But the hoardings went after 1975 and now the eye is caught by the two crosses over a Catholic church. In early evening, the colour returns to the landscape, and sunlight reflects from the other bank. Ships of every description pass the Majestic café, huge freighters, rice barges low in the water, ferries and motor sampans from the Mekong Delta villages. The saddest sight on the river are barges of logs from what is left of the rain forest. Once in the 1960s I watched President Thieu inspecting the fleet of South Vietnam in the river in front of this café. There is no sign of the Communist navy, which spends much of its time patrolling the off-shore oil sites claimed by Vietnam, and also by China, the Philippines and other countries.

Although I had known the Majestic for almost a quarter century, I knew it still longer by reputation. My old Corsican friend M. Ottavj had worked there in the 1930s, and during a dinner to celebrate getting the Légion d'Honneur in January 1974, he brought out not only his old wines but some of the old Majestic menus running to ten or eleven courses. He also produced a programme of music played by the all-women orchestra of Miss Edna Barrett, an English lady of virtue and severity. This detail always delighted me because it recalled the British all-women orchestra in Conrad's *Victory*, set in colonial Java. According to M. Ottavj, when Edna Barrett's orchestra played at a *thé dansant*, an *apéritif dansant* or an evening ball: '*Tout Saigon était là, Monsieur West, les femmes en tenue de soirées, les messieurs en smoking.*' (All Saigon was there, the women in evening dress and the men in dinner jackets.)

When France fell in 1940, the Japanese moved into Vietnam, billeting some of their officers in the Majestic. Since the hotel was near the docks and the ships in the river, it later came under attack from Allied bombers. The Japanese behaved with relative kindness till March 1945, when they arrested or murdered all the French and started to plunder the countryside, causing a famine which led to the death of two million Vietnamese. When Japan surrendered, the British Army took control of Saigon and stationed its officers in the Majestic Hotel. The one British journalist present was Tom Driberg, a socialist politician and putative Soviet agent, who was also a friend of the South-east Asia Allied commander, Lord Louis Mountbatten. When I asked Tom Driberg, shortly before his death, if he had any letters or documents from that period, he answered: 'How curious that you should ask that! Only last night I was looking through a sheaf of letters from Louis addressed to me in Saigon, each one beginning, "Dear Tom, please burn this as soon as you have read it." '

In Graham Greene's novel *The Quiet American*, the *Times* correspondent Thomas Fowler sees an American ship in the river, unloading bombers. The United States was just then starting to get involved. The real-life journalist Stanley Karnow witnessed the same thing about ten years later, as he describes in *Vietnam: A History*: 'One morning in December 1961, I was sipping coffee with a US army press officer on the terrace of Saigon's Majestic Hotel as an American aircraft carrier, the *Core*, turned a bend in the river and steamed towards us, the first shipment of forty-seven helicopters strapped to its deck. Astonished, I grabbed the officer's arm shouting: "Look at that carrier!" He directed a mock squint in the direction of the gigantic vessel and replied: "I don't see nothing." '

That was the start of what came to be called the American War. However, in 1966, when I knew it first, the Majestic was not a popular place with American servicemen, or with journalists. For one thing it was patronised by the CIA, the Quiet Americans now in their hundreds and thousands. Proximity to the river made the Majestic dangerous, as was shown when Vietcong frogmen twice blew up the floating restaurant. The rats from the river also invaded the old hotel; a Greek woman journalist told me that after a trip up country she came back to find a nest of baby rats under her pillow.

After 1973, when the servicemen and most of the CIA had left, the Majestic perked up. The municipal authorities cleared the military debris from the waterfront, and a children's playground opened between the hotel and the river. It was at the Majestic in 1973 that I first met Peter Kemp, the legendary soldier-adventurer who had started fighting the Vietnamese Communists as early as 1945, in Laos. Quite late in life Peter took on a new career, writing for the *Spectator* from some of the places where he had fought in the past such as Spain, Albania and Laos as well as some of the more recent trouble spots such as Rhodesia and Guatemala. I was with him in 1985 in the town of León in Nicaragua, when we spotted a story in one of the papers recording the death of Peter's old enemy, the Albanian Communist leader Enver Hoxha. Peter rose to his feet, lifted his beer mug high and exclaimed: 'Stoke well, the furnaces of Hell!'

The voluptuous Sarah Webb Barrell, with whom I had gone in search of the Chams, was also a patron of the Majestic Hotel and was said to have thrown a boyfriend's typewriter into the Saigon River, during a lovers' tiff. Four years after the end of the Vietnam War I met Sarah again in Salisbury, Rhodesia, where she had fallen in love with a gallant Yorkshireman, Andre Dennison, who was by general consensus the finest officer in Ian Smith's army. In the course of a very long day I spent with them both, Sarah spilled her handbag in the bar of the Monomotapa Hotel, sending skidding a lady's pistol given to her by Andre. I remarked semi-seriously that only a few weeks earlier in this very bar, a Rhodesian soldier had killed himself playing Russian roulette, in the fashion popularised by the Vietnam War film *The Deer Hunter*. A few weeks later, Andre was killed in an attack on the Zimbabwe Ruins Motel, and afterwards Sarah committed suicide with her pistol.

The first time I stayed in the Majestic was in April 1975, only a fortnight before the fall of Saigon. Even at that fateful time, the keep-fit people were still doing their physical jerks on the waterfront, and since it was April, the windy month, the children were flying their kites above the river. I remembered the sad receptionist with the pock-marked face who begged for reassurance about the future: 'We have lost our country. Do you think we shall lose our lives?' As it happened, almost the only shell that landed in downtown Saigon during the final offensive hit the Majestic Hotel and killed a night porter. Before leaving Saigon with the camera crew, Tony de Lotbiniere insisted on booking a room in the

Majestic for Liz Thomas the English nurse, but she went back to her lane in Cholon before the Communists arrived. After staying on in Vietnam for another six months, Liz went back to England but she could not manage to settle down. After a stab at marriage she ended her life in tragic circumstances.

During my first, depressing visit to South Vietnam under Communism, in 1980, I called at the Majestic, bought a drink and said hello to the only other man at the bar, a European of saturnine appearance. When I asked what country he came from, he answered, 'What do you think?' in a self-satisfied, irritating manner.

'Russia?' I ventured, then went on: 'What are you doing here?'
'What do you think?'
'KGB?'

He just went on smiling. Coming back in 1988, and this time staying at the Majestic, I found that the Russians were no longer feared or even respected. They were 'Americans without dollars', and dupes to be sold moonshine vodka.

By the summer of 1990, the Russians had vanished from the Majestic and the East Germans came only as citizens of a now united country. The Australians, who had provided Vietnam with a telecommunications system, were much in evidence in the hotel bar, huge, swag-bellied diggers facetiously wearing the local conical hats. The Japanese were also conspicuous. There was a regular, known to the staff as 'Mr White Horse' because of the whisky he drank from morning till night, and a young man in a 'Checkpoint Charlie' T-shirt, showing Berlin as it used to be before the Wall was taken down. 'I've been to sixteen countries,' he told me, 'and Vietnam is the best. That is a Japanese watch you are wearing, same as mine. Next year there will be many Japanese in this country.'

The French, who unlike the English do not suffer from guilt about their colonial past, were also conspicuous in the Majestic. A young man whose father had been a colonial civil servant in Saigon was trying to set up an advertising agency. He and some Viet Kieu friends had an investment in a textile factory making millions of shirts and items of underwear for the French market. He said that the cost of labour was even lower in Vietnam than in Communist China; moreover the French could remit most of their profits. He did not hold the usual left-liberal views on the Vietnam War, or anything else. He told me that at his *lycée* he had poured petrol over two of his set books, by Jean-Paul Sartre and Simone de Beauvoir, and ostentatiously burnt them in the courtyard.

Another Frenchman I came across in the café of the Majestic was an old friend, Jean-Claude Labbé, the excitable photographer who had travelled with James Fention in the Highlands, and then in April 1975 had lectured Liz Thomas and me on why we should welcome the North Vietnamese. He was stouter and slightly milder in manner, although he still waved his arms about as he talked. But his Stalinist views had not survived long after liberation:

> It was terrible here from 1975 to 1986. They were sending people to prison and camps. And the Boat People! Shit! It was worse here than in Romania. In Romania at least you could get into people's homes, talk to the women, even *boom, boom* [banging one hand on the other]. Here it was f—ing terrible. Yes, you are right, terrible but no f—ing. Shit! And do you know they would not let me into the country. They said I was CIA, and do you know who denounced me? A French journalist who said I was CIA because I took pictures for *Time* magazine. Me, CIA! Me, a member of French f—ing Communist Party! But since 1986, all is changed. I have done a book on Vietnam. And I have bought a house here in Saigon, for $100,000, in a slum.

The Majestic was now the main hotel for the foreign correspondents who came to cover the never-ending war in Cambodia. On the night I arrived in July 1990, the talk was all of a Khmer Rouge ambush against a train, in which they apparently massacred most of the passengers. I met a young Englishman who was going to spend six weeks there photographing the victims of land-mines. The Majestic also housed the staff of the Orderly Departure Programme, by which the United States was accepting as immigrants all those Vietnamese compromised by working with the Americans. Millions more Vietnamese were anxious to join them, as could be seen from the still enormous exodus of Boat People.

Tens of thousands of former Boat People were now coming back as Viet Kieu. In the Majestic I met a woman who had escaped to Thailand in 1979, the year I went to Songkhla to write about the refugees. She had been robbed by pirates (and probably raped, although she did not say this) but now she was back with a US passport and dollars. Some of the Viet Kieu put on airs, even pretending they no longer spoke their language. One woman in the Majestic boasted of earning $60,000 a year, which was not tactful talk in a country where you could meet English-language graduates earning a mere $100 a year, selling custards from a stall.

There were even a few Americans, most of whom had come to Vietnam burdened with guilt about the war, and were startled to find themselves objects of admiration. At the Majestic one day in 1990 I met a delightful couple from North Carolina who during the 1960s had fostered a wounded little girl until she returned to her village in Vietnam. Early that year they had received a letter from her, out of the blue, and had come to Vietnam to try to get her to the United States. When they went to her village in Quang Ngai Province, near the scene of the My Lai massacre, they were astonished by the popularity of Americans. The girl, now a woman in her twenties, had forgotten her English but she remembered her foster-parents and even the names of all their friends. At first the Americans encountered hassle from the local Party officials, but this was resolved when the woman was given permission to leave. In fact the local police chief asked, if he married the young woman, whether he too could emigrate to the United States.

On looking out of my bedroom window, in 1990, I saw what appeared to be a five-deck cruise ship moored in the river. Was

Saigon now on the millionaire holiday circuit? And then I remembered reading about a floating hotel, which somehow or other had reached Saigon from Australia. I walked down to take a look. A sign on the quayside said that the Floating Hotel was under the management of the Southern Hotel Corporation of Sydney, 'the largest hotel company in the Southern Pacific'. The amenities included two hundred guest rooms, a conference centre, two bars, a tennis court and a swimming pool, the last two of which were under construction on the quay. Crossing the gangplank on to the Floating Hotel, I found myself welcomed aboard by smiling Vietnamese porters, dressed as French matelots in pale green sailor suits, with pompoms to match. While they went off to find one of the management, I stared in wonder at the enormous foyer in chrome, plastic and stainless steel. A matelot returned with the Front Office Manager, Patricia Healy, a glamorous young Australian in a black leather skirt. She ordered coffee from 'the only cappuccino machine in Vietnam', then told me the story of the Floating Hotel.

The idea came from a group of businessmen in Townsville, northern Queensland, who wanted to boost the tourist trade on the Great Barrier Reef. There had been cruise ships built like hotels, and even a floating prison in the Hudson River, but no one before had built a floating hotel. However, a Swedish architect had designed such a vessel, and the Bethlehem shipyards in Singapore were ready to do the construction. By the end of 1988, this ship of 12,000 tonnes was ready for towing from Singapore to its destination, seventy-two kilometres from the Queensland coast. When it opened next year, it soon became evident that the promoters had not envisaged some of the problems involved, of which the most vexing was transport. A one-way journey out to the reef by helicopter cost $250. It was cheaper by catamaran but as Miss Healy said: 'The channel is rough, so most of the people who reached the hotel arrived sea-sick, and stayed sea-sick, because it rocked a bit.' The Townsville businessmen sold most of their holding to an aggressive Japanese corporation, keen to expand in Australia and South-east Asia. The vessel went back to Singapore for adaptation into a business hotel. The Japanese considered taking it to Hong Kong, Bangkok and Honolulu, then plumped for Saigon. 'Even with us,' Miss Healy said, 'there are only two thousand hotel rooms in Saigon, of which only 700 are five-star, the Rex, the Caravelle and the Continental. Lots of people prefer to stay at the Rex or the Continental because Vietnam is seen as an adventure destination. But business travellers like hot water and soft pillows.' She described some of the problems facing the Floating Hotel:

> We decided to recruit the 300 local staff from people who hadn't worked in hotels before and learned local habits. You know how the waiters come and sit at your table and smoke cigarettes? We didn't want to have to tell them, 'take that finger out of your nose', so we taught them ourselves. The matelot suits emphasise the old French influence here. We haven't told them they look silly. They think they're gorgeous. They're the most photographed people in Saigon.
>
> We still have a security problem. We have an ex-policeman in charge of security. He knows the kind of thing people will get up to, like swimming across the river and trying to board. We've had three security people at a time just knocking them off the side of the ship. We get big ships sailing right alongside us, blacking us out. The engineer says that anywhere else in the world they'd get prosecuted for sailing too near a moored ship. Maybe they sail their ships the same way they drive their cars.

In the early mornings, before it became too hot, I would take a walk through some of the quieter streets to the zoo, always my favourite place in Saigon. All over the world, I have noticed, you learn a lot about human beings by how they regard and respond to other creatures. The Berlin Zoo, for example, is scholarly and scientific, telling you all you could wish to know of its great and varied collection. The San Diego Zoo has almost abandoned cages in order to let the creatures roam in what appear to be natural conditions. The Rangoon Zoo has reverted to semi-jungle. The once great London Zoo has descended to anthropomorphic whimsicality, giving the animals comic names, and even including rabbits and sheep, to show that Nature is not just red in tooth and claw.

Coming back to Saigon Zoo, almost a quarter century since I had been there first, I noticed that the museum and pagoda were newly painted, while the botanic garden still did credit to Louis Pierre who started the zoo in 1864. Then walking a little further I saw with dismay a concrete playground of swings and roundabout, a kiddies' paddling pool, a miniature railway and worst of all a video theatre showing a film of mythological beasts. However, I soon found that this new amusement park deformed only one side of the zoo, which was bigger than I remembered. The area with the animals was as pleasant as ever. The courting couples were still there in abundance; there were still lines of schoolchildren, each holding the shirt or dress of the one in front; I saw no Boy Scouts but the Communist Pioneers keep up the tradition of tying knots and lighting camp-fires. Several groups of men played *boule*, a French amusement going back to colonial times. After a while I got used to the noise of cassettes from the coffee and soft-drink stall, especially since it was mostly tango music, a Vietnamese favourite that I also like very much.

Having met the zoo's former director Vu Ngoc Tan in 1966, I was eager to meet the present incumbent, Nguyen Quoc Thang. Although Saigon zoo directors, like London policemen, seem to be very young these days, Nguyen Quoc Thang impressed me by his knowledge and enthusiasm. Although a botanist, like the Frenchman who founded the zoo, Thang had a lively concern for the fauna as well as the flora in his care, and the country's wildlife in general. He had studied and worked at zoos in Leipzig and Dresden, so we conversed in German, and when I was stuck for a word like 'goat' I solved the problem by pointing at it.

Before making a tour of the zoo, I asked Nguyen Quoc Thang about the effect of the war on Vietnam's wildlife. He seemed to be generally optimistic. The elephants now flourished again in the region of Ban Me Thuot, where Philip Jones Griffiths and I rode them in 1967. There were still many tigers, said Thang, although people hunted them in hope of gaining their strength. The wild ox survived along the Cambodian border, and of the animals no longer found in Vietnam, he had acquired two black bears from Thailand and hoped to get a tapir. Even during the war I was told that many species of birds had fled the noise of the guns, especially in the Mekong Delta. Among the birds that were now returning were cranes, a national favourite and one of the symbols of longevity. Cranes are also admired, especially by women, because they are faithful to one partner and show their affection by dancing duets. Among the returning cranes was the rare, red-headed variety Grus Antigone, which once used to breed in the cajeput forests of the Plain of Reeds, north of My Tho in the Mekong Delta, a Vietcong haven and therefore once saturated with bombs, shells and defoliant chemicals. The authorities there had replanted cajeput trees, built embankments to hold in water, and generally made the right conditions for cranes.

Like Vu Ngoc Tan in 1966, Nguyen Quoc Thang was keen to build up a bigger and better zoo, which meant making more profit. The entrance fee of five piastres was high by the standards of this impoverished city, so Thang had to give the public its money's-worth:

> We have about two million visitors a year, including 6,000 to 10,000 on Sundays and 60,000 a day during the Tet, or New Year, festival. But I want more. For instance that music from the cafés would be firmly forbidden [*streng verboten*] in any zoo in Europe. But the stallholders say they would lose business without it. Above all the visitors want more animals. They tell me they won't come back unless I get something new. The animals I would really like are a zebra, a giraffe and dolphins. Above all I'd like an open zoo, like the one at San Diego . . .

At the thought of San Diego Zoo, which is indeed a place of enchantment, Thang lapsed into a kind of trance, from which he aroused himself to discuss economics: 'In order to get more animals, we have to sell or exchange our own, no, not the Phu

Quoc dog, I think that's really a cross-breed, but elephants for example. We've sent four to the DDR and CSR [he still used the Communist names for East Germany and Czechoslovakia] and we are very rich in reptiles.'

Like his predecessor in 1966, Thang had to practise economy. He continued the custom of cutting off the antlers of deer to sell for traditional medicine. He saved on cages and wire mesh by clipping the wings of the storks so they could not escape, and putting the gibbons inside a moat. 'Gibbons are afraid of water,' he told me, 'but apes can swim so you have to cage them.' And he added with a sly smile: 'Did you notice we keep the lion and the lioness in separate cages? We don't want them to have cubs because meat is so expensive.'

In a walk round the zoo, Thang showed me the pelicans from Cambodia, a tamarind tree 'as old as the gardener, seventy years', a baby hippo, the largest tree in Vietnam and a bearded German goat, which strangely resembled the late Communist leader Ho Chi Minh. Some of the animals had not adapted well to the climate. The camels got ill from the damp. The Shetland pony from Leipzig looked to me thin and unhappy. The elephants were as always shackled, to stop them trying to jump the moat.

It was when we got to the crocodiles that I sensed for the first time that politics might have intruded into the zoo. As might be imagined, most of the animals over the past fifteen years had come from what used to be called the Socialist bloc, above all from East Germany and Czechoslovakia. One of the few tropical countries in the bloc, Fidel Castro's Cuba, had given Vietnam a number of crocodiles, which is what we call carrying coals to Newcastle, and Germans call sending owls to Athens. Both Cuba and Vietnam had been for a long time client states of the Soviet Union but now were receiving no aid. However, whereas Vietnam remained on civil terms with its former patron, Cuba was highly critical of the reforms in East Europe. On the very day I went to the Saigon Zoo, Fidel Castro had yelled defiance both of the Soviet Union and the United States, proclaiming his slogan, 'Socialism or Death'.

The Vietnamese had little regard for Castro or, it appeared, the Cuban crocodiles. We stopped first at a hatchery where dozens of baby crocs were clambering over each other's backs. 'This is where we have tried to interbreed Cuban and Vietnamese crocodiles,' Nguyen Quoc Thang informed me, 'but it hasn't worked out well. One must always keep the blood pure.' Since he was speaking German, these last words had an eerie ring of the Hitler period: *'Man muß das Blut rein halten.'* Near to the hatchery was a pool for a pair of adults who were about to be fed. One of these monsters was Vietnamese; the other, a darker beast, was Cuban. When the keeper threw in a long fish, the pool burst into a boiling mess of jaws and lashing tails and reptile fury. When the turmoil subsided, I saw that the two creatures were facing in different directions but with their jaws alongside, the Cuban holding the head of the fish and the Vietnamese the tail. Neither had enough in its mouth for more than a snack yet neither dared open its mouth to get a bigger purchase. Occasionally one or the other would give a sideways tug, but for several minutes they lay still and glared at each other with hatred, out of the corners of their eyes.

It seemed to be stalemate when, all of a sudden, the Vietnamese crocodile, still gripping the fish, rolled on its side, then on its back. The Cuban crocodile lost leverage and, as the Vietnamese rotated, the Cuban's head was pulled out of the water and bit off the head of the fish. The Cuban crocodile was left sulking with just its morsel of food and sank under water. The Vietnamese crocodile raised its jaws and part of its body out of the water, tossed the great fish in the air, then caught it and gulped it down with two great crunches. The triumph of the Vietnamese in the battle of the crocodiles seemed to endorse the racial theory that *man muß das Blut rein halten.*

During this stay in Saigon in 1990, I treated myself to yet another re-reading of Graham Greene's novel *The Quiet American*, which had delighted me when it first appeared in 1955, perhaps arousing my interest in Vietnam. When I was doing the commentary for a film on the Mekong Delta in 1969, the director Richard

Taylor urged me to quote one of Greene's remarks on the peasants, not a remark I entirely agreed with even then, and still less later. At any rate, one of the television critics seized on this reference to the Graham Greene book to suggest that I saw Vietnam with a second-hand imagination. Since I was and remain a devotee of *The Quiet American*, I have to ask myself whether the critic was not right, that I see Vietnam through Greene-tinted spectacles.

The question is even harder to answer since Thomas Fowler, the principal character in the book, is an English reporter whose working life in the 1950s bears some resemblance to mine in the 1960s and 1970s. He is captivated by Vietnam and its people, especially the women. Although sympathising both with the French and the insurgents, Fowler is not an ideologue and distrusts efforts to foist Western ideas on South-east Asia. And although Greene was writing about a time when France alone was engaged in the war, *The Quiet American* came to be seen as a prophecy of the US involvement.

The character of the title, Alden Pyle, is said to be based on the CIA agent Colonel Edward Lansdale, who wanted to save democracy with the 'psychological warfare' methods that he had studied during his peacetime career as an advertising executive. Lansdale had helped to subdue a revolt in the Philippines, afterwards going to South Vietnam to assist the regime of Ngo Dinh Diem. Two American authors, William J. Lederer and Eugene Burdick, glorified Lansdale in the novel *The Ugly American*, where he appears as Colonel Edwin Hillendale, who wins hearts and minds by playing the mouth organ.

The Quiet American, Alden Pyle, arrives in Vietnam full of the theories of an absurd pundit, York Harding, author of *The Advance of Red China*. The Englishman Fowler teases him and derides his hope of building a Third Force between Communism and French colonialism. When Fowler discovers that Pyle has imported the plastic explosive to make the bomb that went off in a main Saigon square – this was a real atrocity – he sets him up to be murdered by the Communists. The French policeman assigned to the case knows that Fowler was also jealous of Pyle for taking his girlfriend, Phuong.

The plot of *The Quiet American* could have unfolded in any country in Asia or Latin America where the United States was fighting the spread of Communism. However, in this as in so many of Greene's best books, the place figures as large as the characters. When I see or hear the name of the book, I think at once not of Fowler or Pyle or even Phuong, but Saigon, this garish, wicked but ever enchanting city, which Greene had obviously come to love during the winters he spent here.

Saigon has remained unspoilt by war and the still greater menace of property development, so that not only the atmosphere but the very buildings remain as Greene described them forty years ago. Much of the action takes place in Tu Do, where Greene stayed, and the introduction to two Saigon friends confesses that he has 'quite shamelessly borrowed the location of your flat to house one of my characters'. Fowler first introduces Pyle to Phuong at the Continental Hotel, one evening 'in the momentary cool when the sun has just gone down, and the candles were lit on the stalls in the side streets'. Although, in 1990, the Continental terrace café had been glassed over, the cigarette girls and shoeshine boys had taken their trade to Givral's café across the street. This is the milk bar and ice-cream parlour where every morning Phuong went for a chocolate shake. On the day of the bomb explosion, Pyle had warned her to stay away, thus clinching Fowler's suspicion about his involvement. The Givral still offers good ice-cream and patisserie, an appropriate fare in the city of Ho Chi Minh, who once was assistant pastry cook in the Carlton Hotel in London.

Fowler, the disillusioned journalist, does not believe in God, but Greene, we assume, attended the red-brick cathedral which stands at the top of Rue Catinat. He knew the Majestic Hotel which stands at the bottom. It was here that Fowler was first able to talk to Phuong away from the scrutiny of her older sister. On the night that Pyle is murdered, while on his way to a restaurant by the Dakao Bridge, Fowler provides an alibi at the Majestic bar, and stays to watch the unloading of US planes from a ship in the Saigon River.

Perhaps that restaurant by the Dakao Bridge was the one still popular in the 1960s, when the manageress was a tough Alsatian lady, and some of the clientele were Senegalese, who had settled this quarter as soldiers for France. I went there once with an English journalist, almost a caricature of Fowler, who aired his outrageous views in a braying, upper-class accent. As we entered the crowded restaurant, the journalist said to the manageress in his awful French: '*Pouvez-vous nous mettre à une table très loin des américains, surtout des nègres?*' Fortunately, he was not overheard or understood.

Unlike almost every other foreigner who has written about Vietnam, Greene actually loved the country and its people, or to be more precise, its women. As Fowler lies beside Phuong, he thinks that 'if I smelt her skin it would have the faintest fragrance of opium, and her colour was that of the small flame. I had seen the flowers on her dress beside the canals in the north; she was indigenous, and I never wanted to go home.' Because so many of Greene's novels are set in tropical, nasty places – the Congo, Sierra Leone, Haiti and southern Mexico – some people imagine that Vietnam too was part of his hellish geography. On the contrary, it was a place of sensuous beauty and peopled by French and Vietnamese, two races Greene admired. *The Quiet American* can be enjoyed as a very affecting story of love and murder in an exotic setting, with echoes of Conrad's *Victory*, except that the hero, Fowler, fights for and wins his woman. It is at the same time a very political book, though not of course an ideological tract.

It is Pyle, not Fowler, whose head is bursting with liberal-leftist passion. In fact Fowler, like Greene at the time, was inclined to side with the French. Taxed by Pyle with his indulgence towards the colonialists, Fowler replies: 'Isms and ocracies. Give me facts. A rubber planter beats his labourers – all right, I'm against him. He hasn't been instructed to do it by the Minister of the Colonies. In France I expect he'd beat his wife.' Fowler goes on to describe a French priest, eating nothing but rice and salt fish, who works fifteen hours a day in a cholera epidemic, saying his Mass with a wooden platter. Would Pyle call that priest part of colonialism? Pyle quotes his mentor, York Harding, to the effect that good individuals make it hard to get rid of a bad system. To this Fowler replies with a memorable outburst which may be the key to Greene's thinking on politics:

'Anyway the French are dying every day – that's not a mental concept . . . They aren't leading these people on with half-lies like your politicians – and ours. I've been in India, Pyle, and I know the harm liberals do. We haven't a liberal party any more – liberalism's infected all the other parties. We are all either liberal conservatives or liberal socialists: we all have a good conscience. I'd rather be an exploiter who fights for what he exploits and dies with it.'

A visit to Mexico in 1938 gave Greene his life-long distaste for American liberalism. It was the liberal American President Woodrow Wilson who said, on invading Mexico, that it was 'our duty to teach these people to elect good governments'. It was liberal Americans like Pyle who did so much damage in Vietnam. They got into the war, like Pyle, to build a Third Force between the Communists and colonialists. They got out of the war because the deaths and wounds offended their sensitive conscience, leaving the South Vietnamese to massacre or re-education camp. Pyle, planting his bomb in front of the Continental Hotel, was forerunner of those who rained millions of bombs on North Vietnam, still with the best intentions.

In one of their long discussions, Pyle advances what later came to be known as the Domino Theory, that if Indo-China falls to the Communists, so does all Asia. Greene had himself advanced this theory in *Paris-Match* (12 July 1952). Not even Greene could have prophesied that Red China in 1979 would fight a brief war against Communist Vietnam, nor that the modern Pyles would take the Chinese side. Whatever his later commitments, Greene in the 1950s was not a man of the left in politics. Unlike so many writers of his age, he had not become mixed up in the Spanish

Civil War, going instead to Mexico to report on the persecution of Christians by a Marxist government. He had spent much time in sub-Saharan Africa without becoming enthusiastic for black majority rule. Although he lived in France, Greene did not show any public concern over the problems of Algeria, or the return to power of Charles de Gaulle. *The Quiet American,* when it came out, was seen as a defence of European colonialism against the United States.

Greene understood the brutality of the war but he showed more sympathy to the Frenchmen who fought it than other, later writers showed to the Americans. When Fowler goes out on patrol and sees the French accidentally shoot a woman and child: 'The lieutenant said, "Have you seen enough?" speaking savagely, almost as though I had been responsible for their deaths. Perhaps to the soldier the civilian is the man who employs him to kill, who includes the guilt of murder in the pay envelope and escapes responsibility.' That is a just perception, but it was seldom applied to American troops, who also felt ashamed and disgusted when they had killed women and children.

Fowler goes with the French on a dive-bombing, machine-gunning mission, at the end of which they destroy a sampan, 'adding our little quota to the world's dead'. Afterwards the pilot, Captain Trouin, makes a detour to show Fowler the sunset over the limestone cliffs. Later still, at an opium den, Captain Trouin remarks that the war is lost: 'But we are professionals: we have to go on fighting till the politicians tell us to stop. Probably they will get together and agree to the same peace that we could have had at the beginning, making nonsense of all these years.' Many American pilots probably felt that way and were proved right, but no great novelists put their thoughts in writing.

Inspector Vigot, who questions Fowler about the death of Pyle, has a copy of Pascal's *Pensées* on his desk. Although the sympathetic policeman is one of the stock Greene characters, I nevertheless find Vigot unbelievable. The French police in Indo-China systematically locked up, tortured and even killed political suspects. Many were brutes who would not have read a Simenon story, let alone Pascal. French Indo-China had been from the start a commercial racket, exploiting virtually forced labour to work in the paddy fields, mines and rubber plantations. The colonial government raised a third of its revenue through its monopoly of opium, which was systematically pushed to the native community, as well as the Chinese and French. The British anthropologist Geoffrey Gorer wrote of Saigon in the 1930s: 'Alongside all the solid respectability goes a violence which equals if it does not surpass the old port of Marseilles, or Cairo, or Suez. Every rickshaw boy, and there must be thousands of them, is a pimp: "Madame français, missou? Madame métisse? Madame Annamite? Boy français? Fumer? Moi connais bon." The whole place and most of the inhabitants have the sweet and acrid smell of opium hanging over them. As far as I could see, there was nothing genuine, nothing spontaneous, nothing that was not wholly commercial in the whole town. I personally prefer a nice, marshy swamp.'

Yet Greene, through Fowler, says he prefers the 'honest exploiters' of French Indo-China to the liberal Englishmen who had given India its freedom. Certainly it can be argued that Britain left India in far too much of a hurry, and might have avoided partition with its attendant massacres. Nevertheless the former British possessions in Asia have so far worked better than those of the French or the Dutch, who also ruled on commercial principles. Americans like Pyle may have been innocents but they were surely right to condemn the sheer brutality of the French in Vietnam, as indeed in Algeria.

Greene loved Vietnam but his attitude to its inhabitants verged on the condescending. Fowler's girlfriend Phuong is a bird-brain, who reads nothing but magazine articles on the British royal family. If you had mentioned Hitler, she would have asked who he was. Fowler sneers at the Cao Dai religious sect, whose saints include Christ, Buddha and Victor Hugo, but he neglects to explain that the Cao Dai have a following only among the poor and ignorant of a part of the Mekong Delta region. They are comparable with some holy-roller sect in the southern United

States. During their talk in a watch-tower, coming back from the Cao Dai Cathedral, Fowler tells Pyle that the Vietnamese peasants are only concerned with getting their rice, to which Pyle says that they want to think for themselves. 'Thought's a luxury,' Fowler replies. 'Do you think a peasant sits and thinks of God and democracy, when he gets inside his mud hut at night?' Having apparently lost this point, Pyle argues that not all the country are peasants. What about the educated? Would they be happy under a Communist system? 'Oh no,' said Fowler, 'we've brought them up in our ideas.'

In this debate, I find myself whole-heartedly on the side of Pyle. It is wrong and arrogant to suppose that because a man lives in a mud hut, he cannot think about God or indeed democracy. Although I once spent three weeks making a film in a Delta village, the film in which I was made to quote Greene's comment about the peasants, I would not set myself up as an expert on their thinking. However, I got the impression that most of these villagers took a keen interest in the outside world. Throughout the French time, the Mekong Delta was always a centre of discontent, and it was there, not Saigon, that rebellion broke out in 1930. As well as the Communists, there were Greene's fellow Catholics and three major Buddhist sects, all very active up to the point of militancy. As Pyle rightly predicted, the peasants now greatly resent Communist government, partly perhaps because they want to think for themselves.

Fowler says that the educated would not be happy under the Communists because 'we've brought them up in our ideas'. It is true that the French tried to force their language and education upon the Vietnamese, obliging the children to chant in school: '*Nos ancêstres les gaulois habitaient jadis la Gaule.*' However, this French education was not a success. When the French arrived in the country, some eighty per cent of the people knew the Chinese ideographs for writing Vietnamese. The French prohibited Chinese characters and forced people to use the Latin transliteration devised by a missionary in the seventeenth century. The young Vietnamese protested by simply refusing to go to school:

at the end of the 1930s, eighty per cent of boys of school age were not attending classes. The old-fashioned Mandarins and the new generation of left-wing rebels joined in rejecting what Fowler calls 'our ideas'. From reading *The Quiet American*, no one would guess that the Vietnamese had a civilisation, literature and national pride when 'our ancestors the Gauls' were still savages painted in woad.

If Graham Greene sentimentalises the French and patronises the Vietnamese his attitude to the Americans sometimes verges on snobbery. Dislike of American liberalism sounds very often like simple dislike of Americans. Fowler says that Pyle belongs to the dude ranch, the skyscraper and the express elevator, the ice-cream, the martini and milk at lunch with a chicken sandwich. Pyle had taken a good degree in – 'well, one of those subjects that Americans can take degrees in: perhaps public relations or theatrecraft, perhaps even Far Eastern studies (he had read a lot of books)'.

Greene's anti-Americanism had little to do, in those days, with left-wing sentiment. It belonged to an older, often Tory tradition. The anti-American founding father was Samuel Johnson, scourge of the 'patriots', by which he meant those who believed in Rousseau's '*patrie*', the all-powerful state or government. As a champion of the African race, Dr Johnson asked with reference to the Americans: 'How is it that we hear the loudest yelps for liberty among the drivers of negroes?' Charles Dickens laboured the same point in *Martin Chuzzlewit*, which also makes sport of windy American orators and journalists such as Cyrus Choak, Jefferson Brick and Lafayette Kettle. Greene's friend Evelyn Waugh indulged in anti-American feeling that joined Dickens's mockery to Johnson's Toryism. In the 1930s, when Greene and Waugh were getting into their writing stride, the United States was more popular with the Left than the Right in Britain. Liberals and socialists (and also the Fascists) admired Roosevelt's New Deal as intervention by the State (*la patrie*) to help the poor and unemployed. The Conservatives, with the exception of Winston Churchill, looked down on Americans as vulgar parvenus.

Soon after the publication of *The Quiet American*, Hollywood turned the story into a film, with Michael Redgrave as Fowler and Audie Murphy as Pyle. To the fury of Greene and most of the critics, the scriptwriters and the director turned the story inside out, making Pyle innocent of the bombing, and Fowler a Communist dupe. Having read the reviews, I did not see the film at the time it came out and for thirty years I accepted the general opinion that it was worthless. Quite recently, when I saw the film on late-night television, I had to change my mind. The film is not only well directed and acted but sticks as far as possible to the plot and dialogue of the novel. But whereas Pyle appears as a good-natured idealist, Fowler appears as a bitter and rather arrogant English snob, moved largely by sexual jealousy. Greene's anti-American jibes, spoken in Redgrave's petulant whine, serve to condemn Fowler.

It was perhaps unfortunate for Greene that the film of *The Quiet American* came out shortly after the two British diplomats Guy Burgess and Donald Maclean had defected to Russia. They too were upper-class, snobbish and virulently anti-American. The third of these Communist spies, Kim Philby, was also a close friend of Greene. Of course the film perverted the book of *The Quiet American*, but it did so cleverly, in a way that almost improved the plot. Seeing the film, I began to ask myself, 'Did Fowler really have proof that Pyle was behind the bombing?' The book says so, but then the narrator is Fowler himself. Perhaps the narrator should have been the detective, Inspector Vigot.

About seven or eight years after its publication, *The Quiet American* came to be seen as both a prophetic and left-wing book. In the meantime, Greene had gone to live for a time in Cuba and written *Our Man in Havana* about an amateur spy who pretends that diagrams of the vacuum cleaners he sells are plans of Soviet nuclear rockets. When the Cuba Crisis followed, Greene started to gain his reputation for having political second sight. By that year, 1962, the American presence was growing in Vietnam, and hundreds of real-life Pyles were building a Third Force, and winning the hearts and minds of the people. In November 1963, the CIA mounted a *coup d'état* against South Vietnam's President Ngo Dinh Diem, who was later shot. President Kennedy, like Pyle, was playing at God with the lives of the Vietnamese. Three weeks after the death of Diem, President Kennedy too was killed, like Pyle. As the war progressed, *The Quiet American* entered the anti-war scriptures.

Meanwhile Greene had become politically militant, taking the side of anti-United States rebels in Haiti, Argentina, Panama and eventually Nicaragua. In December 1985, I spent a few days in the small Nicaraguan town of Rivas, during the Feast of the Assumption, when everyone lets off thunder-flashes, locally known as *bombas*. One of these was a real bomb which went off on the church steps during Mass. On the way back to Managua next day, I thought of that much bigger bomb that went off in front of the Continental. That evening, in the bar of the main hotel in Managua, I saw Graham Greene with one of the Sandinista leaders, and later I introduced myself. He was very friendly, talking of people we knew in London, but would not move onto Nicaraguan politics, on which we disagreed. I told him about the bomb at Rivas, hoping to lure him into revealing what he now thought of the bomb in *The Quiet American*. Was Pyle really guilty? Alas, Mr Greene would not be drawn.

Reading *The Quiet American* once again in 1990, here in my bedroom in the Majestic, or over a beer at Givral's café, I get the impression of having been frozen in time. Saigon is immutable. It is the outside world that changes. At one point in the story, Phuong asks Fowler, 'Are there skyscrapers in London?' and Fowler, who knows she is thinking of Pyle, says gently that no, the skyscrapers are in New York. Reading that passage in 1990, when London was studded with skyscrapers, I realised just what an age had passed since Greene was in Saigon writing this novel, and how magnificently it had weathered the test of time.

10

Vietnam: 1994

At the time of my visits to Vietnam in 1990, the news was full of the dissolution of Communism in Eastern Europe. In Poland, Hungary, Romania and Bulgaria, the governments broke with their former Soviet masters, though local Communists clung to a measure of power. In Yugoslavia and Czechoslovakia, the process of change re-awoke religious and cultural differences, and led to an end of the federations formed after the First World War from the wreck of the Austro-Hungarian Empire. By 1991 the Communist system had virtually come to an end in tiny Albania and in the mighty Soviet Union itself, which also fragmented into a number of breakaway states of Slav, Baltic or Asiatic race. The counter-revolution that I had hoped and believed would happen first in Vietnam, early in 1989, had still not arrived there five years later.

The collapse of the Soviet Union meant the end of the Cold War, of which I had been an observer all my adult life. As a teenage national service soldier in Trieste, in 1949–50, I heard the stories of newly arrived refugees from Tito's Yugoslavia, and from the far crueller tyrannies of the Soviet satellite states. I read many accounts of the Soviet Union, notably Viktor Kravchenko's *I Chose Freedom*, and Gustav Herling's *A World Apart*, on his experiences in the Gulag Archipelago. In 1953 I went for a post-graduate year to Yugoslavia, while Milovan Djilas was starting his brave rebellion against the Communist system he once had helped to create. In Yugoslavia and then on journeys to Poland, Czechoslovakia, Hungary and the Soviet Union itself, I came to see that political theories could never replace the need of the human heart for religion, the family and love of country. This realisation became complete on reading Solzhenitsyn's novel *The First Circle* and later *The Gulag Archipelago*.

Foreign fellow-travellers of the Soviet Union, who had been numerous in Western Europe and the United States during the life of Stalin, grew disillusioned after the intervention in Hungary in 1956 and again in Czechoslovakia twelve years later. But loss of faith in Russia did not cause them to lose their faith in the revolutionary dreams of Paris in 1789. The novelist Evelyn Waugh remarked of the foreign radicals in Mexico in 1939:

> These are the ideologues; first in Moscow, then in Barcelona, now in Mexico, these credulous pilgrims pursue their quest for the promised land; continually disappointed, never disillusioned, ever thirsty for the phrases in which they find refreshment, they have flocked to Mexico in the last few months, since the present rulers have picked up a Marxist vocabulary.

So in the 1960s and 1970s, the credulous pilgrims turned towards new variants of the revolutionary dream. One of these was Mao Zedong's economic 'Great Leap Forward' during the early 1960s and his Cultural Revolution which started in 1966. The other phenomenon was that movement in the West, variously known as the New Left, the Sexual Revolution or the Permissive Society, at times embracing the theories of Trotsky, Che Guevara, Frantz Fanon, Herbert Marcuse and Sigmund Freud; lending support to the often terrorist 'liberation movements' in Latin America, southern Africa, Ireland and Palestine, as well as a social revolt against the accepted rules on sexual behaviour and drug abuse; developing in the 1970s into a fresh assault on family life from the feminists, the militant homosexuals, and the inquisitors into allegations of rape, sexual harassment and child abuse.

This last became the pretext for a campaign of denunciations, house arrests and removal of children by the state, often followed by show trials held in an atmosphere of hysteria with the young denouncing their parents and teachers. At one trial in New Jersey, a nursery school teacher found guilty of charges of sexual assault on children in her care was sentenced to 137 years in prison. For want of a better term I shall call this amorphous movement the 'Sixties Revolution', after the decade in which it began and enjoyed its most famous triumph, the Paris *événements* of 1968.

In the frenzy and frivolity of the Sixties Revolution, with its Flower People, its Beatles music and omnipresent reek of marijuana, the West heard little and cared less about the horrific Cultural Revolution in China, coming after the thirty million deaths of the 'Great Leap Forward'. The man-made famine, followed by a more fearful orgy of persecution, torture, lynching, burning of books and smashing of works of beauty, then mass deportation to slave camps, were almost as bad as Stalin's forced collectivisation during the 1930s, the treason trials and the setting up of the Gulag Archipelago.

Partly because of the difficulty of access to Communist China, the West had no idea at the time of the scale of the horror of the 'Great Leap Forward', and how it should have affected our attitude to the Vietnam War. The South Vietnamese, especially the ethnic Chinese minority, were very aware of the danger posed by Mao and his influence over the Hanoi Communists. The Cambodian Communists, nicknamed 'Khmer Rouge' by Prince Norodom Sihanouk, had modelled themselves on Mao and later would institute in the 'Killing Fields' their local Cultural Revolution. But just as it took the West thirty years to grasp what Stalin had done in the 1930s, so it took another thirty years to grasp the evil of Mao in the 1960s.

In retrospect I can see I was quite as guilty as other Westerners of failing to see the significance of the events in China. Like many, I read with a certain amusement of Mao's 'Great Leap Forward' by mobilising the masses to the production of steel. I did not know that in order to fuel these back-yard furnaces, the countryside was stripped of its forest cover, and tens of millions of peasants and factory workers were turned into steel-makers. I certainly did not know that as a result of neglect of agriculture in favour of steel, a famine arose in which at the very least thirty million died.

Mao Zedong started his Cultural Revolution in 1966, the year that I first went to South Vietnam. Far from appreciating its dire significance, I looked on it merely with disdain. Once, in 1967, I actually witnessed some of the Red Guards in action, on a French plane bound from Djakarta to China, via Saigon and Phnom Penh. The majority of the passengers on the flight were young Chinese Indonesians, who had decided, or more probably been compelled, to return to the country of their ancestors. This was only a year after the overthrow of Sukarno and the wholesale massacre of the Indonesian Communists, many of whom were ethnic Chinese. Even before they boarded the plane at Djakarta, these young Chinese in their blue jackets and caps were clutching Mao's *Little Red Book* and shouting his slogans. They kept up their shouting all the way to Saigon, to the great dismay of the French air hostess who plied me with free champagne to compensate for the noise of 'these brats'. When we reached Saigon, the Red Guards brandished their books and yelled Mao's thoughts at the military might of the US Air Force, to such an extent that the airline staff refused to come out to pick up my luggage. Finally I had to climb into the hold of the plane to extract my case from the tin trunks of the Maoists.

Mao remained in power in China throughout the Vietnam War till his death in 1976, a year after the fall of Saigon. There followed the imprisonment of his widow Madame Mao and the rest of the 'Gang of Four' from Shanghai, the gradual abandonment of the Cultural Revolution, the liberalisation of agriculture and the economy, and the opening up of China to the outside world.

President Nixon, having abandoned South Vietnam in the Paris negotiations of 1972, made an historic visit to China, and after his fall from power he maintained the connection, becoming with

Kissinger a leading light of the new China Lobby. From 1979, when Communist China briefly went to war with Communist Vietnam, Nixon and Kissinger used the China Lobby for the pursuit of their feud against the Hanoi government, denouncing its intervention in Cambodia, and lending support to the legend of the two thousand Missing in Action. Out of the bitterness of their wounded pride, Nixon, Kissinger and other United States politicians supported the still Maoist regime in China, and even their murderous clients, the Khmer Rouge, against the more reasonable Vietnamese Communists. The very Americans who once had propounded the Domino Theory, and vowed to prevent the advance of Red China in South-east Asia, were now Red China's supporters.

My only visit to Communist China, in 1983, came about as part of a cruise on a Scandinavian luxury liner, to which I had been invited as representative of *The Field*, a journal of hunting, shooting and fishing for which I wrote at the time. The trip included three nights in Peking and two in Shanghai, and I read all I could of China's recent history. Even from such a cursory visit I got some idea of Mao's Cultural Revolution simply from seeing the physical devastation of Peking. What had apparently been a medieval city of parks, gardens, market-places, tree-lined avenues and crowded lanes between houses and shops, was now a collection of concrete blocks surrounding the central horror of Tiananmen Square. It occurred to me that this vast, empty parade ground in front of Mao's tomb was still more menacing and totalitarian than even the tallest monuments of other dictators.

By contrast Shanghai, the residence of the Gang of Four, had been physically left unchanged from its days as a western treaty port, so that architecturally it remains a mixture of French Third Republic and Edwardian Surrey or Hampstead Garden Suburb. I was also pleased to find that Shanghai had preserved or rediscovered much of its old commercial spirit, with busy shops, markets, tea-rooms and restaurants, even a con-man, who stopped me and offered to go into business, trading tea for photographic equipment. It seemed clear that the coastal Chinese were rapidly moving back to a market economy, leaving the North to the bureaucrats and the Communists. Moreover the Chinese I met showed no sign of having been cowed or brainwashed, as still was the case in some of the countries of Eastern Europe.

At the Peace Hotel I bought one of the two delightful books on old Shanghai by Lynn Pan, who had left her native city as a child to be educated in England. Far from dwelling upon the undoubted horrors of the old regime, Lynn Pan is charmed by the sleazy gangsters and sing-song girls, the brothels and gambling hells, the White Russian *émigrés* and American adventurers, and of course Marlene Dietrich telling us that it took more than one man to give her the name 'Shanghai Lillie'. Lynn Pan, who went on to write excellent books on the Yellow River and on the overseas Chinese, is one of several bright and articulate young authors (most of them women) who have helped to explain their country to Westerners.

Chinese writers such as Lynn Pan, who had lived abroad during the Cultural Revolution, could convey its horrors only at second hand, from the accounts of relatives and friends. For me, as for millions of Western readers, the first partial comprehension of what it was like to live in Mao Zedong's China came with the publication in 1991 of Jung Chang's *Wild Swans*. This is the chronicle of the experiences of her grandmother, her mother and herself, through the civil wars of the 1920s, the Japanese occupation of Manchuria, the rule of the Kuomintang, the Communist capture of power, the early days of the new regime in Sichuan Province, the 'Great Leap Forward' and then the hell of the Cultural Revolution, in which Jung Chang and her family were tormented almost to death.

Jung Chang has written a family chronicle comparable in its tragic intensity to a novel by Tolstoy or Balzac, and yet it is not a work of fiction. With its Eastern concern for family ties and filial duty, *Wild Swans* has echoes of two other books already mentioned, the eighteenth-century Vietnamese epic poem *Kim Van Kieu*, and Kukrit Pramoj's delightful saga about the Thai royal court, *Four Reigns*. Yet although the success of *Wild Swans* comes from the human drama and power to arouse our pity and terror, this is also, and almost in spite of itself, a major political document. Only two other writers, Milovan Djilas and Alexander Solzhenitsyn, have given us comparable insight into the nature of Communism. All three, in their different ways, began as Marxist believers, then suffered persecution, yet emerged with the strength of mind and wisdom to analyse their experiences. One of the side-effects on me of Jung Chang's book was to put the Vietnam War in a wholly different perspective, by relating it to the tragedy of China.

The early chapters of *Wild Swans* recounting the story of Jung Chang's grandmother caused me to reconsider what China was like between the two world wars, and how it compared with Vietnam before the Communist victory. The opening words of her book proclaim that Jung Chang does not romanticise the olden days:

> At the age of fifteen my grandmother became the concubine of a warlord general, the police chief of a tenuous national government of China. The year was 1924 and China was in chaos.

She goes on to describe the various miseries of a woman's life, such as foot-binding, arranged marriage or concubinage, poor education and physical toil. Foreign intervention, followed by the collapse of the Empire and Sun Yat Sen's revolution, had led to brigandage and civil war, in which the two main armies were led by Chiang Kai Shek and Mao Zedong. The Japanese invaded and occupied Manchuria, the home of Jung Chang's grandmother and mother, and after the Japanese came civil war between Chiang's Nationalists and Mao's Communists.

When Chiang and the remnants of his Kuomintang army fled the Chinese mainland in 1949 and established themselves on Formosa, now called Taiwan, Western liberal opinion saw this as good riddance. The historian Barbara Tuchman, who wrote a book on the efforts of General Stilwell to save China both from Japan and Communism, was always contemptuous of Chiang Kai

Shek and his followers, seeing Mao's victory as inevitable. Perhaps unconsciously, when writing her later book *The March of Folly: From Troy to Vietnam*, Barbara Tuchman saw the Saigon regime as another Nationalist China.

The United States, in its efforts to save Chiang in 1945, had sent in 50,000 Marines to northern China, occupying Peking and Tianjin. The memory that in spite of their military help, China had fallen to Communism, haunted Americans during the Vietnam War. For several decades after the Second World War, the anti-Communist Vietnamese found it hard to resist the determined army of Ho Chi Minh, and after the French defeat at Dien Bien Phu, could barely retain their grip on the southern half of the country. The regime of Ngo Dinh Diem, and his sinister brother and sister-in-law, partook of some of the vices of Chiang and his Kuomintang. But during the second half of the 1960s and up till the fall of Saigon in 1975, South Vietnam was a stronger and better-run country, motivated by faith in tradition, family and religion. The South Vietnam I knew bore little resemblance to pre-Communist China as described in *Wild Swans*.

If Communism triumphed in China because of the misery of the old regime, how did the Khmer Rouge come to power in peaceful, prosperous Cambodia? After the overthrow of Sihanouk in March 1970, the apologists for the new Lon Nol government talked of the Prince's egotistical style and his failure to deal with social problems, especially amoebic dysentery. But Sihanouk's critics could not pretend that Cambodia in the 1960s suffered the woes of China under the Kuomintang. The country was calm and content, and I wrote after my first visit in 1963 that 'only a war or grotesque mismanagement could produce real hunger or poverty'. This was partly due to the blessings of Nature. Whereas in China, the vagaries of the Yellow and Yangtse rivers often resulted in flooding or famine, and millions of deaths, the River Tonle Sap, which waters the central rice lands of Cambodia, brings nothing but riches, thanks to its habit of changing direction. During the dry season, it flows north to south into the Mekong, but during the Mekong flood it flows upstream, creating the Tonle Sap lake. The peasants get two floods for their rice paddies and two runs of fish for their nets. And yet these prosperous as well as happy people saw their country turned into the 'Killing Fields'.

When the full horror of what had happened was first revealed to the Western public in 1979, the left wing tried to suggest that the Khmer Rouge were not really Communists but Fascists. Yet anyone who has studied Communism can see that Pol Pot and Ieng Sary belong to the spirit of the Revolution first proposed by Rousseau, then put into action by Robespierre and reaching apotheosis in Stalin's Russia and Mao's China. All these revolutionaries saw in terror, show trials, and the denunciation of parents by children, the means of destroying the opposition and even the thought of opposition to the totalitarian state. Through fear of accusation, torture, prison and an anonymous death, the revolutionaries roused the people themselves to destroy all vestiges of the old regime, starting with noblemen, landlords, the middle classes, priests, men and women of learning, and at last the family. Having destroyed all opposition, the revolutionaries in France, Russia, China and Cambodia started to torture and murder each other.

From Jung Chang's book we see how the revolutionary hatred extends from human beings to Nature itself, so that Mao decreed the abolition of grass, flowers and animals kept as pets. At one time Mao took a dislike to sparrows, so that every household was mobilised into banging metal objects, from cymbals to saucepans, scaring the birds from the trees till they died from exhaustion. In his total war against human pleasure, Mao said that 'relaxation' was obsolete:

> Books, paintings, musical instruments, sports, cards, chess, teahouses, bars – all had disappeared. The parks were desolate, vandalised wastelands, in which the flowers and the grass had been uprooted and the tame birds and goldfish killed. Films, plays and concerts had all been banned: Mme Mao had cleared the stages and the screens for the eight 'revolutionary operas' which she had

had a hand in producing, and which were all anyone was allowed to put on.

Believers in revolution, those 'credulous pilgrims' whom Waugh encountered in Mexico in the 1930s, refuse to see that all efforts to build a heaven on earth are vain, because of man's fallen nature. Yet throughout the twentieth century, each new failure of revolution, in Russia, East Europe, China, Cambodia, North Korea, Cuba and Nicaragua, was blamed not on the Marxist theory but on its 'distortion' or 'betrayal' by various deviationists. Among those very few Communist leaders who died before they came to be branded as 'counter-revolutionaries' were Lenin himself and Ho Chi Minh. Throughout the war and even up to the present day, apologists for the Vietnamese Communists have lauded Ho as a wise, noble and selfless idealist, incapable of becoming a Stalin or Mao Zedong. They have also claimed, probably rightly, that Ho disapproved of the Cultural Revolution which started three years before his death in 1969. It may well be true that Ho was one of those rare dictators (Tito and Atatürk come to mind) who did not suffer from megalomania and morbid suspicion of their colleagues.

Except during the forced collectivisation of North Vietnam in the second half of the 1950s, Ho did not resort to terror and mass murder to maintain revolutionary zeal. He had no need to. From 1946 to 1954 and again from 1960 to 1975, all-out war was the driving force of Communism in Vietnam. As Burke had once predicted, the French Revolution flourished under the threat from external enemies, and set out 'to disturb and distract all other governments'. Jung Chang wrote of another revolution two centuries later:

> Mao found the idea of peaceful progress suffocating. A restless military leader, a warrior-poet, he needed action – violent action – and regarded permanent human struggle as necessary for social development. His own Communists had become too tolerant and soft for his taste, seeking to bring harmony rather than conflict.

There had been no political campaign, in which people fought each other, since 1959.

Since China faced no real political enemies, Mao had to create them by his Cultural Revolution, but Ho Chi Minh had an ever-present enemy in the French, the South Vietnamese and later the Americans. Having risen to power by guerrilla warfare against the French and the Saigon government, Ho established himself as a national hero defying the military might of a super-power. Through the sacrifice of hundreds of thousands of soldiers, as well as civilians killed in the US bombing, Communist Vietnam was a revolutionary nation at war, like France under Napoleon. Ho Chi Minh's successors continued fighting against the Chinese and Cambodian Communists.

Reading *Wild Swans* gave me another insight, this one into the reason why the United States failed in Vietnam. As I mentioned already, Mao's Cultural Revolution came at the same time as what I have called the Sixties Revolution in the United States, and both had in common an enmity to the principles of the South Vietnamese, such as respect for tradition, religious belief and family feeling. But the resemblance does not end there. Indeed, after I finished *Wild Swans*, I had the uneasy sense that whereas China has now recovered its sanity after the Cultural Revolution, the Sixties Revolution has taken over America and most of Western Europe.

From the fall of Saigon in 1975 till the liberalisation began in the late 1980s, I had neither the chance nor the wish to revisit Vietnam, except for the tourist outing of 1980. However, during this time I resumed and extended my old connection with Yugoslavia, visiting there for work and pleasure. The more I grew to dislike modern Britain, the more I appreciated Yugoslavia, so blessedly free of sociological cant and welfare state interference. I even considered emigration to Zagreb or the Dalmatian coast.

At the end of the 1980s, as I saw the revival of hope in South Vietnam, I saw with dread the reappearance in Yugoslavia of hatreds based on the ancient divisions of Catholic and Orthodox

Christians, and of both with Islam. After a happy sojourn in Saigon in the summer of 1990, I sensed in Zagreb in October the unmistakable presence of the Ustasha, the Croatian terrorist movement from the Second World War. In the summer of 1991, in Sarajevo and Mostar, I had the same sense of approaching catastrophe that I knew from Saigon in 1975.

In knowledge of their impending fate, people tried to divert their minds by making plans for a holiday, starting a new job, or even getting married. Again I recalled Tolstoy's metaphor of the mood in Moscow in 1812, as a criminal on his way to the gallows, who knows that in a minute he will die, yet stares about him and even straightens his cap sitting awry on his head. Such was the mood in Sarajevo in 1991, as it had been in Saigon in 1975, yet for seemingly opposite reasons. While the South Vietnamese were losing a civil war and dreading the onset of Communism, the Yugoslavs had been peaceful and happy under Communism, and dreaded the onset of civil war.

My view that the breakup of Yugoslavia would lead to a civil war, first in Croatia and then in Bosnia-Hercegovina, did not conform to the popular wisdom, so that I found it almost impossible to get articles on Yugoslavia published, let alone raise the money to go there. So I wrote a life of Tito instead. Afterwards, in the hope of shaking off the sorrow I felt at the ruin of Yugoslavia, I wrote this memoir of Vietnam, a country whose fortunes had changed in the opposite way, as though in a game of snakes and ladders.

Having completed the first draft of this book, I longed to go back to Vietnam to bring the story up to date and perhaps to give it a happy ending. I canvassed magazines and newspapers, hoping to get a commission towards my expenses. Only one editor made me an offer, and then took it back. However, by this time I had bought my visa as well as a cheap return ticket to Bangkok. And so it was that I stepped off a plane at Tan Son Nhut airport, more than twenty-eight years after my first visit in 1966.

Coming back to Saigon for the fifth time since the war, I was once more amazed by its ever-increasing prosperity and contentment. The road from the airport, which during the 1960s presented a dismal prospect of slums, scrapyards, dusty building sites, black-market stalls and girlie bars, now runs through a clean, smart suburb of private villas, offices and factories, shops, hotels, restaurant and above all trees, for Saigon is becoming again what it was in the 1930s, a *ville-parc* of greenery, under the care of botanists from the zoological gardens.

The Chinese sister-city of Cholon was always neater and cleaner than Saigon, but it suffered during the state-sponsored Sinophobia after 1975, when tens of thousands of Hoa were stripped of their savings and forced to flee the country as Boat People. The persecution was started by Northerners, who feared that their own Hoa might serve as a Fifth Column for China; the Saigon people got on well with their Cholon neighbours. When a Southerner, Nguyen Van Linh, became General Secretary of the Communist Party in 1986, he not only brought in the *Doi Moi* reforms but dropped the harassment of Hoa. Many ethnic Chinese were among the Viet Kieu who started to stream back to the country with foreign passports and money for their protection.

Among them was Philip Chow, who persuaded the Saigon authorities to allow racing again at the Phu Tho hippodrome, built by the French and opened in 1932, as an Asian Chantilly. 'The people had money but the government didn't,' he told a newspaper reporter, 'and I thought it would be easier to get the money from people through legal betting than through higher taxes.' Early in 1994, two famous international racing men, Prince Khalid and Robert Sangster, donated two colts and a mare, with the aim of giving Saigon a bloodstock to rival Hong Kong and Singapore. But even the swiftest animals of Arabia or Ireland would find the going difficult at Phu Tho during the rainy season, when much of the course is under water. As in the 1960s, I noticed that some of the horses failed to keep up a gallop to the finishing post.

At the end of the previous chapter concerning *The Quiet American*, I wrote that the atmosphere of Saigon and even the very buildings remained as Greene had described them forty years earlier. Now, alas, this has changed. A Hong Kong company has bulldozed an entire block of houses between Tu Do and Hai Ba Trung to make way for a giant, high-rise complex behind and towering over the Caravelle Hotel. Besides throwing hundreds of people out of their homes and spoiling the Tu Do skyline, the Hong Kong wreckers have incidentally removed a well-known landmark from the American days, the house of those hippy reporters who went to the war on motor-bikes, high on rock and roll, marijuana and danger. One of the few survivors of that band is the English photographer Tim Page, who figures large in Michael Herr's book *Dispatches*, in Francis Coppola's *Apocalypse Now*, and in a television serial set in the house on Tu Do.

Although threatened by high-rise building, Saigon has so far resisted plans to turn it into a city for the motor car, with highways, ring-roads, flyovers, underpasses and multi-storey car parks. It is still well served by public transport, scooters, push bikes and the cyclo pedicabs; the ruination of Bangkok started when the city fathers banned the tricycle *samlor*. It seems that resistance to the motor car is a deliberate policy, not just a financial necessity, since Singapore and Hong Kong are also dedicated to public transport. I am told that the Asians in New York City are popularising the bicycle.

Coming from London, a city infested with able-bodied and sometimes menacing pan-handlers, it is neartening to find that in Saigon the only remaining beggars are maimed victims of war. There are plenty of touts but they all have something to sell, for instance a shoe-shine, a packet of postcards, a model ship or the *International Herald-Tribune*. The gangs of child pickpockets who used to mob passers-by in the 1960s, and seemed to have reappeared in the 1980s, now seem to have vanished; foreign residents do not complain of a crime problem. The Saigon police have exchanged their guns for truncheons, just when ours are doing the opposite. Since there are now no girlie bars, the prostitutes ply for trade from their scooters.

Tu Do is the place to test the political mood of Saigon, as it was in 1934 when a procession of French and Vietnamese businessmen marched on the hated Banque de l'Indochine, 'the temple of the golden calf', shouting 'Down with the sharks' and 'Down with the gold standard'. The scooter and bicycle processions on Sunday evenings, a feature of Saigon life in 1988 and 1990, still continue but now in a muted form, with less of a spirit of confrontation and no honking of horns. At the time of my second visit in 1990, the secret police were cracking down on dissidents and I was warned against talking to strangers. Even in 1990, not many foreigners went to Saigon, but since then it has become once more a very cosmopolitan city. There are so many foreigners that no secret police force could hope to monitor all their conversations.

None of the many Vietnamese I met on this visit showed any sign of fear or constraint. Furthermore they are no longer obsessed by anger against the regime and the Northerners. They are anti-Communist but they are now cheerful and optimistic. Nor are they any longer starry-eyed about the West. 'Can you get a good education in England?' two students asked me, and when I had to admit that the state schools were rotten, they nodded. This was what they had heard on the grapevine from the Vietnamese abroad. On the other hand they had heard that education was better in France and Australia. From the Vietnamese in California, they know all about America's drug, crime and race problems.

Since most of the people I met were youngsters hoping to practise their English, I made a point of asking if they had ever wanted to emigrate. Without exception they all said they were happy and proud to have grown up in Vietnam. Some of them even volunteered a few words of praise for the government, not for its ideology but for its Vietnamese patriotism, especially standing up to China. In these five visits to Vietnam under the Communists, this was the first time I had heard anything favourable said of them.

It is a paradox of Saigon today that the new spirit of optimism and national pride has come when the city appears to be once more swarming with foreigners. There are daily flights to Saigon from most of the countries of eastern Asia, as well as further afield. The English-language daily *Vietnam News* is supplemented by newspapers from all over the world. The television set in the bedroom of even my modest hotel receives the British, French and Hong Kong news and feature service and no doubt will soon have CNN from America. In Tu Do alone there are restaurants offering Vietnamese, Chinese, Japanese, Indian, Korean, French, German, Italian, Spanish and Swiss food, cooked by chefs of the relevant nationality. In the opening up of Saigon to the outside world, it is hard at first to detect which countries are playing the major part, and the answers are rather surprising. Here I examine the presence today of the five foreign countries that have in the past played a major role in Saigon, in chronological order: France, Japan, Britain, the United States and Russia.

After the fall of Saigon in 1975, the few French residents left, but France maintained a consulate here and economic and cultural links. In 1980 I met French textile experts from Lille, advising a state-run factory, and patronising a café in Nguyen Thiep Street that offered them moonshine Pernod. Ten years later I met a young Frenchman in partnership with a Viet Kieu, running a lucrative private enterprise textile factory. He was also engaged in the property business and trying to set up an advertising agency.

In Saigon today there are said to be two thousand Frenchmen and women, compared to twelve thousand before the Second World War. They tend to be self-employed or in small private businesses, sometimes in partnership with Viet Kieu from France. Besides those in trade and manufacture, many French are engaged in service industries such as banking, insurance, advertising, real estate, airlines and shipping, tourism, hotels and catering. The French are the Europeans best equipped to compete in the restaurant business in Asia. One of the several French chefs in Saigon told me he likes the country so much, he intends to open his own restaurant.

The French run and patronise one of the liveliest restaurants in Saigon, Le P'tit Bistro, also the River Bar, which like the Continental terrace in the old days dispenses with air-conditioning to enjoy the cool of the evening breeze. With its bamboo bar and furniture, overhead fans and abundant greenery, it has the atmosphere of an old film set in the tropics, waiting for Humphrey Bogart or Jean Gabin. This was the first time I had met French people who really seemed to enjoy living abroad. One young man, who has a factory making pet accessories, said how much he preferred Saigon to Paris, with its high taxation, traffic jams, crime, drugs and North African immigrants. Saigon is also chic to the French, who are now indulging the same nostalgia for Indo-China that many Englishmen feel for the Indian Raj. French women especially enjoyed such recent romantic films as *Indochine*, with Catherine Deneuve appearing in many changes of tropical dress and background.

As well as rediscovering the glamour of the East, the French have started to reappraise the history of their involvement in Indo-China, especially the delicate question of what went on during the Second World War. This gap in my own knowledge of Vietnamese history was partly filled by two excellent books I discovered here, Philippe Franchini's *Continental Saigon* and a volume of essays edited and in part written by M. Franchini, *Saigon 1925–1945: De la "Belle Colonie" à l'éclosion révolutionnaire, ou la fin des dieux blancs*. Having known Franchini as the proprietor of the Continental Hotel, as an artist, film-maker and sardonic wit, I did not realise till now that he took a serious interest in Vietnamese history. He relates in his memoirs how, after the Second World War, he enrolled at the Sorbonne, hoping to learn about Indo-China:

> I discovered with astonishment the strange conception that France had of its colonies, the lack of interest it showed, in a general way, to colonial history. At the courses I attended – this was at the height of the Indo-China crisis – there were a few blacks and North Africans, a Canadian missionary, some foreigners from countries in process of decolonisation ... and one solitary Frenchman. It was hardly surprising that the French, in their ignorance, were prey to all sorts of propaganda. Metropolitan prejudice was

such, that in order to see the archives of the Ministry of Foreign Affairs from 1850 to 1870 – indispensible for my work – I had to get the backing of the dean of the faculty.

On the few occasions I met Philippe Franchini during the 1970s, it did not occur to me that he worried about his being a *métis*, the son of a Corsican father and Vietnamese mother. Now, from his memoirs, I find that Franchini has always been painfully conscious of his *métissage*, and had endured slights still more from his mother's than from his father's people. His maternal grandmother never forgave her Corsican son-in-law and always referred to him not as 'son' but as 'Mr Westerner'. Philip Franchini drily remarks of his father: 'Final irony ... "Mr Westerner" was unaware of the insult because he spoke no Vietnamese.'

Throughout his childhood, Philippe Franchini endured the taunts of *'métis'* from his French schoolmates, and from the Vietnamese the traditional insult, 'chicken's head, duck's arse'. Although his parents were married, he suffered the same contumely as the more numerous children born to a Frenchman's *con gai*, or 'girl' in the sense of mistress, often a poor peasant sold by her family to a procuress. Phuong in *The Quiet American* is a *con gai* rather than *co*, or girl in the ordinary sense. Mixed marriage or sexual liaison has always been far less acceptable in Vietnam than it is in the racially tolerant Europe or United States. The North Vietnamese, with their puritanism and pride of race, were still more opposed to miscegenation. Philippe Franchini thinks that the Northern conquerors of 30 April 1975 'wanted to cleanse Saigon, to chastise its naughtiness and above all to purge it of *métissage*'.

The Hanoi government's brutal treatment of half-caste children, and then their expulsion in the 1980s, failed to dislodge from the liberal Western mind the deep-rooted delusion that only white people are 'racists'. In fact the whites are outstandingly tolerant. To understand this, one only has to imagine what the reaction would have been if the United States had expelled from the country children of white mothers and Asian fathers, the obverse of what Hanoi did in the 1980s.

Philippe Franchini is at his best in describing the odd and even surreal events in Indo-China during the Second World War. He says that during the 'Phoney War' in the winter of 1939–40, the French in Saigon felt remote from trouble, and even after Hitler had launched his blitzkrieg on Paris, they held their annual Turf Club ball at the Continental Hotel. After the fall of France and Charles de Gaulle's call to continue the struggle, the French in Saigon were overwhelmingly Gaullist, and gathered to cheer the Union Jack at the British Consulate. The Gaullist cause suffered a set-back when Churchill ordered the Royal Navy to shell the French fleet at Mers el-Kébir in Algeria, 'strewing the sea with pom-poms', especially since the new Governor-General of Indo-China was a naval officer, Admiral Decoux.

Soon after the fall of France, Japan demanded the right to station troops in Indo-China and use its airfields for military planes. When Decoux demurred, in September 1940, the Japanese Army launched a punitive raid across Vietnam's border, killing 800 French troops at Lan Son, the scene of a French débâcle in 1885 and a Chinese débâcle in 1979. While French Indo-China was under threat from Japan, the Thais invaded from the west to 'reclaim' parts of Laos and Cambodia. Among those who served in this brief war was the future novelist and statesman Kukrit Pramoj, who as Thailand's Prime Minister in 1975 closed down the American bases and formed an alliance with Communist China. During that difficult autumn of 1940, Admiral Decoux was faced as well by a peasant revolt in the Mekong Delta. Perhaps out of pique at France's humiliation by Japan and Thailand, Decoux punished the rebels with needless cruelty.

Vietnam provided the jungle training ground and the air and naval base for Japan's invasion of South-east Asia beginning on 6 December 1941. Even after the war had started, Japan permitted the French in Indo-China to carry on running the civil government, though now under the scrutiny of the Kempetai, or secret police.

In Japan's new empire and Co-Prosperity Sphere in South-east Asia, the only countries retaining a measure of independence were Thailand and French Indo-China. As the British and Dutch were starved in concentration camps, or worked to death on the Burma Railway, their former allies the French continued to taste the delights of the opium pipe, the aperitif and the beautiful *con gai*. Admiral Decoux was not content with keeping the government ticking over. He embarked on a programme of social reform and moral uplift based on the ideals of Marshal Pétain in Vichy France. The programme included road-building and public works, the setting up of co-operatives, the extension of primary schools in the countryside, the teaching of Vietnamese cultural history in the *lycées*, and the expansion of the university. The administration condemned the practice of Europeans addressing the Vietnamese as *tu*, the familiar 'thou', and banned the word *indigène*, 'native', in all official pronouncements. Ceremonies were staged to honour the monarchies of Vietnam, Laos and Cambodia, suggesting that they could flourish only under the aegis of France.

A naval captain, Ducoroy, the Commissioner of Youth and Sport, mounted a series of propaganda rallies and demonstrations to foster patriotism. In 1941 he organised a relay race of runners bearing a lighted torch from Hanoi round the peninsula to the temple of Angkor Wat, its flame to be seen as a symbol of still living France. A series of athletic events in 1942 was followed in 1943 by the first 'Tour de l'Indochine' cycle race, which proved as popular as the 'Tour de France' in the homeland, now abandoned because of the war. The success of the race was eclipsed in May 1944 by Captain Ducoroy's gigantic 'Festival of Joan of Arc', staged on the broad Boulevard Norodom behind the red-brick Notre Dame Cathedral. One of those taking part was the sixteen-year-old schoolboy Philippe Franchini.

In his memoirs, *Continental Saigon*, Franchini says that even before the Joan of Arc celebrations, the pupils at the *lycée* Chasseloup-Laubat had grown accustomed to hymning the praises of Marshal Pétain, for whom, as an old man, the Vietnamese anyway felt respect. To prepare for the so-called 'J-Day', which strangely enough came shortly before the D-Day of France's liberation, the schoolboys were trained to march in step and to chant in unison *Maréchal, nous voilà!* or 'Marshal, present and correct!', which sounded in Vietnamese French as *Mareçang, nous vouala!*' When 'J-Day' arrived, Franchini with thousands of other young people and children in white shirts and shorts assembled on Boulevard Norodom, where an enormous statue of Joan had been erected under an equally grandiose French flag. The saint was portrayed as a shepherdess, escorted by lambs, to avoid any reminder of her military role, and her hands were shown joined in a gesture of prayer like the Virgin Mary, or Kuan Yin, the Chinese goddess of mercy. Two placards bearing the arms of France, a sword and a fleur-de-lys were there to remind the crowd of the mother country's protection. There was a stand for the notables, dressed in white, except for some of the Vietnamese bourgeois who wore their heavy dark suits at the risk of suffocation under the broiling May sun. Franchini says that he and his schoolmates could scarcely smother their mirth when one of these gentlemen stood to reveal that under his black jacket and tie he was wearing white shorts. Franchini continues:

> At last Captain Ducoroy arrived, visibly proud of this vast assembly. One could sense he was moved to see, standing side by side, French, Vietnamese, Indians and *métis*, children and young people, singing together *Maréchal, nous voilà!* to which was added a certain local colour. Certainly it did not occur to him that the young Vietnamese had made a connection in their minds between Joan and the Vietnamese heroines, the Two Sisters Trung.

How could Captain Ducoroy have known, asks M. Franchini, with hindsight, that this manifestation of loyalty to Joan and France would be followed in little over a year by a larger and still more enthusiastic gathering, calling for the expulsion of the French?

Everything was there to convince him that he had won all hearts to the great cause of an Indo-China joined to the French Empire. Communal restaurants, public baths, centres for the young blind, homes for waifs and strays, civil defence and first aid units, schools for physical training instructors, all these things done on behalf of the young were beyond count. One only had to consider the carnival atmosphere of the tour of Indo-China cycle race, or the torch carried by volunteer runners . . . Yes, definitely his work had been a success.

Franchini says that the young people who took part in the demonstrations were far more nationalist than Ducoroy realised. It was not enough to make gestures like banning the use of *tu* as a form of address – a ban largely ignored by the French – in order to satisfy nationalistic feelings:

If Ducoroy had attended a football match in the public stands, he would have understood. I remember the underlying tensions I observed during a game between the 11th Colonial Infantry Regiment and the Vietnamese team Star of Gia Dinh. The slightest knock, the slightest friction, not to mention a brutal foul, was the signal for shouts and abuse, going far beyond the normal barracking from supporters.

There is something fantastic about the complacency of the French in holding their bicycle races, Olympic runs and Joan of Arc festival, right at the heart of Japan's Asian Empire, now approaching its nemesis. By the end of 1944, the Allies had liberated France itself, and were fighting their way north through the Philippines and east through Burma, preparing for an attack on the Malay Peninsula, Thailand and Indo-China. In one of the Allied air raids on Saigon, a bomb gutted the National Theatre, yards away from the Continental terrace café, whose patrons now were reduced to drinking rice-spirit whisky or *paddy soda*, and murky concoctions brewed from the mangosteen fruit. American OSS agents had crossed from China to northern Vietnam and made contact with Ho Chi Minh's Communists. The Kempetai in Saigon believed that Gaullist supporters were acting as spies for British or Free French intelligence. On 9 March 1945, Japan dismissed Admiral Decoux and his administration, arresting thousands of Frenchmen, some of whom were later tortured to death by the same Vietnamese police thugs who once tormented the Communists on behalf of France.

At this point, very late in the war, Japan attempted to play on racial hatred to gain the support of the Vietnamese populace. The Japanese had already befriended Prince Cuong De, a pretender to the throne at Hue, the leaders of the Cao Dai and Hoa Hao religious sects, and various nationalist politicians such as the lawyer and future President Ngo Dinh Diem. From 9 March 1945, the Japanese stepped up their appeals to racial feeling, summed up in a favourite metaphor: 'Take an egg, there is a white and a yellow part. The yellow is better, nobody doubts that. If you mix them together the yellow will come out on top. Nobody doubts that.'

Some nationalist Vietnamese took the chance to humble their former masters, as Pierre Brocheux recalls in an essay in *Saigon 1925–1945*:

> For me the revolution had already begun between March and August 1945. Going up Paul-Blanchy Street, behind the central park, I witnessed the daily spectacle of post office workers, wearing the caps of the Party of National Renewal, forcing all European men and women to get off their bicycle or cyclo (pedicab) to salute the yellow flag with three horizontal orange stripes, which was to become the emblem of the Republic of Vietnam in the 1950s.

The Japanese tried to arouse contempt for the white man by marching half-starved Dutch and Australian prisoners through Saigon, but according to M. Franchini this excited pity rather than hatred among the Vietnamese.

There were many Vietnamese in the war who admired Japan, and in one of the best essays in *Saigon 1925–1945*, Bui Xuan Quang suggests that the two countries may be coming together again. He argues that the Japanese have always regarded Saigon as the natural base for obtaining control of the peninsulas and islands of South-east Asia, with their abundant cheap labour and rich resources of oil, precious woods and strategic metals. During the war the city was glad to perform its role in Japan's Co-Prosperity Sphere. Then Bui continues:

> Fifty years later, when the time has come to debaptise Ho Chi Minh City, Saigon is asking the Japanese to return. To *invest*. To serve as a *model*. Historical irony: the sphere of co-existence and of economic co-prosperity, once so despised, now rallies everyone to its cause.

Bui Xuan Quang, who lectures and writes on international affairs in Paris, believes that Japan has taken into its long-term calculations the geographical, ideological and temperamental differences between the North and South Vietnamese:

> North Vietnam, monolithic, austere, less rich and resourceful than the South, should be integrated materially, economically and financially with southern China, notably with the coastal provinces, the Special Economic Zones of Yunan, Fujan, Quangdong, Guangsi and Hainan, to benefit from the dynamism of Hongkong, Canton and Taiwan. As for South Vietnam, more open, more developed than former Tonkin, it should naturally be joined to the prosperous community of the countries of ASEAN [Association of South-east Asian Nations], where Tokyo already has freedom of access and an important voice [*a déjà ses entrées et son mot à dire*].

It was startling to find on sale and to read in Ho Chi Minh City a book predicting its rebaptism as Saigon, as well as advancing the theory that North Vietnam might be joined with China, and South Vietnam with the ASEAN countries of Thailand, Malaysia, Singapore, Indonesia and the Philippines.

It is the ASEAN countries, as well as Hong Kong, Taiwan and South Korea, that make the running in Saigon's booming economy; yet oddly enough the British are now the most prominent foreign community. There are pubs with dart boards, billiard tables and video tapes of television soap operas set in Liverpool or London. The *Vietnam News* has a cricket correspondent, 'The Infielder', reporting on local matches between British, Australasian and Indian teams. But I soon came to see that most of the British in Saigon were not entrepreneurs but skilled workers on contract to non-British companies. For example the British long-term residents at the hotel where I stay are working either for a Hong Kong construction firm, or helping to install a boiler for a glass works owned by Chinese Malaysians.

The changed relationship between Britain and its former eastern empire is shown by an article in the *Vietnam Investment Review* (3–9 October 1994), listing thirty countries by the amount they invested in Vietnam in the first nine months of 1994. The list, in descending amounts of money invested, opens with Hong Kong, Taiwan, Singapore, Switzerland, Japan, USA, South Korea, Malaysia and France, down to numbers twenty-nine and thirty, respectively North Korea and the United Kingdom.

Britain's remaining colony, Hong Kong, and its two ex-colonies of Singapore and Malaysia are now far more prosperous than the mother country, thanks to their low taxation and government spending. As Asian immigrants have taken over Britain's textile, retail and catering businesses, so thousands of unemployed British are looking for work in Asia. In Hong Kong there are now more than 25,000 white British immigrants, most of them doing low-paid work as English-language teachers, waiters at table, kitchen staff and in services such as removal, delivery and decorating. One Hong Kong Chinese-language newspaper has called the British the 'new coolies'.

Another highly successful Asian country, Singapore, is proud to explain why it is now overtaking Britain and the United States. The Singapore Prime Minister Goh Chok Teng told a rally on 21 August 1994:

> America's and Britain's social troubles – a growing underclass which is violence-prone, uneducated, drug-taking and sexually

promiscuous – are the direct result of their family unit becoming redundant or non-functional. Our institutions and basic policies are in place to sustain high economic growth. But if we lose our traditional values, our family strength and cohesion, we will lose our vibrancy and decline. This is the intangible factor in the success of East Asian economies.

In the same speech, Prime Minister Goh revoked the right of unmarried mothers to buy public housing on favourable terms, saying that this had implicitly recognised unmarried motherhood as a respectable part of Singapore society. Yet in Singapore, only one in a hundred children is born out of wedlock compared to one in three in Britain and the United States. Singapore's contempt for Western liberal values was shown in 1994 when a court ordered the caning of an American youth for acts of vandalism.

Singapore's former Prime Minister and respected elder statesman, Lee Kuan Yew, is now a trusted friend and adviser to Vietnam's government. After the fall of Saigon in 1975, Lee was foremost among those warning that Communist Vietnam intended to conquer all South-east Asia, presumably driving out the Chinese and subjugating people of other races. Like all the ASEAN countries, Singapore opposed Vietnam's military intervention against the Khmer Rouge in Cambodia. Lee Kuan Yew's conversion into a friend of Hanoi has helped to bring Vietnam into the East Asian community, if not yet into ASEAN.

However, Lee Kuan Yew has theories on race, whose application to Vietnam could cause trouble. He believes that because of 'innate ethnic qualities', combined with climate and diet, the East Asians – meaning the Chinese, Japanese and Koreans – have a cultural edge over the Indians and South-east Asians. Lee regards the East Asians as 'disciplined, calculating, intense, achievement-oriented and sceptical', the Indians and South-east Asians as 'soft, intuitive, pleasure-loving and easy-going' – in everything but religion. Give an 'un-intense' people a surface-to-air missile, Lee once said disdainfully of the Thais, 'and you will have to have the instructor there till the end of time'. Lee Kuan

Yew's theory of a division between the 'disciplined' East Asians and 'pleasure-loving' South-east Asians could encourage renewed demands for the separation of North and South Vietnam.

To those who remember the war, the strangest feature of modern Saigon is the absence of an American influence. There are T-shirts on sale reading 'Good Morning, Vietnam', after a Hollywood film, and even a bar called 'Apocalypse Now', but most of the customers for both are European tourists on side trips from Bangkok. Two Americans work at the elegant 'Q Bar', built into the side of the National Theatre, the former Assembly, but here again most of the patrons are European or Vietnamese. Although President Clinton has lifted the trade embargo, there has been no rush to change from buying Asian cars, computers and stereophonic gadgetry. A hamburger and fried chicken restaurant has opened on Hai Ba Trung, but it does not flourish because the Vietnamese, like all Asians, prefer their traditional food. Nor have the Vietnamese taken to US clothes, sports, films, pornography or feminism.

During the US intervention, the Vietnamese resisted American popular music, preferring their own composers such as Trinh Cong Son, or the melancholy strain of the tango. Then, on returning to Saigon in 1980, I heard Western pop music booming from every public place. I thought then and think still that this was a form of political statement, a way of proclaiming 'Come back, Americans!' Today the Vietnamese still love tango music and Trinh Cong Son – who incidentally now owns an elegant restaurant serving 'Imperial' food in the style of Hue. But young Vietnamese adore American pop music. When I went to cash a traveller's cheque at the bank across the road from the Continental Hotel, I found the staff of two young men and two young women singing along in English to a tape at the back of the room. 'Nobody's going to change my love for you,' the two girls trilled from a printed sheet of the words, and continued to sing as they noted my passport details and counted the money. 'It's a George Benson song,' one of them told me during a pause between verses.

'We like it because it's very sad.' Although George Benson's is not my kind of music, I rather enjoyed this singing bank.

Although young people admire the United States, there is no longer a general craving to get to California. Even in 1990, the Vietnamese were so infatuated with the United States that I noticed the faces fall when I had to admit I was merely an Englishman. Now, I believe, the United States has left it too late to enjoy the affection and gratitude of the South Vietnamese. The Americans chiefly to blame are the Rambos who demonised the Communist Vietnamese, accused them of holding two thousand Missing in Action, and dreamed of a bloody revenge. Almost as harmful was the opposing delusion that US intervention had been a mistake and crime. Americans who thought that way could not accept or even believe in the gratitude and affection of the South Vietnamese.

The first American Vietnam veteran to open a bar in Saigon does not suffer from either delusion. Former Captain Bob Shibley, who runs 'Bob and Hien's Place' with his Vietnamese wife, did two terms of service here, learnt Vietnamese and came to admire the people. Even during the war he attended concerts of songs by Trinh Cong Son and was thrilled to hear that the great man had opened a restaurant in the same street, Hai Ba Trung. Shibley believes that US commanders such as General William Westmoreland fought the war in the wrong way, but he does not regret his own involvement. He says that most of the veterans who opposed the war belonged to that great majority who were never in combat. When I mentioned the name of Jane Fonda the actress and anti-war campaigner, Shibley said in a wistful fashion: 'I'd love for her to come into this bar, so I could have the pleasure of throwing her out.'

The Russians were always a forlorn presence in Saigon, and I had not expected to see them after the breakup of the Soviet Union. Then, in a German bar on Tu Do, I heard Russian spoken by three burly women. What were they doing here? I asked the Frenchman next to me. 'They're prostitutes,' he said, 'you find them all over the East these days. In Delhi, Bangkok, above all

Hong Kong.' Later, another French resident of Saigon explained that these women were also traders: 'They fly from Moscow with caviar and Cuban cigars. The woman I buy from comes to Saigon for a week, works as a prostitute, then flies back to Moscow with snow suits made in Vietnam.'

Epilogue

One of the books I read during that last stay in Saigon was the volume of Conrad stories I brought on my first visit to Indo-China, more than thirty years ago. The opening story, *Youth*, still perfectly captures the way I remember Thailand and Cambodia, 'the first sigh of the East on my face...' But over the years Bangkok had changed into just a squalid traffic jam. Cambodia suffered the horrors of the Killing Fields. Now, mysteriously, it is Vietnam and above all Saigon that has taken the place of Thailand and Cambodia as the East of Conrad's *Youth*. The second of Conrad's stories, *Heart of Darkness*, has little to do with the Vietnam of *Apocalypse Now*, though it remains a powerful metaphor of Africa and England.

The third story in the volume, *The End of the Tether*, is set in the East and serves as a gloomy antidote to the optimism of *Youth*. It concerns an old sailor, Captain Whalley, 'otherwise Daredevil Whalley of the *Condor*, a famous clipper in her day... Fifty years at sea, and forty out in the East had made him honourably known to a generation of shipowners and merchants in all the ports from Bombay clean over to where the East merges with the West upon the coast of the two Americas.' Captain Whalley has long since buried his wife in the Gulf of Petchile, has seen his daughter marry a profligate, and lost all his money in the crash of the Travancore and Deccan Bank, 'whose downfall had struck the

East like an earthquake'. He is forced to come out of retirement to sail his barque the *Fair Maid*, trading around the East Indian archipelago.

Three years before the action begins, his daughter has asked Captain Whalley for £200 to open a boarding-house in Melbourne. He sells his barque in a great port, probably Singapore, and looks around for employment, however humble, in somebody else's ship. But times have changed: 'There was no longer for Captain Whalley an armchair and a welcome in the private office, with a bit of business ready to be put in the way of an old friend, for the sake of bygone services.' He meets a contemporary from the old days, Captain Elliott, now rich and important as the Master-Attendant of shipping, who laughs out loud when Whalley shyly suggests he would like the job Elliott has mentioned, of taking charge of a Glasgow ship at Saigon.

At this point Captain Elliott stops laughing. Has he not heard that Whalley had been cleaned out by the Travancore and Deccan smash? Can he be penniless? Impossible, he must have something put by. Rather than help Whalley to find some work, Elliott says to him: 'We old fellows ought to take a rest now.' In desperation, Whalley invests his remaining money in taking command of a steamer owned by a psychopath, one of those terrifying Conrad villains. Before Captain Whalley can serve out his three-year contract, he starts to go blind, and the story ends in disaster.

The disappointment of age has never been better described than in *The End of the Tether*. Many can identify with Captain Whalley in his continual financial worry, although nowadays the cause of the trouble is likely to be the Inland Revenue, rather than the Travancore and Deccan Bank. People who tout for casual employment are used to the smug advice of those in assured positions: 'We old fellows ought to take a rest now.' Yet even *The End of the Tether* could not spoil the delight of my stay in Saigon; the only bad hour occurred when I casually switched on the television set in my hotel room, and found myself watching an almost unbearable documentary film on Sarajevo, with music by Shostakovich and Samuel Barber – the same *Adagio* used by

Oliver Stone in *Platoon*. It was Conrad's story of youth rather than old age that set the mood of this visit.

To complete my happiness during this stay in Saigon, I spent many hours in the resurrected premises of Monsieur Ottavj's Royale Hotel. When I had first come back under the Communists, in 1980, the Royale's former restaurant and bar had been converted into a workshop making Communist flags, with a yellow star on a red background. In 1988 and again in 1990, the premises were a women's dress shop. This year I found that the door on the corner of Nguyen Hue and Nguyen Thiep Street carried the sign: 'Ciao Café – Ice Cream – Pizza – Cake.'

The sombre old room has been recreated around a circular bar with a coffee machine, assorted bottles of liquor and an inviting cake-stand. The interior decorator has covered the walls with Vietnamese variations of Pre-Raphaelite, impressionist and cubist art, and has added stained-glass pictures of fruit to the windows. The yellow-and-green check dresses of the waitresses add to the general impression of vivid colour, as do the two television sets flashing American pop groups. After a few minutes of culture shock, I grew very fond of the Ciao Café and the young men and women who run it, most of them university students, not old enough to remember the war. Like most of their generation, the staff of the Ciao Café are very proud of their country and glad to have grown up here instead of in exile. They made much of me, partly I fear because of my age, but partly, I think, because I had stayed with the country through war and tribulation. Once they invited me to join them at their own evening meal, after business was over, as Monsieur Ottavj had so often invited me to his table beneath the plaque to Saint-Exupéry and the other French air force 'Old Joysticks'.

Sitting over a beer in the Ciao Café, I naturally thought back to the many people I knew in its previous incarnation. At the table where a Vietnamese businessman was chattering down his portable phone, I had dined with Pat Burgess during the May Offensive of 1968, while the Royale staff and their families camped on the other side of the room, as refugees from the fighting in the suburbs. Gerald Scarfe had drawn a wicked caricature of myself at the Royale bar, with Philip Jones Griffiths and Monsieur Ottavj. Later *habitués* were Murray Sayle, Stuart Dalby and James Fenton, writing his Indo-Chinese version of *Don Juan*. It was here that I first met Liz Thomas, the English nurse and her colleague Father Hoang. The Royale also held its romantic memories from the 1960s. There was K the Laotian, who turned out to be carrying on simultaneously with a Corsican gangster, and melancholy D, from the North, who married an American and went to live in Thailand.

The Ciao Café caused me to ponder especially on the years after 1972, when the gallant South Vietnamese fought on their own against all odds, until they were overwhelmed by the North in 1975. That was the period when the mood of the country was summed up by Saint-Exupéry's words on the fall of France: 'Defeat... Victory... Terms I do not know what to make of. One victory exalts, another corrupts. One defeat kills, another brings life. Tell me what seed is lodged in your victory or your defeat, and I will tell you its future.' After the fall of Saigon came grim years of re-education camps, the expulsion of the Chinese, the suffering of the Boat People, and ten more years of war in Cambodia, leaving another 55,000 dead and many more maimed. Then came the reforms of 1986, since when Vietnam has become an increasingly pleasant country. It does not matter much that the regime still calls itself Communist; at least it is honest by South-east Asian standards. And socialism may help to postpone the ravages of the motor car, the tourist trade and the sexual depravity that have destroyed Bangkok.

And so, in the café where I got my first impressions of Vietnam, I bring this story to a close. There has been no consistent theme, for I am not an ideologue and have never believed that any side was entirely right or wrong. Throughout this book I have tried to describe how I thought and felt at the time, rather than with the advantage of hindsight. Today, as I see the optimism and cheerfulness of the new generation of Vietnamese, I think and feel that Saint-Exupéry's words have proved correct, and that in the defeat of 1975 were lodged the seeds of a victory that is now in bloom.

The happiness of the visit remained with me in the airport departure lounge, where as well as the usual duty-free shop, I found an arresting display of local products. There were paintings, sculptures and video tapes of the music of Trinh Cong Son and others. There were packets of shark's fin, swallow's nest, dried pork tendon and jewfish's air bladder, for Chinese and Japanese gourmets. There were trays of glassware, ceramics, lacquer, jade, amber, silverware, tortoiseshell goods and the carved tusks of boar, bear and tiger.

Then I noticed a small collection of archaeological artefacts – the metal cigarette lighters once sold to American servicemen, and now on sale to departing passengers at $32 apiece. The salesgirl took out three to let me note the inscriptions on the cases: 'The Unwilling working for the Unable to do the Unnecessary for the Ungrateful', 'Vietnam Phu Bai 69–70. Cong Executioners', and the familiar, 'Yea, though I walk through the Valley of the Shadow of Death I shall fear no evil, for I am the evilest son of a bitch in the Valley'.

The inscriptions may serve as an epilogue to this chronicle of war and peace in Vietnam.

Index

In Vietnamese, the family name is written first, as in Ho Chi Minh. Where individuals have become known in the West by their given names, e.g. Presidents Diem or Thieu, these have been entered with cross references to their full names.

Adair, Gilbert: *Hollywood's Vietnam*, 72
Agnew, Spiro: visits Laos, 107–8
Allen, Woody, 90
Americal Division, 55
An Quang Pagoda, 21–2, 126
Anne, Princess, 187
Apocalypse Now (film), 50, 53, 58, 61, 215, 241–5, 339
Arnett, Peter, 82

Bangkok Post (newspaper), 106
Barrell, Sarah Webb, 138–9, 306
Benge, Mike, 42, 61, 251
Blue, Vida, 92
Bontawee, Kampoon: *A Child of the Northeast*, 119
Botan: *Letters from Thailand*, 120–3
Brando, Marlon, 97, 182
Bryan, Ann (editor *Overseas Weekly*), 70–1
Bui The Lan, General, 146
Bui Xuan Quang: *Saigon 1925–45*, 348–9
Bulletin of Counter-Government (journal), 98–100
Burdick, Eugene *see* Lederer, William, J.

Burgess, Guy, 324
Burgess, Pat, 63–4, 357
Burke, Edmund, quoted, 335

Cao Dai (religious sect), 152, 321–2, 348
Carter, Rowly, 139, 181
Castro, Fidel, 314
Cavalleri (Vientiane hotelier), 107
Cawthorne, Nigel: *The Bamboo Cage*, 250–4
Chang, Jung: *The Wild Swans*, 331–6
Chin Peng (Malayan Communist), 95
Chou En-lai (Chinese Communist), 184
Chow, Philip, 338
Chu Tu: *War*, 15–7
CIA (US Central Intelligence Agency), 77–8; in Cambodia, 101, 219, 305
Cimino, Michael (director *The Deer Hunter*), 236–7, 306
Conrad, Joseph: *Youth*, 2, 355; *Heart of Darkness*, 2, 241–5, 256, 355; *The End of the Tether*, 2, 355–7; *Lord Jim*, 175, 245; *The Rescue*, 188; *Victory*, 140, 304
Clinton, Bill, 352

Cooper, Gary, 39
Coppola, Francis (director *Apocalypse Now*), 50, 241
Cornwell, David (author under name John Le Carré), 125–6
Corson, Lt Col W. R., 32
Crookston, Peter, 198
Crossman Richard, 94

Daily Mail (London newspaper), 6, 22
Dalby, Stuart, 125, 141, 358
Davies, Greg, 298–9
Decoux, Admiral (French Governor-General of Indo-China in Second World War), 344–5, 348
Deer Hunter, The (film), 255–6, 258
Deneuve, Catherine; in film *Indochine*, 342
Dennison, Andre, 306
Detoradiyuth, Narmedol, 189
Diehl, William: *Thai Horse*, 255–6, 258
Diem, Ngo Dinh *see* Ngo Dinh Diem
Dien Bien Phu, battle of, 56, 96
Djilas, Milovan, 326, 332
Donovan, David (pseudonymous author *Once a Warrior King*), 76–7, 300–2
Dostoevsky, Fyodor: *The Brothers Karamazov*, 32
Driberg, Tom, 304–5
Ducoroy, Captain (French official in Second World War), 304–5, 345–7
Dung, Van Tien *see* Van Tien Dung
Duong Quang Thang, 282–4, 296–7

Eisenhower, Dwight D., 96
Ellsberg, Daniel, 216
Erlanger, Steve, 271, 281
Ewell, General Julian, 75–6

Fall, Bernard: *Street Without Joy*, 28, 145, 286
Fenton, James, 104–5, 125, 157, 164, 167, 308, 358
Field, The (London journal), 330
First Air Cavalry, 55
Flynn, Sean, 11, 104
Fonda, Jane, 91–2, 353
Fournier, Edith, 108–10
Franchini, Philippe (proprietor of Continental Hotel), 142–3; *Continental Saigon*, 247, 342–9; editor *Saigon 1925–1945*, 342
Frankland, Mark, 82, 172, 176

Garwood, Bobby, 251–2
Giap, Vo Nguyen *see* Vo Nguyen Giap, General
Goh Chok Teng, 350
Gorbachev, Mikhail, 266, 270, 275
Gorer, Geoffrey: on Angkor, 4; on opium, 231
Gott, Richard: on Khmer Rouge, 193
Green Berets *see* Special Forces
Greene, Graham, 105, 217; *The Quiet American*, 1, 7, 46, 48, 96, 142, 163, 262, 284, 298, 305, 315–25, 338, 343
Griffiths, Philip Jones, 42–5, 50–3, 55, 64–6, 150, 312, 358; *Vietnam Inc*, 243

Hackworth, David: *About Face*, 76
Halberstam, David, 46, 299
Hastings, Max, 176
Healy, Patricia, 310–11
Heath, David, 148
Hemingway, Ernest, 234–5, 241
Herald-Tribune, International, 341
Herling, Gustav: *A World Apart*, 326
Herr, Michael: *Dispatches*, 198–9, 235–6, 237, 339
Ho Chi Minh, 46, 95, 113, 179, 211, 218, 229, 231–2, 273–4, 290, 294, 303, 314, 333, 335–6
Ho Xuan Huang, 268–9
Hoa Hao (religious sect), 45, 348
Hoa in Vietnam Dossier (1978) (Hanoi publication), 204–6, 210
Hoang, Father (colleague of Liz Thomas), 151–2, 173, 174, 358
Holt, Estelle 108
Hope, Bob, 89–93
Hoxha, Enver, 306
Hughes, Dick, 151

Indochine (film), 343
Ingrams, Richard, 124
Irish Times (Dublin newspaper), 158, 177

Jensen-Stevenson, Monika: *Kiss the*

Index

Boys Goodbye (with William H. Stevenson), 251–3
Johnson, General H. K., 45
Johnson, Lyndon B., 40, 45, 83, 91, 149
Johnson, Samuel, quoted, 220, 323
Joyaux, François: *La Chine et le règlement du premier conflit d'Indochine*, 219

Karnow, Stanley: *Vietnam: A History*, 73–4, 168, 216–20, 227, 305
Kemp, Peter, 108–11, 125, 254, 305–6
Kennedy, John F., 2, 40, 82, 96, 267, 325
Kepner, Susan, 119–20
Khalid, Prince, 338
Khmer Rouge (Cambodian Communists): named by Sihanouk, 98; rise to power, 101–4; their reign or terror, 191–8; and Mao Zedong, 333–4
Kieu Chinh (Vietnamese actress), 69
King, Martin Luther, 239
Kissinger, Henry, 83–4, 94–5, 124, 194–5, 234, 249, 330
Klotz François, 108–10, 254
Kravchenko, Viktor: *I Chose Freedom*, 326
Kukrit *see* Pramoj, Kukrit

Labbé, Jean-Claude, 164–5, 170–1, 308
Lansdale, Edward G., 96, 316
Le Canard Enchainé (Paris journal), 223
Le Duc Tho, 94–5, 124
Le Monde (Paris newspaper), 56
Le Nouvel Observateur (Paris journal), 224
Lederer, William J.: *The Ugly American* (with Eugene Burdick), 96–7, 166, 200, 316
Lee Kuan Yew, 97, 182, 351–2
Lewis, Norman: *A Dragon Apparent*, 1, 46, 49
Lewy, Guenther: *America in Vietnam*, 239
Linh, Nguyen Van *see* Nguyen Van Linh

Loan, Nguyen Ngoc *see* Nguyen Ngoc Loan, General
Look (American journal), 23
Lotbiniere, Tony de, 141, 144, 150, 152, 158, 170, 172, 178, 306

McCarthy, Joseph, 232
McCarthy, Mary, 28, 32
McCoy, Alfred: *The Politics of Heroin in Southeast Asia*, 130
Maclean, Donald, 324
Mao Zedong (or Mao Tse Tung), 183, 193, 232, 273; significance to Vietnam of his Great Leap Forward and Cultural Revolution, 327–36
Mao, Madame (Jing Qing), 329
Marcos, Ferdinand, 216
Marine Corps (United States), 27–33, 55, 124, 289
Martin, Graham, 226
Mayréna, David de, 245–7
Menges, Chris, 79, 195
MIA (or Missing in Action), 248–58, 276–7, 278
Michener, James: *South Pacific*, 15
Mooney, Jerry, 252–3
Moore, Robin: *The Green Berets*, 40–2, 44
Moreau, Ron, 224
Mountbatten, Lord Louis, 218, 305
Muggeridge, Malcolm, 193
Mullin, Chris: *The Last Man out of Saigon*, 279–80
Murphy, Audie, 324
My Lai, massacre at, 55, 71, 73

Naipaul, V. S., *A Bend in the River*, 244
Nation (Bangkok newspaper), 189
New Statesman (London journal), 1, 56, 72, 86, 104, 137, 141, 157, 172, 177, 179–80, 224
Newsweek (US journal), 1
Ngo Dinh Diem, 1, 46, 96, 325, 348; and drug traffic, 130–1; overthrow, 126–7, 221–2
Ngo Dinh Ho, 52
Ngor, Haing S.: *Surviving the Killing Fields*, 196–8
Nguyen Kao Ky, Air Marshal, 21, 160

Nguyen Ngoc Loan, General, 54, 60, 64
Nguyen Quang Di (diplomat), 264–5
Nguyen Quoc Thang (zoo director), 312–15
Nguyen Van Linh: and *Doi Moi* reforms, 259, 271, 273–4, 338
Nguyen Van Thieu (President of South Vietnam till 1975), 21, 62, 84, 87, 203, 211, 299, 304
Nixon, Richard, 83–4, 94–5, 149, 194–5, 226, 234; and MIA, 249–50; and China Lobby 329–30

O'Brien, Tim: *Going After Cacciato*, 235
Operation Phoenix (also known as Phoenix Program), 79–80, 219, 300
O'Toolis, Sean, 253
Ottavj, Jean (proprietor of Royale Hotel, Saigon), 6, 7–12, 63, 82, 125, 127, 135, 139–41, 304; Royale lives on as Ciao Café, 357–8
Overseas Weekly (US forces journal), 70–1

Page, Tim, 143, 198–9, 212, 236, 339
Pan, Lynn (also Pan Ling) (Chinese author), 331
Parker, Dorothy: on Hollywood, 243
Peng, Chin *see* Chin Peng
Philby, Kim, 324
Phoenix Program *see* Operation Phoenix
Phom Hong Cuc, 189
Pol Pot, 193, 334
Ponchaud, Father Francis: *Cambodia Year Zero*, 193–4
Pramoj, Kukrit, 97; *Four Reigns*, 114–18; Thailand's Prime Minister, 182–5, 331, 344
Pramoj, Seni, 118, 120, 180, 185
Pran, Dith, 195–6
Private Eye (London satirical journal), 6, 223

Quang Phuoc, 153
Quan Doi Nhan Dan (Hanoi army newspaper), 276

Rambo: First Blood Part II (film), 187, 248
Ray, Martha, 93
Reagan, Ronald, 89; and MIA, 249, 253, 278
Redgrave, Michael, 324
Rosie, George: *The British in Vietnam*, 67
Roubaud, Louis: *Christiane de Saigon*, 141

Saigon Daily News, 34
Saint-Exupéry, Antoine de: *Pilote de Guerre*, 135–6, 140, 357–9; *Vol de Nuit*, 140; *Terre des Hommes*, 140–1
Sangster, Robert, 338
Sanlaville, Jacques, 35, 58–9, 84–5, 134–5, 163
Santilli (Italian coffee planter), 133–4
Sary, Ieng, 193, 334
Sayle, Murray, 55, 57–8, 60, 163, 167–8, 176, 243, 258
Scarfe, Gerald, 6, 22, 24, 157, 358
Schanberg, Sydney, 195–6
Scholl-Latour, Peter: *Eyewitness Vietnam*, 220–4, 227
Shawcross, William: *Sideshow*, 194–5
Sheehan, Neil, 46; *A Bright Shining Lie*, 46, 299
Shibley, Bob, 353
Sihanouk, Norodom (at various times King, Prince and Prime Minister of Cambodia), 4–5; in late 1960s, 97–100; attitude to Lon Nol regime, 100–4; relations with Khmer Rouge, 197; in exile, 223–4, 264, 328, 333–4
Smith, Colin, 168
Smiley, David, 186
Solzhenitsyn, Alexander, 190, 202, 220, 327, 332
Sot, Colonel (Laotian Communist), 107
Special Forces (or Green Berets): in Highlands, 39–45; on Phu Quoc Island, 50–3, 61, 82, 88; in *Apocalypse Now*, 242–3
Spellman, Cardinal Francis, 232–3
Stallone, Sylvester, 187, 248
Stepinac, Cardinal Alojzije, 233
Stevenson, William H., *see* Jensen-Stevenson, Monika

Stone, Oliver, 237–41, 258, 357
Stone, Robert, 237
Strong, Colonel G. G., 161
Swain, Jon, 125, 169–70, 193, 195, 260, 263
Sydney Morning Herald, 6

Taylor, Richard, 77, 79, 82, 144, 195, 315
Thatcher, Margaret, 265, 270
Thieu, Nguyen Van *see* Nguyen Van Thieu
Thomas, Liz, 150–6, 158, 163–7, 173–4, 207, 306–8, 358
Thompson, Dr Hunter S., 170–1, 174, 235
Thompson, Sir Robert, 157–8
Thorez, Maurice, 208
Tito, Josip Broz, 233
Todd, Olivier: *Cruel April*, 224–7
Tolstoy, Leo: *War and Peace*, 83, 179, 337
Tran Bach Dang, 271–4
Tran Van Don, 161, 220
Tran Van Lan, 225
Trinh Cong Son, 147–8, 352–3, 359
Tuchman, Barbara: *The March of Folly*, 215, 228–34, 258, 332–3

Van Tien Dung, General, 168, 221
Vann, Lt Col John Paul, 299
Vatthana, King Savang, of Laos, 223
Vietnam Guardian, 17, 34
Vietnam Investment Review, 350
Vietnam News, 341, 350
Viollis, Andrée: *L'Indochine S.O.S.*, 142, 203
Vo Nguyen Giap, General, 55–6
Vo Thi Kho, 78–9
Vo Thi That, 79
Vu Ngoc Tan, 20–1, 312–13

Wall Street Journal, 32
Walters, Captain Jerry, 42–5
Wayne, John, 39, 88–9, 165
Westmoreland, General William, 249, 353
Wilson, Ed, 253
Winter Soldier (film), 72
Wise, Donald, 67
Wolfe, Tom, 235
Woollacott, Martin, 162

Young, Gavin, 259
Young, Phil, 86

Zhou Enlai *see* Chou En-lai
Ziemer, Robert, 39, 61